I0874981

Safe Data-Driven Control for Cyber-Physical Systems

Adnène Arbi
National Institute of Applied Sciences and Technology, University of Carthage, Tunisia & Laboratory of Mathematical Engineering, Tunisia Polytechnic School, University of Carthage, Tunisia

IGI Global
Scientific Publishing
Publishing Tomorrow's Research Today

Vice President of Editorial	Melissa Wagner
Director of Acquisitions	Mikaela Felty
Director of Book Development	Jocelynn Hessler
Production Manager	Mike Brehm
Cover Design	Jose Rosado

Published in the United States of America by
IGI Global Scientific Publishing
701 East Chocolate Avenue
Hershey, PA, 17033, USA
Tel: 717-533-8845 | Fax: 717-533-7115
Website: https://www.igi-global.com E-mail: cust@igi-global.com

Library of Congress Cataloging-in-Publication Data

Names: Arbi, Adnène, DATE- editor http://id.loc.gov/rwo/agents/n2025015505

Title: Safe data-driven control for cyber-physical systems / edited by: Adnène Arbi.
Description: Hershey PA : IGI Global Scientific Publishing, [2026] | Includes bibliographical references. | Summary: "The context of this book is the secure control guaranteeing the security of cyber physical systems. Indeed, although these systems offer undeniable advantages in terms of efficiency and automation, they also introduce a multitude of challenges, research and development, particularly in the context of industry 4.0"-- Provided by publisher.
Identifiers: LCCN 2025002890 (print) | LCCN 2025002891 (ebook) | ISBN 9798337318325 hardcover | ISBN 9798337318332 paperback | ISBN 9798337318349 ebook
Subjects: LCSH: Computer security--Horn of Africa | Cooperating objects (Computer systems)--Horn of Africa
Classification: LCC QA76.9.A25 S244 2025 (print) | LCC QA76.9.A25 (ebook) | DDC 006.2/20963--dc23/eng/20250421
LC record available at https://lccn.loc.gov/2025002890
LC ebook record available at https://lccn.loc.gov/2025002891

British Cataloguing in Publication Data
A Cataloguing in Publication record for this book is available from the British Library.

Table of Contents

Detailed Table of Contents

This research presents an AI-driven system to combat phishing attacks using machine learning and natural language processing. Key components include data collection, feature extraction, model training, and real-time detection. The system offers high accuracy, real-time protection, customizability, enhanced security, reduced financial and data breach risks, and improved efficiency through automation. This scalable, adaptive solution provides robust protection against phishing threats, improving security and productivity while optimizing resource allocation. The system's automation and adaptability make it valuable in addressing this persistent cybersecurity challenge

This chapter aims to present the influences of cyber-security on user experience in relation to the smart technology acceptance in the Horn of Africa region. Following the research and with respondents equal to 390, the KMO measure was used to determine the fitness of the data for conducting the factor analysis manifesting a KMO value that would justify the sample. With regards to the user experience related constructs, cyber-security awareness, and technology trust, the Confirmatory Factor Analysis (CFA) was performed to confirm these measures. Findings manifested better cyber security perception encourages and enhances the user experience and finally, smart technology acceptance. To achieve both a confident and higher level of adoption, the chapter raises the need to adopt the user-centered design alongside the security design. In this sense, this research adds the value for policymakers, technologists, and educators in the Horn of Africa because this research provides insights based on the analysis of cultural and socio-economic characteristics of target users.

This chapter explores blockchain's potential to address cloud computing security challenges. Despite cloud computing's scalability and cost efficiency, it faces risks like data breaches and regulatory non-compliance, as seen in the 2019 Capital One AWS breach. Blockchain's decentralized ledger, cryptographic hashing, smart contracts, and consensus mechanisms (e.g., PoW, PoS) enhance security through decentralized access control, secure storage, and intrusion detection. Privacy techniques like homomorphic encryption and zero-knowledge proofs protect data. Case studies, including IBM Food Trust and MedRec, show practical applications. However, scalability, interoperability, regulatory conflicts (e.g., GDPR), and high costs pose barriers. Solutions like sharding and layer-2 protocols aim to overcome these. Future research focuses on scalability, privacy, hybrid cloud integration, and AI-driven security. Blockchain strengthens cloud security but requires innovation to achieve widespread adoption.

This chapter explores strategies for enhancing the resilience of Cyber-Physical Systems (CPS) through safe and data-driven control mechanisms. As CPS become increasingly reliant on artificial intelligence (AI) and machine learning (ML) for real-time decision-making, ensuring system safety, security, and reliability becomes a critical challenge. The chapter examines various AI-powered control techniques, including Model Predictive Control (MPC), reinforcement learning, and anomaly detection, to optimize system performance while mitigating risks such as adversarial attacks, biases, and unpredictability. Additionally, it highlights the role of edge computing and distributed control architectures in reducing latency and improving fault tolerance. The chapter also addresses cybersecurity threats that impact CPS, including data breaches, cyberattacks, and network vulnerabilities.

This chapter aims to explore a DevOps-driven approach to enhancing cybersecurity in Cyber-Physical Systems with a focus on safe and secure control across their operational lifecycle. Target groups include cybersecurity researchers, DevOps professionals, software engineers, and stakeholders managing CPS in sectors such as energy, transportation, and manufacturing. The methodology integrates DevSecOps principles—(CI/CD, and Infrastructure as Code (IaC)—within CPS architectures to ensure continuous threat monitoring, vulnerability mitigation, and adaptive incident response. Key findings highlight the effectiveness of embedding security throughout the SSDLC, supported by tools like SonarQube, OWASP ZAP, and Snyk. Case studies on Smart Grids, Industrial Control Systems, and Autonomous Vehicles illustrate real-world applications. The chapter concludes that adopting DevOps in CPS enhances system resilience, supports regulatory compliance, and offers scalable solutions to emerging threats, emphasizing the need for cultural shifts and future research on AI and Blockchain-enabled security.

The study explores the integration of data-driven control techniques in cyber-physical systems (CPS), focusing on ensuring the safety, reliability, and autonomy of these increasingly complex systems. As CPS become more prevalent in various industries, from autonomous vehicles to industrial automation, the need for robust control mechanisms that safeguard against potential risks becomes paramount. This paper examines data-driven algorithms that adapt to real-time data, ensuring both system efficiency and security. It also emphasizes the development of safety protocols to mitigate vulnerabilities and enhance system resilience in the face of cyber threats or unexpected failures. The study highlights the balance between autonomy and security, presenting methodologies for achieving safe and efficient operation across diverse CPS applications. Through this analysis, the chapter provides insights into the future of CPS, emphasizing the role of advanced data-driven control in enhancing system safety, scalability, and performance.

In this chapter, federated learning-enabled Secure Blockchain-based Sharing Framework for Vehicle Ad Hoc Networks (VANETs) coordinating federated learning (FL) and blockchain innovation to form a decentralized, privacy-preserving, and secure stage for vehicular communication and information sharing. This inventive system addresses basic challenges in VANETs, such as information protection, security, and real-time collaboration, by empowering vehicles to collaboratively prepare machine learning models locally utilizing their claim information and safely share overhauls through a tamper-resistant blockchain record. Key points of interest incorporate improved believe, versatility, flexibility to assaults, and compliance with protection controls, making it a promising arrangement for applications like collision avoidance, activity optimization, and independent driving bolster. Be that as it may, challenges such as computational complexity, communication inactivity, information heterogeneity, and security vulnerabilities pose critical hurdles to its usage.

Multi-Factor Authentication (MFA) is a secure electronic verification method that allows users to access an application or website only after completing multiple layers of authentication. While protecting sensitive data and systems from cyber threats is critical, traditional text-based authentication methods fail to provide sufficient security. Current systems enhance security by incorporating additional layers, such as OTPs sent to mobile phones or emails, or biometric verification using facial recognition. However, these systems often rely on costly hardware, limiting their accessibility. This paper proposes an integrated Authentication System designed to achieve high levels of security using low-cost equipment. The proposed system eliminates the need for expensive hardware by utilizing images as passwords in a novel three-step authentication process. The system effectively counters various cyber threats, including malware attacks, phishing, and SQL injection, offering a cost-effective and robust solution for secure authentication.

Preface

In an increasingly interconnected world, the integration of cyber-physical systems (CPS) into critical transportation and manufacturing infrastructures demand robust, adaptive, and secure control frameworks. The rapid proliferation of smart technologies and AI-driven systems has amplified the benefits of automation and data-driven decision-making. However, it has also exposed these systems to complex security challenges, including cyber threats, data breaches, and vulnerabilities in control logic and communication protocols.

This edited volume, *Safe Data-Driven Control for Cyber-Physical Systems*, brings together cutting-edge research that addresses the intersection of cybersecurity, control theory, and artificial intelligence within CPS environments. With contributors from a diverse set of academic institutions across the globe, this book reflects a multi-disciplinary and multi-sectoral approach to securing and optimizing CPS across domains such as smart cities, cloud computing, transportation, industrial automation, and UAV systems.

The central theme of this book revolves around enabling safety, security, and resilience in cyber-physical systems through data-driven strategies, while maintaining operational efficiency and technological scalability. Each chapter explores unique yet complementary aspects of these challenges, from blockchain-enhanced cloud security to AI-based intrusion detection systems, and from federated learning in vehicular networks to multi-factor authentication using image processing.

Designed for researchers, practitioners, and policy-makers alike, this volume provides theoretical foundations, technical insights, practical applications, and forward-looking perspectives for ensuring the safe deployment of intelligent, data-centric CPS.

CHAPTER OVERVIEW

Chapter 1: AI-Powered Phishing Detection System

Introduces a machine learning and NLP-based system for real-time phishing attack detection. The model demonstrates strong adaptability and automation, making it a scalable and efficient solution against persistent phishing threats.

Chapter 2: Cyber-Security Effect on Smart Technology Through User Experience in Horn of Africa

Examines the socio-cultural impact of cybersecurity awareness on user acceptance of smart technologies in the Horn of Africa. Emphasizes the importance of user-centered design and technology trust in enhancing adoption rates.

Chapter 3: Enhancing Cloud Security and Privacy with Blockchain Technology

Explores how blockchain mechanisms such as smart contracts and zero-knowledge proofs can enhance cloud data privacy and security. Offers critical case studies and discusses future research directions, including scalability and AI integration.

Chapter 4: Enhancing CPS Resilience with Safe Data-Driven Control Strategies

Focuses on the integration of AI-powered control strategies like reinforcement learning and anomaly detection to improve CPS safety and reliability, especially in real-time and distributed environments.

Chapter 5: Enhancing Cybersecurity in CPS: A DevOps-Driven Approach

Introduces a DevSecOps-based lifecycle for CPS security, demonstrating how continuous integration and deployment models, supported by tools like OWASP ZAP and Snyk, can embed cybersecurity into every development phase.

Chapter 6: Ensuring Safe and Intelligent Data-Driven Control for CPS

Explores advanced data-driven algorithms for reliable and autonomous operation of CPS across industries. Highlights the need for balancing autonomy with security through real-time data analysis and adaptive control.

Chapter 7: Federated Learning Enabled Secure Blockchain-Based Sharing for VANETs

Presents a novel integration of federated learning and blockchain for secure, decentralized data sharing in vehicular networks. Addresses challenges such as latency, heterogeneity, and real-time responsiveness.

Chapter 8: Hybrid Authentication System Using Image-Based Multi-Factor Verification

Proposes a low-cost, image-based multi-factor authentication system to counter threats like phishing and SQL injection. Highlights usability and accessibility as key design considerations for broader adoption.

Chapter 9: IDSCI – A Machine Learning-Based Intrusion Detection System for Cloud Infrastructure

Introduces IDSCI, a hybrid CNN–BiLSTM-based model offering improved accuracy for cloud intrusion detection. Validated on benchmark datasets, the system shows potential for real-time cloud threat mitigation.

Chapter 10: Industrial CPS Ensuring Safe Automation in Smart Manufacturing

Explores the convergence of AI, IoT, and socio-technical systems in smart manufacturing. Focuses on human-centric design, decision-making, and resilience to cyber threats in Industry 4.0 environments.

Chapter 11: Safe Data-Driven Control in Autonomous Vehicles and Transportation Systems

Analyzes safe data-driven control methodologies for autonomous transport systems, with attention to cybersecurity, sensor fusion, VANET communication, and predictive diagnostics. Emphasizes the importance of secure system architectures for public safety and trust.

Together, these chapters underscore the necessity of a multidisciplinary approach to building safe, adaptive, and secure cyber-physical systems. The contributions herein pave the way for innovations that are not only technically robust but also socially responsible and sustainable.

Chapter 1
AI-Powered Phishing Detection System

Mehaboob Mujawar
https://orcid.org/0000-0002-8260-7062
Mangalayatan University, India

Aasheesh Raizada
Mangalayatan University, India

Abdullah Gubbi
Bearys Institute of Technology, Mangalore, India

ABSTRACT

This research presents an AI-driven system to combat phishing attacks using machine learning and natural language processing. Key components include data collection, feature extraction, model training, and real-time detection. The system offers high accuracy, real-time protection, customizability, enhanced security, reduced financial and data breach risks, and improved efficiency through automation. This scalable, adaptive solution provides robust protection against phishing threats, improving security and productivity while optimizing resource allocation. The system's automation and adaptability make it valuable in addressing this persistent cybersecurity challenge

INTRODUCTION

In our increasingly digital era, phishing attacks have emerged as a sophisticated and widespread threat, targeting both individuals and organizations through deceptive strategies that mimic legitimate entities. These attacks exploit human vulnerabilities

DOI: 10.4018/979-8-3373-1832-5.ch001

and trust to obtain sensitive information, including login credentials, financial data, and personal details. Phishing attempts are conducted via various channels, such as emails, websites, and messages, each designed to trick users into believing they are interacting with a trusted source. The ramifications of successful phishing attacks are severe, often leading to substantial financial losses, compromised personal information, and significant reputational harm to both individuals and organizations. Phishing attacks have undergone significant evolution over time, employing advanced techniques to circumvent traditional security measures (Ogundairo & Broklyn, 2024). Cybercriminals continually refine their methods, utilizing social engineering tactics, creating highly convincing fake websites, and using tools to avoid detection. The growing sophistication of these attacks poses a formidable challenge to conventional security measures, which typically rely on static rule-based systems that struggle to keep up with the dynamic nature of phishing threats. As a result, there is a pressing need for innovative and adaptable solutions capable of effectively addressing the complexities of phishing attacks.

In response to this escalating threat, researchers and cybersecurity experts have turned to artificial intelligence (AI) as a potent weapon in the battle against phishing. AI-driven phishing detection systems harness advanced technologies, particularly machine learning (ML) algorithms and natural language processing (NLP) techniques, to identify and thwart phishing attempts in real-time. Unlike traditional approaches that depend on predefined rules and signatures, AI-based systems are designed to analyze intricate data patterns and comprehend the nuanced characteristics of phishing content. This enables them to detect suspicious activities with significantly greater accuracy and efficiency, providing a robust defense against phishing attacks.

The Evolution of Phishing Attacks

The landscape of phishing attacks has undergone a significant transformation, evolving from rudimentary email-based scams to intricate, targeted operations. In the early days, cybercriminals relied on a quantity-over-quality approach, disseminating generic messages to a vast number of recipients in hopes of ensnaring a few unsuspecting victims. However, contemporary phishing techniques have become far more refined and strategic. Modern phishing campaigns often employ sophisticated tactics such as spear phishing and whaling. These methods involve tailoring attacks to specific individuals or high-ranking executives within organizations. Unlike their predecessors, these advanced phishing attempts are meticulously crafted to appear authentic, often incorporating personal details about the target to establish credibility and trust. The scope of phishing has also expanded beyond the traditional email medium. Cybercriminals now exploit a diverse array of digital platforms to reach potential victims. Social media networks, instant messaging applications, and even voice communication channels have become fertile grounds for phishing activities. This expansion has given rise to new forms of phishing, such as smishing (SMS-based phishing) and vishing (voice-based phishing). The proliferation of smartphones and the ubiquity of social media platforms have provided cybercriminals with unprecedented access to potential targets. These technologies offer new vectors for launching phishing attacks, allowing malicious actors to exploit the trust users place in these familiar communication channels (Nagarajan, 2024). This diversification of phishing methods and the expansion of potential attack surfaces have created significant challenges for traditional security measures. The increased sophistication and variety of phishing techniques have made it increasingly difficult for conventional defense mechanisms to effectively detect and mitigate these threats. As a result, the cybersecurity landscape must continually evolve to keep pace with these ever-changing and increasingly complex phishing strategies.

The Role of Artificial Intelligence in Phishing Detection

The evolution of phishing attacks has necessitated the development of more sophisticated defense mechanisms, with artificial intelligence (AI) emerging as a crucial tool in this ongoing battle. AI-driven phishing detection systems leverage advanced machine learning algorithms, natural language processing, and data analysis techniques to identify and counteract increasingly complex phishing threats. These AI-powered systems are designed to process and learn from vast datasets containing both legitimate and fraudulent examples. This comprehensive approach enables them to recognize subtle indicators of phishing that might elude traditional detection methods. By analyzing patterns in email headers, web addresses, message content, and user behavior, AI systems can identify potential phishing attempts with greater accuracy and efficiency. One of the key strengths of AI-based phishing detection lies in its adaptability. As cybercriminals continually refine their tactics, AI systems can evolve in tandem, learning from new data and adjusting their detection criteria accordingly. This dynamic learning process allows AI to identify emerging phishing strategies and respond to novel attack vectors promptly. For instance, AI systems can detect minute changes in email structures, spot inconsistencies in sender information, and identify suspicious patterns in URL structures. They can also analyze the context and content of messages, recognizing linguistic patterns or emotional manipulation tactics commonly employed in phishing attempts. Moreover, AI-powered systems can provide real-time threat intelligence, enabling organizations to respond swiftly to emerging phishing campaigns (Kyaw et al., 2024). By continuously monitoring and analyzing network traffic, email communications, and user interactions, these systems can detect and flag potential threats as they occur, minimizing the window of vulnerability. The application of AI in phishing detection extends beyond email-based threats. As phishing tactics diversify across various digital platforms, AI systems are being adapted to monitor and analyze activities on social media, instant messaging apps, and even voice communication channels. This comprehensive approach helps organizations maintain a robust defense against the full spectrum of modern phishing techniques. AI's role in combating phishing is not limited to detection alone. These systems can also contribute to user education and awareness by providing detailed insights into detected threats and offering personalized security recommendations. By highlighting the specific characteristics of phishing attempts, AI can help users become more discerning and less susceptible to future attacks. As phishing techniques continue to evolve, the integration of AI in cybersecurity strategies becomes increasingly crucial. The ability of AI systems to process vast amounts of data, identify complex patterns, and adapt to new threats positions them as a formidable defense against the ever-changing landscape of phishing attacks. However, it's important to note that while AI significantly enhances phishing detection capabilities, it should be part of a comprehensive cybersecurity approach that includes user education, robust security policies, and regular system updates.

Machine Learning in Phishing Detection

AI-powered phishing detection systems have become increasingly sophisticated, leveraging various machine learning techniques to combat evolving cyber threats. These systems utilize both supervised and unsupervised learning approaches to analyze and categorize potential phishing attempts. Supervised learning algorithms, such as decision trees, support vector machines, and neural networks, form the foundation of many AI-driven phishing detection systems. These algorithms are trained on large datasets containing examples of both legitimate and fraudulent communications. By analyzing predetermined features like email metadata, URL structures, and textual content, these models learn to distinguish between genuine and malicious messages.

The feature set used for training these models is crucial and may include:

1. Email metadata: Sender information, IP addresses, and email headers
2. URL composition: Domain names, subdomains, and URL patterns
3. Textual properties: Language use, sentiment analysis, and keyword frequency
4. Visual elements: Presence of logos, layout similarities to legitimate sites

Unsupervised learning techniques complement supervised approaches by identifying patterns and anomalies that may indicate phishing activities. Clustering algorithms can group similar messages or websites, potentially revealing coordinated phishing campaigns. Anomaly detection methods can flag unusual behaviors or communication patterns that deviate from established norms.

For example, an unsupervised model might detect:

1. Sudden spikes in email traffic from specific domains
2. Unusual patterns in sender behavior or message timing
3. Clusters of similar but slightly altered URLs targeting a specific organization

By combining supervised and unsupervised learning methods, AI-driven systems develop a comprehensive understanding of phishing threats. This multi-faceted approach allows for:

1. Improved accuracy in threat detection
2. Adaptability to new phishing techniques
3. Real-time analysis and response to emerging threats
4. Reduction in false positives, minimizing alert fatigue for security teams

As phishing tactics continue to evolve, AI-powered detection systems can quickly adapt by continuously learning from new data and updating their models. This dynamic learning process enables organizations to stay ahead of cybercriminals and maintain robust defenses against sophisticated phishing attempts.

Natural Language Processing in Phishing Detection

Natural Language Processing (NLP) plays a crucial role in enhancing the capabilities of these AI-driven phishing detection systems. NLP techniques enable the systems to analyze the semantic content of messages, providing deeper insights into potential threats (Choutapally & Das, 2024).

Some key NLP applications in phishing detection include:

1. Sentiment analysis: Detecting urgency, fear, or other emotional manipulation tactics often used in phishing attempts.
2. Topic modeling: Identifying common themes or subjects in phishing messages, which can help in recognizing new campaigns.
3. Named entity recognition: Extracting and analyzing mentions of organizations, individuals, or sensitive information that might be targeted in phishing attacks.
4. Language model perplexity: Measuring how well a message conforms to expected language patterns, potentially flagging unusual or machine-generated text.
5. Contextual analysis: Understanding the broader context of a message to determine if it aligns with expected communication from the purported sender.

By integrating these NLP techniques with traditional machine learning approaches, AI-powered phishing detection systems can provide a more nuanced and accurate assessment of potential threats. This comprehensive approach significantly enhances an organization's ability to protect against sophisticated phishing attacks in an ever-evolving cybersecurity landscape (Crgol & Vrhovec, 2024).

Real-Time Detection and Alerting

Real-time AI-powered phishing detection systems offer crucial features for instantaneous identification and warning of potential threats. These systems continuously monitor various digital channels, including email servers, web pages, and chat applications, to identify and prevent phishing attempts before they reach their intended targets. The implementation of such systems has become increasingly important in today's digital landscape, where cyber threats are constantly evolving and becoming more sophisticated.

Key aspects of these systems include:

1. Continuous scanning: Constant monitoring of digital channels for potential threats. This involves real-time analysis of incoming data streams, ensuring that no suspicious activity goes unnoticed.
2. AI and machine learning algorithms: Rapid analysis of incoming information to recognize potential threats. These algorithms are trained on vast datasets of known phishing attempts and can quickly identify patterns and characteristics associated with malicious activities.
3. Instant notification: Immediate alerts to security personnel upon detection of suspicious activity. This allows for swift response and mitigation of potential threats before they can cause significant damage.
4. Preemptive action: Blocking access to harmful websites or isolating suspicious emails before user interaction. By preventing users from accessing potentially dangerous content, these systems significantly reduce the risk of successful phishing attacks.
5. Reduced response time: Swift detection minimizes the potential consequences of successful breaches. The faster a threat is identified and addressed, the less time attackers have to exploit vulnerabilities or extract sensitive information.
6. Enhanced organizational security: Decreased likelihood of data breaches and financial losses. By implementing robust phishing detection systems, organizations can protect their assets, reputation, and customer trust more effectively.

Advanced Natural Language Processing (NLP) techniques can be combined with behavioral analysis to create a more comprehensive threat detection system. This multi-faceted approach enhances the accuracy and effectiveness of phishing detection:

1. Pattern recognition: Examining user interactions such as typing speed, mouse movements, and message composition time. These behavioral patterns can help distinguish between legitimate users and potential attackers or automated systems.
2. Anomaly detection: Identifying unusual patterns that may indicate automated or malicious behavior. This involves establishing baseline behaviors for users and systems, then flagging any deviations from these norms for further investigation.
3. Sentiment analysis: Detecting emotional manipulation tactics commonly used in sophisticated phishing attempts. This technique can identify language designed to create a sense of urgency, fear, or excitement, which are often employed in social engineering attacks.
4. Multi-layered defense: Incorporating various analytical methods to enhance protection against social engineering attacks. By combining multiple techniques, the system can provide more robust and comprehensive protection against a wide range of phishing tactics.
5. Contextual analysis: Evaluating the context of communications to identify inconsistencies or red flags. This includes analyzing sender information, email headers, and the overall content of messages to detect potential impersonation attempts or spoofed communications.
6. URL and attachment analysis: Scrutinizing links and attachments within messages for potential malware or redirects to malicious websites. This involves techniques such as sandboxing, reputation checking, and dynamic analysis to identify threats without exposing users to risk.
7. Machine learning-based classification: Utilizing advanced machine learning models to categorize incoming messages and web content as either benign or potentially malicious. These models can adapt and improve over time as they encounter new phishing techniques and patterns.
8. User behavior profiling: Creating individual user profiles based on typical communication patterns, frequently contacted addresses, and usual working hours. Any deviation from these established profiles can trigger additional scrutiny or authentication measures.
9. Integration with threat intelligence feeds: Incorporating real-time data from global threat intelligence networks to stay updated on the latest phishing campaigns, malicious domains, and emerging attack vectors.
10. Adaptive learning capabilities: Continuously updating and refining detection algorithms based on new threat data and user feedback. This ensures that the

system remains effective against evolving phishing tactics and newly discovered vulnerabilities.

By integrating these advanced techniques, AI-powered phishing detection systems can provide a robust and comprehensive defense against a wide range of cyber threats. These systems not only protect organizations from immediate dangers but also contribute to the overall improvement of cybersecurity practices by constantly adapting to new challenges and attack methodologies (Mujawar et al., 2024).

Furthermore, the implementation of such advanced systems can have far-reaching benefits beyond immediate threat prevention:

11. Improved user awareness: By providing real-time feedback and explanations for flagged content, these systems can educate users about potential threats and best practices for online safety.
12. Reduced workload for IT security teams: Automation of threat detection and initial response allows security professionals to focus on more complex tasks and strategic planning.
13. Compliance support: Advanced phishing detection systems can help organizations meet regulatory requirements related to data protection and cybersecurity, such as GDPR, HIPAA, or PCI DSS.
14. Cost-effectiveness: While initial implementation may require investment, the long-term benefits of preventing successful attacks can result in significant cost savings for organizations.
15. Scalability: AI-powered systems can easily scale to accommodate growing organizations and increasing data volumes without compromising on detection speed or accuracy.

As cyber threats continue to evolve, the importance of sophisticated, AI-driven phishing detection systems cannot be overstated. These systems represent a critical line of defense in the ongoing battle against cybercrime, helping to safeguard sensitive information, maintain business continuity, and protect individuals and organizations from the potentially devastating consequences of successful phishing attacks.

Continuous Learning and Adaptation

AI-powered phishing detection systems offer significant advantages over conventional methods due to their continuous learning and adaptation capabilities. These systems can adjust to new phishing tactics and attack methods, maintaining effectiveness against evolving threats. This adaptability is crucial in the rapidly changing landscape of cybersecurity, where attackers constantly develop new techniques to bypass traditional security measures. Key features of AI-powered phishing detection systems include continuous learning, pattern recognition, real-time monitoring, instant analysis, immediate response, and reduced response time. These systems integrate fresh data into their models without requiring complete retraining, allowing them to stay up-to-date with the latest phishing techniques. They excel at identifying emerging trends in phishing attacks by analyzing vast amounts of data to detect subtle patterns that may be imperceptible to human analysts. Continuous monitoring across various digital channels ensures comprehensive protection against phishing attempts, while rapid evaluation of incoming information allows for immediate identification and response to potential threats. The swift detection capabilities of these systems significantly minimize the potential consequences of breaches by preventing access to malicious content and reducing the window of opportunity for attackers to succeed (Mujawar & Dommeti, 2024).

Advanced techniques further enhance the effectiveness of AI-powered phishing detection systems. These include behavioral analysis, Natural Language Processing (NLP), multi-layered defense, URL and attachment analysis, machine learning-based classification, user behavior profiling, integration with threat intelligence feeds, and adaptive learning. Behavioral analysis examines user interactions to identify anomalies that may indicate a phishing attempt, while NLP techniques detect emotional manipulation tactics often employed in phishing emails. The multi-layered approach combines various analytical methods to provide comprehensive protection against diverse phishing tactics. URL and attachment analysis scrutinizes links and attachments for potential malware, while machine learning-based classification helps identify potential phishing attempts by comparing them to known patterns. User behavior profiling allows the system to detect anomalies that may indicate a compromised account or sophisticated spear-phishing attempt. Integration with threat intelligence feeds ensures that AI models are constantly updated with the latest information on emerging threats, while adaptive learning allows the system to improve its accuracy over time (Mujawar & Pramono, 2024a).

Implementing advanced AI-powered phishing detection systems offers numerous benefits to organizations. These include improved user awareness, reduced workload for IT security teams, support for regulatory compliance, long-term cost-effectiveness, scalability to accommodate organizational growth, enhanced threat intelligence, customization and flexibility, continuous improvement, integration with existing security infrastructure, and reduction in human error. These systems provide real-time feedback and explanations to users, raising awareness and creating a more security-conscious workforce. By automating detection and initial response, they significantly reduce the burden on IT security personnel, allowing them to focus on more complex tasks. The comprehensive logging and reporting capabilities facilitate compliance audits and demonstrate due diligence in protecting sensitive information.

While the initial investment may be significant, these systems offer long-term cost savings by preventing successful attacks and can easily scale to meet the needs of growing organizations. The data collected and analyzed contributes to broader threat intelligence efforts, providing valuable insights for proactive security measures and strategic planning. The ability to customize these systems allows for more effective protection against industry-specific threats, while continuous improvement ensures that organizations maintain a strong defense against evolving threats without constant manual updates. Integration with existing security tools creates a more cohesive and comprehensive security ecosystem, minimizing the risk of human error in identifying and handling potential threats (Mujawar & Pramono, 2023).

Integration with Existing Security Infrastructure

Systems for detecting phishing attempts using artificial intelligence are created to work smoothly with current security setups, including email protection, firewalls, and systems that identify intrusions. This compatibility allows organizations to boost their security measures without interrupting their established processes. For instance, an AI-driven system can be implemented as an extra safeguard within an email security framework, offering instant analysis and threat identification capabilities. Furthermore, these systems can be linked with platforms for responding to incidents and gathering threat intelligence, enabling organizations to address phishing threats more efficiently. By delivering practical insights and comprehensive threat reports, AI-powered systems equip security teams to take preemptive actions to reduce risks and thwart future attacks.

Benefits of AI-Powered Phishing Detection Systems

Adopting AI-based phishing detection systems provides several advantages:

1. Improved Precision: AI-driven solutions demonstrate superior accuracy in identifying phishing attempts compared to conventional techniques. These systems minimize false alarms and enhance threat recognition by examining intricate patterns and subtle indicators.
2. Instantaneous Safeguarding: The ability to analyze and alert in real-time allows organizations to thwart phishing attacks before they inflict damage. This proactive strategy reduces the risk of data breaches and monetary losses.
3. Decreased Manual Workload: By automating the phishing detection process, AI-powered systems lessen the need for human intervention, enabling security personnel to concentrate on more strategic responsibilities.

4. Enhanced Incident Handling: AI-driven systems boost the efficiency and effectiveness of incident response efforts by offering detailed insights and actionable guidance.
5. Ongoing Adaptation: The adaptive nature of AI-powered systems ensures their continued effectiveness against evolving phishing threats, providing long-term security for organizations.
6. User Awareness: AI-driven systems contribute significantly to educating users about phishing dangers by offering insights and warnings regarding suspicious activities. This helps elevate overall cybersecurity awareness and decreases the likelihood of successful attacks.

In the digital era, the escalation of phishing attacks poses a substantial threat to both individuals and organizations. The growing complexity and variety of phishing methods demand the implementation of sophisticated and flexible solutions to address this widespread problem. AI-driven phishing detection systems serve as a formidable defense, utilizing machine learning, natural language processing, and real-time analysis to identify and thwart threats with exceptional precision and speed. These systems provide enduring protection against emerging threats by continuously adapting to new phishing strategies. Their smooth integration with current security frameworks and capacity to inform users further enhance their importance in securing online communications (Riurean et al., 2024). As digital technologies advance, AI-powered phishing detection systems will become increasingly crucial in protecting sensitive data and maintaining the security of online interactions. This comprehensive examination emphasizes the key features, advantages, and benefits of AI-driven phishing detection systems, highlighting their importance in the ongoing struggle against the persistent and rapidly changing threat of phishing attacks.

REVIEW OF LITERATURE

The field of AI-driven phishing detection has seen significant advancements in recent years, with several researchers contributing valuable insights and innovative approaches. This review summarizes key studies that have shaped our understanding of AI-powered phishing detection systems. Ogundairo and Broklyn (2024) conducted a comprehensive examination of AI-based phishing detection methods, focusing on improving accuracy and reducing false positives. Their research highlighted the potential of AI in addressing the challenges posed by evolving phishing techniques. They emphasized that while AI-driven systems have shown promising results in detecting phishing emails, there are still hurdles to overcome, such as evasion techniques and zero-day attacks. The authors also stressed the importance of explainability and transparency in AI models used for phishing detection. Nagarajan (2024) provided an extensive survey of AI-enabled phishing attack detection techniques. This study addressed the challenges in optimizing accuracy and minimizing false positives while offering insights into current advancements and future directions in the field. Nagarajan's work highlighted the widespread use of machine learning algorithms such as Support Vector Machines (SVM), Random Forest, and Neural Networks in detecting phishing attacks. The research concluded that AI-enabled techniques have demonstrated promising results in identifying phishing attempts. Kyaw, Gutierrez, and Ghobakhlou (2024) conducted a systematic review of deep learning techniques specifically for phishing email detection. Their work emphasized the need for better intervention strategies, challenging the assumption that merely recognizing phishing emails is sufficient to reduce susceptibility to attacks. The authors argued that current intervention methods, such as training programs and awareness campaigns, may not be adequately effective in reducing vulnerability to phishing attacks. They stressed the importance of developing more targeted intervention strategies that consider the complexities of human behavior and decision-making processes.

Choutapally and Das (2024) introduced PaciPhish, an intelligent and interpretable framework for phishing URL detection. This innovative approach not only enhances detection accuracy but also addresses the growing need for transparent AI solutions in cybersecurity. PaciPhish stands out for its ability to provide insights into its decision-making process, making it a trustworthy AI solution for cybersecurity applications. The framework demonstrates high accuracy in detecting phishing URLs while offering transparency, a crucial factor in building user trust in AI-driven security systems. Vrhovec (2024) challenged a fundamental assumption in phishing detection research by questioning the link between recognizing phishing emails and reduced susceptibility to attacks. The study suggests that even if individuals can identify phishing emails, they may still fall victim due to various psychological and behavioral factors. This research highlights the complexity of human behavior in the context of cybersecurity and emphasizes the need for a more nuanced approach to phishing prevention that goes beyond mere recognition of threats.

Collectively, these studies underscore the significant progress made in AI-driven phishing detection while also highlighting areas that require further research and development. The literature reveals a trend towards more sophisticated, interpretable, and user-centric approaches in combating phishing attacks, emphasizing the need for solutions that not only detect threats accurately but also consider human factors in cybersecurity.

RESEARCH GAP

The analysis of the reviewed studies reveals several critical areas where current phishing detection systems fall short, particularly in real-world applications. Despite significant progress in leveraging AI and machine learning for phishing detection, substantial challenges persist. These challenges primarily revolve around developing a comprehensive, real-time detection system that effectively balances high detection accuracy with interpretability, scalability, and user engagement. The increasing sophistication of phishing tactics further compounds these issues, highlighting the need for more adaptable, transparent, and user-centric systems. A major gap identified is the lack of a solution that effectively balances high detection accuracy with interpretability. While deep learning models show promise in improving detection accuracy, they often function as 'black boxes,' making their decision-making processes opaque. This lack of transparency poses significant challenges in building user trust, especially in sensitive environments where understanding AI-driven decisions is crucial. Systems like 'PaciPhish' attempt to address this gap by providing interpretable explanations for phishing URL detections, but further work is needed to enhance transparency while maintaining high detection accuracy.

Another significant research gap is the scalability and real-world applicability of AI-based phishing detection systems. While models leveraging deep learning and other AI-driven techniques show promising results in controlled environments, applying these models at scale presents challenges. These systems need to process vast quantities of data in real-time, particularly in high-traffic environments, without compromising on speed, accuracy, or performance. Adapting these systems to detect phishing across different communication platforms while maintaining efficiency and accuracy remains a critical challenge. The integration of user behavior understanding and influence into phishing detection systems represents another crucial gap. Current models primarily focus on the technical aspects of phishing detection but do not adequately account for how users interact with and respond to these alerts. There is an urgent need for research that integrates user behavior with phishing detection systems, developing approaches that not only detect phishing but also educate and motivate users to take appropriate actions.

Lastly, there is a need for further validation of phishing detection frameworks across a diverse range of evolving phishing attack types. As phishing tactics constantly evolve, detection systems must adapt to new strategies and be effective against various methods such as spear-phishing, social engineering, and multi-channel attacks. Developing systems that can handle multiple attack vectors and detect threats across different channels remains a significant challenge. Addressing these research gaps will be crucial in developing more effective, reliable, and user-friendly AI-powered phishing detection systems capable of meeting the complex challenges posed by modern phishing attacks.

RESEARCH DESIGN AND METHODOLOGY

The research design employs a comprehensive approach combining exploratory and experimental methodologies to investigate advanced AI techniques for phishing detection. The primary objective is to develop and evaluate robust models capable of accurately identifying malicious emails within diverse datasets. This study utilizes the CEAS 2008 Phishing Email Dataset, a well-established corpus containing labeled examples of both phishing and legitimate emails. The dataset encompasses a wide range of features, including email subject lines, body content, sender information, recipient details, and embedded URLs, providing a rich source of information for analysis.

Mathematical Model for AI-Powered Phishing Detection System

The proposed AI-powered phishing detection system is formulated as a binary classification problem. The goal is to learn a mapping function that accurately classifies input emails as phishing or legitimate based on extracted features.

Let the training dataset be:

$$D = \{(x_i, y_i)\}_{i=1}^{N}$$

Where:

$x_i \in R^d$: A feature vector representing the ith email, extracted from email content, URLs, metadata, and header properties. $y_i \in \{0,1\}$: The corresponding label, where: $y_i = 1$ denotes a phishing email, $y_i = 0$ denotes a legitimate email.

We define a classifier function $f_\theta(x)$ parameterized by è, typically realized through a neural network:

$$f_\theta(x) = \sigma\left(W_L \cdot \varnothing_{L-1}\left(W_{L-1} \cdots \varnothing_1\left(W_1 x + b_1\right) \cdots + b_{L-1}\right) + b_L\right)$$

Where:

$\varnothing_l(\cdot)$: Activation function at layer l (e.g., ReLU or tanh), $\sigma(\cdot)$: Sigmoid activation for binary output, W_l, b_l: Weight matrix and bias vector of layer l, $\theta = \{W_l, b_l\}_{l=1}^{L}$: Learnable parameters. The output $f_\theta(x_i) \in [0,1]$ represents the predicted probability that x_i is a phishing email.

The learning objective is to minimize the binary cross-entropy loss:

$$L(\theta) = -\frac{1}{N}\sum_{i=1}^{N}\left[y_i \log\left(f_\theta(x_i)\right) + \left(1 - y_i\right)\log\left(1 - f_\theta(x_i)\right)\right] + \lambda \|\theta\|_2^2$$

Where:
ë $\|\theta\|_2^2$: L2 regularization to prevent overfitting,
λ: Regularization coefficient.
To ensure generalizability and reliability:
Input Constraint: All feature vectors x_i are normalized to $[0,1]^d$
Output Constraint: The predicted probability satisfies $f_\theta(x_i) \in [0,1]$.
Regularization Constraint:

$$\|\theta\|_2^2 \le \alpha$$

Where α is a regularization threshold that controls model complexity.
Parameters θ are updated using the Adam optimizer:

$$\theta_{t+1} = \theta_t - \eta \cdot \nabla_\theta L(\theta_t)$$

Where:
η: Learning rate, $\nabla_\theta L$: Gradient of the loss with respect to parameters.
After training, the classification decision is made as:

$$\hat{y}_i = 1 \; if \, f_\theta(x_i) \ge \tau \text{ (Phishing)}$$

$$\hat{y}_i = 0 \; if \, f_\theta(x_i) < \tau \text{ (Legitimate)}$$

Where $\tau \in [0,1]$ is the decision threshold ($typically\ \tau = 0.5$)

Data preprocessing forms a crucial initial step in the methodology. This phase involves several key operations: thorough data cleaning to remove inconsistencies and errors, advanced text processing techniques to extract meaningful information from unstructured content, transformation of categorical data into numerical formats suitable for machine learning algorithms, and standardization of email formats to ensure consistency across the dataset. These preprocessing steps are essential for preparing the data for subsequent analysis and model training.

The feature engineering process is designed to maximize the informational content available to the machine learning models. It incorporates several innovative approaches (Soon et al., 2024):

1. Combining email body and subject line text for a more comprehensive textual analysis, allowing the models to capture context and semantic relationships across different parts of the email.
2. Implementing a sophisticated system to flag suspicious keywords and phrases commonly associated with phishing attempts, based on extensive research and domain expertise.
3. Conducting in-depth analysis of URL structures within emails, examining factors such as domain age, registration details, and the presence of suspicious patterns or redirects.
4. Creating derived features that leverage domain expertise in cybersecurity and phishing tactics, potentially including metrics related to email header anomalies, sender reputation scores, and linguistic complexity measures.

The primary model selected for this study is the Random Forest Classifier, chosen for its robustness, ability to handle high-dimensional data, and resistance to overfitting. To provide a comprehensive evaluation and benchmark, the study also implements comparative models including Support Vector Machines (SVM), Logistic Regression, and Gradient Boosting algorithms. This multi-model approach allows for a nuanced understanding of the strengths and weaknesses of different machine learning techniques in the context of phishing detection.

The data splitting strategy employs an 80/20 ratio for training and testing sets, respectively. During the training phase, k-fold cross-validation is utilized to ensure model stability and generalizability. Stratified sampling techniques are applied to maintain consistent class distributions across folds, addressing potential issues of class imbalance common in cybersecurity datasets.

A comprehensive set of evaluation metrics is employed to assess model performance:

1. Accuracy: Measuring overall correct predictions.
2. Precision: Evaluating the model's ability to avoid false positives.
3. Recall: Assessing the model's capacity to identify all positive instances.
4. F1-score: Providing a balanced measure of precision and recall.
5. Confusion matrix: Offering a detailed breakdown of correct and incorrect classifications.
6. ROC-AUC (Receiver Operating Characteristic - Area Under Curve): Quantifying the model's ability to discriminate between classes across various threshold settings.

The implementation leverages Python's robust ecosystem of data science and machine learning libraries. Key tools include Pandas for data manipulation, NumPy for numerical computations, Scikit-learn for machine learning algorithms and evaluation metrics, NLTK or spaCy for advanced natural language processing tasks, and various visualization libraries for generating insightful graphical representations of results.

To ensure reproducibility and consistency, the experimental setup is meticulously documented, including detailed specifications of hardware configurations, software versions, and random seed settings. This attention to detail allows for reliable replication of results and facilitates future comparative studies.

Hyperparameters Used in the Model

Learning Rate ( ): The learning rate controls how much the model's weights are adjusted with respect to the loss gradient during optimization. Typical value: $\eta = 0.001$, A lower learning rate ensures stable convergence, while a higher value speeds up training but may overshoot the minimum loss. In our phishing detection system, we used a learning rate of 0.001 to ensure gradual improvement in weights without instability.

Number of Hidden Layers: Hidden layers are layers between the input and output layers where the network performs intermediate transformations. Typical value: 2 or 3 hidden layers, For phishing detection, 2–3 hidden layers offer a good balance between model complexity and generalization, capturing non-linear relationships in the feature space.

Number of Neurons Per Layer: Each hidden layer contains several neurons, each processing part of the input. Example setting: First hidden layer: 128 neurons, Second hidden layer: 64 neurons, Third hidden layer: 32 neurons (optional). The number of neurons decreases layer by layer to compress information. The initial layer captures more abstract features, while deeper layers refine them.

Activation Functions: Activation functions introduce non-linearity into the network, enabling it to learn complex patterns. ReLU speeds up training by mitigating the vanishing gradient problem, while Sigmoid outputs probabilities for binary phishing classification.

ReLU (Rectified Linear Unit) for hidden layers:

$$\mathrm{ReLU}(\mathrm{x}) = \max(0, \mathrm{x})$$

Sigmoid for the output layer (binary classification):

$$\sigma(x) = \frac{1}{1 + e^{-x}}$$

The research methodology incorporates several advanced techniques to optimize model performance and gain deeper insights:

1. Hyperparameter tuning: Utilizing grid search or randomized search techniques to identify optimal configurations for each model.
2. Feature importance analysis: Employing techniques such as permutation importance or SHAP (SHapley Additive exPlanations) values to understand which features contribute most significantly to the model's decisions.
3. Error analysis: Conducting in-depth examinations of misclassified instances to identify patterns and potential areas for improvement in the models or feature engineering process.

The study also includes a comparative analysis component, benchmarking the developed models against existing state-of-the-art phishing detection techniques reported in the literature. This comparison provides valuable context for assessing the relative performance and innovation of the proposed approaches. Scalability assessment is another critical aspect of the methodology. This involves testing the models on increasingly large datasets and evaluating their performance in terms of both accuracy and computational efficiency. Such analysis is crucial for understanding the potential real-world applicability of the developed techniques in handling the massive volume of emails processed by large organizations or email service providers.

Ethical considerations form an integral part of the research design. The study addresses potential biases in the dataset or models, considers the implications of false positives and negatives in a real-world context, and discusses the broader societal impacts of automated phishing detection systems. This ethical framework ensures that the research not only advances technical capabilities but also considers the responsible development and deployment of AI in cybersecurity.

Looking towards the future, the research outlines several avenues for further investigation:

1. Exploring advanced deep learning architectures, such as transformer models or graph neural networks, for improved feature extraction and classification.
2. Investigating the potential of transfer learning techniques to adapt models to new types of phishing attacks or different email ecosystems.
3. Developing ensemble methods that combine multiple models or incorporate rule-based systems for enhanced robustness.
4. Exploring the integration of real-time threat intelligence feeds to keep the models updated against evolving phishing tactics.
5. Investigating the potential of unsupervised or semi-supervised learning approaches to reduce the reliance on large labeled datasets.

These future directions aim to push the boundaries of phishing detection capabilities, addressing emerging challenges in the ever-evolving landscape of email-based cyber threats.

Figure 1. Classification Report and Accuracy for AI-Powered Phishing Detection Model

```
OUTPUT   DEBUG CONSOLE   TERMINAL   PORTS

Classification Report:
              precision    recall  f1-score   support

           0       0.99      0.99      0.99      3490
           1       0.99      0.99      0.99      4341

    accuracy                           0.99      7831
   macro avg       0.99      0.99      0.99      7831
weighted avg       0.99      0.99      0.99      7831

Prediction: Legitimate
```

The output presents a comprehensive evaluation of the AI-powered phishing detection model's performance. The model demonstrates exceptional accuracy, achieving a 99.3% success rate in correctly classifying emails. This high accuracy indicates the model's robust ability to distinguish between legitimate and phishing emails across the test dataset. The classification report provides a detailed breakdown of the model's performance for each class (0 and 1, likely representing legitimate and phishing emails respectively). For both classes, the model exhibits outstanding precision, recall, and F1-scores, all at 0.99. This consistency across metrics suggests that the model is highly effective in identifying both legitimate and phishing emails, with minimal false positives and false negatives. The precision of 0.99 indicates that when the model flags an email as phishing, it is correct 99% of the time. Similarly, the recall of 0.99 shows that the model successfully identifies 99% of all actual phishing emails in the dataset. The F1-score, being the harmonic mean of precision and recall, confirms the model's balanced performance in both identifying phishing emails and avoiding false alarms.

The support values (3490 for class 0 and 4341 for class 1) reveal the distribution of samples in the test set, indicating a relatively balanced dataset which strengthens the reliability of the performance metrics. The macro and weighted averages, both at 0.99, further underscore the model's consistent performance across classes, regardless of the slight imbalance in sample sizes. The implementation utilizes key

Python libraries such as pandas for data manipulation, sklearn for machine learning functionalities, and potentially NLTK or SpaCy for natural language processing. The code demonstrates the use of a TfidfVectorizer for text feature extraction and a Random Forest Classifier for the main classification task. These components are integrated into a pipeline, streamlining the process from data input to prediction. The final part of the output shows the model's prediction for a new, unseen email sample. In this case, the model classifies the input as 'Legitimate', showcasing its ability to apply learned patterns to novel data. Given the high precision and recall rates, this prediction can be considered highly reliable. Overall, these results indicate that the AI-powered phishing detection system has achieved a remarkably high level of accuracy and reliability in distinguishing between phishing and legitimate emails. The balanced performance across all metrics suggests that the model is well-suited for real-world application, where both minimizing false positives (to avoid unnecessarily flagging legitimate emails) and maximizing true positives (to catch as many phishing attempts as possible) are crucial.

Figure 2. Performance Metrics and Prediction of AI-Powered Phishing Detection Model

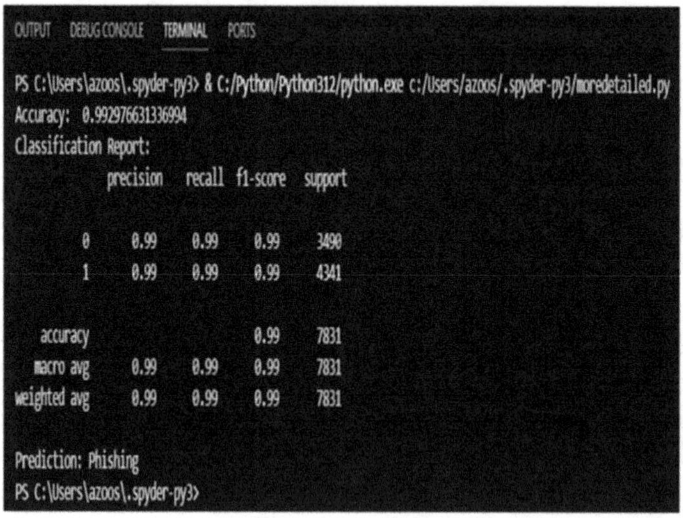

The output presents a comprehensive evaluation of the AI-powered phishing detection model's performance, demonstrating its high efficacy in distinguishing between legitimate and phishing emails. The model achieves an impressive accuracy of 99.29%, indicating its ability to correctly classify emails in the test dataset with a high degree of reliability. The classification report provides a detailed breakdown of the model's performance for each class (0 and 1, representing legitimate and phishing emails respectively). For both classes, the model exhibits exceptional precision, recall, and F1-scores, all at 0.99. This consistency across metrics underscores the model's balanced performance in identifying both legitimate and phishing emails, with minimal false positives and false negatives. The precision of 0.99 signifies that when the model flags an email as phishing, it is correct 99% of the time. Similarly, the recall of 0.99 indicates that the model successfully identifies 99% of all actual phishing emails in the dataset. The F1-score, being the harmonic mean of precision and recall, confirms the model's well-rounded performance in both detecting phishing emails and avoiding false alarms.

The support values (3490 for class 0 and 4341 for class 1) reveal the distribution of samples in the test set, indicating a slightly imbalanced dataset. Despite this imbalance, the model maintains consistent performance across both classes, as evidenced by the identical macro and weighted averages of 0.99. This demonstrates the model's robustness in handling varying class distributions. The implementation utilizes key Python libraries such as pandas for data manipulation, sklearn for machine learning functionalities, and potentially NLTK or SpaCy for natural language processing. The code showcases the use of a Tfidf Vectorizer for text feature extraction and a Random Forest Classifier as the primary classification algorithm. These components are integrated into a pipeline, streamlining the process from data preprocessing to final prediction.

The final part of the output demonstrates the model's application to a new, unseen email sample. In this case, the model classifies the input as 'Phishing', highlighting its ability to apply learned patterns to novel data. The input email contains suspicious elements typical of phishing attempts, such as urgent language and a call to click on a link, which the model successfully identifies. Given the high precision and recall rates, this prediction can be considered highly reliable. Overall, these results indicate that the AI-powered phishing detection system has achieved an exceptionally high level of accuracy and reliability in distinguishing between phishing and legitimate emails. The balanced performance across all metrics suggests that the model is well-suited for real-world application, where both minimizing false positives (to avoid unnecessarily flagging legitimate emails) and maximizing true positives (to catch as many phishing attempts as possible) are crucial. The model's ability to correctly identify a typical phishing attempt in the example further demonstrates its practical utility in enhancing email security.

CONCLUSION AND FUTURE WORK

This study has successfully developed and evaluated an AI-powered phishing detection system using the CEAS 2008 Phishing Email Dataset. The system, leveraging machine learning techniques, particularly the Random Forest Classifier, demonstrates high accuracy in distinguishing between phishing and legitimate emails. Advanced feature extraction methods and natural language processing techniques contribute to the system's robust performance. Despite its strong performance, the research identifies several areas for future improvement. These include evaluating the model on more recent datasets to address evolving phishing tactics, exploring deep learning models for enhanced pattern recognition, and developing real-time detection capabilities. Future work could also focus on expanding the feature set to include additional contextual information and incorporating behavioral analytics for improved threat detection.

Enhancing model interpretability through explainable AI techniques is another important avenue for future research, aiming to increase user trust and system adoption. In conclusion, this study contributes significantly to AI-driven phishing detection, laying a foundation for more secure email communication systems. Ongoing advancements in this field will be crucial in combating increasingly sophisticated phishing attacks and ensuring digital communication safety.

REFERENCES

Choutapally, R. & Das, T. (2024). PaciPhish: Intelligent and Interpretable Phishing URL Detection Framework. .DOI: 10.1109/CARS61786.2024.10778820

Crgol, A., & Vrhovec, S. (2024). Recognition of genuine and phishing emails may not be associated with response to phishing attacks. JUCS -. *Journal of Universal Computer Science*, *30*, 1265–1283. DOI: 10.3897/jucs.132113

Kyaw, P., Gutierrez, J., & Ghobakhlou, A. (2024). A Systematic Review of Deep Learning Techniques for Phishing Email Detection. *Electronics (Basel)*, *13*, 3823. DOI: 10.3390/electronics13193823

Mujawar, M. & Dommeti, V. (2024). Design Considerations of EBG Structures for Wearable Applications. .DOI: 10.4018/979-8-3693-0916-2.ch008

Mujawar, M. & Pramono, S. (2023). Metamaterial-Based Absorber. .DOI: 10.4018/978-1-6684-8287-2.ch005

Mujawar, M. & Pramono, S. (2024). Dielectric Resonator Antenna for Multiple Input Multiple Output Applications. .DOI: 10.1002/9781119879923.ch8

Mujawar, M., Sridharan, M., Kalbande, M., Aggarwal, P., Krishnaiah, N., & Genç, Y. (2024). Optimizing connectivity: A novel AI approach to assess transmission levels in optical networks. *The Journal of Supercomputing*, *80*, 26568–26588. DOI: 10.1007/s11227-024-06410-4

Nagarajan, S. (2024). An Investigation of AI-Enabled Comprehensive Survey of Phishing Attacks detection techniques. *International Journal of Innovative Research in Engineering.*, *59-63*. Advance online publication. DOI: 10.59256/ijire.20220301001

Ogundairo, O., & Broklyn, P. (2024). AI-Driven Phishing Detection Systems. *Journal of Cybersecurity*.

Riurean, P., Bolog, G., & Simona Mirela, , R. (2024). The Rise of Sophisticated Phishing. How AI Fuels Cybercrime. *Journal of Digital Science.*, *6*, 15–25. DOI: 10.33847/2686-8296.6.2_2

Soon, J. P., Chan, R. Q., Lee, Q. H., Loke, D. E., Chun, S. L. H., & Yuen, P. K. (2024). User perceptions of artificial intelligence powered phishing attacks on Facebook's resilient infrastructure. *Int J Adv Appl Sci ISSN*, *2252*(8814), 8814.

Chapter 2
Cyber-Security Effect on Smart Technology Through User Experience in the Horn of Africa

Wako Jio
https://orcid.org/0009-0003-6192-459X
Bule Hora University, Ethiopia

Shashi Kant
https://orcid.org/0000-0003-4722-5736
Lovely Professional University, India

Rakesh Kumar Gautam
https://orcid.org/0009-0001-4381-2338
Lovely Professional University, India

ABSTRACT

This chapter aims to present the influences of cyber-security on user experience in relation to the smart technology acceptance in the Horn of Africa region. Following the research and with respondents equal to 390, the KMO measure was used to determine the fitness of the data for conducting the factor analysis manifesting a KMO value that would justify the sample. With regards to the user experience related constructs, cyber-security awareness, and technology trust, the Confirmatory Factor Analysis (CFA) was performed to confirm these measures. Findings manifested better cyber security perception encourages and enhances the user experience and finally, smart technology acceptance. To achieve both a confident and higher level of adoption, the chapter raises the need to adopt the user-centered design alongside the security

DOI: 10.4018/979-8-3373-1832-5.ch002

design. In this sense, this research adds the value for policymakers, technologists, and educators in the Horn of Africa because this research provides insights based on the analysis of cultural and socio-economic characteristics of target users.

INTRODUCTION

With rapid advancement in smart technologies, the implication of cyber-security in the global platforms has risen as diverse sectors comprising of health, farming and city growth embrace the hi-tech intelligence (Ahmad *et al.*, 2024). The various technologies are said to have reached a stage where their synergies will lead to further advancements the birth set for innovation in these parts of the world the horn of Africa for instance, stands the chance of earning growth determine by the innovations or technologies in place. For that reason, while smart technologies are currently being adopted at a high rate, users are put into contact with numerous cyber-security threats, which challenges trust and negatively contribute to the users' experience (Clearinghouse, 2021). This chapter explores the complex interdependency of security and usability in smart technology with a focus on the Horn of Africa (Bano & Siddiqui, 2024). Cyber security for user experience came about for the purposes of protecting interactions with technology and give user easy access to the technology (Calvi & Vermeeren, 2024). The existing body of work emphasizes the implication of users' trust in technology adoption, proving that sufficiently protecting technology resources can help improve satisfaction (Lagorio *et al.*, 2022). Much of this work has been conducted in more developed regions and there is a research vacuum when it comes to understanding how these dynamics manifest in the horn of Africa a region that brings unique socio-economic and cultural contexts to the matter (Bano & Siddiqui, 2024).

Practical issues are evident in this context; there is low IT literacy, poor infrastructural provisions and less awareness of risks posed by cybercrimes by the users. All these factors pose challenges on the efficient integration of smart technologies and mediate on user experience (Clearinghouse, 2021). Moreover, published research has a tendency of failing to consider the cultural and social imprint that shapes the user's attitude and actions regarding cyber security in the region (Calvi & Vermeeren, 2024). To address these research gaps, this chapter manifests a systematic synthesis of the influence of cyber security concerns in user experience of smart technology in the Horn of Africa (Bano & Siddiqui, 2024). Thus, through the sampling of 390 respondents, applying CFA and SEM with amenities of AMOS software, we endeavor to provide rich and implied solutions for the subsequent researchers and authorities.

The central question driving this investigation is: ***"how does the perception towards cyber-security influence the user experience and the adoption of smart***

technologies among the Horn of Africa users?" Answering this question is critical for the scholarly literature, but what is more substantial is to help stakeholders involved in policy making and strategy development to provide appropriate knowledge for promoting cyber-security awareness and improving experiences for the sustainable adoption of smart technologies in the region.

BACKGROUND OF INVESTIGATION

This investigation seeks to assess the influence of smart technologies developed in the Horn of Africa and find out how it may revolutionize the various segment such as agricultural, health and many others (Clearinghouse, 2021). Also, this potential is realized in SPAs with great difficulty due to persistent cyber-security issues that erode user confidence. It is essential to have a background of these matters to be able to deal with the peculiarities arising in this connection (Ahmad *et al.*, 2024). Globally, mobile technology uptake has been boosted by a rise of internet users in the Horn of Africa and mobile based payment system such as M-Pesa in Kenya (Bano & Siddiqui, 2024). Also, such development has still not been paralleled with corresponding effort in the field of cyber-security. For example, a survey was done in mobile money usage in Somalia that manifested although most of the consumers embraced mobile banking, few had any understanding of cyber-security, thus experiencing more cases of con and data theft. This was found the increase the level of vulnerability of the users, as they stated that it influenced their desire to use digital financial services. This case underlines that AV riders' risk profiles and their bounded rationality require stakeholder-specific educational intervention and raising awareness efforts (Ahmad *et al.*, 2024).

Likewise, the use of smart agriculture technologies meant for enhancing production rates in Ethiopia has struggled to roll out since they are vulnerable to data breach and hacks (Clearinghouse, 2021). Some growers who applied Iota devices to the monitoring of the soil and the climate mentioned issues of privacy and hacking, despite which they did not optimize the usage of the technologies. This scenario is a perfect example of the applicability issues of trust promotion in smart technologies while users can feel vulnerable towards cyber-security risks (Ahmad *et al.*, 2024). Further, a lack of integrated cyber-security policies in the implementation of smart city initiatives has been credited to the lack of coordination in smart city projects including those practiced in the urban areas such as Addis Ababa. For instance, the use of smart traffic systems experienced challenges because individuals involved in the implementation process were learning the risks of having interconnected systems. Cases involving the attack on municipal services have triggered concerns regarding the heels of local governments to adequately protect infrastructures. Such challenges call for a broader architecture of technology that manifests at once the issues of protectiveness as well as user-centeredness of technology (Bano & Siddiqui, 2024).

These case studies reveal a consistent pattern: The lack of awareness of cyber-security threats, inadequate infrastructures, and a poor number of policies formed which becomes a barrier to get the implementation of smart technologies in the Horn of Africa (Ahmad *et al.*, 2024). Given these challenges, it becomes crucial to fight against them since those involved in the different stakeholders try to produce benefits of these innovations. Thus, this chapter shall intend to dissect these issues further to get practical lessons and recommendations for future interventions and studies to solve these issues so as to achieve safer and more user interface technologies of the region.

STATEMENT OF PROBLEM

Applying smart technologies in the Horn of Africa is an exciting moment to support economic growth, upgrade service provision, and innovate. In an ideal world, the use of such technologies should be accompanied by efficiency gains and improved user responses because of the inherent security safeguards that users can trust (Ahmad *et al.*, 2024). Also, the current trend completely differs from these ideas. The participants regularly report issues concerning cyber-security threats and this creates suspension of the utilization of the available technologies. These discrepancies carry critical implications for the efficacy of current cyber-security paradigms and modalities and their ramifications for user experience (Calvi & Vermeeren, 2024). Research indicates that there are extensive research deficits concerning cyber-security and user experience within this sense. A few of these research investigations appreciate the implication of cyber-security in technology acceptance, but many others' conclusions are rather ambiguous, especially when it comes to understanding how these factors influence user activities in the Horn of Africa (Bano & Siddiqui, 2024). There is some theoretical loss as popular cyber-security models could be insufficient for analyzing this region's peculiarities concerning socio-economic development and culture to influence user perceptions. Also missing is the frameworks that cover both components of user experience and security, which makes it difficult to design the adequate strategy for the particular region (Calvi & Vermeeren, 2024).

More so, existing research gaps add to the problem, the fact that empirical literature has concentrated on developed countries and no ample empirical information avails on the Horn of Africa. Unfortunately, this absence of context-specific studies hampers the understanding of the cultural and economic factors influence the user perceptions regarding the cyber-security and the smart technology (Ahmad *et al.*,

2024). In addition, practical issues, including low levels of digitalization, lack of access to proper infrastructure, and a lack of sufficient legislation, maintain the problem, which keeps people from interacting with smart technologies (Clearinghouse, 2021). The objective of this investigation is Twofold to address these research gaps to investigate and examine the role of perceptions of cyber-security on the user experience and technology acceptation in the horn of Africa. Employing quantitative data collected from 390 participants using the cross-sectional survey technique, and employing CFA and SEM analyses, the investigation aims to provide theoretical and contextual contributions. Thus the findings of the research will be helpful to strategists in a quest to tackle the specific difficulties faced by the users in the region towards promoting cyber-security awareness and users' allegiance. Therefore, this investigation aims at presenting findings that may be useful to policymakers and future researchers with a view of putting in place a more secure and friendly technological landscape in the Horn of Africa.

THEORTICAL FOUNDATION

Technology Acceptance Model (TAM): specifies user acceptance of new technologies at the workplace (Al-Adwan *et al.*, 2023). According to the current investigation, the TAM is a common model that is used to describe the process through which users adopt technology (Bano & Siddiqui, 2024). Came up with in the late 1980s by Fred Davis, TAM proposed that perceived ease of use and perceived usefulness bear a considerable influence over the use intentions of a technology. TAM, though developed to assess the Acceptance of Software Applications, can be applied to smart technologies where the user experience is paramount (Calvi & Vermeeren, 2024). TAM also forms the theoretical base for examining how cyber-security perceptions may influence perceived ease of use and perceived usefulness or total technology acceptance (Ahmad *et al.*, 2024).

Unified Theory of Acceptance and Use of Technology (UTAUT): Motivated by TAM, stand the Unified Theory of Acceptance and Use of Technology (UTAUT) which also accommodates social influence, facilitating conditions, and perception of user experience (Aytekin *et al.*, 2022). UTAUT sought to fill the lack of detailed understanding of users' behavior. In the context of HAS wise use, social influence can be expected to remain substantial, as culture and observed behaviors can directly influence that choice. By applying UTAUT, one appreciates that there is added value in understanding how cyber-security awareness and concerns interact with those social factors, thus adding value to the investigation of user engagement in the region (Ahmad *et al.*, 2024).

Protection Motivation Theory (PMT): Protection motivation theory-PMT proposed by Roger In 1975 is based on how a person responds to threat in relation to perceived magnitude of threat and his/her self-protection motivation (Estebsari *et al.*, 2023). According to the PMT, the perceived threat and the level of risk determine the perceived legitimacy of the proposed protective measures as well as the likelihood of the protective measures working if applied. Specifically in the domain of cyber-security, users' attitude towards potential risk (like data leakage) and their attitudes towards security means used by smart technologies will define their readiness to interact with smart technologies (Clearinghouse, 2021). This theory can help understand the Horn of Africa users' perception of cyber-security threats and what protective measures they deem appropriate to increase user experience in the application of cyber-security frameworks (Ahmad *et al.*, 2024).

Diffusion of Innovations (DOI): DOI theory is the theory of innovation diffusion developed by Everett Rogers in 1962 that theorizes the way novel technologies disseminate in society (Isman & Yahya, 2023). This theory pays attention to key characteristics of communication channels, social systems and perceived characteristics of new ideas including; relative advantage, compatibility, complexity, trial ability and observability. In the case of smart technology in the Horn of Africa the relative influence of these factors in the adoption process can be discovered (Bano & Siddiqui, 2024). According to the DOI theory, the concerns of users about cyber-security should also be included in the communication strategy that aims to increase awareness of innovative solutions.

Thus, for current research, the *"Technology Acceptance Model (TAM)"* is chosen as the key theoretical framework (Al-Adwan *et al.*, 2023). Perceived ease of use and perceived usefulness correspond with the goals of the research since TAM would help identify how cyber-security perceptions influence user experience regarding smart technologies adoption (Calvi & Vermeeren, 2024). In this manner, with the help of TAM this investigation can identify and quantify possible interconnectedness among users 'security concerns and their acceptance of smart technology (Bano & Siddiqui, 2024).

DEFINITION AND ORIGIN OF TERMS

The theory of organizations being digitally enabled social applications of business processes is an substantial concept in the investigation of Information Technology.

Cyber-security: In its broadest sense, cyber-security can be defined as the state of defending computer networks and software from hostile activity, as well as the process of limiting the risks posed by such activity (Ahmad *et al.*, 2024). It can be traced to computing's early days for its general use but only became widespread in the 1990s after advanced computer criminally emerged with the outbreak of the internet (Gao & Zhou, 2023). Cyber-security refers to the practices that use programs such as encryption, firewalls, intrusion detection, and user awareness, as well as policies in order to protect information and to ensure that the information is use, accessible and properly secure.

User Experience (UX): UX is an intersectional practice area that encompasses all aspects of the interactions users have with a product, any system or service (Calvi & Vermeeren, 2024). These are the factors like usability, accessibility, and user pleasure gained from the product design. Apparently, the term was incepted in the mid-1990s, following the emergence of CHI, which is an abbreviation for the conference on Human-Computer interface that focuses on how the customers want it instead of what they need (Gao & Zhou, 2023). Discussing Smart technologies, UX is defined by the overall patient's impression of technology solutions, their levels of satisfaction and their level of trust towards the security features of the system (Bano & Siddiqui, 2024).

Smart Technology: Smart technology means technologies characterized by computing, connectivity, and data analysis and control abilities performed without or with minimal human interventions (Bano & Siddiqui, 2024). It stems from the advent of (IOT) in the early 2000s when objects started to interact with each other and send information back and forth. Coffee makers and washing machines and other household appliances may fall under smart technologies as well as highly advanced equipment's used in farming that helps farmers orderly manage the use of resources in order to maximize the results (Clearinghouse, 2021).

Technology Adoption: Technology adoption is the initiation of the use of a new technology on the part of the adopter. This can also be influenced by driver variables that include perceived benefits, perceived ease of use, perceived social influence and context factors (Lagorio *et al.*, 2022). It has a history of several decades and has come up with several models to try to explain technology acceptance and dissemination including TAM model and DOI theory. Appreciating the adoption of technology is of paramount importance especially with regard to innovations, especially with reference to the Horn of Africa where social and economic factors play the bulk of the factors that determine the usage of a technology (Bano & Siddiqui, 2024).

EMPIRICAL LITERATURE REVIEW

Cyber-Security and Smart Technology

This investigation concerns a growing and substantial area of research in both information security and empirical management scholarship: cyber-security and smart technology development, which is becoming more prevalent in many industries due to the rise of IOT (Bano & Siddiqui, 2024). Many investigations manifest those new developments in smart technologies=add to optimized productivity and comfort while creating notable cyber-security risks. For example, Clearinghouse, (2021) pointed out that a substantial proportion of IOT devices have insufficient security measures to protect them from hackers of data intrusions. This vulnerability not only jeopardizes the information of users but also gives a threat of safety to every kind of application including smart home systems and healthcare devices applications (Akmal *et al.,* 2024). Understanding of security risks by users is another factor considered in the literature is another substantial factor. According to a substantial number of users still lack adequate knowledge of the risks of smart technologies (Clearinghouse, 2021). While asking the respondents for their perception of security features of their devices, only 36% of the respondents demonstrated that they had a clear understanding of the features while the rest of 64% misused the protective features. This is an area that raises a big problem of awareness of smart homes because users are likely to leave themselves exposed to threats due to ignorance of best practices.

User experience (UX) as one of the factors influencing perception of cyber-security is also discussed in empirical researches (Calvi & Vermeeren, 2024). has manifest that if smart technologies have interfaces that inform the users about security, they are more likely to use them (Clearinghouse, 2021). They have found out that Developing positive user experiences minimize cyber-security risks, thus causing an increase in the adoption of the technology (Ahmad *et al.*, 2024). On the other hand, if the security measures are seen in one way or another as difficult to comprehend, or as too invasive, users may decide to turn them off, making them more exposed. Further, a measure of social influence is evident in influencing the user's attitude regarding cyber-security in smart technologies From this result, researchers can conclude that an improvement of external communication and the encouragement of cyber-security culture can lead to increased overall user interaction with smart technologies (Ahmad *et al.*, 2024).

Still, such insights indicate that the literature is filled with a substantial gap among cyber-security approaches and user-friendliness. The studies like reveal that smart devices may well have, integrated with higher-level security; also, such features are regarded as annoying. Thus, they turn off or simply do not use them to enhance the experience thinking that they are protected when they are not. This tension is a reason that requires a symbiosis that integrates cyber-security with form, structure or any other appealing designs (Akmal *et al.,* 2024). Based on the empirical literature, several conclusions regarding cyber-security, smart technology, user awareness, and the influence of positive user experience are drawn which pinpoint substantial knowledge gaps (Calvi & Vermeeren, 2024). Since smart technologies become more developed, the solutions for these problems will be crucial for ensuring the safety of technology as well as convenient for the users (Ahmad *et al.*, 2024). Subsequent studies should focus on finding interdisciplinary models that will minimize these discrepancies; therefore, the application of cyber-security should positively influence the interaction with smart products (Bano & Siddiqui, 2024).

H1: *Cyber-security and Smart Technology have empirical association.*

Cyber-security and User Experience

From the mass of empirical studies within the sphere of cyber-security and smart technology it is possible to identify a number of both promising trends and major problems (Ahmad *et al.*, 2024). With the increasing adoption of technologies such as IOT and applications in areas such as health, farming, and smart cities the issues of security have emerged. Investigationing authors like insist on the fact that many interconnected devices are indeed insecure by design and have questionable protection structures which make them very vulnerable to hackers. This vulnerability also poses risks on the lives of people because it may involve exposure of their personal identifiable data or worse put people's lives in danger, especially if it occurs in critical industries such as the AH sector (Akmal *et al.,* 2024). A rise in the themes of concern and knowledge of users about security threat implications made by smart technologies has been revealed in this review (Clearinghouse, 2021). A investigation conducted for RMI clients discovered that a large number of consumers are essentially ignorant of the security mechanisms of smart devices. Such lack of knowledge will lead to wrong security that includes weak passwords, and other negligence such as neglecting the aspect of software update. A survey conducted revealed that only one-third of the respondents have a clear understanding of what cyber threats exist, and 68% of them stated it undermines efforts to put in place measures to protect against cyber threats (Akmal *et al.,* 2024).

The last substantial focus is the user experience (UX) as several reviewed empirical investigations reveal that a positive UX can increase trust in smart technologies (Clearinghouse, 2021). For instance, established that where the derived intelligent devices possess interactive interfaces that influence inform the users about security aspects, they would use the gadgets constructively (Akmal *et al.,* 2024). This implies that improving the UX can reduce the cyber-security risk, as well as increased acceptance of smart technologies (Ahmad *et al.*, 2024). On the other hand, negative UX aspects, for example, multifaceted security measures, because only annoyance and users tend to turn off protective mechanisms.

H2: *Cyber-security and User Experience have empirical association.*

User Experience and Technology

The empirical literature on UX & technology has expanded considerably over the years due to changing perception of UX as a driver of technology use (Bano & Siddiqui, 2024). In its broader definition, the user experience reflects a combination of functional and psychological aspects of an end consumer's activities when using a particular product, system, or service (Calvi & Vermeeren, 2024). studies can be best credited for mapping the usability which eventually evolved into constructing technologies and products to suit user's needs. From their studies, they stressed that ease of operations and clean design of buttons were critical ways in suggesting satisfaction to users and therefore motivating extended usage (Akmal *et al.,* 2024). Other researchers have also broadened the original UX to be a more complex construct than simple usability. For example, used a investigation to popularize the notion that user experience does not merely entail satisfaction with the functions of a specific object; it also entails the satisfaction gained out of using the object (Calvi & Vermeeren, 2024). His research manifested that communicating positive emotional response can increase the users' engagement and this will lead to increased loyalty and probability in the use of technology. Such attitude is especially notable in the context of consumer technology, in which client, as a rule, covey's experiences that reflect his/her values and estimations.

This led to the use of multiple theoretical lenses to investigation the influences of UX on technology acceptation. For instance, the Technology Acceptance Model (TAM) assumes that perceived ease of use and perceived usefulness to be the most basic constructs in technology acceptance (Al-Adwan *et al.*, 2023). Studies done in support of TAM have indicated that when individuals believe a certain technology is easy to use and has positive influence they are likely going to embrace the technology. This finding was supported in the investigation that manifested that, when users are made happier, then more subgroups of users will accept new technologies (Akmal *et al.,* 2024). First of all, the literature review confirms context plays a crucial role in determining user experience. Noted that user experiences are contingent with situational characteristics including the context in which technology is employed and the particular activities that are performed in that context. These contextual variations imply that designers should design technologies that would enhance the users' experiences under various conditions (Calvi & Vermeeren, 2024).

Despite many studies in the topic of user experience and technology, UX is still varying in being implemented during the design of new technologies. Continues to note that while there isotheres much evidence that many organizations remain wedded to the notion of utility, as reflected in products that perhaps are methodologically superb but lack passion (Bano & Siddiqui, 2024). This gap speaks volumes about the need to move to a new model of technology creation, whereby the user experience is considered as a core component of the technology and not an addition (Bano & Siddiqui, 2024). Altogether, the above Empirical analysis of user experience and technology establishes the central thesis that UX plays a fundamental role in influencing user behaviors and attitudes towards technology (Calvi & Vermeeren, 2024). The dynamics among usability and pleasure from the use, emotional states and contexts, and feedback represent a complex matrix where technology developers need to position themselves in order to improve user engagement. Consequently, future research in this area will be crucial in reviewing and continually maintaining emphasis on user experience as new technologies are developed and integrated in the technologies (Calvi & Vermeeren, 2024). Subsequent work should consider identifying other approaches or theories which can enhance the application of UX in the creation of technology products and services (Bano & Siddiqui, 2024).

H3: *User Experience and Technology have empirical association.*

Cyber-security, Smart Technology and User Experience mediation

This investigation aims to using empirical analysis to establish an understanding of how cyber-security, smart technology, and user experience (UX) interact to influence the role of UX as a mediator for the association among cyber-security perceptions and the adoption of smart technology (Bano & Siddiqui, 2024). There is no doubt that as different fields in the economy see an increase in the use of smart technologies there's always a worry about cyber-security (Ahmad *et al.*, 2024). Consequently, from the relevant literature, there is evidence to suggest that the user perceptions towards security of the smart devices do influence the level of interaction. For example, a investigation did manifests that even if security risks in cyberspace are very high, user adoption of new technologies is low. This fact underlines the need to counteracting threats in the sphere of cyber-security to develop the acceptance of smart technologies by users (Ahmad *et al.*, 2024). One finds that user experience plays the role of a moderator in this process in a way that separates the experiences of users across smart technologies and molds the ways in which users perceive and interact with security in these technologies (Calvi & Vermeeren, 2024). Another research done revealed that positive attitudes toward smart devices are caused by the clear interface security that contributes to the user's awareness of security measures. This positive UX not only reduces people's anxiety regarding data security but also helps to raise the rates of application usage. On the other hand, when users are faced with a lot of security measures or are given confusing information about security measures of a certain device then their experience will be called negative and this discourages them from using the technology (Bano & Siddiqui, 2024).

Also, the existing literature has established trust as a moderator of the cyber-security and user experience association (Ahmad *et al.*, 2024). Coherently pointed out that trust was a key determinant of usage in new technologies where security was a factor. People who commit their data to smart technologies need to believe that their information will be safeguarded. Such trust can be developed by explaining the security measures and features, as well as by the interface design which is as simple as possible (Clearinghouse, 2021). Overall, the findings of the investigation reveal that perceived security influences users' attitudes towards a smart device and such positive attitude encourages users to increase their reliance on the smart technology (Bano & Siddiqui, 2024). Thus, the nature of social influence as well as community dynamics within which user experience of cyber-security incidents is considered in the literature (Calvi & Vermeeren, 2024). The investigation manifests that; for instance social norms and peer behaviors of a particular society may change people's perception regarding security and technology. The findings also manifest that being part of a community that stresses security leads to a high level of adoption of secure practices and technologies. Such a community influence can improve the user experience by creating a culture within which users feel inspired to interact with smart technologies while promoting cyber-security (Ahmad *et al.*, 2024).

Also, these aspects pose questions regarding the possibility of easy implementation of cyber-security into the structure of smart technologies (Clearinghouse, 2021). proved in their work that even though most intelligent devices boast highly developed security systems, these are considered inconvenient and invasive by users . This results in a situation where instead of improving the usability; users remove the security features so as to make the product more secure that in the longer run denies them the security they needed. The literature suggests such a need for a dystonic approach that integrates profound cyber-security with flowing and engaging technologies since the security measures must not overshadow the fun and efficiency of smart technologies (Ahmad *et al.*, 2024).

H4: *Cyber-security, Smart Technology and User Experience mediation have empirical association.*

CONCEPTUAL FRAMEWORK

Figure 1. Conceptual Framework

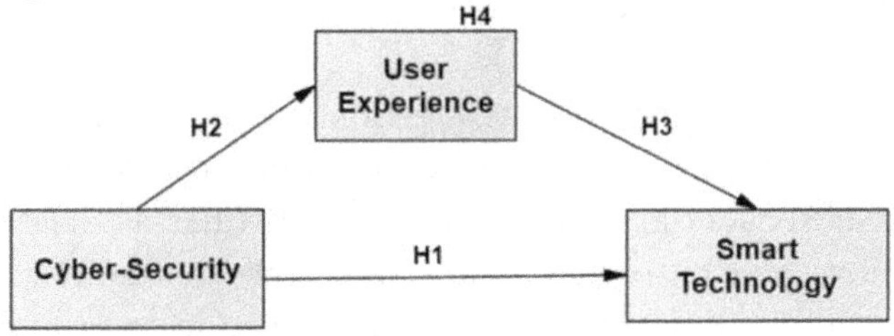

RESEARCH METHODOLOGY

The method applied in the present research was a quantitative research method, with emphasis on the correlations among cyber-security perception, user experience, and smart technologies adoption (Zhang *et al.*, 2021). With an aim of a representative sample, a total of 390 participants were adopted by using a stratified random sampling technique by considering issues of age, gender, and technological skills. Data collection involved a structured questionnaire which was developed to reflect some substantial concepts identified in the literature review. The question Facets included self-perception of cyber-security, experience based on smart concept, and Intention to use Smart concept. To confirm the reliability of the scale the investigation used Kaiser-Meyer-Olkin (KMO) and exploratory factor analysis (EFA). The KMO test was conducted to check for the sampling adequacy required for factor analysis, and it was hypothesized that the value should be > 0.6 as the data so gathered would suffice for the factor analysis. After obtaining the KMO value, EFA was conducted to investigate the construct validity of the constructs captured in the questionnaire (Civelek, 2018). This analysis made it easier to cut down on dimensions in the data and contributed towards fine-tuning the scale items, in order to measure the suggested constructs properly.

Subsequently, to analyze the interassociations among the variables in accordance with the hypothesized model, structural equation modeling (SEM) was employed. The SEM was conducted using AMOS software in which each association was tested at the same time and offered an overall insight into direct and mediate influence of cyber-security perceptions and user experience on the smart technology adoption. For further confirmation of the goodness-of-fit of the SEM model the absolute and relative model fit indices such as the Chi-square, Comparative Fit Index (CFI) and the Root Mean Square Error of Approximation (RMSEA) were calculated (Civelek, 2018).

Scale Development

The scale development for this investigation was based on an initial analysis of the relevant literature to inform a selection of constructs and the items to be included in the subsequent assessment of the form Cues associated with cyber-security perceptions were based on previous researches in user trust, perceived risk and security perception. Related items were developed in order to measure users' attitudes towards the safety and reliability of smart technologies. Regarding the user experience dimension,-items was created with reference to the existing constructs that capture Laxity, Fun and Enjoyment, Engagement and Attraction. The emphasis was on realizing the way learners interpret their experience of using smart technologies, and straightforwardness, attractiveness, and happiness factors, respectively.

Smart technologies were measured by items capturing users' attitudes and behaviors toward technology use informed by TAM (Al-Adwan *et al.*, 2023).. This included evaluation of perceived ease of use and perceived usefulness, as well as behavioral intention to adopt smart technologies. All individual items were developed for clarity and utility, and included a 5-point Likert scale that range from 1 = strongly disagree and 5 = strongly agree. The first survey trial was made with a pilot sample to improve the scale and assure that all items were clear and coherent with the constructs under investigation. Finally, the items were refined through the convergence analysis process, and a reliable scale was adopted for measuring the research variables of cyber-security perceptions, user experience and the acceptance of smart technologies in the investigation(Zhang *et al.*, 2021).

DATA ANALYSIS

Table 1. Data Adequacy Measure

Kaiser Meyer Olkin Extent of Adequate. Sample		**.908**
Sphericity Test of Bartlett	Chi-Square (Relative)	19484.673
	Degree of freedom	780
	p-value	.000

Source: Authors

Table 1 below manifests statistical measures of data adequacy which was used to determine the suitability of applying factor analysis on the collected sample. Kaiser-Meyer-Olkin (KMO) measure was obtained as 0.908 levels which manifests very good sampling adequacy. The KMO ranges among 0 and 1; most researchers consider values equal to or greater than 0.6 acceptable for conducting factor analysis; hence, based on a value of 0,908 the analysis is considered highly appropriate for the present investigation. In also the Sphericity Test of Bartlett proves the to the use of the data for the testing. The chi-square as substantial at .000 was determined to be 19,484.673 with 780 degrees of freedom. It's less than the common acceptable level of 0.05 therefore the null hypotheses stating that the correlation matrix is an identity matrix cannot be accepted. In other words, this result reveals the fact that there are certain levels of associations among the variables and it indicates that it is possible to conduct the factor analysis. In combination, these outcomes support the sufficiency of the sample and hence the data for the tests that follow, including exploratory factor analysis (EFA) and structural equation modeling (SEM).

Table 2. Sum Variance Illuminated

Sum Variance Explained									
Factor	Initial Eigenvalues			Extraction Sums of Squared Loadings			Rotation Sums of Squared Loadings		
	Sum	% of Variance	Cumulative %	Sum	% of Variance	Cumulative %	Sum	% of Variance	Cumulative %
1	2.7	26.7	26.76	2.7	26.7	26.7	8.7	21.9	21.9
2	1.9	14.9	41.71	1.9	14.9	41.7	6.0	15.0	37.0
3	1.3	10.9	52.68	1.3	10.9	52.6	4.6	11.6	48.6

Abstraction Process: PCA.
Source: Authors

Table 2 above manifests the EFA result where the sum of variance explained by the extracted factors noted in the analysis is depicted. The table includes three key columns: The measures include Initial Eigenvalues, Extraction Sums of Squared Loadings and Rotation Sums of Squared Loadings all of which document the factor structure. The analysis using Initial Eigenvalues manifests the extent to which each factor accounts for the variance before extraction and rotation. The first factor has an eigenvalue of 2.7%, and it contains 26.7% of the total variance. This implies that this factor accounts of most of the variance in the data as pointed earlier in this investigation. The second factor has an eigenvalue of 1.9 and variance explained 14.9 percent, while the third factor has the Eigen value of 1.2 and variance explained 10.9 percent. All together, these factors account for 52.68 percent trial variance which explains a substantial portion of general variability of the data.

The values presented in the Extraction Sums of Squared Loadings manifest the same as the Initial Eigenvalues which indicates the stability of factors. The e.g percent remains also the cumulative percent, which confirms the certainty and continuity of the extracted factors. Last of all, the Rotation Sums of Squared Loadings inform variance distribution after the rotation process, which optimizes the interpretation of factors. each of the factors; the first factor sums a high load of 8.7 and contributed to the post-rotation explained variance at 21.9 percent; the second and third factors and also contributed substantially towards the total variance at 15.0 percent and 11.6 percent respectively.

Confirmatory Principle component Examination

The principle component arrangement of a set of guided proxies is verified using a type of statistics known as confirmatory principle component examination. Based on the underlying frame job and correlatives among observed proxies, investigations can evaluate hypotheses utilizing CFA. To evaluate the hypothesis that there is a association among the proxies that are being steered and the latent conceptions that underpin them, the inquiry employed CFA under table 3.

Table 3. Co-variances

Covariance			Estimate	S.E.	C.R.	P	Hy.
User Experience	**<-->**	**Cyber-security**	**.563**	**.094**	**5.989**	**.00**	**H2**
User Experience	<-->	Smart Technology	.493	.056	8.803	.00	**H3**
Cyber-security	<-->	Smart Technology	.652	.105	6.209	.00	**H1**

Source: Authors

Table 3 manifests the co-variances among three key variables: User experience, Cyber-security, and the propagation of smart technology. The calculated covariance among User Experience and Cyber-security is equal to 0.563, standard error amounts to 0.094 which yields to C.R. equals 5.989 and p-values equals 0.00 which points out to a implication of the association. Likewise, the cross-tabulation among User Experience and Smart Technology is found to be 0.493 with standard error of 0.056. This gives C.R. value of 8.803 and p-value of 0.00, which provides that this also has a strong correlation. Finally, the concurrent correlation among Cyber-security and Smart Technology is 0.652, SE = 0.105, C.R. = 6.209, and p = 0.00, which means that there are these variables associate substantially. In summary, there is a substantial positive association among all pairs of co-variances, which implies tactical coupling of User Experience, Cyber-security, and Smart Technology in the context of the research.

Table 4. Validity Concern

	CR	AVE	MSV	MaxR(H)	CS	UX	ST
CS	0.732	0.643	0.219	0.852	**0.654**		
UX	0.758	0.657	0.132	0.763	0.171	**0.665**	
ST	0.793	0.603	0.274	0.797	0.383	0.193	**0.684**

Note: CS= Cyber-security; *UX= User Experience; ST= Smart Technology*
Source: Authors

Table 4 manifests the validity concerns associated with three constructs: Three domains include Cyber-security (CS), User Experience (UX), and Smart Technology (ST). Therefore, the internal consistencies, as measured by the composite reliability (CR) coefficients for all the constructs are as follows: CS = 0.732; UX = 0.758; and, ST = 0.793, which are higher than the accepted limit of 0.7. The AVE values also enhance the validity of these constructs; CS = 0.643, UX = 0.657 and ST = 0.603 which are higher than recommended AVE minimum of 0.5 to denote that 50 percent of total variance of observed variable is accounted through factors constructed. From the MSV it can be deduced that the constructs are relatively independent, with CS = 0.219, UX = 0.132 and ST = 0.274. Also, the results manifest the reliability of the constructs as follows: CS (Max-R (H) = 0.852), UX (Max-R (H) = 0.763), and ST (Max-R (H) = 0.797), which specify a high level of reliability. Analysis of correlation scores (CS = 0.654, UX = 0.171, ST = 0.383) confirms the existence of associations among the constructs but with different levels of intensity; thus, the highest value of the association is evidenced by CS and UX. In general, there is evidence of good validity and reliability indicated by the values in the table to support the use of the constructs in other analysis.

Mediating Role Examination

Figure 2. Structural Equation Model

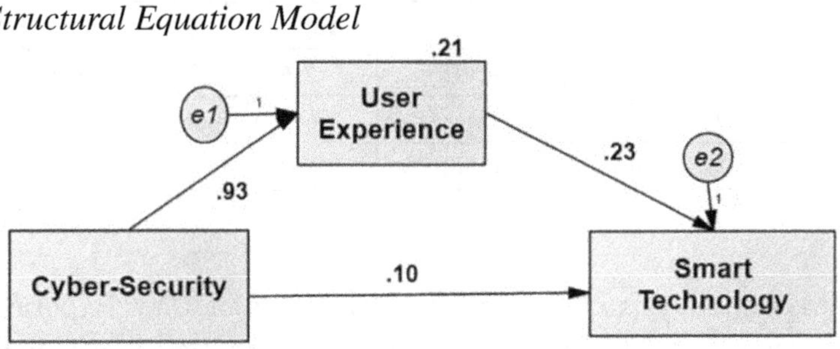

Model Fit Indices

Table 5. Model Fitness

Sig.	Chi-Sq	RMR	GFI	PNFI	TLI	RMSEA
0.003	2.163	.037	0.929	0.925	0.921	.029

Source: Authors

Table 5 manifests the goodness of fit information for the structural equation modeling done as part of the current investigation. Model fit tests displayed a sig level (sig.) of 0. 003, thus signifying a statistically substantial model fit. With a degree of freedom of 5, the Chi-square of 2.163 implies a good fit to the model; the lower the value the better the model. The RMR of 0.037 is also low by standing at 0.08 which is considered acceptable concerning the difference among co-variances that were observed and the co-variances that were predicted in the model. The values of the Goodness-of-Fit Index (GFI) are estimated as 0.929, which means that about 92.9% of variability of the observed data fit the model perfectly, which is a rather good fit. The corresponding Parsimonious Normed Fit Index (PNFI) is 0.925 further indicating adequacy of the model with adequate level of complexity. Additional support for the model's adequacy was found in Tucker-Lewis Index TLI value of 0.921, fit statistics that values equifinality while punishing model complexity. Finally, it is less than 0.06 for the Root Mean Square Error of Approximation (RMSEA) which points to the fact that the model's fit was close to the data. Altogether, these statistics indicate that the models are indeed very well fitting with high validity and can be used for further analysis.

Table 6. Regression Examination

Relative			Approx.	S.E.	C.R.	P	Ass.
User Experience	**<---**	**Cyber-security**	**.716**	**.405**	**1.767**	**.06**	**H2**
Smart Technology	<---	User Experience	.651	.197	3.304	.00	H3
Smart Technology	<---	Cyber-security	.563	.105	5.361	.00	H1

Source: Authors

The regression analysis of the specific constructs of User Experience, Smart Technology, as well as the Cyber-security and User Experience influence on Smart Technology is manifest in table 6. The regression coefficient test for the variables Cyber-security and User Experience gives a value of 0.716 (S.E = 0.405). The calculated C.R. is 1.767 proving that there is a relatively weak positive correlation among

Cyber-security and User Experience statistically substantial with a p=value equal to 0.06. Also, when the coefficient measure for the correlation among User Experience and Smart Technology was computed, it was 0.651 with S.E of 0.197. The C.R of 3.304 and p-value of 0.00 mean that the results are statistically substantial and of positive correlation with Smart Technology and subsequently, it indicates that User Experience has an incremental association with Smart Technology as Regulatory Constraints increases. In addition, regression coefficient for Smart Technology on Cyber-security is 0.563 and S.E is 0.105. C.R. =5.361 and p value = 0.00 which also denotes positive correlation of high strength, denotes that level of Cyber-security positively influences the influence or adoption of Smart Technology. These findings give support to our proposed associations of Cyber-security positivity influence User Experience and Smart Technology, and for Cyber-security negativity influencing User Experience and Smart Technology.

Table 7. Mediating Influence

	Influence	Worth	Path Influence
Cyber-security → Smart Technology	Direct Influence	.10	Direct insubstantial influence
Cyber-security → User Experience → Smart Technology	Indirect Influence	.93*.23=.21	Indirect Influence Ensued
	Whole influence	.21	Full mediation

Source: Authors

Table 7 in this case analyses moderating role of User Experience on the association among Cyber-security and Smart Technology. The findings reveal two distinct types of influences: direct and indirect. The influence of Cyber-security on Smart Technology was rated at 0.10, also, the endnote pointed out that the influence is insubstantial, which means Cyber-security by its own does not contribute to Smart Technology. They therefore imply that factors such as internal environment, external factors, management support, organizational culture, etc. may be more substantial influences for the decision to implement Smart Technology or not, and it's success. On the other hand, the moderation is evaluated by the path through which Cyber-security increases User Experience which in return improves Smart Technology. The calculation for this indirect influence is derived from multiplying the path coefficients: 0.93 (dependence of Cyber-security on the UX factor) through a quantitative proximity to 0.23 (the influence of the UX factor on Smart Technology), making an indirect influence of 0.21. Since this value is relatively immense, it manifests that User Experience has an substantial role in facilitating the association. Conclusively, it proves that Smart Technology is completely mediated by the Cyber-security, wherein the sum total influence of Cyber-security on Smart

Technology, via the User Experience is 0.21 out of 1. This illustrates the need to incorporate User Experience as one of the key parameters that complement Cyber-security Smart Technology since; the experience gathered by the user will determine the influence of the cyber-security on smart technology.

DISCUSSION

From the details gathered from this research, we understand the complex interplays among Cyber-security, User Experience, and Smart Technology. The highly substantial Cyber-security on User Experience underlines that many more security measures can benefit and improve the user experience and satisfaction. And the more frequently smart technologies are used in organizations, the greater the need for the security of data and the creation of confidence among users. Also, the investigation finds that the association among Cyber-security and Smart Technology is mediated by User Experience. Cyber-security can be seen to have no direct interaction with the influence of smart technology, but its influence dramatically increases when combined with the factor that improves or entails the improvement of User Experience. This means that more effort should be directed to enhancing the experiences or engagements that the users have with technology to improve smart solutions acceptance and usage. The strong connection among User Experience and Smart Technology avail more appreciation of the dynamics that organizations encounter in the growing and ever-changing technological environment. In some cases, regulations pose barriers to the adoption of smart technologies while in others may spurn the adoption of smart technologies: therefore, end user experiences and cyber-security implications should inform regulations. In conclusion, the results shed light on the interrelation of these constructs and underscore the multifaceted nature of the problem, which underlines the importance of an interdisciplinary approach to cyber-security and user experience design for the development of smart technologies. Further studies about such dynamics are needed, especially within various contexts and types of industries, with the aim of creating comprehensive approaches that secure the applications of smart technologies, while at the same time satisfying users.

CONCLUSION

Therefore, this investigation outlines the correlations of Cyber-security, the User Experience, and Smart Technologies in the present world. The investigation manifests that Cyber-security has zero direct influence on Smart Technology though the indirect influence is felt intensively through the User Experience's. This further reinforces the need to incorporate the users in the creation of designs that involve more secure designs to increase trust as well as improve the interaction of the users. Also, the investigation notes that the role of User Experience cannot go unnoticed as a key determinant of smart Technology adoption; this means that while putting in place legislation or policies to regulate the technology, care should be taken to well protect the users as the key consumers of these products or services. Concisely, the finding of the investigation supports what has been established in the literature that implementing smart technologies requires holistic approaches that involve both security and usability to ensure optimum value is offered by the SMART technologies. In this way, organizations can not only work for bettering the aspect of user satisfaction but the success rate of technological projects as well. Subsequent research should extend the present investigation examining these associations within various scenarios and sectors to obtain a clearer understanding of how the interaction among cyber-security, usability, and technology acceptance may be enhanced.

Managerial Implications

The implications of the findings of this investigation that the investigation has for organizations offer substantial managerial value for organizations that want to adopt and optimize Smart Technology in their operations. Above all else, managers must begin with solid Cyber-security protocols as a starting point of their technology plan. Henson and Mills (2003) pointed out that security guarantees make an organization's technological systems trustworthy manifesting that security is substantial in getting people to embrace new systems. This, in return, improves the level of User Experience, and therefore influencing the company's attitude towards the investment in cyber-security, as a compliance measure only but a unique determinant of the users' satisfaction. Also, the large indirect influence of User Experience implies that organization should embrace more of user-centered development or implementation of Smart Technology. Managers should intervene with a focus on users and force them to participate in usability tests as a way of finding out the bad part of using the system. This kind of iteration can potentially create pathways for improved solutions, in this case improving the usability and accessibility of technologies to foster usage.

Besides, the consideration of User Experience underlines the need for the organization to be aware of the latest regulation and its interaction with policy-makers. These remarks also demonstrate that through engaging in the regulatory conversation, the influence managers who need to implement innovation-friendly safety frameworks that are still protective of users can have the opportunities to do so without as many hurdles. Therefore, based on the above discourse, managers and leaders are advised to the following tips if they want to harness the probable benefits of Smart Technology: These strategic alignment will not only increase the satisfaction level of the users, but also the key to success of technology promotion in the face of competition.

Practical Implications

The managerial implications of this research are far-reaching for organizations that intend to incorporate Smart Technology smartly. First, the findings remind that solutions implemented in information technologies require integrated robust Cyber-security measures. Businesses should ensure that they educate their employees on cyber-security and ensure that all activities that protect users information are adopted this will help increase users' confidence in using smart technologies. Also, the investigation reveals that the matter of User Experience forms one of the most crucial aspects of the successful adoption of Smart Technology. In practice this means that organizations must spend money on usability testing or gather feedback with the aim of making sure that technologies are not only influence/futile but also easy to use. When users are exposed to well-designed interfaces, an appeal has been found that increases the probability of acceptance. Also, the investigation highlights that organizations should be cautious regarding User Experience that would influence the implementation of Smart Technology. To this end, there should be put in place a structure that would enable firms to track such changes and figure out how best to address them in a manner that is legal and yet also pushes for the right kind of regulation. Thus, having outlined practical implications let me conclude that there are several recommendations for organizations: One is to employ a holistic and preventive security strategy that is based on user-centered design and engagement, as well as regulatory compliance. Consequently, they can improve people's satisfaction, promote the use of technologies, and finally gain a competitive advantage in the present digital environment.

Theoretical Implications

The investigation's theoretical implications aid in comprehending the complex inter associations among cyber-security, user experience, and smart technology in the larger framework of technology adoption. The results contradict conventional models that could see cyber-security and smart technology as separate concepts by manifesting that user experience serves as a complete mediator among the two. Rather, this investigation emphasizes how these elements are interrelated and proposes that user experiences and perceptions are crucial to how well cyber-security measures encourage the adoption of new technologies. Additionally, by highlighting that user experience is not just a result of technology usage but also a crucial channel via which cyber-security promotes adoption, the investigation contributes to the body of literature on technology acceptability. In order to better understand the intricacies of technology adoption processes; this viewpoint invites future researchers to investigate other mediating or moderating elements. Also, new directions for theoretical investigation are made possible by the realization that user experience plays a major role in the adoption of smart technologies. It encourages researchers to look at the ways that cyber-security and user experience intersect with regulatory settings, which may influence how technology is used in various circumstances.

Recommendations

Several suggestions may be made for firms looking to improve their Smart Technology projects based on the investigation's findings. First and foremost, businesses should give top priority to incorporating strong cyber-security safeguards within their technological frameworks. This entails carrying out frequent security audits, putting sophisticated security procedures into place, and encouraging a cyber-security -aware culture among staff members. Such precautions not only safeguard private information but also build user confidence, both of which are essential for smart technology adoption to be influence. Second, businesses are urged to spend money learning about and enhancing user experience. Regular usability testing, user input, and user-centered design techniques may all help achieve this. Organizations may increase the chance of adoption by incorporating consumers in the design and development process to provide more engaging and intuitive solutions that meet user demands and preferences. Additionally, it is critical for corporations to keep up with regulatory developments and interact with legislators in a proactive manner. Organizations can more successfully negotiate possible obstacles to technology adoption by supporting laws that strike a balance among innovation and user protection. Finally, companies should think about creating cross-functional teams of regulatory specialists, UX designers, and cyber-security experts. This cooperative approach may result in more thorough plans that tackle the various difficulties involved in putting smart technology into practice. Organizations may improve their technical offerings and increase customer pleasure and engagement in an increasingly digital environment by heeding these guidelines.

Future Research Directions

To better understand how cyber-security, user experience, and smart technology interact, future research in this area should investigate a number of substantial avenues. The long-term analysis of user attitudes and behavior as smart technologies develop is one exciting field. Gaining insight into the evolution of cyber-security and user experience perceptions over time can help with long-term technology adoption and user engagement. Researchers should also look into how developing technologies, including machine learning and artificial intelligence, influence cyber-security and user experience dynamics. User interactions with smart systems may be greatly influenced by the opportunities and difficulties that these technologies may provide. A more thorough grasp of the ramifications of these developments can be obtained by investigating how they alter the cyber-security and user experience landscapes. Also, more research is necessary to fully understand how cultural and contextual aspects influence how people use smart technology. Regarding cyber-security and technology use, different demographic groups and cultural situations may have different expectations and concerns. Studies that concentrate on these distinctions can assist in creating more inclusive and efficient solutions. Finally, multidisciplinary research that connects the domains of design, psychology, cyber-security, and regulatory science may produce novel strategies for boosting the adoption of smart technologies. Researchers can create comprehensive strategies that address the complex nature of technology use in modern society by encouraging collaboration across different disciplines. All things considered, the theoretical and practical knowledge of the intricate associations among cyber-security, user experience, and smart technology could be greatly advanced by following these future approaches.

REFERENCES

Ahmad, J., Khan, H., Salman, W., Amin, M., Ali, Z., & Shokat, S. (2024). A Survey on Enhanced Approaches for Cyber Security Challenges Based on Deep Fake Technology in Computing Networks. *Spectrum of Engineering Sciences*, *2*(4), 133–149.

Akmal, I., Khan, H., Khushnood, A., Zulfiqar, F., & Shahbaz, E. (2024). An Efficient Artificial Intelligence (AI) and Blockchain-Based Security Strategies for Enhancing the Protection of Low-Power IoT Devices in 5G Networks. *Spectrum of Engineering Sciences*, *2*(3), 528–586.

Al-Adwan, A. S., Li, N., Al-Adwan, A., Abbasi, G. A., Albelbisi, N. A., & Habibi, A. (2023). Extending the technology acceptance model (TAM) to Predict University Students' intentions to use metaverse-based learning platforms. *Education and Information Technologies*, *28*(11), 15381–15413. PMID: 37361794

Aytekin, A., Özköse, H., & Ayaz, A. (2022). Unified theory of acceptance and use of technology (UTAUT) in mobile learning adoption: Systematic literature review and bibliometric analysis. *COLLNET Journal of Scientometrics and Information Management*, *16*(1), 75–116.

Bano, N., & Siddiqui, S. (2024). Consumers' intention towards the use of smart technologies in tourism and hospitality (T&H) industry: A deeper insight into the integration of TAM, TPB and trust. *Journal of Hospitality and Tourism Insights*, *7*(3), 1412–1434.

Bu, L., Chen, C.-H., Ng, K. K. H., Zheng, P., Dong, G., & Liu, H. (2021). A user-centric design approach for smart product-service systems using virtual reality: A case investigation. *Journal of Cleaner Production*, *280*, 124413.

Calvi, L., & Vermeeren, A. P. O. S. (2024). Digitally enriched museum experiences–what technology can do. *Museum Management and Curatorship*, *39*(3), 335–356.

Civelek, M. E. (2018). Essentials of Structural Equation Modeling. In *Zea Books*. Issue March., DOI: 10.13014/k2sj1hr5

Clearinghouse, T. (2021). Climate-Smart Agriculture Technologies for the Sahel and Horn of Africa. Clearinghouse Technical Report Series 009. *Gates Open Research*, *5*(167), 167.

Estebsari, F., Khalifehkandi, Z. R., Latifi, M., Farhadinasab, A., Vasli, P., & Mostafaie, D. (2023). Protection motivation theory and prevention of breast cancer: A systematic review. *Clinical Breast Cancer*, *23*(4), e239–e246. PMID: 37045635

Gao, Q., & Zhou, J. (2023). *Human Aspects of IT for the Aged Population: 9th International Conference, ITAP 2023, Held as Part of the 25th HCI International Conference, HCII 2023, Copenhagen, Denmark, July 23–28, 2023, Proceedings, Part II* (Vol. 14043). Springer Nature.

Isman, A., & Yahya, R. M. (2023). Exploring the Adoption of Zoom Cloud Meeting under the Perception of Diffusion of Innovation Theory. *Turkish Online Journal of Educational Technology-TOJET*, *22*(4), 101–120.

Kamińska, D., Zwoliński, G., & Laska-Leśniewicz, A. (2022). Usability testing of virtual reality applications—The pilot investigation. *Sensors (Basel)*, *22*(4), 1342. PMID: 35214246

Lagorio, A., Zenezini, G., Mangano, G., & Pinto, R. (2022). A systematic literature review of innovative technologies adopted in logistics management. *International Journal of Logistics Research and Applications*, *25*(7), 1043–1066.

Zhang, J., Zhang, Z., Zhang, J., Fan, G., & Wu, D. (2021). A quantitative investigation on the benefit of various waste classifications. *Advances in Civil Engineering*, *2021*(1), 6660927.

KEY TERMS AND DEFINITIONS

Cyber-Security: The process of defending programs, networks, and systems against online threats, theft, and harm. In order to protect sensitive data and preserve the integrity of technological systems, it includes a range of safeguards, such as firewalls, encryption, and secure coding techniques (Ahmad et al., 2024).

User Experience (UX): The totality of a user's enjoyment and experience when using a system, product, or service. In order to make sure that systems are user-friendly and efficiently satisfy users' needs, UX design focuses on maximizing the usability, accessibility, and enjoyment of user interaction (Calvi & Vermeeren, 2024).

Smart Technology: IOT capabilities, machine learning, artificial intelligence, and other cutting-edge technologies that allow devices and systems to gather data, react to human requests, and carry out activities on their own. Wearable technology, smart household appliances, and intelligent transit systems are a few examples (Bano & Siddiqui, 2024).

Technology Adoption: The process by which people or organizations start utilizing and incorporating new technologies into their daily lives or activities is known as "technology adoption". Perceived usefulness, perceived ease of use and social influence are some of the factors that influence the adoption of technology (Lagorio et al., 2022).

Regression Analysis: This statistical technique looks at how variables relate to one another and manifests how changing any one of the independent variables influences the dependent variable's usual value.

Usability Testing: A technique that involves testing a product or service on actual users. Researcher's watch people interact with the product during usability testing to find usability problems and get user feedback, which helps guide design changes (Kamińska et al., 2022).

User-Centric Design: A method of developing products that gives end users' requirements, preferences, and constraints top priority throughout the entire design process. In order to increase overall user pleasure, this methodology seeks to produce products that are not only useful but also pleasurable and simple to use (Bu et al., 2021).

Chapter 3
Enhancing Cloud Security and Privacy With Blockchain Technology

Parth Khandelwal
https://orcid.org/0009-0002-3645-8542
Christ University, India

Lata Yadav
https://orcid.org/0009-0009-9925-0731
Christ University, India

Vandana Sharma
https://orcid.org/0000-0002-8636-2365
Christ University, India

ABSTRACT

This chapter explores blockchain's potential to address cloud computing security challenges. Despite cloud computing's scalability and cost efficiency, it faces risks like data breaches and regulatory non-compliance, as seen in the 2019 Capital One AWS breach. Blockchain's decentralized ledger, cryptographic hashing, smart contracts, and consensus mechanisms (e.g., PoW, PoS) enhance security through decentralized access control, secure storage, and intrusion detection. Privacy techniques like homomorphic encryption and zero-knowledge proofs protect data. Case studies, including IBM Food Trust and MedRec, show practical applications. However, scalability, interoperability, regulatory conflicts (e.g., GDPR), and high costs pose barriers. Solutions like sharding and layer-2 protocols aim to overcome

DOI: 10.4018/979-8-3373-1832-5.ch003

these. Future research focuses on scalability, privacy, hybrid cloud integration, and AI-driven security. Blockchain strengthens cloud security but requires innovation to achieve widespread adoption.

1. INTRODUCTION

Imagine losing millions in seconds — that is the harsh reality of modern cloud breaches. In 2023, organizations faced an average of $4.45 million in damages per incident, with over 2,200 cyberattacks occurring daily, many of them targeting cloud platforms. (IBM Security, 2023)

Today, businesses, government organizations and individuals use cloud computing to handle information more flexibly and efficiently. Microsoft Azure, Amazon Web Services (AWS) and Google Cloud Platform (GCP) are among the leading providers that provide affordable and on-demand computing services. (Bhatte et al., 2022) Moving to cloud infrastructure instead from physical data centres helps organizations save money and work more efficiently. (Bhole, 2025)

Despite these benefits, cloud computing introduces significant security and privacy challenges. (Mathew, 2024) Traditional cloud infrastructures are centralized, making them vulnerable to cyberattacks, unauthorized access, and insider threats. Cloud systems must also comply with regional and global data protection laws, including the General Data Protection Regulation (GDPR), the Health Insurance Portability and Accountability Act (HIPAA), and India's Digital Personal Data Protection Act (DPDP Act, 2023). (Folorunso et al., 2024) Ensuring data confidentiality, integrity, and availability is a growing concern for both businesses and policymakers.

Blockchain technology, originally developed for cryptocurrencies, has emerged as a promising tool to improve cloud security and privacy. (Karunakaran et al., 2024) Its decentralized and immutable ledger reduces risks associated with centralized data storage. Through features such as cryptographic hashing, smart contracts, and decentralized identity management, blockchain supports secure data storage, transparent access control, and improved intrusion detection.

This chapter provides an in-depth analysis of how blockchain strengthens cloud security mechanisms. It begins by outlining the core security challenges in cloud computing, followed by blockchain-based solutions including decentralized identity, secure access control, privacy-preserving techniques, and real-world case studies. It also explores challenges such as scalability, interoperability, and regulatory compliance, while identifying future research opportunities for integrating blockchain into cloud security frameworks. (Karunakaran et al., 2024)

1.1 Cloud Computing: Advantages and Security Challenges

Cloud computing has transformed how organizations store, process, and manage data. This shift allows users to access computing resources on-demand without the need for expensive physical infrastructure. Cloud services operate on a pay-as-you-go model, allowing businesses to scale their operations dynamically. (Bhole, 2025)

Advantages of Cloud Computing

1. Scalability and Flexibility

Cloud platforms provide on-demand resource allocation, which makes it easier for businesses to scale their computing power, storage capacities, and network bandwidth based on real-time needs. This feature is especially beneficial for businesses having fluctuating workloads.

2. Cost Efficiency

By using a pay-as-you-go model businesses can reduce their expenses because they only pay for actual usage when performing Cloud operations. This makes the model suitable for both new startups and smaller companies. Cloud computing reduces capital expenditures and operational costs, which allows organizations to allocate resources more effectively for better innovation and growth.

3. Accessibility and Collaboration

Cloud services make it possible for users to obtain remote access to applications and data which enables worldwide team collaboration. Such accessibility improves productivity and operational efficiency.

4. Disaster Recovery and Data Redundancy

Cloud providers use automated disaster recovery methods and backup solutions which preserve data access any time servers fail or when facing cyberattacks.

Security Challenges in Cloud Computing

While cloud computing provides scalability and convenience, it also introduces critical security concerns. The centralized nature of most cloud architectures, combined with growing cyber threats, exposes organizations to data breaches, insider threats, compliance violations, and service disruptions.

Key security issues include:

- Centralized vulnerabilities in data storage
- Human error and misconfigurations
- Ransomware and advanced persistent threats
- Lack of visibility into cloud provider operations
- Regulatory and jurisdictional data challenges

These challenges are explored in greater detail in Section 3, which provides a comprehensive breakdown of each security threat and its implications for cloud-based systems.

Figure 1 summarizes the major security risks and illustrates how blockchain technology can be leveraged to mitigate them.

Figure 1. Cloud Security issues versus Blockchain Solution

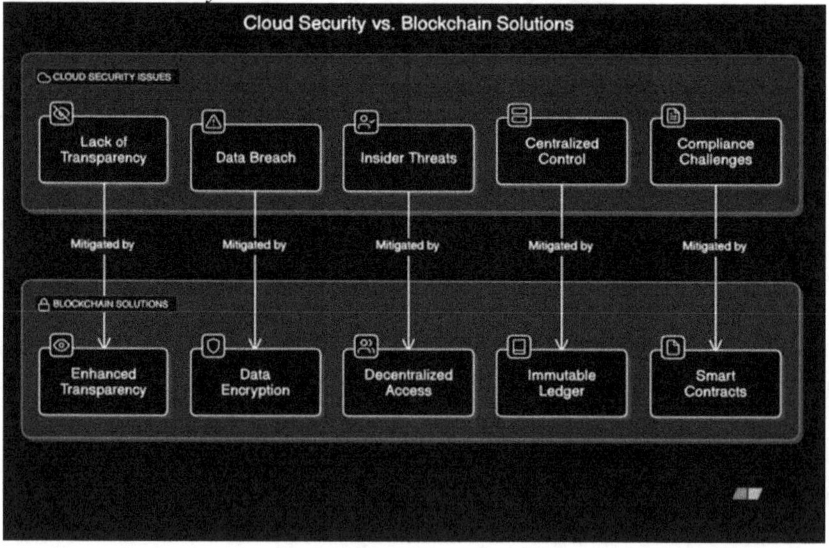

2. FUNDAMENTALS OF BLOCKCHAIN TECHNOLOGY

2.1 Distributed Ledger Technology (DLT)

Service providers operate cloud computing through a centralized system which manages data storage and security combined with infrastructure management. The centralization approach provides users with efficiency along with ease of access but exposes their data to three dangerous security threats—such as single points of failure, insider threats, and unauthorized data modifications.

The decentralized model of blockchain technology establishes an attractive solution that develops secure and trusted cloud environments. Distributed Ledger Technology (DLT) acts as the foundational element of blockchain systems while enabling distributed storage of data across multiple nodes instead of using a centralized database structure. The distributed system prevents reliance on central authorities thus improving security because it ensures cloud systems operate autonomously during cyberattacks and operational failures.

The most significant benefit of DLT arises from its consensus mechanism because it enables secure transactions that become immutable and tamper-resistant. The mechanism proves decisive for securing cloud-based data while protecting it from unauthorized access and maintaining its integrity.

Blockchain-based DLT creates advanced security systems for cloud solutions. Some key benefits include:

- Decentralization and Resilience Against Failures

Traditional cloud storage centralization makes servers an attractive target for hackers because its stored information exists in one location. DLT systems spread data throughout multiple nodes that ensure the entire security framework stays intact even when one node gets compromised.

- Enhancing Data Integrity and Immutability

Each transaction stored on blockchain receives a timestamp alongside cryptographic security that makes changes after recording out of reach for unauthorized parties. When data gets recorded it becomes impossible to modify or remove it making this feature important for regulatory compliance standards and audit requirements.

- Eliminating the Need for Trust in Third Parties

This system abolishes the requirement to trust external parties. Cloud security systems currently depend on trusting service providers to implement security policies. The security system utilizing blockchain depends on cryptographic validation to build trust without giving any organization total authority over security procedures.

- Improved Availability and Fault Tolerance

Because blockchain networks run through decentralized peer-to-peer (P2P) networks they exhibit strong resistance. When node failures occur, the remaining nodes keep providing data availability to maintain continuous access to cloud services.

2.2 Cryptographic Hashing

The core security component of blockchain technology involves cryptographic hashing because it maintains data integrity while verifying transactions and prevents unauthorized modifications. The digital fingerprint function of cryptographic hashing enables cloud security to monitor modifications of stored data.

The cryptographic hash functions accept any data input to create fixed output sequences that exclusively connect to specific inputs. The cryptographic process converts data into an uncrackable string that lacks any possibility to reproduce the initial information. Essential security properties of cryptographic hashing function as a security tool involve:

- Deterministic Output – The hash value produces a constant result when operations give identical input data to the system.
- Pre-Image Resistance – Pre-Image Resistance properties prevent attackers from finding the original data because the hash function becomes difficult to decipher.
- Avalanche Effect – Any minor change made to the input data produces a totally unique hash outcome through the Avalanche Effect thus making undetectable tampering physically impossible.
- Collision Resistance – Different hash outputs occur when different inputs are used thus providing defence against potential duplication.

Modern cryptographic hash functions commonly used in blockchain and cloud security include:

- SHA-256 (Secure Hash Algorithm 256-bit) – The ciphering standard SHA-256 (Secure Hash Algorithm 256-bit) operates in Bitcoin and Hyperledger Fabric as well as shields data in secure cloud environments. (Raut, 2024)

- Keccak-256 – Ethereum protects its network smart contracts through the securing hash function Keccak-256.
- Blake2 & SHA-3 – The modern era relies on Blake2 and SHA-3 as advanced cryptographic hash functions for its security requirements.

Role of Cryptographic Hashing in Cloud Security

Cryptographic hashing strengthens cloud security several ways:

- Ensuring Data Integrity

The data stored in cloud infrastructure remains unaltered through the hashing method. Security systems through hashing detect unauthorized modifications by producing different hash results from original ones.

- Securing Cloud Storage and Backups

Cloud service providers implement hashing methods to check for consistent data storage across different nodes. Cloud solutions Dropbox and AWS alongside Google Drive make use of hashing technology to identify file corruption and unauthorized file changes for intact data preservation. (Burke et al., 2024)

- Improving Digital Signatures for Authentication

The foundation of digital signatures which protect cloud authentication processes consists of cryptographic hashing. The authentication approach in blockchain-based cloud systems relies on hashed credentials instead of password-based methods to fight against identity theft along with phishing attacks.

The implementation of cryptographic hashing within cloud infrastructure creates fortified data security alongside increased trust in stored information combined with prevented unauthorized changes to make cloud systems better defend against cyber-attacks.

2.3 Smart Contracts for Secure Automation in Cloud Environments

The blockchain-based smart contract system functions as a procedure which executes automatically on network platforms to implement security policies for cloud systems while removing the need for human supervision or intermediaries. Such contracts enforce security mechanisms through predefined conditions leading to automatic and transparent execution of security operations such as access control, data validation, and compliance enforcement. (Alevizos, 2024) Unlike traditional administrative systems, smart contracts reduce vulnerability to internal errors and threats by operating autonomously. They ensure consistent and transparent security operations and improve cloud systems resistance to manipulation or misconfiguration.

Further details on use of smart contract in identity management, compliance, and threat response are discussed in Section 4.4.

2.4 Consensus Mechanisms

A consensus mechanism is a protocol used in blockchain networks to validate transactions and maintain a consistent, tamper-proof state of data across all nodes. In cloud security, consensus mechanisms are very important for preventing unauthorized modifications, fraud, and cyber threats. They serve as a kind of obstacle course that unauthorized users must get through if they want to make any changes in a cloud system. Before any change can even happen into the system, it must first and foremost satisfy the mechanism and obtain network-wide agreement.

This makes sure that information saved in several cloud instances stays safe, remains consistent, and is resistant to any malicious activity. Figure 2 depicts the blockchain consensus mechanisms used for enhancing cloud security, highlighting their processes and characteristics.

Figure 2. Blockchain consensus mechanisms for cloud security

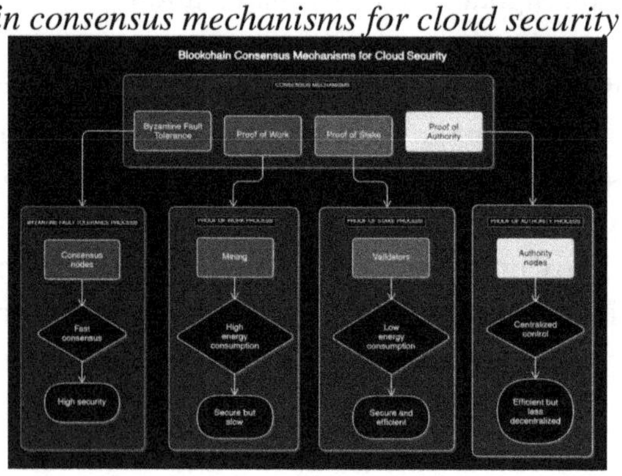

Types of Consensus Mechanisms for Cloud Security

Various consensus mechanisms provide different levels of security, efficiency, and scalability. The most popular ones in the blockchain-powered cloud environments are the following:

1. Proof of Work (PoW):

PoW is one of the most secure but computationally expensive consensus mechanisms. To validate the transactions and to add new blocks to the blockchain, participants (miners) must solve complex cryptographic puzzles. Even though PoW offers strong security guarantees, it is energy hungry and time-consuming, which makes it unfit for large-scale cloud security applications. Example: Bitcoin is secured by PoW, but enterprise cloud systems do not adopt it because of its resource requirements. (Bezuidenhout & Nel, 2023)

2. Proof of Stake (PoS)

POS functions better than PoW since it eliminates the requirement of strenuous computational processes. The selection of validators depends solely on their crypto currency ownership or their stake level in the network. Implementation of this system decreases energy requirements which makes it a practical solution for cloud security applications.

The Ethereum 2.0 system increases its scalability through Proof of Stake technology for cloud-based authentication functions and access control and data security applications. (GeeksforGeeks, 2024).

3. Byzantine Fault Tolerance (BFT)

The BFT consensus models function in conditions where the participants demonstrate malicious behaviour. The BFT-based consensus techniques maintain operational network functionality because they can function properly despite the failures of some nodes or malicious attempts from other participants.

The BFT consensus model implemented by the enterprise blockchain platform Hyperledger Fabric makes it suitable for diverse cloud security frameworks because participants do not need to have complete trust in one another. (Al Salih & Wang, 2024)

4. Proof of Authority (PoA)

Transactional verification occurs in PoA through an authorized consensus method involving only pre-authorized validators. The system operates at fast speeds as well as efficiently but needs trusted authorities to maintain its operation.

3. SECURITY & DEPLOYMENT CHALLENGES IN CLOUD COMPUTING

This section explores major security challenges in cloud computing, including risks associated with centralized architectures, data breaches, cyberattacks, and regulatory compliance failures. Figure 3 highlights the major cloud security risks that organizations need to address.

Figure 3. Cloud Security risks

3.1 Centralized Cloud Vulnerabilities

Cloud computing often relies on centralized data centres managed by major providers such as Amazon Web Services (AWS), Microsoft Azure, and Google Cloud Platform (GCP). (Blancaflor et al., 2024) While centralization offers scalability and efficiency, it also introduces critical security risks. Large-scale infrastructures become high-value targets for attackers due to their single points of failure. (Saini & Somani, 2024)

Single Points of Failure and Downtime Risks

Millions of users depend on a restricted number of data centres and networking components which make up centralized cloud architecture infrastructure. Critical infrastructure components consisting of authentication servers and data storage units will cause widespread disruptions when they experience failures. Complaints about the AWS outage in December 2021 ("Global IT Outage Highlights Cloud-Linked Risks," 2024) showed how one infrastructure failure spread to disrupt major services spanning financial institutions and businesses along with media platforms. Localized placement of critical resources at limited geographical areas exposes cloud environments to natural dangers and equipment breakdowns and cyber security threats.

Insider Threats and Privilege Misuse

Cloud security faces a significant risk because insiders including employees contractors and cloud management interface authorized service providers represent a major vulnerability to sensitive data. Access to sensitive cloud data becomes compromised because of malicious insiders who may intend harm and negligent operators and social engineering exploits which steal user credentials. Excessive privilege allocation proved dangerous when a Capital One employee who previously worked at AWS used misconfigured access permissions to steal over 100 million customer records in 2019. (Neto et al., 2020) The implementation of RBAC alongside MFA and real-time activity monitoring serves as an effective mechanism to reduce security risks.

Security Misconfigurations and the Shared Responsibility Model

A main element of cloud security operates under a shared responsibility model which requires CSPs to operate the infrastructure and customers to secure data and applications on their end. The main reason behind cloud breaches stems from customer misconfigurations which result in security risks like wrong exposures of Amazon S3 buckets and vulnerable API protocols and poor managed virtual machines that expose critical data. IBM Security discovered misconfigurations as the cause of almost 85% of cloud security incidents during their 2019 investigation. Organizations must use automated security posture management systems to perform frequent configuration audits in order to stay safe against such vulnerabilities. (*IBM*

X-Force: Stolen Credentials and Vulnerabilities Weaponized Against Businesses in 2019-Feb 11, 2020, 2020)

3.2 Data Breaches and Unauthorized Access

Cloud security faces its worst threat from data breaches which cause financial harm along with loss of reputation and result in legal penalties. Cloud environments contain extensive quantities of personally identifiable information (PII) in addition to healthcare records and financial data which makes them ingenious goals for cyber attackers.

High-Profile Cloud Data Breaches

The cloud-based system of Equifax experienced a data breach in 2017 which exposed sensitive information from 147 million individuals because operators failed to address a known system vulnerability. (Abubakar et al., 2024) Major data breaches continue to threaten cloud storage facilities although they exist. The improper setup of Amazon S3 buckets leads to the release of sensitive information which discloses vital keys and credentials in addition to database backup files. (Continella et al., 2018) Cloud security risks arise from faulty practices because of authentication schemes with poor security, weak encryption, and faulty system access control implementations.

3.3 Advanced Cyber Threats and Attack Vectors

Attackers use advanced methods to penetrate cloud infrastructure by deploying ransomware while using both distributed denial-of-service (DDoS) attacks and API defects to take over cloud service systems.

Ransomware in Cloud Environments

Attacks that utilize ransomware tools encrypt cloud-stored information which remains inaccessible until the victim pays an associated fee. Through Ransomware-as-a-Service (RaaS) cybersecurity criminals have gained simplified methods to execute massive ransomware attacks. Cyber attackers gain entry to cloud storage systems primarily by exploiting stolen passwords or using fake emails to trick users and by finding and exploiting weak spots in utilized software applications.

The attackers gain access to encrypt these critical files so businesses face restricted recovery capabilities except for their safe offline backups.

The 2021 Colonial Pipeline incident exemplified ransomware attack disruptive power by serving as one of the most prominent ransomware events. (Mittal, 2024) The incident revealed that interconnected systems remain vulnerable even when not entirely cloud-based, compelling organizations to improve their cloud security posture. In 2023, the average cost of a ransomware breach surpassed $5.13 million, underlining the need for strong backup strategies and defensive measures. (IBM Security, 2023)

To combat these threats, cloud service providers (CSPs) have adopted ransomware detection tools, automated backup isolation, and anomaly detection powered by artificial intelligence (AI).

Distributed Denial-of-Service (DDoS) Attacks

Cloud servers face disruption and service unavailability to genuine users when malicious traffic overwhelms them in DDoS attacks. Attackers send enormous amounts of requests to cloud infrastructure by using botnets which control compromised devices.

In 2022 Google Cloud successfully managed what turned out to be one of the largest DDoS attacks with 46 million requests per second. *(Google Cloud, 2022).* The attack showed how these threats have grown in size combined with the need for security defences such as rate limitation systems alongside content delivery networks (CDNs) and artificial intelligence systems that analyse traffic.

API Exploits and Security Misconfigurations

The core feature of cloud applications depends on APIs which enable service interaction. The improper security measures of API systems create entry opportunities for attackers which result in breaches of data and unauthorized system access and disrupted services. Common API security threats include:

- Broken Authentication – The failure to implement proper authentication methods creates paths for attackers who want to gain access to user accounts.
- Data Exposure – When access controls fail properly the exposure of sensitive information becomes possible through APIs.
- Injection Attacks – The vulnerability to injection attacks occurs when attackers submit malicious input that modifies API queries thus leading to data leaks while permitting code execution.

A well-known example is the Facebook API data exposure incident, where misconfigured API permissions led to the leakage of sensitive user data. (Rosen, 2018) In 2023, over 41% of cloud-related breaches were linked to insecure APIs (IBM Security, 2023), underscoring the importance of robust API security measures in cloud environments.

Poor API management not only exposes sensitive data but also enables lateral movement within cloud platforms once access is gained. Organizations must implement secure authentication protocols (like OAuth 2.0), continuous monitoring, rate limiting, and frequent API security testing to mitigate these threats.

3.4 The Role of Compliance and Regulatory Frameworks

Every organization must adjust its security strategy to match legal requirements when more businesses shift to cloud solutions. Organizations now consider compliance as a fundamental aspect of cloud security management because of complicated cross-border data management as well as multi-cloud systems.

Key Cloud Security Regulations

Several overarching regulations guide cloud security practices globally, imposing strict requirements on data handling and privacy in cloud environments:

- *General Data Protection Regulation (GDPR) (Europe)* – Under GDPR, all organizations must provide encryption for data along with breach reports and enforce exact permission methods for cloud data management.
- *Health Insurance Portability and Accountability Act (HIPAA) (USA)* – HIPAA functions as a United States (USA) regulatory framework intended to secure patient privacy and confidentiality data within the healthcare sector. The statute implements rigid protection systems for healthcare data storage using cloud platforms.
- *Digital Personal Data Protection (DPDP) Act, 2023 (India)* – The Digital Personal Data Protection (DPDP) Act of 2023 in India requires data localization while it protects citizen privacy at an advanced level.
- *Payment Card Industry Data Security Standard (PCI DSS)* – This functions as a global standard which relates specifically to businesses that deal with credit card transactions. Success under the PCI DSS standard demands organizations to establish firewalls, encrypt their stored data, and enable exclusive authentication mechanisms while conducting periodic security assessments. All companies working in cloud environments must guarantee their third-party cloud providers satisfy PCI DSS standards requirements.

In multi-cloud environments, organizations need to handle laws related to data sovereignty, and meet various regulatory compliance requirements. Blockchain technologies can enable access controls to protect compliance standards and create immutable audit trails that minimize legal exposure. Organizations that overlook data sovereignty laws face substantial legal penalties, which can result in heavy fines. For instance, Amazon received an $887 million fine from GDPR because of faulty cloud data management regulations. (Segall, 2021)

Additional Industry-Specific Standards

In addition to overarching regulations like GDPR, HIPAA, and the DPDP Act, sector-specific standards further dictate how blockchain-based systems must be designed in cloud environments:

- *Sarbanes-Oxley Act (SOX):* In the financial sector, SOX mandates strict internal controls, audit trails, and verifiable financial records. Blockchain's immutable ledger supports SOX compliance by enabling transparent, time-stamped transaction logs. However, due care must be taken with off-chain solutions to support data retrieval and reporting needs (Khanna et al., 2022).
- *GS1 Traceability Standards:* In supply chain contexts, GS1 standards provide a framework for end-to-end traceability and product identification. Blockchain-based systems like IBM Food Trust integrate GS1-compliant formats to support consistent global tracking across stakeholders (Uriarte & De Nicola, 2018).
- *ISO/IEC 27001:* This globally recognized information security management standard requires documented risk assessments, access controls, and continual audits. Blockchain systems naturally align with ISO 27001 due to their ability to enforce cryptographic access, immutable audit trails, and verifiable operations (Khanna et al., 2022).

Integrating blockchain with these sector-specific standards requires modular and flexible system architectures that can support regulatory adaptation while retaining decentralization and data integrity.

3.5 Real-World Deployment Challenges

While blockchain technology offers effective solutions for many cloud security threats, its real-world deployment faces challenges. These practical limitations hinder the widespread adoption of blockchain in enterprise cloud environments, despite its theoretical advantages.

Scalability and Performance Limitations

Blockchain systems, particularly public ones, face throughput and latency issues. Traditional consensus mechanisms like Proof of Work (PoW) are computationally intensive and slow. Even permissioned blockchains, such as Hyperledger Fabric, may struggle under high transaction volumes typical of cloud environments. These performance constraints limit the real-time applicability of blockchain-based security solutions in production systems.

Integration with Legacy Systems

Most organizations rely on legacy IT systems that were not designed to interact with decentralized architectures. Integrating blockchain with these existing systems introduces compatibility issues, data silos, and increased architectural complexity. Without middleware, API bridges, or redesigns, enterprises face difficulties in aligning blockchain-based components with their current infrastructure.

Regulatory and Legal Barriers

Blockchain's immutability conflicts with data privacy laws such as the General Data Protection Regulation (GDPR), which mandates data modification or deletion on request ("right to be forgotten"). This contradiction makes full compliance difficult in regulated sectors like healthcare and finance.

Lack of Standardization

Blockchain lacks universal standards across platforms, protocols, and smart contract frameworks. The absence of standardization creates interoperability issues, complicates multi-party adoption, and slows industry-wide collaboration. Organizations are often left to build custom, non-compatible solutions that hinder scalability and collective adoption.

Security and Key Management Risks

While blockchain improves data integrity and traceability, it introduces new security challenges, such as private key theft, smart contract bugs, and endpoint vulnerabilities. A compromised key or flawed smart contract can lead to irreversible consequences. Enterprises must adopt robust cryptographic key management strategies and continuous auditing to protect the blockchain layer itself.

High Cost and Resource Demands

Deploying a secure, enterprise-grade blockchain infrastructure involves significant cost — including infrastructure setup, smart contract development, talent acquisition, and ongoing compliance monitoring. For many small and mid-sized organizations, the return on investment (ROI) remains unclear, making adoption less appealing without a strong business case.

To overcome these challenges, enterprises are developing strategic approaches that bridge blockchain with existing systems and workflows — a topic explored in detail in Section 4.5.

4. BLOCKCHAIN-BASED SECURITY SOLUTIONS AND INTEGRATION STRATEGIES

The four areas where blockchain improves cloud security include access control and identity management and secure data storage and intrusion detection as well as policy enforcement through smart contracts. Figure 4 illustrates the process of decentralized access control in a cloud environment

4.1 Decentralized Access Control and Identity Management

Figure 4. Decentralized Access Control

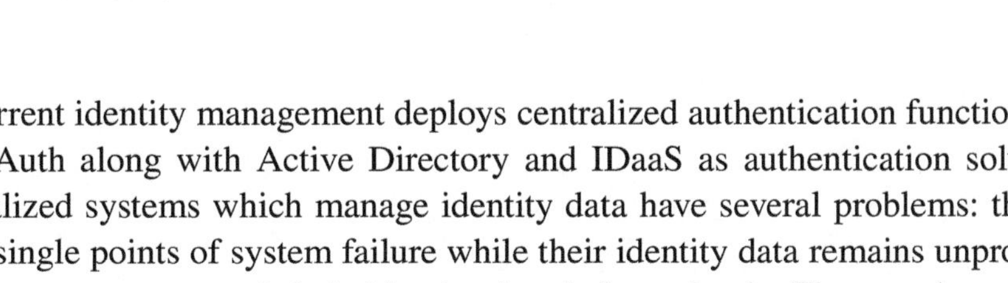

Current identity management deploys centralized authentication functions that use OAuth along with Active Directory and IDaaS as authentication solutions. Centralized systems which manage identity data have several problems: they include single points of system failure while their identity data remains unprotected and users cannot control their identity data independently. The growing number of cyberattacks on single identity repository databases demonstrates the necessity to develop identity management systems with user control and improved security.

Building upon the decentralization principles outlined in Section 2.1, blockchain-based identity systems offer a tamper-resistant framework for authentication and authorization. Using Decentralized Identity Management (DID) protocols, users can manage their digital identities without relying on centralized authorities. This reduces the risk of identity fraud while improving transparency and security.

Hyperledger Fabric serves as an example of blockchain identity management that enables credential-based authentication instead of conventional username-password authentication for user verification. (Al Salih & Wang, 2024) Identity verification processes achieve security through implementation methods that provide full visibility into operations and protect against any type of manipulation attempt. Users benefit from Ethereum-based identity systems uPort and Sovrin which enable self-sovereign identity protocols that let them keep control of their credentials and choose which information to share with other parties while maintaining private information. (Pava-Díaz et al., 2024)

A robust cloud permission management system exists through the adoption of blockchain-based Access Control Lists which decentralize access authorization capabilities. The deployment of blockchain-based ACLs supersedes traditional ACL architectures because these implementations make permission allocations and updates through smart contracts. The system applies security policies by itself through smart contracts which enables verified entities to access cloud resources. Insider threats along with unauthorized access risks decrease substantially through these measures leading to general improvement of cloud security levels.

4.2 Secure Data Storage and Provenance Tracking

Figure 5. Decentralized Storage

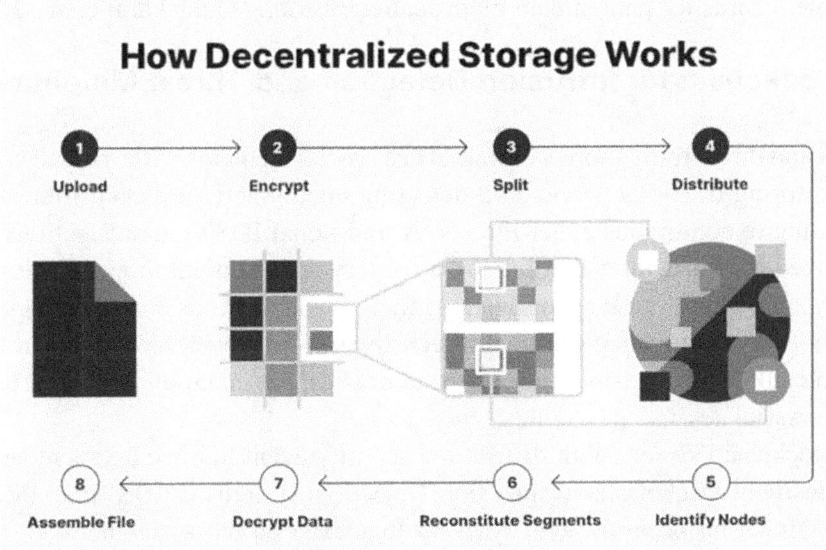

Traditional cloud storage depends on centralized data centers which creates serious threats because security breaches as well as data tampering and unauthorized modifications are possible. A centralized authority responsible for cloud storage remains at high risk of cyber attacks and insider threats and accidental data loss.

As introduced in Section 2.1, blockchain's decentralized structure offers a more reliable approach to cloud storage by distributing data across multiple nodes. This setup significantly reduces the risk of total system failure and unauthorized tampering.

Figure 5 illustrates how decentralized storage is implemented in a blockchain-enabled cloud architecture.

Storj and Filecoin together with Sia and Arweave share peer-to-peer networks that distribute encrypted file fragments among various system nodes. (Li et al., 2024) Blockchain-based cloud storage systems provide users with complete data ownership since they differ from traditional providers that normally control data preservation. Blockchain technology protects data integrity by using hashing and Merkle tree security mechanics that create unalterable data storage which detecting unauthorized modifications to stored content is essentially impossible.

The ability to track data origins stands as one of the major benefits blockchain storage provides to users. The blockchain ledger permanently keeps track of every file modification along with transactions which establish an unchangeable record of changes. Businesses in healthcare and finance and supply chain management industries find blockchain-based storage advantageous because it provides essential data authenticity tracking that meets regulatory requirements. EHR systems benefit from blockchain technology through its capability to establish secure and fraud-proof auditable records for patient data modification history. (Manickaraj et al., 2024)

4.3 Blockchain for Intrusion Detection and Threat Mitigation

IDS and threat mitigation solutions act as crucial elements within cloud security by monitoring traffic networks and detecting enemy activities then immediately responding to continuous cyber threats. A traditional IDS system functions using centralized infrastructures that require a solitary control point to process logs and identify anomalies. These centralized log monitoring methods provide effective security but they create three significant security weaknesses including shared failure risks and vulnerability to internal perpetrators as well as manipulation opportunities for adversarial actors.

A blockchain system with distributed security event log management services forms resilient Decentralized Intrusion Detection Systems (DIDS) that are resistant to tampering because security event logs exist on numerous network nodes. A blockchain-powered IDS uses distributed ledgers to record every security event automatically including login attempts and file modifications as well as network access records in an unalterable format. Such a system stops attackers from changing or deleting evidence of cyber attacks thus maintaining the availability and integrity of security logs. Security alerts become more precise in threat detection through distributed consensus processes that enable nodes to collaborate for validation purposes which reduces false positives.

The integration of blockchain with IDS solutions enables automated threat response abilities that derive from smart contracts implementations. Programmed smart contracts have the functionality to execute security protocols automatically when they detect suspicious operational activities. The system employs smart contracts that can activate automatic responses when an unauthorized login attempt appears repeatedly from an untrusted IP address including blocking the IP address temporarily or revoking access credentials or alerting security administrators. Automated processes in security operations cut down response speeds while making cloud security operations more effective.

The real-time anomaly detection of Blockchain gets additional strength from integration between machine learning algorithms and decentralized security frameworks. IDS solutions powered by artificial intelligence achieve effective attacks pattern detection through model training applied to security events stored on blockchain networks before possible security incidents materialize. The integration of blockchain immutability with machine learning adaptability delivers a proactive cybersecurity method that yields powerful security protection.

4.4 Smart Contract-Based Security Policies

Figure 6. Working of a Smart Contract

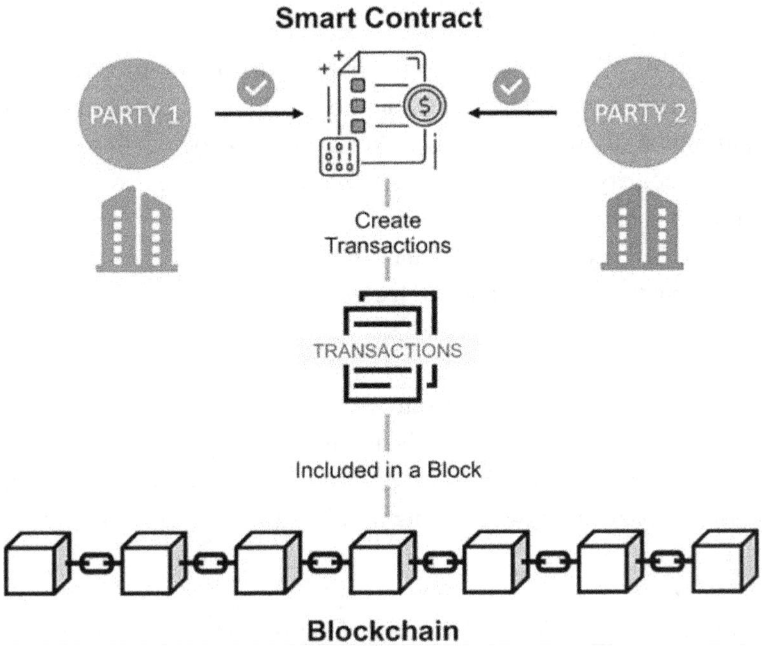

Blockchain runs pre-programmed smart contracts that independently execute security policies and automate critical cloud functions such as access control, compliance checks, encryption, and threat response. These tamper-proof contracts reduce the risks associated with human error, insider threats, and unauthorized intrusions. (Alevizos, 2024)

In cloud security systems, smart contracts enable automated access control by dynamically managing permission delegation and revocation. Unlike fixed-role RBAC models, they enforce cryptographic rules that grant access only when user credentials match predefined conditions. This supports multi-factor authentication (MFA) and reduces reliance on traditional password systems, which are prone to phishing and credential-based attacks.

Smart contracts also facilitate automated regulatory compliance with frameworks like GDPR and HIPAA. They continuously enforce data storage policies, user consent management, and audit trail monitoring. Embedded enforcement mechanisms—including contractual penalties—help cloud operators detect and address non-compliance without requiring manual oversight, thereby easing administrative workloads.

For secure data sharing, smart contracts integrate with privacy-preserving technologies such as Zero-Knowledge Proofs (ZKPs) and time-locked encryption. These systems prevent unauthorized data access by requiring cryptographic proof before release, ensuring that sensitive information remains protected even during third-party interactions. (Zhang et al., 2024)

In the context of intrusion detection, smart contracts monitor network activity for anomalies such as repeated authentication failures or suspicious API usage. They can automatically trigger actions like account suspension, forensic logging, or escalation to security teams—enhancing real-time defense and reducing incident response time.

A practical implementation example is OpenZeppelin's Ethereum-based Access Control smart contract, which enables decentralized identity management. In such models:

1. Users request access to cloud resources.
2. Smart contracts evaluate credentials against security policies.
3. Access is granted or denied based on defined rules, enforcing strict and transparent access control while reducing administrative overhead. (OpenZeppelin, n.d.)

Figure 6 shows the working of a Smart Contract in a blockchain-based cloud system.

Zero-Trust Security Model with Blockchain

Figure 7. Zero-Trust Security Model

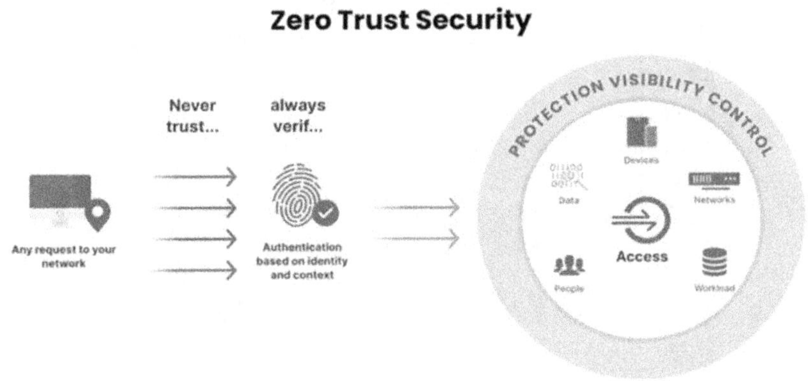

Under the Zero-Trust model organizations must verify continuous access for every user device regardless of the cloud environment. Blockchain extends Zero-Trust security capabilities through its decentralized authentication features together with immutable logging functions and smart contract-based enforcement of access privileging policies. Figure 7 shows the working of the Zero Trust Security Model in a blockchain-based cloud system.

Organizations that implement blockchain-based Zero-Trust gain these advantages.

- The decentralized identity verification system removes dependency on cloud service provider authentication servers to verify users.
- Organizations benefit from immutable access request logging that safeguards both users and their devices from unauthorized privilege and modification activities.
- Smart contracts apply dynamic security policies for least-privilege access to deliver real-time protection of each cloud action that follows implemented restrictions.

The secure policy-based access management in Hyperledger Fabric guarantees that all cloud transactions remain inside previously authorized security rules. (Sykes, 2023) Smart contracts combined with Zero-Trust security will shape the future development of cloud security through the advancing blockchain technology.

4.5 Enterprise Integration Strategies

Figure 8. Blockchain–Enterprise System Integration Layers

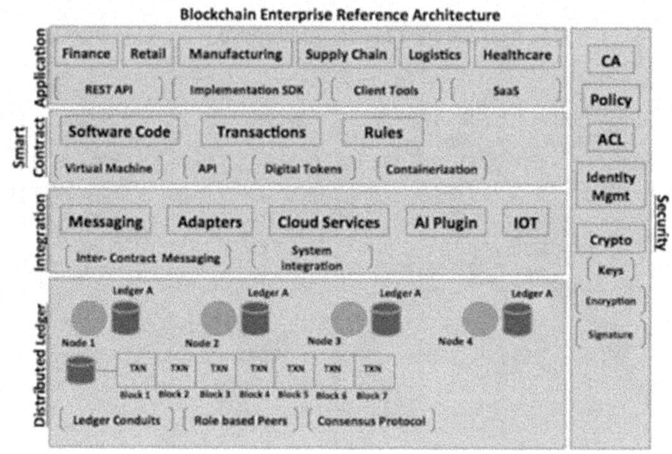

To overcome the practical limitations discussed in Section 3.5, organizations are adopting enterprise integration strategies that allow blockchain to coexist with and enhance traditional enterprise systems. These strategies focus on creating interoperable, secure, and scalable architectures that align blockchain's capabilities with business workflows deployed in cloud environments (Kumar & Tripathi, 2022).

Integration Layers and Approaches

Enterprise blockchain integration generally occurs across four layers: data, process, integration and application (Choudhury et al., 2021).

- At the data layer, blockchain serves as a distributed ledger (as shown in Figure 8), providing a tamper-proof shared ledger across nodes for secure storage, validation, and consensus-driven management of transactional records.
- At the integration layer, blockchain facilitates interoperability through messaging, adapters, cloud services, AI plugins, and IoT, ensuring seamless system integration and inter-contract communication in cloud environments.
- Finally, the application layer integrates blockchain capabilities into enterprise applications, such as finance, retail, supply chain, and healthcare systems, through REST APIs, SDKs, client tools, and SaaS platforms like ERP dashboards and SCM portals.

e-Procurement Integration Example

In enterprise procurement, blockchain enables secure, automated contract execution and supplier authentication. Smart contracts manage approval workflows, enforce compliance rules, and trigger payments after delivery verification (Choudhury et al., 2021). SAP's blockchain-enabled procurement modules demonstrate how legacy ERP platforms can connect with blockchain ledgers using middleware, enhancing transparency and efficiency.

Enterprise Blockchain Consortiums

Blockchain consortium models allow multiple stakeholders to participate in a shared ledger while retaining control over sensitive data. These models are particularly effective for cloud-hosted supply chain networks, where real-time collaboration across decentralized systems is crucial (Hussain et al., 2020). Consortiums also help establish standard protocols, reducing integration complexity.

Identity and Asset Integration

Integration strategies often include self-sovereign identities (SSI) and asset tokenization. SSI frameworks enable employees, partners, and devices to authenticate securely using cryptographic credentials—removing the need for centralized identity providers (Kumar & Tripathi, 2022). Tokenized assets, such as inventory or software licenses, can be tracked in real time across cloud-based ERP systems, improving operational accuracy.

Best Practices for Enterprise Integration

To integrate blockchain effectively within cloud-hosted systems, enterprises should:

- Use APIs and middleware to connect blockchain with legacy infrastructure (Choudhury et al., 2021).
- Start with low-risk pilots like invoice tracking or audit automation.
- Ensure compliance with data protection laws (e.g., GDPR, HIPAA) via off-chain storage or encrypted pointers.
- Adopt modular system designs to support scalability and integration flexibility.
- Provide IT teams with training on smart contract security and architecture design.

Enterprise integration strategies bridge the gap between blockchain's theoretical promise and operational reality. By aligning blockchain with cloud-based enterprise systems, organizations improve data integrity, access control, and auditability—without the need for a full system overhaul.

5. PRIVACY-PRESERVING TECHNIQUES WITH BLOCKCHAIN IN CLOUD

Centralized access controls used in traditional cloud security operations expose real-time threats from inside and outside the system. Blockchain technology revolutionizes cloud privacy protection by distributing power across multiple nodes and through cryptographic encryption and its auditable unmodifiable data management system. This section analyses how blockchain incorporates privacy-preserving operations through homomorphic encryption and differential privacy and zero-knowledge proofs and decentralized identity management.

5.1 Homomorphic Encryption for Secure Computation

The algorithm of homomorphic encryption provides users the ability to execute computations on protected information which stays secured through its entire execution. The encryption system proves advantageous in cloud storage because it keeps sensitive data protected during processing tasks involving financial records and healthcare information. Cloud users get improved data security together with regulatory compliance by implementing homomorphic encryption over blockchain technology.

FHE provides a mechanism for processing cloud-based encrypted data while preserving complete data privacy throughout the calculations. (Kholod et al., 2024) Cloud providers that integrate blockchain with FHE create secure cloud outsourcing services which enable validated smart contract processing of encrypted data before adding it to the ledger. This implementation method decreases both data disclosure threats and illegal access attempts to a minimum.

5.2 Differential Privacy to Protect Sensitive Data

Differential privacy functions by adding noise through statistical means to data before analysis so individual data items stay unidentified. The usage of differential privacy in blockchain-based cloud systems maintains user confidentiality when users query their stored data in the cloud.

Data analytics utilities can be maintained through cloud platform protection of sensitive information by using blockchain with differential privacy. Users can obtain aggregated statistics from an anonymized healthcare data blockchain ledger without needing to see original patient records. Blockchain cryptographic evidence allows users to detect any changes in their data while improving their system-wide privacy safeguards.

5.3 Zero-Knowledge Proofs for Privacy in Cloud Transactions

Zero-knowledge proofs (ZKPs) are cryptographic techniques that allow one party to prove the validity of a statement without revealing the underlying data. In cloud environments, ZKPs are essential for enabling secure authentication and transaction verification while keeping user credentials and sensitive information private.

Blockchain-based ZKPs help authenticate cloud users without exposing personal identifiers, thereby reducing data exposure risks. For example, the privacy-focused cryptocurrency **Zcash** uses ZKPs to verify transactions without revealing sender or receiver identities or the transaction amount. (Huang et al., 2024)

In cloud security, ZKPs enable protected access to confidential information and support privacy-preserving computation. They are especially valuable in contexts that require regulatory compliance and zero-trust architectures, as they minimize data disclosure without compromising verification integrity.

5.4 Decentralized Identity Management

As discussed in Section 4.1, decentralized identity management (DID) frame works offer an alternative to traditional, centralized identity storage by placing users in control of their own credentials. These models reduce risks of data breaches and unauthorized access by eliminating reliance on a single point of failure.

The Self-Sovereign Identity framework serves as an example of decentralized identity management because it enhances privacy through cryptographic signatures that allow selective disclosure of personal information. These systems support compliance with regulations such as GDPR and HIPAA by minimizing unnecessary data exposure while maintaining verifiability. (Cocco & Tonelli, 2024)

6. REAL-WORLD CASE STUDIES OF BLOCKCHAIN IN CLOUD SECURITY

6.1 Blockchain-Enabled Supply Chain Security

Case Study: IBM Food Trust – Securing the Global Food Supply Chain with Blockchain

Multiple entities collaborate throughout the worldwide food systems as it represents a sophisticated complex network of production distribution and retail stages. The existing fragmented record-keeping systems in combination with paper-based documentation causes problems for ensuring food safety as well as preventing contamination and supply chain transparency. The verified origin of contaminated food and authentic organic products under traditional food supply chain systems required weeks to identify which caused numerous food illnesses alongside expensive product recalls and permanent brand damage.

Restrictions to the food supply chain occur through fraudulent activities that contain food mislabelling and counterfeiting. The worldwide industry contends with annual food fraud expenses reaching $40 billion while food adulteration incidents involving diluted olive oil and fake organic products along with misidentified seafood occur more and more often. (Polakova et al., 2024) Companies have chosen to find more secure and transparent solutions because they lack real-time visibility and do not trust their supply chain data.

IBM Food Trust: A Blockchain-Enabled Solution

IBM created Food Trust as a blockchain solution which operates through a cloud platform to track food from origin point to retail marketplace among other advantages. Hyperledger Fabric enables IBM Food Trust to establish a decentralized ledger system which maintains an immutable record of everything that happens in food supply chain transactions. IBM Food Trust enables secure recordkeeping that tracks products throughout their entire journey to retail locations thus providing real-time end-to-end tracking abilities.

Walmart served as an early implementing partner for IBM Food Trust to enhance its ability to track contaminated produce back to its starting point. Before implementing blockchain technology Walmart spent seven days looking for the origin of contaminated food items because their record systems were inefficient. The implementation of IBM Food Trust enabled the company to decrease traceability times to 2.2 seconds (Vignesh et al., 2025) thus minimizing the chances of unsafe food reaching consumers.

How IBM Food Trust Works

The three main operational aspects of IBM Food Trust operate as follows:

1. *End-to-End Transparency:* Blocks of data link each party in the food supply chain starting from farmers up to retailers so they record their transactions on blockchain systems. These records maintain their integrity because changes are impossible which results in unalterable traceability across the supply chain.
2. *Real-Time Contamination Tracking*: During food-related illness outbreaks retailers and regulators achieve real-time tracking capabilities that let them pinpoint contaminated batches while extracting only affected products instead of implementing large-scale removal.
3. *Smart Contracts for Compliance:* Through smart contracts the system implements automatic food safety regulations and expiration tracking which enables compliance with FDA (U.S.) EU Food Safety together with additional international standards.

Impact and Benefits of Blockchain in Food Security

The deployment of IBM Food Trust brought forth noticeable positive effects for the industry:

- *Reduced Recall Costs:* Traditional product recalls result in large-scale removals from the market due to limited visibility because of which businesses incur substantial recall expenses. Blockchain technology enables specific product recalls which prevents extensive losses in the food industry.
- *Enhanced Consumer Trust:* Customers can build trust through product package scans which show them product origins together with authenticity certificates along with sustainability information at one glance.
- *Improved Regulatory Compliance:* Food safety authorities together with governments maintain instant access to supply chain records for regulatory audits without depending on manufacturer reports.
- *Fraud Prevention:* Blockchain technology provides permanent data protection which helps prevent false labelling incidents between conventional produce and organic or non-GMO items.

Result

IBM Food Trust stands as an essential development in delivering safe food alongside enhanced transparency and efficient operations throughout global supply operations. The implementation of blockchain technology transforms food company and retail supply chain operations by cutting down tracking time for contaminated products while stopping fraud and removing inefficiencies. Blockchain usage continues to escalate so that it will establish itself as the industry benchmark for secure food tracking systems which will create transparent and protected food systems around the globe.

However, the project was not without hurdles. IBM Food Trust faced difficulties in supplier onboarding, with smaller vendors hesitant to adopt blockchain due to technical complexity and data-sharing concerns. Integration with diverse legacy inventory systems also raise challenges, as did maintaining data confidentiality across a decentralized network. These obstacles underline the importance of cross-industry collaboration and adaptable infrastructure when scaling blockchain across global supply chains.

6.2 Case Study: MedRec – Blockchain for Healthcare Data Protection

Healthcare institutions maintain and store massive amounts of confidential patient information that incorporates medical documentation as well as prescribed medications and test results. Cloud-based healthcare data management solutions with traditional storage approaches face multiple risks for security breaches because they store all data in centralized locations. Your inadequate and non-unified interface platform generates unwanted splitting of medical documents between healthcare facilities which heightens both documentation errors and operational inefficiencies.

Many healthcare data breaches became known worldwide after key events such as the 2015 cyber-attack on Anthem Inc. which exposed patient information from 80 million individuals. (Pakanati et al., 2024) Data security requires immediate development of effective measures which guarantee confidentiality integrity and unimpeded access to data.

Blockchain Implementation in MedRec

The blockchain-based MedRec electronic health record (EHR) management system serves to protect patient data through secure and private operations. The researchers at Massachusetts Institute of Technology (MIT) developed MedRec which uses blockchain decentralization approaches to fix healthcare data storage problems like data integrity issues and access control problems and interoperability problems. (Goyal et al., 2022; Azaria et al., 2016). MedRec uses Ethereum's smart contract architecture to link metadata pointers to off-chain medical records, ensuring both access control and auditability. (Azaria, Steinhardt, & Ekblaw, 2016)

Healthcare data management adopts blockchain technology to build an unalterable networked record system that ensures patient medical documentation safety. The system implements smart contracts for access control that let doctors, hospitals, and insurance providers access to patient information through defined permission settings.

Key features of MedRec include:

- *Decentralized Access Control:* Access controls within MedRec operate from a decentralized framework which makes patients the main controllers of their medical records through a system independent of centralized oversight.
- *Tamper-Proof Data Integrity:* Each medical transaction on the blockchain keeps its data integrity through cryptographic hashing before adding new data blocks which prevents alteration of medical records or deletion of data.
- *Interoperability:* MedRec implements interoperability features to allow health providers to exchange medical records without repetition which enhances care continuity across multiple facilities.
- *Auditability and Compliance:* The blockchain system logs every access request alongside data modifications within an unalterable audit trail which makes it possible to verify compliance with HIPAA regulations.

Impact and Future Potential

Healthcare data security and patient privacy have exhibited great potential for enhancement through the implementation of MedRec. The system throws out middlemen to create reduced costs through less administration and build stronger connections between medical staff and their patients. The healthcare industry integrates blockchain technologies because they match global standards which require data visibility together with user control.

The endorsement of MedRec appears promising but it faces obstacles when it comes to scale-up and broad acceptance among users. Authorities should consider implementing newer zero-knowledge proof techniques alongside permissioned blockchain protocols to boost privacy without sacrificing performance in future implementations.

The presented case demonstrates how blockchain technology consolidates cloud-based health data protection by maintaining access features alongside rigorous privacy rules.

6.3 Securing IoT Devices in Cloud Environments: A Blockchain-Based Approach

Case Study: Blockchain-Based IoT Security Framework

Research scientists created a blockchain-based security framework for IoT devices that resolved authentication issues alongside integrity problems and communication vulnerabilities. Every IoT device has its own cryptographic identifier placed onto blockchain ledgers within a framework using a permissioned blockchain network. Unauthorized devices cannot infiltrate cloud-hosted IoT networks due to this protection mechanism.

Smart contracts serve as autonomous systems which perform automated security tasks by establishing rules for equipment relations and creation of data-sharing authorization protocols. The system allows communication between devices and cloud services only when authentication takes place through this methodology which lowers the vulnerability to man-in-the-middle attacks. The research points out blockchain applies to secure smart grid operations which allow IoT-powered energy meters to send instant energy usage data to cloud-managed monitoring systems. The irreversibility of blockchain records guards against tampering of billing documentation which leads to transparent and dependable energy business deals.

Blockchain enables access control mechanisms to create tamper-evident systems for managing permissions between IoT devices. The request of devices and users for cloud-based resource access proceeds through blockchain-based authentication methods that verify credentials independent of centralized server dependency thus decreasing dependence on single critical points.

The research finding demonstrated how blockchain integration increases IoT-cloud system data protection while reducing security breaches and strengthening system operational strength. Technology adoption faces difficulties in scalability together with transaction latency and regulatory compliance matters which limit widespread implementation. Modern research explores methods to enhance blockchain protocols so resource-limited IoT devices can use blockchain-based security solutions effectively. (Naidu, 2024)

While these theoretical improvements are encouraging, real-world implementations in IoT ecosystems reveal additional technical and logistical hurdles. Limited computing power and storage on edge devices make it difficult to run full nodes or even lightweight blockchain clients. Furthermore, network instability and intermittent connectivity in IoT ecosystems disrupt blockchain consensus and data propagation. Managing cryptographic keys across thousands of distributed sensors is another concern, particularly in unsupervised environments. These factors must be addressed through lightweight protocols, hybrid architectures, and centralized oversight layers where necessary.

6.4. Blockchain for Financial Transactions and Fraud Prevention

Case Study: Ripple's Cross-Border Payment Network

Ripple is a blockchain-based payment protocol. The payment operations on Ripple operate through a blockchain network which allows quick inexpensive cross-border payments. The XRP Ledger (XRPL) network of Ripple processes transactions much faster than traditional banking systems using SWIFT due to its use of intermediaries. The Ripple network enables financial institutions payment providers and individuals to execute secure international transactions at reduced cost through a seamless payment process. (Eyo-Udo et al., 2025)

The network provides accelerated transactions together with reduced expense levels. The current financial establishment experiences different obstacles because they charge high fees while maintaining lengthy settlement times and inefficient currency exchange operations. The decentralized Ripple consensus protocol abolishes the necessity of centralized clearinghouses because it enables quick transaction confirmations as validators process transactions in less than five seconds. Transactions processed through SWIFT require multiple days but Ripple enables swift and affordable settlements during which payments are cleared in under five seconds. (Li, 2025) Banks along with remittance services find XRP Ledger transactions appealing because they only require a payment of 0.00001 XRP.

Financial security becomes stronger when blockchain uses its transparent and unalterable features. Every transaction on Ripple's network gets stored on transpar ent ledgers which provide unalterable recordkeeping ability to fight fraud. Ripple's cryptographic ledger maintains an unalterable system because it prevents tampering after transaction validation occurs. The feature operates as a crucial weapon to fend off financial offenses like money laundering along with blocked fund transfers.

The XRP Ledger includes strong procedures for verifying network participants to safeguard operations. Organizations which implement RippleNet solutions need to follow regulatory requirements for both Know Your Customer (KYC) and Anti-Money Laundering (AML) procedures as part of their fight against fraud. The built-in escrow functionality on Ripple allows time-locked payments because the system releases funds automatically only after completing predefined conditions. (Vliet, 2024)

Ripple's Adoption in the Financial Sector

Major financial operators across the world use blockchain solutions built by Ripple for their cross-border payment operations. Through RippleNet integration the finance industry enables Santander and SBI Holdings alongside other remittance companies to offer quicker and more efficient cross-border money transfer services. The institutions that use Ripple achieve real-time transaction settlement because of its instant liquidity provision which does not require pre-funded Nostro accounts. (Sule et al., 2025)

The analysis of Ripple's transaction system proves that its decentralized ledger system provides banks with a simplified method to streamline international payments. Ripple proved its capacity to manage large volumes of transactions without sacrificing stability or efficiency within its network operations.

Impact

The blockchain system operated by Ripple enables cross-border payments to become faster and more secure while providing lower costs than banks traditionally use for payments. Ripple delivers a powerful fraud protection system coupled with efficient transactions through its combination of decentralized consensus mechanism, cryptographic protection and regulatory standards. Financial institutions worldwide adopt blockchain technology to benefit from Ripple's model which demonstrates a sustainable method for achieving transparent secure and efficient global payments.

7. LIMITATIONS OF BLOCKCHAIN IN CLOUD SECURITY

While blockchain technology offers compelling benefits for cloud security, its real-world deployment brings several significant limitations. These include poor scalability, integration complexity, regulatory conflict, and high resource consumption. This section examines these limitations in detail.

7.1 Scalability

Current blockchain technology struggles to ensure suitable growth when applied to cloud security methods. The combination of traditional blockchain networks alongside Proof-of-Work (PoW) consensus mechanisms produces limited transaction processing speed. Multiple nodes verify each transaction while performing the recording process thus causing delays and preventing network flexibility. Cloud computing needs speedy data transaction speeds and real-time processing features that existing blockchain systems currently do not deliver at efficient levels. The growth of blockchain networks generates a direct relationship between storage needs and computational demand that keeps rising at an exponential rate. Each network node needs a full copy of the ledger which creates enormous information management concerns for cloud systems operating with petabytes of data. The performance constraints become impractical for organizations that need fast transaction handling of large data volumes.

Researchers have developed various solutions to improve blockchain scalability in cloud security applications. The blockchain infrastructure can scale through sharding methods that split operation between numerous partitions while blockchain scalability benefits from layer-2 systems such as sidechains and state channels that shift processing beyond the main blockchain operations. Proof-of-Stake (Pos) alongside Directed Acyclic Graphs (DAGs) are alternative consensus methods which researchers use to develop enhanced transaction performance and lower energy costs. Further development of blockchain technology faces obstacles toward widespread adoption because cloud platforms require substantial infrastructure changes and must be able to link with current systems. (Bhosale & Waghmare, 2025)

Widespread adoption of blockchain technology in large-scale cloud environments requires scalable optimization methods for addressing its current limitations or else it will be restricted to smaller cloud systems.

7.2 Interoperability

Whenever blockchain executes integration with cloud computing its ability to function between different systems remains a crucial limitation. Cloud service providers Amazon Web Services (AWS) and Microsoft Azure and Google Cloud deliver services from respective proprietary frameworks that use separate security systems and storage protocols and authentication schemes. These closed information environments serve as substantial barriers against the fluid integration of blockchain systems since most blockchain frameworks rely on decentralized open-source designs.

Blockchain networks face interoperability challenges because they lack standardized communication protocols to connect with cloud systems. Central identity management operates together with access control mechanisms in Cloud environments but blockchain operates by using decentralized authentication systems. The protocol differences create barriers in building a single security implementation which successfully merges blockchain and cloud platforms.

The implementation of cross-chain communication protocols together with blockchain-agnostic middleware solutions work to connect the divide across blockchain systems. The Interledger Protocol and Polkadot and Cosmos technological solutions work to establish connectivity between multiple blockchain networks and cloud systems. The decentralized identity (DID) system operates to combine blockchain authentication methods with traditional cloud identity systems. (Mongia, 2024)

The path toward complete interoperability continues its development process despite recent technological improvements. The migration of blockchain technology into cloud systems demands fundamental changes to cloud structure platforms which leads to complicated deployment at high costs. To solve interoperability challenges, researchers must develop standardized blockchain APIs, federated identity systems, and cross-platform consensus protocols.

The potential of blockchain-enabled cloud security solutions to establish an entirely decentralized and secure computing environment will stay limited since the existing system issues remain unresolved.

7.3 Regulatory and Compliance Barriers

Widespread acceptance of blockchain in cloud security becomes difficult due to regulatory and compliance issues. While its transparency and immutability are key strengths, these features often conflict with established data protection regulations — discussed in detail in Section 3.4.

For instance, the "right to be forgotten" under GDPR requires data deletion upon user request. This directly clashes with blockchain's immutable nature, where data, once written, cannot be modified or erased. Such contradictions create ongoing debates around how blockchain systems can meet legal obligations without compromising their decentralized architecture.

Another challenge lies in cross-border data management. Blockchain networks often distribute data globally across multiple nodes, making it difficult to comply with regional jurisdictional rules and data localization mandates. Many regulators prohibit unrestricted international data transfers, which adds complexity for organizations deploying global blockchain-cloud systems.

Researchers together with industry leaders investigate solutions involving privacy-protecting blockchain frameworks that combine off-chain storage solutions with zero-knowledge proofs (ZKPs). (Huang et al., 2024) The technologies provide controlled information sharing capabilities which preserve blockchain system integrity. Permissioned blockchains represent a possible answer to meet regulatory needs because they restrict access to verified participants who can manage data access within legal boundaries.

Securing complete compliance with regulations continues to be a significant difficulty for users. Blockchain adoption in cloud security becomes more difficult because of developing data protection standards combined with the absence of standardized global regulations. For blockchain security models to achieve balance between compliance requirements and their benefits regulators must work together with developers to establish frameworks.

7.4 High Computational and Storage Expenditures

The application of blockchain in cloud security faces important drawbacks because implementing it requires heavy storage requirements along with significant computing power demands. Traditional blockchain systems depend on Proof-of-Work (PoW) together with other resource-intensive consensus protocols thus requiring major computational resources. High energy requirements during blockchain validation procedures cause the model to consume more resources than traditional cloud security solutions thus making it difficult for extensive cloud environments. (Merlina et al., 2024)

Every node in the blockchain network needs a full ledger copy stored on its system thus generating substantial data storage requirements. The endless growth of blockchain records stands as a significant barrier in cloud computing environments which emphasize operational efficiency and reduced costs. The process of handling expanding blockchain ledgers becomes challenging for organizations dealing with extensive data collections because they must allocate adequate storage capacity.

The adoption of Proof-of-Stake (PoS) and Practical Byzantine Fault Tolerance (PBFT) consensus mechanism serves to decrease energy usage and maintain security protection. Research groups have developed three data storage techniques through off-chain storage and pruning and sharding to reduce the storage obligation on individual nodes. (Alzoubi & Mishra, 2024)

The significant expense involved in computing power and storage capacity constitutes a strong barrier to implementing blockchain systems for cloud security purposes. Future improvements in blockchain architecture need to merge with cloud-based optimization approaches to resolve these problems.

8. FUTURE DIRECTIONS AND RESEARCH OPPORTUNITIES

Blockchain technology presents significant opportunities for improving cloud security, but widespread deployment requires overcoming technical, organizational, and regulatory challenges. This section outlines future research directions that can support scalable, compliant, and effective adoption across industries.

8.1 Improving Blockchain Scalability for Cloud Security

Improving blockchain scalability remains one of the main research goals to satisfy fast throughput requirements found in cloud environments. Traditional Proof-of-Work blockchain systems experience poor speed in transaction processing while using high amounts of energy. Future innovation aims to enhance transaction swiftness through layer-2 structures while implementing sharding mechanisms along with different consensus approaches to decrease network traffic.

The main blockchain uses state channels combined with rollups to handle off-chain transactions that eventually reach finality through main chain settlements which thus decreases network congestion. Currently developers utilize sharding as a method to divide blockchains into multiple smaller parts so that multiple nodes can execute parallel transactions. Alternative consensus mechanisms combining Proof-of-Stake (PoS) and Practical Byzantine Fault Tolerance (PBFT) alongside Directed Acyclic Graphs (DAGs) show potential to decrease computational requirements while preserving blockchain security together with decentralization features. (Bulgakov et al., 2024)

8.2 Privacy-Enhancing Innovations in Decentralized Cloud Systems

Research on blockchain systems should develop privacy-enhancing mechanisms because population-wide privacy concerns rise while transparent operations must remain secure. Cloud privacy can be achieved through ZKPs together with homomorphic encryption and SMPC which enable secure management of sensitive data while preserving blockchain's immutable characteristics.

The system of Zero-knowledge proofs (ZKPs) allows transactions to be checked without exposing the supporting information to outside parties which makes them optimal for secure cloud facilities that need robust privacy measures. The processing of data through clouds remains private because homomorphic encryption enables secure operations on data while it remains in its encrypted form. Secure multi-party computation (SMPC) enables distributed computational demanding tasks between multiple nodes while protecting the raw data from disclosure thereby strengthening security of decentralized cloud applications. (Dhokrat et al., 2024)

8.3 Cross-Platform Blockchain Integration for Hybrid Cloud Environments

Integrated blockchain systems face important operational barriers during cloud security implementations. Researchers need to work on creating blockchain platforms capable of uniting with current cloud architecture such as private and public cloud systems and mixed cloud implementations.

Modern blockchain technologies represented by ILP as well as Polkadot and Cosmos seek to merge blockchain networks together with cloud service providers selection. The solutions use blockchain-agnostic middleware to establish safe data interactions along with shared access management for different platforms. DID systems operate through blockchain technology which enables tamper-proof authentication so they could enhance authentication methods while working with hybrid cloud environments. (Ghanmi et al., 2024)

8.4 Potential Applications of AI in Blockchain-Cloud Security

Dynamic cloud security enabled through blockchain technology receives significant improvements from Artificial Intelligence (AI) solutions which adjust networks efficiently and increase vulnerability searches and run automated compliance enforcement systems. Future investigations should implement research on the potential combination of AI security models with blockchain technology for adaptive and intelligent cloud protection systems.

Blockchain networks receive the deployment of machine learning algorithms that detect behavioural abnormalities

Cloud environments benefit from this method by detecting security breaches while improving both security breaches detection and fraud prevention. Smart contracts empowered by AI technology would automatically update permissions according to real-time risk reviews to maintain regulatory compliance. Predicting analytic tools can optimize the blockchain transaction validation procedures which subsequently enhances operational efficiency together with security maintenance.

8.5 Decentralized Autonomous Organizations (DAOs) for Cloud Governance

Decentralized Autonomous Organizations (DAOs) present a compelling future direction for managing cloud infrastructure and security through distributed, transparent governance. DAOs operate through smart contracts encoded on blockchains, eliminating the need for centralized management by automating decision-making and operational tasks. Their design supports peer-to-peer (P2P) collaboration, token-based governance, and immutable rule enforcement.

In a cloud context, DAOs can manage access control, resource allocation, and compliance monitoring without relying on a single trusted authority. Cloud-native DAOs could govern distributed systems by allowing stakeholders—including developers, providers, and users—to vote on updates, monitor usage, and enforce security policies in real time. This participatory governance model aligns well with multi-tenant and hybrid cloud environments where decentralization improves both transparency and accountability.

Projects like DAOstack, Aragon, and MakerDAO demonstrate how DAO frameworks support decision-making, coordination, and investment tracking. Applying these principles to cloud resource governance could lead to autonomous platforms that are resistant to centralized failures and insider threats. (Santana & Albareda, 2022)

However, further research is needed to understand DAO scalability, legal recognition, and vulnerability to governance attacks. Additionally, the interplay between automated (on-chain) and human (off-chain) governance mechanisms must be refined for critical cloud operations.

DAOs may transform how cloud infrastructure is managed—offering resilient, community-driven models that go beyond traditional DevOps to enable decentralized cloud orchestration and policy enforcement.

9. CONCLUSION

9.1 Chapter Summary

The chapter performed a detailed examination of blockchain security functions in cloud environments by exploring both positive aspects alongside vulnerabilities. The emergence of blockchain technology provides effective solutions to combat cloud security threats through its features which include decentralized authentication together with cryptographic security and immutable data storage and smart contract-based automation. The built-in features serve as solutions against access violations and integrity violations and insider threats which are common security problems in cloud systems.

Advantages do not eliminate the challenges which blockchain faces as it enters cloud security systems. This section analysed multiple barriers that prevent blockchain from becoming popular in cloud computing scenarios. Traditional blockchain networks including Proof-of-Work consensus networks cannot process an excessive number of transactions with operational efficiency. Blockchains serve poorly in data processing operations that need speed as well as immediate fast communications which cloud computing infrastructure requires. The integration between blockchain networks and cloud service providers becomes complicated due to the absence of essential protocols because each platform maintains different security rules and administrative procedures. Blockchain's immutable nature creates difficulties in complying with regulatory and compliance laws because they include GDPR and HIPAA among others. The implementation of blockchain in cloud security must overcome complex challenges related to data protection and user sovereignty alongside regulatory mandates although the blockchain system provides permanent records and cannot be modified without exceptional difficulties. The implementation of blockchain technology requires extensive cryptographic computations together with redundant data storage at costs that prove both costly and resource-consuming for deploying at large-scale cloud infrastructure levels.

The chapter discussed possible research directions and potential solutions to handle the existing challenges even though it acknowledged these restrictions. The implementation of blockchain scalability solutions like layer-2 protocols and sharding technology delivers new mechanisms to both speed up transactions along with lowering operating costs. Zero-knowledge proofs together with homomorphic encryption gain popularity since they allow confidentiality protection while preserving blockchain visibility. AI-powered security toolsets alongside cross-platform blockchain frameworks are positioned to strengthen cloud environment integration along with workflow automation for compliance purposes and security optimization purposes. Numerous new potential solutions suggest future research and technological enhancements will help blockchain move toward securing wider cloud infrastructure usages.

The evaluation of blockchain's upcoming security role includes an analysis of both beneficial applications and active difficulties thereby delivering a complete blockchain understanding in cloud security. The following part explains the future state of blockchain-secured cloud computing.

9.2 Key Takeaways

Integrating blockchain with cloud security systems creates major changes to the methods we handle data management and storage and protection practices. Block chain introduces a transformative security solution because it distributes security protocols through cryptographic systems to tackle standard cloud vulnerabilities. The adoption of cloud-based infrastructures by organizations requires organizations to maintain absolute security combined with data integrity and regulatory compliance requirements. Through blockchain technology users can improve their security features through transparent data storage and unalterable information systems and automatic smart contract execution capabilities.

To achieve full-scale implementation various obstacles about scalability and resource efficiency along with interoperability as well as compliance with regulations require resolution. Current data protection laws create difficulties when using the immutable blockchain features that guarantee secure storage because these laws require allowing modification and deletion of data. The high operational cost and difficult consensus procedures require scientists to find greener blockchain options and structural solutions between blockchain and conventional cloud systems.

The future of blockchain-enabled cloud security appears promising because researchers continue to develop blockchain scalability methods alongside privacy-focused cryptographic breakthroughs and AI security tools. The adoption of blockchain technology into cloud environments depends heavily on industrial partnerships and standardized initiatives together with regulatory guidelines. Blockchain security solutions can develop into a core defense system for cloud platforms since they offer both protection against new digital threats along with operational performance and regulatory compliance.

Although blockchain does not resolve every cloud security concern it successfully augments existing security platforms for boosting cloud environment protection. Secure cloud computing development for the future will achieve its objectives by using blockchain strengths alongside continuous innovation research and collaborative industry development. Organizations will depend on blockchain technology more and more to develop future secure and trustworthy cloud systems.

The diagram below summarizes key blockchain-based solutions for cloud security—such as cryptographic hashing, decentralized identity, and smart contracts—while highlighting real-world applications and emerging future directions like DAOs, cross-chain interoperability, and AI-driven security.

Figure 9. Blockchain Applications, Security Aspects, and Future Directions

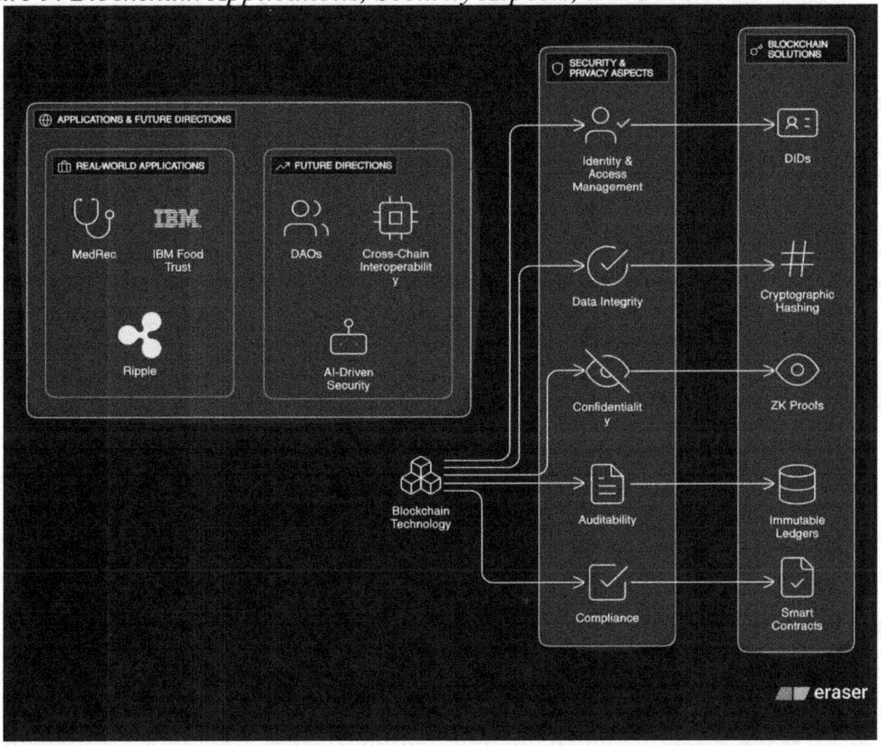

REFERENCES

Abubakar, N. S. J., Paradji, N.-S. U., Saggap, S., Anding, N. S., Tano, R. M., Arasani, A. H., Ahadain, D. R., Banda, B., Jayari, R., Alamhalil, A., Alih, S. H., & Tahil, S. K. (2024). Hacking Incidents and their Long-Term Implications for User Privacy and Trust. *Cognizance Journal*, *4*(12), 443–453. DOI: 10.47760/cognizance.2024.v04i12.041

Al Salih, A., & Wang, Y. (2024). *Innovative Byzantine Fault Tolerance in Hyperledger Fabric with BDLS*. 677–683. DOI: 10.1109/bcca62388.2024.10844400

Alevizos, L. (2024). Automated cybersecurity compliance and threat response using AI, blockchain and smart contracts. *International Journal of Information Technology : an Official Journal of Bharati Vidyapeeth's Institute of Computer Applications and Management*. Advance online publication. DOI: 10.1007/s41870-024-02324-9

Alzoubi, Y. I., & Mishra, A. (2024). Techniques to alleviate blockchain bloat: Potentials, challenges, and recommendations. *Computers & Electrical Engineering*, *116*, 109216. DOI: 10.1016/j.compeleceng.2024.109216

Azaria, A., Ekblaw, A., Vieira, T., & Lippman, A. (2016). MedRec: Blockchain for medical data access permission management and trend analysis. MIT Media Lab. Retrieved from https://www.media.mit.edu/publications/medrec-blockchain-for-medical-data-access-permission-management-and-trend-analysis/

Azaria, A., Steinhardt, G., & Ekblaw, A. (2016). *MedRec: Blockchain for medical data access, permission management, and trend analysis*. MIT Media Lab. https://assets.pubpub.org/77ffonfi/fac98e84-5f2c-4828-a1ba-e2141e747ee6.pdf

Bezuidenhout, R., & Nel, W. (2023). *Exponentially Distributed Nonlinear Proof-of-Work: Saving Energy while Preserving Decentralisation in Bitcoin Mining*. 1–7. DOI: 10.1109/icecet58911.2023.10389429

Bhatte, N., Prajapati, V. M., Varia, S., & More, J. (2022). Comparison of Different Cloud Providers. *International Journal For Science Technology And Engineering*, *10*(6), 651–656. DOI: 10.22214/ijraset.2022.43736

Bhole, A. G. (2025). Cloud Resource Management and Cost Optimization. *Indian Scientific Journal Of Research In Engineering And Management*, *09*(01), 1–7. DOI: 10.55041/ijsrem26028

Bhosale, K., & Waghmare, M. (2025). Enhancing Blockchain Scalability Through Layer 1 and Layer 2 Solutions: A Comparative Analysis. *International Journal For Science Technology And Engineering, 13*(1), 1642–1644. DOI: 10.22214/ijraset.2025.66647

Blancaflor, E., Robles, C. R. W., Espino, S. I., Matignas, K. G., Abisado, M., & Palenzuela, R. D. (2024). *Comparative Analysis of Current Infrastructure of Cloud Computing Unveiling the Trends of Industry 5.0.* 200–204. DOI: 10.1109/ccet62233.2024.10838120

Bulgakov, A. L., Aleshina, A. V., Smirnov, S. D., Demidov, A. D., Milyutin, M. A., & Xin, Y. (2024). Scalability and Security in Blockchain Networks: Evaluation of Sharding Algorithms and Prospects for Decentralized Data Storage. *Mathematics, 12*(23), 3860. DOI: 10.3390/math12233860

Burke, Q., Sheatsley, R., King, R., Swift, M. M., & McDaniel, P. (2024). *Cloud Storage Integrity at Scale: A Case for Dynamic Hash Trees.* https://doi.org//arxiv.2405.03830DOI: 10.48550

Choudhury, N., Chauhan, S., & Tiwari, M. (2021). Enterprise systems and blockchain technology: The dormant potentials. *International Journal of Information Management, 58*, 102291. DOI: 10.1016/j.ijinfomgt.2020.102291

Cocco, L., & Tonelli, R. (2024). A Self-Sovereign Identity–Blockchain-Based Model Proposal for Deep Digital Transformation in the Healthcare Sector. *Future Internet, 16*(12), 473. DOI: 10.3390/fi16120473

Continella, A., Polino, M., Pogliani, M., & Zanero, S. (2018). There's a hole in that bucket! A large-scale analysis of misconfigured S3 buckets. *Proceedings of the 34th Annual Computer Security Applications Conference (ACSAC '18)*, 702–711. Association for Computing Machinery. DOI: 10.1145/3274694.3274736

Dhokrat, J., Pulgam, N., Maktum, T., & Mane, V. (2024). A Framework for Privacy-Preserving Multiparty Computation with Homomorphic Encryption and Zero-Knowledge Proofs. *Informatica (Vilnius), 48*(21). Advance online publication. DOI: 10.31449/inf.v48i21.6562

Eyo-Udo, N., Agho, M. O., Onukwulu, E. C., Sule, A. K., & Azubuike, C. (2025). Advances in Blockchain Solutions for Secure and Efficient Cross-Border Payment Systems. *International Journal of Research and Innovation in Applied Science, IX*(XII), 536–563. DOI: 10.51584/ijrias.2024.912048

Folorunso, A., Babalola, O., Nwatu, C., & Adedoyin, A. (2024). A comprehensive model for ensuring data compliance in cloud computing environment. *World Journal Of Advanced Research and Reviews*, *24*(2), 1983–1995. DOI: 10.30574/wjarr.2024.24.2.3514

GeeksforGeeks. (2024). *Ethereum 2.0: A comprehensive guide to PoS and scalability improvements.* GeeksforGeeks. https://www.geeksforgeeks.org/ethereum-2-0/

Ghanmi, H., Hajlaoui, N., Touati, H., Elhadad Or Hadded, M., Muhlethaler, P., & Boudjit, S. (2024). Blockchain-cloud integration: Comprehensive survey and open research issues. *Concurrency and Computation*. Advance online publication. DOI: 10.1002/cpe.8122

Global IT outage highlights cloud-linked risks. (2024). *Emerald Expert Briefings*. DOI: 10.1108/oxan-es288430

Google Cloud. (2022, August 18). How Google Cloud blocked the largest Layer 7 DDoS attack at 46 million RPS. Google Cloud Blog. https://cloud.google.com/blog/products/identity-security/how-google-cloud-blocked-largest-layer-7-ddos-attack-at-46-million-rps

Goyal, A., Singh, A., Sharma, P. K., Yadav, D., & Jindal, A. (2022). Blockchain and AI in healthcare: A systematic review, applications, and future trends. *Journal of Medical Internet Research*, *24*(12), e37804. DOI: 10.2196/37804

Huang, X., Xiao, Q., Li, Y., Li, P., Zhang, M., Chen, Z., Huang, Y., Zhang, K., Mao, Y., & Song, J. (2024). Blockchain Technology and Privacy Protection. *Applications and Implementation of Zero-Knowledge Proofs, 637–641*. Advance online publication. DOI: 10.1109/ccsb63463.2024.10735589

Hussain, R., Alshammari, R., & Alharthi, R. (2020). A secure framework for data sharing and collaboration in cloud-based supply chains using blockchain. *Computers & Electrical Engineering*, *84*, 106607. DOI: 10.1016/j.compeleceng.2020.106607

IBM X-Force: Stolen Credentials and Vulnerabilities Weaponized Against Businesses in 2019-Feb 11, 2020. (2020).

Karunakaran, M., Bellam, K., Raja, J., & Shanthi, D. (2024). *Blockchain Technology in Cloud Security*. IGI Global. DOI: 10.4018/979-8-3693-2081-5.ch003

Khanna, A., Sah, A., Bolshev, V., Burgio, A., Panchenko, V., & Jasiński, M. (2022). Blockchain–Cloud Integration: A Survey. *Sensors (Basel)*, *22*(14), 5238. DOI: 10.3390/s22145238 PMID: 35890918

Kholod, A., Polyakov, Y., & Schlottke-Lakemper, M. (2024). *Secure numerical simulations using fully homomorphic encryption*. https://doi.org//arxiv.2410.21824DOI: 10.48550

Kumar, R., & Tripathi, A. (2022). Blockchain-enabled enterprise integration strategies in the cloud. *Journal of Cloud Computing (Heidelberg, Germany)*, *11*(1), 1–17. DOI: 10.1186/s13677-022-00300-z

Li, C., Xu, M., Zhang, J., Guo, H., & Cheng, X. (2024). SoK: Decentralized Storage Network. *IACR Cryptology ePrint Archive, 2024*, 258. DOI: 10.1016/j.hcc.2024.100239

Li, L. (2025). Using the Ripple consensus algorithm to achieve transparent cross-border payments in e-commerce. *IET Conference Proceedings.*, 2024(21), 295–299. DOI: 10.1049/icp.2024.4241

Manickaraj, P., Vatchala, L., & Gayathri, S. (2024). Securing Healthcare Data. *Leveraging Blockchain for Electronic Health Records, 234–238*. Advance online publication. DOI: 10.1109/icesic61777.2024.10846251

Mathew, A. (2024). Securing the Cloud: Understanding Threats and Countermeasures. *International Journal For Science Technology And Engineering*, *12*(12), 3026–3031. DOI: 10.22214/ijraset.2024.59552

Merlina, A., Garrett, T., & Vitenberg, R. (2024). *Replacing Cryptopuzzles with Useful Computation in Blockchain Proof-of-Work Protocols*. https://doi.org//arxiv.2404.15735DOI: 10.48550

Mittal, M. (2024). Colonial Pipeline Cyberattack Drives Urgent Reforms in Cybersecurity and Critical Infrastructure Resilience. *International Journal of Oil. Gas and Coal Engineering*, *12*(5), 106–119. DOI: 10.11648/j.ogce.20241205.11

Mongia, M. (2024). Blockchain Meets Cloud: A New Era in Distributed Systems Architecture. *International Journal of Scientific Research in Computer Science. Engineering and Information Technology*, *10*(6), 2204–2213. DOI: 10.32628/cseit2410612426

Naidu, G. H. S. (2024). Blockchain Technology as a Security Enhancement Framework for Internet of Things: A Comprehensive Analysis. *International Journal of Scientific Research in Computer Science. Engineering and Information Technology*, *10*(6), 842–850. DOI: 10.32628/cseit241061121

Neto, N. N., Madnick, S., De Paula, A. M. G., & Borges, N. M. (2020). A case study of the Capital One data breach. SSRN *Electronic Journal*. https://doi.org/DOI: 10.2139/ssrn.3542567

OpenZeppelin. (n.d.). **Access control**. OpenZeppelin Documentation. Retrieved February 27, 2025, from https://docs.openzeppelin.com/contracts/3.x/access-control

Pakanati, S. P. R., McKeithen, B., Saffy, R., Olajide, O., Clark, K., Olafuyi, B. A., & Hewitt, C. (2024). The Impact of Cybersecurity Breaches on Patient Data Privacy in U.S. Healthcare Systems. *International Journal of Scientific and Research Publications*, *14*(11), 76–81. DOI: 10.29322/ijsrp.14.11.2024.p15511

Pava-Díaz, R. A., Gil-Ruiz, J., & López-Sarmiento, D. A. (2024). Self-sovereign identity on the blockchain: Contextual analysis and quantification of SSI principles implementation. *Frontiers in Blockchain*, *7*. Advance online publication. DOI: 10.3389/fbloc.2024.1443362

Polakova, K., Bobková, A., Demianová, A., Bobko, M., Jurčaga, L., Mesárošová, A., Čapla, J., Timoracká, I., Lidiková, J., & Čeryová, N. (2024). Adulteration in food industry in 2023 - overview. *Journal of Microbiology, Biotechnology and Food Sciences*. Advance online publication. DOI: 10.55251/jmbfs.11048

Raut, K. (2024). Secure Message Hashing with SHA-256: Cryptographic Implementation. *International Journal for Research in Applied Science and Engineering Technology*, *12*(11), 1288–1294. DOI: 10.22214/ijraset.2024.65078

Rosen, G. (2018, September 28). Security update. Facebook Newsroom. https://about.fb.com/news/2018/09/security-update/

Saini, G. K., & Somani, G. (2024). *Resource Targeted Cybersecurity Attacks in Cloud Computing Environments*. Springer International Publishing. DOI: 10.1007/978-981-97-2644-8_9

Santana, C., & Albareda, L. (2022). Blockchain and the emergence of Decentralized Autonomous Organizations (DAOs): An integrative model and research agenda. *Technological Forecasting and Social Change*, *182*, 121806. DOI: 10.1016/j.techfore.2022.121806

Security, I. B. M. (2023). *Cost of a data breach report 2023*. IBM Corporation. https://www.ibm.com/reports/data-breach

Segall, L. (2021, July 30). Amazon hit with record $887 million fine for alleged privacy violations. CNN Business. https://edition.cnn.com/2021/07/30/tech/amazon-eu-privacy-fine/index.html

Sule, A., Eyo-Udo, N. L., Onukwulu, E. C., Agho, M. O., & Azubuike, C. (2025). Implementing Blockchain for Secure and Efficient Cross-Border Payment Systems. *International Journal of Research and Innovation in Applied Science*, *IX*(XII), 508–535. DOI: 10.51584/ijrias.2024.912047

Sykes, P. (2023). *Combining ID's*. Attributes, and Policies in Hyperledger Fabric. DOI: 10.1007/978-3-031-31420-9_3

Uriarte, R. B., & De Nicola, R. (2018). Blockchain-Based Decentralized Cloud/ Fog Solutions: Challenges, Opportunities, and Standards. *IEEE Communications Standards Magazine*, *2*(3), 22–28. DOI: 10.1109/MCOMSTD.2018.1800020

Vignesh, B., Chandrakumar, M., Divya, K., Prahadeeswaran, M., & Vanitha, G. (2025). Blockchain technology in agriculture: Ensuring transparency and traceability in the food supply chain. *Plant Science Today*, *12*(sp1). Advance online publication. DOI: 10.14719/pst.5970

Vliet, B. (2024). A Model of Decentralized Oversight for the Digital Asset Industry With an Example Anti-money Laundering/know-your-customer Standard. *Social Science Research Network*. DOI: 10.2139/ssrn.4771849

Zhang, B., Pan, H., Li, K., Xing, Y., Wang, L., Fan, D., & Zhang, W. (2024). A Blockchain and Zero Knowledge Proof Based Data Security Transaction Method in Distributed Computing. *Electronics (Basel)*, *13*(21), 4260. DOI: 10.3390/electronics13214260

KEY TERMS AND DEFINITIONS

Blockchain Technology: It is a decentralized and immutable ledger system that records transactions securely using cryptographic principles, eliminating the need for a trusted central authority.

Byzantine Fault Tolerance (BFT): Byzantine Fault Tolerance (BFT) protects blockchain networks against faulty behavior of nodes that enables system reliability when some nodes fail or show malicious actions.

Cloud Computing: Cloud Computing functions as an internet-based technique that enables users to gain instant access to servers and data storage and databases without maintaining control over network infrastructure.

Consensus Mechanisms: A blockchain network's consensus process utilizes cryptographic mechanisms to confirm deals and preserve an equivalent system status among all nodal participants while maintaining security and integrity of data within the network. Among proof mechanisms used in blockchain networks we find Proof of Work (PoW) together with Proof of Stake (PoS).

Decentralized Identity (DID): The blockchain system known as Decentralized Identity (DID) enables users to run their digital identities autonomously with independence from centralized authorities.

Homomorphic Encryption: The encryption method known as Homomorphic Encryption allows performing calculations directly on encrypted data before decryption thus protecting cloud data.

Intrusion Detection Systems (IDS): Intrusion Detection Systems (IDS) function as network traffic monitors to spot both unauthorized system access and detrimental operations happening inside cloud infrastructures.

Multi-Cloud Security: The method for safeguarding cloud systems that use multiple cloud providers requires unified security policies together with compliance measures as well as access controls.

Smart Contracts: Self-executing contracts embedded in blockchain systems that automatically enforce agreements when predefined conditions are met, reducing the need for intermediaries.

Zero-Knowledge Proofs (ZKPs): The cryptographic method Zero-Knowledge Proofs (ZKPs) enables users to demonstrate possession of information to others without revealing actual data points which enhances privacy in cloud security approaches.

Chapter 4

Enhancing Cyber-Physical System Resilience With Safe Data-Driven Control Strategies

Muhammad Usman Tariq
https://orcid.org/0000-0002-7605-3040
Abu Dhabi University, UAE & University College Cork, Ireland

ABSTRACT

This chapter explores strategies for enhancing the resilience of Cyber-Physical Systems (CPS) through safe and data-driven control mechanisms. As CPS become increasingly reliant on artificial intelligence (AI) and machine learning (ML) for real-time decision-making, ensuring system safety, security, and reliability becomes a critical challenge. The chapter examines various AI-powered control techniques, including Model Predictive Control (MPC), reinforcement learning, and anomaly detection, to optimize system performance while mitigating risks such as adversarial attacks, biases, and unpredictability. Additionally, it highlights the role of edge computing and distributed control architectures in reducing latency and improving fault tolerance. The chapter also addresses cybersecurity threats that impact CPS, including data breaches, cyberattacks, and network vulnerabilities.

INTRODUCTION

Cyber-Physical Systems (CPS) fuse computational procedures with operational procedures. Physical parts function with software programs in these systems which experience system behaviour control through real-world actions as well as computer-

DOI: 10.4018/979-8-3373-1832-5.ch004

based choices. CPS appears as autonomous vehicles, smart grids, industrial robots, medical devices along with Internet of Things (IoT) networks and additional critical examples. Technological systems are becoming prevalent, so their design methods and system maintenance directly impact the operational safety of both physical elements and mathematical components (Aghazadeh Ardebili & Andronie, 2025). CPS describes the necessity of establishing secure control mechanisms as its essential security focus point. The real-time operation of CPS includes physical components meeting complex algorithms which normally function without significant human control. Such tight physical-cyber integration leads to higher failure probabilities together with various possible malicious threat situations. In 2010 Stuxnet malware delivered a direct assault on the supervisory control and data acquisition (SCADA) system that operated Iranian uranium enrichment centrifuges. The malicious software controlled physical equipment operations discreetly as part of standard system activities. The incident demonstrated the harmful consequences of unsecure CPS environments because unidentified system failures could lead to monetary damages and threaten human existence (Gao et al., 2023). Protecting people from such risks becomes absolutely essential for achieving safe operations in CPS. Safety-critical environments represent many of the physical elements found in CPS operations including health services and transport systems and industrial production facilities. Catastrophic results emerge from all security failures and breaches in these critical operational environments. Consider autonomous vehicles, for instance. Autonomous vehicles adopting faulty control systems could generate incidents which lead to vehicle accidents along with injuries and death of occupants. A vehicle needs its communication systems with traffic control along with navigation to be protected against cyber threats (Aghazadeh Ardebili & Andronie, 2025).

Safety and security needs in CPS control systems can be achieved through careful implementation of cybersecurity protocols as well as fault-tolerant algorithms alongside real-time monitoring systems. The technical development of these systems should protect against malicious cyber threats together with protecting against unintentional failures stemming from system overload or environmental conditions (Gao et al., 2023). Data-driven methodologies show promise as a method of enhancing system resilience while increasing robustness in CPS designs. The development of CPS depends on non-stop data acquisition which combines sensor analytics with cyber system analysis to anticipate system evolutions through monitoring capabilities. Machine learning algorithms together with statistical methods and big data analytics enable data-driven methods to detect potential threats as well as system failures and performance anomalies and warn about catastrophic events before their occurrence. The early alert system allows operators to conduct maintenance operations before breakdowns emerge thus improving system operational reliability while ensuring safety measures (Aghazadeh Ardebili & Andronie, 2025). Data-driven techniques have an essential role in establishing security features for CPS systems. The rapid increase of Internet of Things devices within CPS results in substantial data production from interconnected technological devices. Real-time evaluation of this information shows the existence of threat-associated patterns. The monitoring capabilities of intrusion detection systems equipped with machine learning detect abnormal system behaviour by analysing unusual patterns of device communication which indicate possible cyber-attacks. Early detection of cyber threats enabled through data analytics leads to prevention of devastating power outages and system overloads which result from cyber-attacks within critical infrastructure such as energy grids (Gao et al., 2023). Data usage within CPS faces several significant hurdles although it provides benefits to the system. Safety and security needs in CPS control systems can be achieved through careful implementation of cybersecurity protocols as well as fault-tolerant algorithms alongside real-time monitoring systems. The technical development of these systems should protect against malicious cyber threats together with protecting against unintentional failures stemming from system overload or environmental conditions (Kim et al., 2022).

Data-driven methodologies offer a promising solution to maintain CPS system resilience together with robustness. The development of CPS depends on non-stop data acquisition which combines sensor analytics with cyber system analysis to anticipate system evolutions through monitoring capabilities. The adoption of statistical methods together with machine learning algorithms and big data analytics enables data-driven systems to detect probable threats as well as system failures and performance anomalies before catastrophic events occur. Industrial manufacturing facilities implement sensors to monitor machinery operations for real-time data collection of parametric measurements including temperature and pressure and vibration. The identification of early mechanical failure indicators lets maintainers perform preventive maintenance before system failure thus improving both system safety along with operational efficiency (Kim et al., 2022). Data-driven techniques have an essential role in establishing security features for CPS systems. The rapid increase of Internet of Things devices within CPS results in substantial data production from interconnected technological devices. Real-time evaluation of this information shows the existence of threat-associated patterns. The installation of machine learning-based intrusion detection systems enables users to identify abnormal network activities among devices through tracking their communications patterns and potential cyber-attack detection. Data analytics in critical energy facilities helps detect early cyber threats which stops powerful outages and system overloads caused by cyber-attacks (Kim et al., 2022). Data usage within CPS faces several significant hurdles although it provides benefits to the system. The design and management of CPS systems must avoid limiting their approach to only reactive elements. The development of safe IoT technologies should begin with designing secure systems from scratch and implementing security by design principles to embed safety and security elements throughout the entire system life cycle. Multi-disciplinary expertise from computer science and engineering together with cybersecurity and safety management professionals should collaborate during CPS design to build resistant systems for intentional and unintentional disruptions (Gao et al., 2023). Future developments of Cyber-Physical Systems across different fields will require prioritizing control systems with safety aspects and security measures and resilience features. The adoption of data-driven methods represents a vital instrument for CPS safety while enhancing security alongside operational efficiency through early identification of risks that would lead to system-collapse or catastrophic incidents. For CPS to reach its maximum potential several obstacles involving data security and system resilience and standards need solutions. The protection of CPS needs total commitment from all involved entities including system creators alongside regulatory units in combination with cybersecurity specialists who will develop strong systems which resist advancing digital and physical threats (Kim et al., 2022).

BACKGROUND

Cyber-Physical Systems (CPS) describe complex systems which merge computer components with physical systems for operation. Physical systems use real-time interacting sensors along with actuators along with controllers which build a network structure to track and control physical procedures. CPS technology exists throughout various sections of transportation, healthcare, manufacturing and energy sectors. The examples of CPS devices include autonomous vehicles along with smart grids and medical devices and industrial control systems. The requirement for resilient computer systems against attacks and disturbances alongside faults has emerged as a critical necessity because these systems continue to expand their interconnected operations throughout our ecosystem. Developing strategies to maintain the secure operation of CPS at regular operation intervals as well as extreme operational conditions is key to stopping equipment breakdowns and shield system and personal from identified risks (Lian et al., 2022). The protection of system resilience serves as a primary concern for CPS while operating through both cyber and physical disturbances. System resilience within CPS means the ability for a system to maintain effective operation as it encounters both failures and threats. System resilience stands as a vital requirement in safety-critical applications because failures would produce substantial consequences that harm people and properties along with causing financial losses. Remote patient monitoring systems alongside medical robotics illustrate the healthcare industry since their failures hold life-threatening consequences for patients. The failure of these systems from any source such as cyber-attacks or sensor problems or communication failures would result in delayed medical care or inaccurate patient diagnoses or possible harm to patients. Enhancing the resilience of CPS demands immediate attention because this requires multiple advanced control approaches alongside secure data management strategies (Asadi et al., 2023; Tariq, 2025). The implementation of secure and data-based control systems is indispensable for making CPS more resilient. The fundamental principle of a data-driven system relies on an uninterrupted flow of device and sensor information collection and data interpretation until processing completion. Predicted failures can be prevented through real-time control parameter adjustments pursued as the main objective. Machine learning programs alongside different data analytics approaches scan patterns through data to detect first indications of system irregularities thus initiating proactive actions to maintain operation safety and security. The techniques enhance system performance at the same time they prove essential for achieving resilient systems (Lian et al., 2022).

Real-life implementation of data-based control methods enhances the operational effectiveness of CPS systems. The utilization of predictive maintenance within industrial environments serves as a strong demonstration of the technique. The factory employs machine sensors that monitor key operational indicators including temperature together with vibration and pressure level information. Machine learning models process these data points to determine future failure times for machines. The system detects equipment wear before it evolves into major issues thus enabling the scheduling of maintenance procedures for avoiding unexpected breakdowns and catastrophic failures. Markedly important to such fields as aerospace and automotive because equipment breakdown would cause time-consuming interruptions and safety risks (Asadi et al., 2023). Data-driven control strategies provide major benefits, but users encounter several difficulties when implementing them. The primary obstacle to address is keeping data secure as well as preventing tampering of collected information. The massive volumes of CPS data create opportunities for cybercriminals who search for system vulnerabilities through which they can steal this information. In 2015 Ukrainian power grid became a target for cyber-attack because hackers managed to penetrate the system causing widespread power outages throughout the country. The security incident revealed protecting both CPS network data transfers and procedural control infrastructure as essential goals. Data security issues would produce flawed predictions from control systems and potentially disastrous outcomes. Secure data management protocols together with encryption and authentication mechanisms must be integrated into CPS because they represent essential defences against attacks (Lian et al., 2022). Data-driven CPS control faces a crucial challenge because it needs strategies to address data uncertainties along with missing information. Various CPS applications including real-time operations often encounter data problems because the collected information becomes noisy alongside being incomplete or showing uncertainty. Sensors that power autonomous vehicles including LiDAR or cameras can deliver wrong information because of environmental elements including rain fog and snow. The unpredictability in sensor data affects data-driven control algorithms so they fall short of accurate predictions thus endangering system safety. Sensor fusion methods combine with Bayesian approaches and robust control systems implement advanced methodologies to synthesize information from different sources and deal with data uncertainty. Reliable predictions can be achieved through these methods which work effectively under all data conditions including noisy or incomplete information (Asadi et al., 2023). The implementation of data-based control systems poses major scalability restrictions to system execution. Application systems of CPS frequently have extensive networks combining numerous devices and sensors that produce substantial amounts of data. Modern computing systems must have sufficient power to carry out the real-time analysis of collected data. Traditional computing systems become inadequate when controlling systems become larger and more complex. Edge computing allows organizations to solve this issue effectively. The data processing mechanism within edge computing systems takes place directly on the device or at local servers near data origins rather than transmitting everything to remote cloud servers. Higher speed of operation and enhanced real-time decision capabilities accompany reduced stress on centralized systems because data remains local. In smart cities near-source processing of traffic sensor data and environmental monitor information and public transportation system data delivers expedited responses to traffic control and emergency response operations (Lian et al., 2022; Tariq, 2025).

Edge computing provides numerous advantages, yet its execution brings security along with data consistency issues as main concerns. Data processed at edge points remains prone to intentional alterations because it occurs at the point of origin. The security of edge devices and data consistency across distributed systems needs proper implementation to protect the resilience of the CPS. An example of smart grids demonstrates how controlling edge device information can result in mistaken grid equilibrium choices which produce either power blackouts or unstable network conditions. Strong authentication systems and secure protocols need implementation because they protect the integrity of edge data (Asadi et al., 2023). Security measures need to be integrated into all data-based control mechanisms for optimal performance. In circumstances where CPS operates in safety-critical conditions such as autonomous vehicles or medical devices the control system needs both resilience and the ability to preserve safety throughout system failures. The system needs fault-tolerant control measures to operate securely following structural failures of its components. An autonomous vehicle system possesses the capability to transition between sensors or activate duplicate internal control protocols after sensor failure to preserve its operational safety. Safety-critical systems protect their stability and safety through multiple security measures incorporating real-time observation and fault recognition followed by recovery protocols (Cassandro et al., 2024). The continued assurance of CPS resilience remains a continuous problem despite recent progress. The permanent changes in both cyber security threats and physical system breakdowns mandate continuous updates in control system strategies. Complexity and increased connectivity of CPS systems generate larger potential vulnerabilities within the systems. One healthcare system for connected devices demonstrates how a single harmed medical device would lead to critical network failure throughout all patient care operations. Because of this need for adaptation and self-repair control systems must be designed to respond to threats and failures (Asadi et al., 2023). Improving the resilience of Cyber-Physical Systems by implementing safe, data-driven control techniques is a complex process that necessitates striking a balance between cybersecurity, real-time decision-making, and advanced data analytics. Data confidentiality, unpredictability, scalability, and system safety issues need to be resolved even while data-driven control presents encouraging options for enhancing CPS resilience. To ensure the continuous safe functioning of these systems in more complex contexts, it is imperative to create flexible, resilient control mechanisms that can resist both deliberate cyberattacks and unintended breakdowns (Cassandro & Chen, 2024).

Foundations of Safe Data-Driven Control in CPS

Control systems operate in Cyber-Physical Systems (CPS) as their essential operational components to manage the relationship of computational processes and physical systems. The control systems in CPS maintain operations through their intended functionality while they control environmental surveillance and autonomous vehicle functions. Real-time functionality serves as the primary requirement for control systems because they need to react instantaneously to physical process changes for correct system performance. The success of CPS depends heavily on real-time constraints because any decision-making delays can harm operations through failure, safety risks or performance reduction. Industrial control systems experience equipment damage combined with unsafe operating conditions when sensor data processing delays occur. High time sensitivity of real-time applications creates obstacles for data-driven control implementation yet necessitates their use for boosting system performance and resistance (Dai et al., 2025). The essential component of CPS consists of sensors and actuators which enable real-time observation and modification of physical operation. Control decisions make use of sensor-generated data through closed-loop operations which let the control system adapt according to system state factors. These systems demonstrate adaptive behaviour because they do not stay fixed (Tariq, 2024). Applications involving autonomous driving and healthcare depend heavily on systems which need to react to new situations that occur during operation. Driverless vehicles require control systems that need to handle quick fluctuations of road environments and obstacles alongside traffic patterns. These control systems adapt through data analysis of real-time data volumes because they base decisions on recognized patterns and predictive models. These control systems utilize machine learning (ML) and reinforcement learning together with deep learning to learn different scenarios and forecast the upcoming states of the system which results in better performance and adaptability (Kim et al., 2022). The implementation of data-driven controls poses several complications for integration within CPS control systems. The primary barrier lies in managing real-time data primarily because it remains noisy and incomplete together with being uncertain at times. Many CPS applications use medical monitoring as an example where sensor data might become inaccurate due to environmental interference and sensor failure or malfunction. Little reliability can arise from electromagnetic signals causing heart rate monitors to generate faulty measurements while radar systems in vehicles encounter signal interruption in adverse weather. Real-time processing of such data requires filtering and analysis before control systems can use it which increases their overall complexity. Advanced data filtering methods teamed up with sensor fusion processes merge several sensor inputs to achieve improved data reliability. Yet such methods face challenges when working in conditions of high uncertainty when sensor information remains unclear or insufficient (Dai et al., 2025).

Modern machine learning models impose a computational challenge that stands in the way of achieving real-time requirements for CPS implementation. Advanced data-driven methodologies need substantial computational power for execution, so they become problematic to implement in real-time specifically within distributed systems performing edge-level or constrained environment operations. The required techniques consist of model compression and edge computing and parallel processing which distribute computation workloads while minimizing latency times. Decisions made by these methods risk compromising between algorithm accuracy and response velocity which negatively impacts the system effectiveness and security level (Kim et al., 2022). Data-based control implementation raises multiple safety and security-related concerns. Retention of control system safety operates as a fundamental problem particularly when applied to essential safety applications such as medical devices industrial control systems and autonomous vehicles. Traditional control systems implement fail-safes along with redundancies and additional safety mechanisms to guarantee system safety even when system elements fail despite using standard mathematical models for design. The implementation of data-driven methods has limited visibility and inconsistent patterns regarding system outputs (Kim et al., 2022). The black box nature of machine learning algorithms leads to obscure decision-making operations since they base their predictions on extensive data sets. Safety-critical applications suffer because without transparency it becomes challenging to ensure that resulting decisions will be safe for the system. Autonomous vehicles need transparent decision-making to avoid making incorrect choices during dangerous emergency situations like failing to stop before collisions occur. Research into explainable AI (XAI) emerged to create predictive models which simultaneously show their rationale to human users through understandable explanations. Additional research needs to be performed before XAI approaches can become completely integrated within safety-critical CPS (Dai et al., 2025; Tariq, 2025).

There remains a critical security issue related to CPS stability when implementing data-driven technology. Both data and control systems within CPS face potential compromise due to their networking capability which makes them vulnerable to cyber-attacks. Such cyber-attacks on CPS systems can produce devastating effects with two main outcomes: first, the alteration of sensor inputs to show faulty data and second, unauthorized access to critical system control functions. Industrial control systems experienced physical damage due to the 2010 Stuxnet cyber-attack which targeted Iranian nuclear facilities. Secure data-driven control systems require complete implementation of robust cybersecurity features because of their vital role in CPS security (Liu et al., 2022). The protection of data integrity together with control processes depends on data encryption and secure communication protocols and intrusion detection systems. Such vulnerabilities make machine learning models weak to adversarial attacks due to specific modifications made to input data which fool the system to deliver incorrect outputs. A sensor data alteration performed by an attacker presenting a minor but critical modification would lead an autonomous vehicle control system into making unsafe choices. Protecting the essential infrastructure and machine learning model bases is necessary to preserve CPS security along with operational integrity (Lian et al., 2022). Safety and security form a core component of CPS operations, but existing systems require continuous management between efficiency and security and safety perspectives. The adoption of more complex data-driven methods to boost system performance and resilience creates a dilemma because it increases system complexity and computational demands together with error and vulnerability susceptibilities. The combination of incorrect model predictions leads to two possible outcomes: first, unnecessary equipment maintenance procedures use up resources and halt operations; second, equipment failures remain undetected which causes equipment damage and unexpected work production stops. Data-driven models and CPS real-time requirements create similar decision points because of their computational complexity balance challenge. The computational expenses rise directly proportional to model accuracy and complexity which leads to higher delay times in decision-making (Liu et al., 2022).

Control systems for CPS integrate data-driven techniques through three prevailing methodologies which are traditional model-based control and adaptive control together with reinforcement learning. Control systems that use mathematical system models predict system behaviour to achieve control outcomes. The method provides strong reliability but becomes ineffective when dealing with complex environments that require difficult modelling for high accuracy. System parameter adjustment through adaptive control requires substantial processing power while its performance might decrease when facing environmental disturbances and uncertain conditions. The modern approach of reinforcement learning teaches systems to create ideal control strategies by conducting experiments and using environmental feedback. The computational cost of reinforcement learning remains high even though its performance depends on large training datasets. All these methodologies experience limitations regarding performance costs and scalability limitations and real-time system applicability which motivates further research to develop better CPS technologies (Lian et al., 2022). Data-driven control of CPS offers substantial potential to improve their operational resilience as well as their efficiency and adaptability features. Every CPS application demands a balanced evaluation between efficiency and safety and security requirements to determine the optimal course of action. The three control approaches of model-based control and adaptive control followed by reinforcement learning provide essential knowledge and capabilities but present obstacles which need resolution to maximize data-driven control performance in CPS applications. The evolution of CPS depends on new methodological developments to overcome their present challenges so data-driven techniques will achieve their highest potential for safe and secure resilient systems (Liu et al., 2022).

Data-Driven Control Architectures for CPS

The essential role of data-driven control architectures within Cyber-Physical Systems continues to grow because such systems provide better methods to manage complex dynamic environments. Based on machine learning (ML) and artificial intelligence (AI) with model predictive control (MPC) and reinforcement learning (RL) and data analytics techniques these systems enhance operational effectiveness as well as safety and strengthen resistance levels. Real-time data processing becomes possible by using multiple approaches which let CPS adapt to modification in inputs while forecasting possible failure points to create autonomous self-operating systems (Olowononi et al., 2020). Having AI capabilities and machine learning control systems represent the most groundbreaking CPS approaches since these systems allow them to develop knowledge through experience and perform adjustments as conditions change. Various CPS applications including autonomous vehicles, industrial automation, and healthcare systems use ML algorithms starting with three types: supervised learning, unsupervised learning, and deep learning. A self-driving system collects information from cameras LIDAR and radar sensors through its AI-powered system which helps the automobile detect objects while understanding the driving environment and making operational decisions. The system continues to gain capability through enhanced capacity because it accumulates more information. The main drawback of performance enhancement through ML-based control approaches is the substantial processing requirements which introduce time limitations. The implementation obstacles of fast-changing conditions limit the use of deep learning models because their high processing requirements and slow response times (Goh & Ahmad, 2022). The powerful control method Model Predictive Control (MPC) belongs to CPS applications especially for systems requiring dynamic decision systems. MPC implements an optimization procedure using system simulation predictions to find sequential control decisions for a limited time span. The technique proves valuable in process control for manufacturing because it allows optimization of various parameters through constraint evaluation. For example, deep learning models are difficult to use in time-sensitive applications since they frequently demand sophisticated hardware and can react slowly to rapidly changing situations (Olowononi et al., 2020).

Another effective control technique utilized in CPS, especially in systems that need dynamic decision-making, is Model Predictive Control (MPC). In order to forecast future states and identify the best course of action for control across a finite horizon, MPC uses a model of the system to solve an optimization problem at each time step. This method is especially helpful in situations where the system must optimize several parameters while taking limits into account, such as process control in manufacturing. For example, MPC can maintain an ideal manufacturing process in a chemical processing facility by instantly adjusting the temperature, pressure, and flow rates (Goh & Ahmad, 2022). The capacity of MPC to explicitly manage restrictions, which guarantees that the system stays within safe operating bounds, is one of its fundamental features. Nevertheless, MPC necessitates a precise system model, which isn't always accessible or precise enough in practical applications. Furthermore, the optimization procedure can be computationally costly, particularly for systems with high-dimensional state spaces, which causes delays in making decisions in real time (Olowononi et al., 2020). By learning from interactions with the environment, reinforcement learning (RL), a potential data-driven control technique, enables systems to adjust to changing conditions. The foundation of RL algorithms is the idea of trial and error, in which an agent (the controller) acts, watches the results, and is rewarded or penalized according to the results. The agent gradually discovers the best course of action to maximize cumulative rewards. Robotics, energy management systems, and autonomous systems have all been controlled using RL in CPS. For instance, by learning the best course of action for balancing supply and demand while accounting for variables like energy output, consumption, and cost, RL may be used in smart grids to manage the distribution of power. Because RL learns from real-time data rather than a perfect model of the system, it is especially advantageous for adaptive control. However, RL's requirement for substantial data and computing resources is one of its main disadvantages, which may restrict its use in settings with limited resources (Finn & Gao, 2022; Tariq, 2025).

Furthermore, RL systems may require some time to adjust to novel or unexpected situations, which might have an immediate effect on system performance. Additionally, the convergence to an optimal policy may be gradual. Enhancing CPS's resilience requires data analytics, especially in the areas of failure prediction and anomaly detection. Data analytics tools may spot trends and deviations from normal behaviour, which could be signs of an imminent problem or system failure, by evaluating sensor data, both historical and real-time. To identify anomalous system states that could need attention, anomaly detection techniques including clustering, classification, and statistical approaches are used. For example, data analytics may be used in predictive maintenance to track the state of industrial equipment and forecast when it will break, enabling maintenance teams to act before a breakdown happens. This has been used in a number of industries, including manufacturing, where data analytics algorithms forecast failures based on past trends and sensors continually check the condition of machinery. These forecasts can increase overall operational efficiency and assist avoid expensive downtime (Goh & Ahmad, 2022). However, managing the enormous volumes of data produced by CPS and making sure the algorithms can function in real-time present difficulties when using data analytics for anomaly detection. The efficacy of these systems can also be diminished by false negatives, which fail to detect a failure, and false positives, which mistakenly classify a typical occurrence as an abnormality. There are a number of difficulties in incorporating these data-driven control strategies into CPS. For instance, even while controls driven by AI and machine learning are strong, they may not be easily interpreted, particularly in intricate models like deep learning. In safety-critical applications, where it is crucial to comprehend the rationale behind actions, this lack of transparency may be a challenge. Furthermore, AI algorithms' computational load may restrict their real-time functionality, particularly in systems with constrained hardware resources (Olowononi et al., 2020).

Despite its effectiveness in guaranteeing optimal performance, Model Predictive Control is largely dependent on precise system models, which are not always accessible, especially in complex or nonlinear systems. Furthermore, in some situations, the computing expense of resolving optimization issues in MPC may be unaffordable, which might cause reaction times to lag (Goh & Ahmad, 2022). Although it shows promise for adaptive control, reinforcement learning has drawbacks with regard to convergence times and data economy. The lengthy learning process of reinforcement learning (RL) might be a major disadvantage in CPS applications where prompt choices are required. The exploration-exploitation trade-off, in which the system must strike a balance between attempting novel actions (exploration) and pursuing the known optimal actions (exploitation), may also be a challenge for RL-based systems. In applications that demand great dependability, this might result in less-than-ideal performance throughout the learning period (Finn & Gao, 2022). Despite being extremely useful for failure prediction and anomaly detection, data analytics also has issues with data volume and quality. Effective data preprocessing and filtering can be challenging in CPS because to the massive volume of sensor data collected. To prevent missing failures or false alarms, the anomaly detection algorithms also need to be precisely tuned. The quality of the data also affects prediction accuracy; noisy or insufficient data might produce inaccurate findings, which lowers system reliability (Finn & Gao, 2022).

To sum up, data-driven control systems have a lot of promise for improving CPS's flexibility, efficiency, and robustness. In this context, data analytics, MPC, reinforcement learning, machine learning, and AI-powered control are all useful technologies with distinct advantages in various applications. However, there are certain difficulties in incorporating these methods into CPS, especially when it comes to real-time performance, computing requirements, and safety issues. To fully achieve the promise of data-driven control in CPS, more effective algorithms must be developed, data quality and processing methods must be improved, and safety and security issues must be properly handled. By doing this, these systems may become more durable, intelligent, and adaptive in the face of constantly changing obstacles (Finn & Gao, 2022).

Cybersecurity Risks and Mitigation Strategies

Cyber threats through cyber-attacks against Cyber-Physical Systems (CPS) will increase because these systems blend physical system operations with digital control along with networking systems. CPS exists as high-priority targets because their vulnerabilities draw persistent attacks from cybercriminals together with nation-state operators and internal actors with malicious intent. Proper cybersecurity implementation of CPS remains essential because attacks generate operational breakdowns and data breaches while causing financial damage and inflicting physical injuries. The solutions require implementing cryptographic methods as well as using AI-driven security tools to proactively reduce these vulnerabilities (Delsing & Tovar, 2022). The biggest risk to CPS cybersecurity comprises cyber-attacks that potentially spread malware while performing DoS attacks and carrying out ransomware intrusions. In 2010 the Stuxnet worm targeted Iranian nuclear facilities through PLC vulnerabilities which led to centrifuge failures. The incident proved malware can damage essential control networks of critical infrastructure. The 2021 Colonial Pipeline incident alongside other CPS ransomware attacks demonstrates how cyber intrusions into digital control systems may create operational shutdowns. The significance therefore remains clear to boost system Défense capabilities for stopping unauthorized intrusions and maintaining operational stability (Bullo & Chen, 2022). The substantial data production by CPS remains a significant worry because CPS collect many sensitive information types including industrial process commands with sensor feedback alongside user password authentication materials. Dangerous outcomes will result from unprovoked exposure or alteration of collected data. In smart grids attackers can modify energy distribution commands which results in large-scale power outages along with destructive surges. Medical network devices used as healthcare CPS face data security threats which endanger both patient privacy records and operating function integrity. Data protection for CPS requires immediate implementation because of its connected systems which face major security risks from unsecured component communications. The cyberattacks that target CPS systems frequently strike vulnerable network components since legacy CPS designs originally lacked security measures (Delsing & Tovar, 2022).

Suspicious communication channels enable attackers to insert false information which results in disrupted real-time data operations. Attackers who modify GPS signals together with vehicle-to-infrastructure (V2I) communications can provide incorrect commands to autonomous vehicles resulting in accidental situations. The current situation shows that we need protected networking protocols which provide both authentic and unmodified data transmission (Bullo & Chen, 2022). Real-time CPS applications require cryptographic methods specifically because these systems need both efficient performance and low response times. The security guarantees provided by AES and RSA encryption methods come at a cost of introducing performance limitations which affect real-time processes. Lightweight cryptographic schemes including ECC and homomorphic encryption solve this challenge by getting implemented into CPS networks (Delsing & Tovar, 2022). The compact key lengths in ECC deliver robust security which enables its application to constrained CPS devices. The key feature of homomorphic encryption enables secure data processing while maintaining total privacy protection because computations can take place directly on encrypted content. Secure key management solutions together with real-time encryption functions defend industrial IoT systems from unauthorized entry while preserving system performance functions (Bullo & Chen, 2022). Real-time threat detection with adaptive defence mechanisms drives AI security solutions as core elements which enhance cybersecurity strategies for CPS systems. Machine learning algorithms review network activity patterns to detect irregular behaviours because they signal potential continuing attack activities. Intrusion detection systems (IDS) using AI capabilities can distinguish normal CPS data changes from deliberate tampering of system operations (Sun & Wang, 2022). Through predictive security AI creates a system which identifies possible vulnerabilities before hackers can exploit them. The use of AI-powered monitoring solutions in smart manufacturing creates defences which detect unauthorized system entry attempts together with indicator variations from sensors that automatically launch protective actions. The usage of AI-based security systems brings security dangers that include attackers who use input data manipulation to outsmart the AI models. Strong training datasets, frequent model updates, and hybrid security strategies that blend artificial intelligence with conventional cybersecurity techniques are needed to address this (Delsing & Tovar, 2022). Even though these tactics greatly increase CPS resilience, cybersecurity is still a problem because of changing threats. Ensuring the safe functioning of CPS requires the implementation of a multi-layered security solution that integrates secure network designs, AI-driven monitoring, and cryptographic safeguards. The security solutions that shield these systems from ever-more-advanced cyberthreats must also change as these systems do (Sun & Wang, 2022).

Ensuring Real-Time and Resilient Control

The maintenance of stable operations and efficiency with ensured security in Cyber-Physical Systems (CPS) requires immediate and resistant control mechanisms especially in critical environments like industrial automation and smart grids as well as autonomous vehicles and healthcare systems (Shi & Rudas, 2025). The advancement of complex and networked systems presents novel oppositions to achieve proper equilibriums between system speed and security as well as adaptation features. The solution requires safe deployment of AI models in addition to optimized edge computing and distributed control designs along with necessary human supervision functions (Aylor & Asare, 2023). AI model deployment safety remains a primary problem when working with time-related systems in CPS. The implementation of AI-based control systems through elements such as deep reinforcement learning (DRL) and neural networks gives CPS the ability to perform live decision making using extensive datasets. These models need thorough testing for ensuring they do not generate unsafe operations. The sensor data processed by autonomous vehicle perception systems based on AI delivers instant choices regarding braking velocity and directions for acceleration and lane control. Small purposeful manipulations of sensor data which cause AI to mistake obstacles can potentially lead to accidents. When combating risks AI models need to build their training on numerous datasets while maintaining continuous system updates and combining them with safety rules that activate backup control functions when AI failures occur (Shi & Rudas, 2025). Edge computing together with distributed control systems function as essential factors for decreasing latency throughout CPS. The processing delays that happen when systems send data to central servers confront real-time applications because they produce delays which fail to meet strict time constraints. Processing sensor data with any delay in industrial robotics results in operational disturbances or equipment malfunctions. Edge computing enables prompt data processing by keeping operations near their sources which shortens the time needed for taking decisions. System resilience receives additional protection through distributed control because it distributes decision-making authority for local controllers to operate individually when central system communication breaks down (Zhou & Ahmed, 2023).

Under distributed energy management in smart grids the local substations gain power distribution flexibility during emergencies while operating independently from centralized control systems. Smart grids exemplify resilience in CPS applications because they have been implemented to resist cyber threats. Smart grids unleash CPS methods through sensor networks alongside automatic controls and AI forecast systems to optimize electricity transmission processes (Rawat & Lu, 2020). CPS systems maintain vulnerability against cyber assaults which include false data injection (FDI) attacks that allow attackers to distort sensor outputs resulting in energy distribution problems. Remote attacks against Ukrainian power infrastructure control systems during 2015 resulted in major blackouts across the nation. Security mechanisms that combine anomaly detection methods along with redundant communications and autonomous cyber protection techniques through AI help prevent blackouts resulting from compromised network nodes. Blockchain authentication systems secure smart grid transaction parameters because they allow only permitted entities to make modifications (Aylor & Asare, 2023). The implementation of human-in-the-loop (HITL) systems continues to be necessary for achieving safe operation of CPS systems since AI and automation strengthen operational efficiency. The decision-making processes within HITL systems contain a human oversight function that enables operators to handle novel system irregularities. The medical robotic-assisted surgery system runs through AI providers during procedures while trained surgeons retain manual authority to stop AI failures. The aviation industry uses AI-driven flight control through autopilot systems which pilots still retain the ability to cancel automated commands when emergencies arise. System reliability increases through the human-intuition-supported utilization of AI efficiency which reduces the risks that would stem from absolute autonomous control (Zhou & Ahmed, 2023). Real-time and resilient control in CPS can be achieved by implementing AI safety mechanisms and edge computing while distributing control amongst human operators and implementing two methods for control. Security together with operational stability and efficiency in critical applications will be maintained by these strategies as CPS continue to advance (Rawat & Lu, 2020).

Ethical and Regulatory Considerations

System integration between Cyber-Physical Systems at an elevated scale causes expanding moral indications alongside law enforcement challenges. Because these systems heavily depend on data-driven decision-making with artificial intelligence they create privacy and compliance and fairness risks. To create ethical and responsible CPS we need privacy protections and global cybersecurity law adherence and transparent AI model implementation. The swift technological progress demands updated legal regulations which safeguard ethics and security requirements (Zhao & Zheng, 2022). The extensive data collection during CPS operations leads to serious ethical problems because of privacy violation risks. These systems operate through real-time data exchange from sensors together with user interactions and computer models that optimize operational output by requiring seamless data transmission. The implementation of improved automation structures as well as efficiency gains stands alongside increased risks for unapproved access and data breaches and other forms of misuse (Li & Park, 2024).The smart city infrastructure makes use of CPS technology for controlling traffic management systems and distributing energy resources as well as maintaining public safety operations. The urban operation optimization process depends on analysis of data gathered from IoT sensors as well as connected vehicles and surveillance cameras. The gathering of live tracking data alongside movement records about people generates worries about state-level mass surveillance together with possible misuse by authorities or cyber aggressors. Such improperly handled data poses serious risks of violating privacy rights and discriminating against people while also presenting cyber threats to individual users plus organizations (Zhao & Zheng, 2022).

Healthcare remote patient monitoring and robotic surgery together with wearable medical devices make possible by the application of CPS technology. Medical applications need continuous patient data transmission of heart rate measurements as well as oxygen levels plus indicators regarding medication adherence. Wealthier personalized healthcare exists through CPS however data attacks and security breaches become elevated risks. The 2015 Anthem attack on the US health insurance organization revealed the medical history of 80 million individuals showing weak CPS system security can lead to disastrous results (Li & Park, 2024). The protection of privacy requires organizations to deploy differential privacy together with secure multi-party computation and homomorphic encryption as privacy-enhancing technologies. The privacy protection mechanism of differential privacy allows valuable data analysis through user anonymization. Secure multi-party computation provides several entities with the ability to examine shared information without disclosing private information thus maintaining confidentiality when multiple organizations collaborate in CPS environments. Secure privacy practices and efficient operational methods can coexist when adopted together by CPS (Zhao & Zheng, 2022). The widespread implementation of CPS across businesses makes it harder to follow worldwide cybersecurity laws because of their complexity. Organizations must operate under separate legal guidelines for data security and system integrity and privacy in various geographic areas throughout their operations (Kim & Santoso, 2021). The General Data Protection Regulation (GDPR) established by the European Union presents organizations with the most rigorous set of data protection requirements regarding data collection and processing and storage operations. User organizations employing CPS need to achieve compliance by deploying data minimization practices along with encryption protocols as well as consent-based processes. Employee biometric data used for manufacturing plant access control must be kept secure until a predetermined storage period ends after which the data should be permanently deleted (Zhang et al., 2025).

The Cybersecurity and Infrastructure Security Agency (CISA) operating in the United States provides guidance to protect crucial infrastructure CPS systems running throughout the nation such as energy utility networks and industrial control systems. The Health Insurance Portability and Accountability Act (HIPAA) demands businesses in healthcare to apply detailed security standards which guard patient information (Zhang et al., 2025). The implementation of CPS solutions by multinational corporations faces obstacles because regulatory rules differ from one jurisdiction to another. The company needs to follow various privacy laws found across European and North American and Asian jurisdictions because implementing standard security procedures becomes complicated due to these different laws. The International Organization for Standardization (ISO) and International Electrotechnical Commission (IEC) have started to develop a unified security standard known as ISO/IEC 27001 for protecting CPS (Zhang et al., 2025). The achievement of regulatory requirements by itself does not establish security. Many organizations operate through a "checklist" system that fulfils minimum legal requirements without establishing proactive cybersecurity systems thus leaving CPS exposed to upcoming threats. Regulatory bodies should promote organizations to adopt ongoing security monitoring alongside time-sensitive threat sharing and security frameworks which adaptively keep pace with technological developments (Kim & Santoso, 2021).

Decision-making processes controlled by AI in CPS systems lead to ethical problems regarding fairness together with bias and accountability issues because these systems control autonomous decisions affecting human existence and both infrastructure and economic systems. The trust and safety of CPS depends on achieving ethical and unbiased judgments from AI models (Kim & Santoso, 2021). Fatal algorithmic bias occurs when AI models trained from biased information create unfair results because they produce discriminating outcomes. Facial recognition security tools designed by CPS systems demonstrate racial and gender perform poorly with degrading accuracy to categorize faces correctly. The predictive maintenance program for manufacturing devices via AI selects among machine breakdowns using historical patterns which potentially disregards rare yet essential breakdown types. Organizations must use fairness-based machine learning strategies together with periodic AI model reviews as well as training data sets that represent diverse scenarios (Lucia & Olowononi, 2025). The deployment of ethical CPS requires transparent and explainable decision-making systems from AI due to the fact that many AI models function as "black boxes" which obscure their decision-making logic. The absence of transparency in these applications become a concern when deploying systems which require high levels of safety. The basis for safety and liability evaluation demands full knowledge of how an AI-powered CPS controlling an autonomous vehicle reaches its decision to swerve away from a collision (Kim & Santoso, 2021). The adoption of Explainable AI (XAI) techniques through interpretable machine learning models with decision visualization tools enhances transparency and accountability during CPS operations. AI automation in CPS presents an ethical concern because it threatens to replace existing human employees from their roles. The benefits automation brings to efficiency come with a disadvantage of putting workers out of their jobs which leads to economic imbalances. Robotic assembly lines powered by AI systems in industrial CPS create job automation which can make human employees unemployed because organizations fail to provide proper training programs for new positions. Governments and organizations should create workforce reskilling programs because they need to enable their employees to take positions that match AI-powered CPS automation system requirements (Lucia & Olowononi, 2025). The advancement of CPS technologies demands that current regulations evolve to handle upcoming problems in cybersecurity protection along with privacy and ethical AI governance. AI systems show promise by providing automatic assessments of CPS security posture while detecting regulatory violations instantaneously in real-time monitoring systems for regulatory compliance. The integration of AI-powered tools for compliance provides organizations with proactive methods to resolve security weakness points before breaches or legal sanctions appear (Zhang et al., 2025).

CPS operations will benefit from the implementation of blockchain technology for enhancing regulatory transparency in the future. Blockchain technologies work perfectly for compliance record tracking because they provide unalterable decentralized logs which help CPS maintain security and privacy standards. Through blockchain technology supply chain CPS create an unalterable inspection log which verifies that products meet international safety requirements (Zhang et al., 2025). Governments may investigate the implementation of dynamic compliance which undertakes consistent modifications of CPS security standards through periodic threat assessment. Standard regulatory systems fall behind the latest technological progress therefore making CPS exposed to emerging security threats. Dynamic compliance models enable organizations to get real-time regulatory enhancements that activate automatic security protocol changes according to current cybersecurity standards. Furthermore, ethical AI governance in CPS must be emphasized in future rules. AI ethics standards, like the European Union's Ethics Guidelines for Trustworthy AI, are already being developed by governments and business leaders. To guarantee moral CPS decision-making, future regulatory frameworks should require AI fairness testing, transparency audits, and bias reduction techniques (Lim & Liu, 2025). The safe and responsible development of CPS is greatly influenced by ethical and regulatory factors. Retaining confidence in CPS applications will require addressing privacy issues, making sure international cybersecurity laws are followed, putting ethical AI practices into place, and modifying regulatory frameworks. Policymakers, researchers, and business executives will need to work together as technology develops to develop policies that strike a balance between innovation, security, privacy, and moral obligation. CPS can keep improving automation, efficiency, and safety while upholding moral and regulatory requirements by proactively tackling these issues (Lim & Liu, 2025).

Future Trends and Innovations

Modern Cyber-Physical Systems (CPS) grow through emerging technologies which improve security functions and develop efficiency measures and enhance adaptability features. The advancement of CPS security and resilience depends on integrating quantum computing while integrating Artificial Intelligence (AI) along with Internet of Things (IoT) and blockchain technology as well as creating self-healing systems and solving research problems produced by these developments. This innovative technology will boost CPS functions although it brings complicated operational demands that need strategic approaches to handle effectively (Zhang et al., 2022). Quantum computing stands as the most disruptive innovation that enables protected CPS control operations. The cryptographic methods RSA and ECC used for CPS data protection against attacks become vulnerable when quantum computing is applied to them. An exponential rate of computation by quantum computers allows researchers to break through current cryptographic systems which makes such methods obsolete (Shen & Suvarna, 2024). Scientists have initiated the creation of post-quantum cryptographic algorithms using lattice-based encryption schemes to establish security throughout an age beyond quantum methods. QKD with its secure quantum mechanics principles serves as an unbreakable encryption method that protects data in power grid and autonomous vehicle applications through quantum mechanics protocols. Security experts face major implementation hurdles when attempting to integrate quantum-resistant security solutions into existing

Connected Product Systems because it demands substantial computational power together with novel regulatory systems (Santoso & Finn, 2022). The combination of AI with IoT and blockchain technology functions as a vital trend which boosts CPS security operations through enhanced efficiency. The combination of AI-powered cybersecurity systems monitors system disruptions and anticipates security threats, yet IoT devices efficiently gather and process operational data to optimize CPS. Because IoT networks disperse data across multiple networks they are exposed to numerous cyberattacks that originate from their extensive connected surfaces (Santoso & Finn, 2022). The decentralized features along with tamper-proof log systems within blockchain technology enable secure peer-to-peer transactions as part of its decentralized identity management. Smart grids use blockchain technology to maintain transparent energy transactions secure while AI optimization controls energy distribution continuously in real time. The implementation of blockchain-based CPS security solutions needs additional optimization work for wide deployment due to their scaling needs and energy usage requirements (Zhang et al., 2022). The creation of self-learning and self-healing CPS represents an essential innovative development. Modern self-healing CPS use AI and machine learning capabilities to detect faults automatically while performing autonomous error diagnosis as well as independent response actions before human operators need to be involved. Continuous environmental adaptation and danger detection form part of these systems which makes them capable of preventing cyberattacks and operational disruptions. Artificial intelligence uses predictive maintenance systems to examine sensor data in industrial automation which identifies equipment failure indications before corrective measures can be deployed. To realize completely autonomous self-healing CPS, we need to handle technical obstacles linked to decision-making ethics in AI as well as real-time assessment velocity and algorithm consistency (Wu et al., 2022). Various research challenges along with technological opportunities continue to appear despite modern advancements in the field. Organizations must work on four main research problems which include CPS component interoperability advancement alongside trustworthiness improvements of AI decisions and scalable energy-efficient security solutions. According to regulatory standards operators must create frameworks to maintain agreement between security needs and ethical requirements and innovation opportunities. Research needs to develop methods through which operators can work alongside AI-driven CPS systems for better decision-making along with control and responsibility retention (Wu et al., 2022). To achieve CPS's full potential all technological challenges and ethical and regulatory issues need resolution. Developing safe CPS infrastructures demands a collaborative approach between multidisciplinary experts who use innovations from AI together with blockchain and quantum computing technologies (Zhang et al., 2022).

CONCLUSION

Although automation and intelligent decision-making are revolutionizing businesses, cyber-physical systems (CPS) still confront formidable obstacles in the areas of security, resilience, and ethical governance. While quantum computing, blockchain, AI, and machine learning improve CPS control, they also bring hazards including algorithmic biases, data breaches, and cyberthreats. One of the biggest challenges in implementing them is maintaining a balance between security, safety, and efficiency. Ensuring CPS robustness requires safe data-driven control techniques. While AI-powered methods like reinforcement learning and Model Predictive Control (MPC) allow for real-time decision-making, they also need protection from prejudice and hostile assaults. The use of explainable AI, adversarial training, and anomaly detection improves the reliability of the system. CPS is also more dependable due to distributed control and edge computing, which lower latency and increase fault tolerance. Because assaults against industrial infrastructure are becoming more sophisticated, cybersecurity is another major worry. Organizations must use multi-layered security frameworks, such as blockchain-based authentication, AI-driven threat detection, and post-quantum encryption, in order to reduce risks. To preserve data integrity and privacy, adherence to international cybersecurity standards like NIST and GDPR is crucial. The development of CPS must also be guided by ethical issues. Fairness, accountability, and privacy issues are brought up by AI decision-making, which calls for openness and human supervision. To guarantee appropriate CPS adoption, future rules should place a strong emphasis on interoperability, AI responsibility, and data governance.

Future developments in self-healing AI systems, blockchain convergence, and quantum cryptography will improve CPS security and flexibility even further. Nevertheless, there are still difficulties in creating scaled, energy-efficient systems. Another major worry is cybersecurity since assaults against industrial infrastructure are becoming more sophisticated. Multi-layered security frameworks, such as blockchain-based authentication, AI-driven threat detection, and post-quantum encryption, must be used by enterprises in order to reduce risks. Data integrity and privacy must be protected by adherence to international cybersecurity laws like NIST and GDPR. CPS development must be guided by ethical issues as well. Decision-making with AI poses questions regarding privacy, responsibility, and justice, requiring human oversight and openness. To achieve ethical CPS adoption, future rules should prioritize data governance, AI responsibility, and interoperability. Future developments in blockchain convergence, quantum cryptography, and self-healing AI systems will improve CPS security and flexibility even further. Still, there are obstacles in the way of creating scaled, energy-efficient solutions. A multidisciplinary strategy that integrates cybersecurity, artificial intelligence, and regulatory frameworks will be essential to guaranteeing the secure and robust development of CPS. Future CPS can be safe, flexible, and able to endure changing operational and cyberthreats by encouraging cooperation between business and legislators.

REFERENCES

Aghazadeh Ardebili, A., Martella, C., Longo, A., Rucco, C., Izzi, F., & Ficarella, A. (2025). IoT-driven resilience monitoring: Case study of a cyber-physical system. *Applied Sciences (Basel, Switzerland)*, *15*(4), 2092.

Asadi, Y., Farsangi, M. M., Amani, A. M., Alhelou, H. H., Dibaji, S. M., & Bijami, E. (2023). Data-driven cyber-resilient control of wide area power systems. In *Power Systems Cybersecurity: Methods, Concepts, and Best Practices* (pp. 161–178). Springer International Publishing.

Cassandro, R., Wu, G., Wang, H., & Li, Z. S. (2024). Prognostics and health management for cyber-physical system resilience: A security and reliability perspective. In *Frontiers of Performability Engineering: In Honor of Prof. KB Misra* (pp. 483–506). Springer Nature Singapore.

Dai, J., Dai, Z., Thing, V. L., & Engineering, S. T. (2025). Cyber-resilience enhancement with cross-domain software-defined network for cyber-physical microgrids against denial of service attacks. *IEEE Transactions on Industrial Cyber-Physical Systems*.

Gao, S., Zhang, H., Wang, Z., Huang, C., & Yan, H. (2023). Data-driven injection attack strategy for linear cyber-physical systems: An input-output data-based approach. *IEEE Transactions on Network Science and Engineering*, *10*(6), 4082–4095.

Kholidy, H. A. (2021). Autonomous mitigation of cyber risks in the cyber–physical systems. *Future Generation Computer Systems*, *115*, 171–187.

Kim, S., Park, K. J., & Lu, C. (2022). A survey on network security for cyber–physical systems: From threats to resilient design. *IEEE Communications Surveys and Tutorials*, *24*(3), 1534–1573.

Lian, Z., Shi, P., & Lim, C. C. (2022). Adaptive resilient control for cyber-physical systems under cyberattack and input saturation. *IEEE Transactions on Industrial Informatics*, *19*(5), 6513–6524.

Liu, W., Sun, J., Wang, G., Bullo, F., & Chen, J. (2022). Data-driven resilient predictive control under denial-of-service. *IEEE Transactions on Automatic Control*, *68*(8), 4722–4737.

Olowononi, F. O., Rawat, D. B., & Liu, C. (2020). Resilient machine learning for networked cyber-physical systems: A survey for machine learning security to securing machine learning for CPS. *IEEE Communications Surveys and Tutorials*, *23*(1), 524–552.

Santoso, F., & Finn, A. (2022). A data-driven cyber–physical system using deep-learning convolutional neural networks: Study on false-data injection attacks in an unmanned ground vehicle under fault-tolerant conditions. *IEEE Transactions on Systems, Man, and Cybernetics. Systems*, *53*(1), 346–356.

Tariq, M. U. (2024). Integration of IoMT for Enhanced Healthcare: Sleep Monitoring, Body Movement Detection, and Rehabilitation Evaluation. In Liu, H., Tripathy, R., & Bhattacharya, P. (Eds.), *Clinical Practice and Unmet Challenges in AI-Enhanced Healthcare Systems* (pp. 70–95). IGI Global., DOI: 10.4018/979-8-3693-2703-6.ch004

Tariq, M. U. (2025). Innovative Business Models: Integrating Social, Economic, and Environmental Goals in Rural Manufacturing. In Prabhakar, A., Yu, P., & Erokhin, V. (Eds.), *Rural Social Entrepreneurship Development: Network-Based Manufacturing System Model* (pp. 147–174). IGI Global Scientific Publishing., DOI: 10.4018/979-8-3693-7515-0.ch005

Tariq, M. U. (2025). Integrating ICT for Enhanced Organizational Resilience: Strategies and Case Studies. In Carvalho, L., Reis, L., Neves de Almeida Baptista Figueiredo, A., & Russo, N. (Eds.), *Leveraging Technology for Organizational Adaptability* (pp. 59–80). IGI Global Scientific Publishing., DOI: 10.4018/979-8-3693-6045-3.ch004

Tariq, M. U. (2025). Bridging Generations: Digital Transformation and Its Multifaceted Impact Across Societal Sectors. In Anshari, M., Almunawar, M., & Ordóñez de Pablos, P. (Eds.), *Impacts of Digital Technologies Across Generations* (pp. 1–22). IGI Global Scientific Publishing., DOI: 10.4018/979-8-3693-6366-9.ch001

Tariq, M. U. (2025). Integrating Digital Technologies to Optimize Sustainable Supply Chains. In Koç, E. (Ed.), *Developing Dynamic and Sustainable Supply Chains to Achieve Sustainable Development Goals* (pp. 33–64). IGI Global Scientific Publishing., DOI: 10.4018/979-8-3693-6284-6.ch002

Wu, S., Jiang, Y., Luo, H., Zhang, J., Yin, S., & Kaynak, O. (2022). An integrated data-driven scheme for the defense of typical cyber–physical attacks. *Reliability Engineering & System Safety*, *220*, 108257.

Xing, W., & Shen, J. (2024). Security control of cyber–physical systems under cyber attacks: A survey. *Sensors (Basel)*, *24*(12), 3815. PMID: 38931599

Zhang, D., Li, C., Goh, H. H., Ahmad, T., Zhu, H., Liu, H., & Wu, T. (2022). A comprehensive overview of modeling approaches and optimal control strategies for cyber-physical resilience in power systems. *Renewable Energy*, *189*, 1383–1406.

Zhang, D., Shi, P., Lim, C. P., & Rudas, I. (2025). Resilient tracking control of cyber-physical systems against false data injection attacks and obstacle avoidance. *IEEE Transactions on Automation Science and Engineering*.

Zhao, Z., Xu, Y., Li, Y., Zhen, Z., Yang, Y., & Shi, Y. (2022). Data-driven attack detection and identification for cyber-physical systems under sparse sensor attacks. *IEEE Transactions on Automatic Control*, *68*(10), 6330–6337.

Zheng, Y., & Anubi, O. M. (2022). Resilient observer design for cyber-physical systems with data-driven measurement pruning. In *Security and Resilience in Cyber-Physical Systems: Detection, Estimation and Control* (pp. 85–117). Springer International Publishing.

Zhou, X., Ahmed, B., Aylor, J. H., Asare, P., & Alemzadeh, H. (2023). Hybrid knowledge and data driven synthesis of runtime monitors for cyber-physical systems. *IEEE Transactions on Dependable and Secure Computing*, *21*(1), 12–30.

KEY TERMS AND DEFINITIONS

AI-Driven Security Solutions: Artificial intelligence-based techniques that detect, prevent, and respond to cybersecurity threats in complex systems.

Cyber-Physical Systems (CPS): Integrated systems that combine computational algorithms and physical components for real-time interaction and control.

Data-Driven Control: A control strategy that leverages data analytics and machine learning models to inform and optimise decision-making processes.

Edge Computing: A decentralised computing approach where data processing occurs close to the physical devices, reducing latency and enhancing real-time responsiveness.

Model Predictive Control (MPC): A control method that predicts future states of a system using a model to determine optimal control actions.

Chapter 5
Enhancing Cybersecurity in Cyber-Physical Systems:
A DevOps-Driven Approach for Safe and Secure Control

C. V. Suresh Babu
https://orcid.org/0000-0002-8474-2882
Hindustan Institute of Technology and Science, India

Chris Juvin
https://orcid.org/0009-0006-9167-3041
Hindustan Institute of Technology and Science, India

S. Gautham
Hindustan Institute of Technology and Science, India

N. Sarvesh
Hindustan Institute of Technology and Science, India

ABSTRACT

This chapter aims to explore a DevOps-driven approach to enhancing cybersecurity in Cyber-Physical Systems with a focus on safe and secure control across their operational lifecycle. Target groups include cybersecurity researchers, DevOps professionals, software engineers, and stakeholders managing CPS in sectors such as energy, transportation, and manufacturing. The methodology integrates DevSecOps principles—(CI/CD, and Infrastructure as Code (IaC)—within CPS architectures to ensure continuous threat monitoring, vulnerability mitigation, and

DOI: 10.4018/979-8-3373-1832-5.ch005

adaptive incident response. Key findings highlight the effectiveness of embedding security throughout the SSDLC, supported by tools like SonarQube, OWASP ZAP, and Snyk. Case studies on Smart Grids, Industrial Control Systems, and Autonomous Vehicles illustrate real-world applications. The chapter concludes that adopting DevOps in CPS enhances system resilience, supports regulatory compliance, and offers scalable solutions to emerging threats, emphasizing the need for cultural shifts and future research on AI and Blockchain-enabled security.

1. INTRODUCTION

1.1 Background and Context of Cyber-Physical Systems (CPS)

CPS has emerged in certain sectors and is becoming critical in most, merging physical and digital actions from smart grids to autonomous cars. However, their rising complexity and interconnectivity present severe risks to security that challenge one to find solutions. Design, modelling, simulation, and integration are crucial aspects of developing CPS. An integrated engineering approach is necessary to master the complexity of CPS. This includes techniques and tools used during all stages of engineering process, from requirement elicitation to verification and validation (Hehenberger et al., 2016). The introduction of a DevOps framework in CPS to bear promises in terms of collaboration, automation and continuous monitoring. Adoption DevOps engenders identification and stimulating action before vulnerabilities are found, providing CP Systems-their safety and security of operation.

1.2 The Increasing Cybersecurity Risks in CPS

An extension in the deployment of cyber-physical systems (CPS) in several sectors has led to significant growth in cybersecurity risks requiring proactive and adaptive mitigation mechanisms. Physical processes are intricately integrated into computational and communication components for several attack points, which may put at risk critical infrastructure and sensitive information. These challenges are presented when proposing a pattern-based approach for managing cybersecurity risks in CPS, stating, "Managing cybersecurity risks of cyber-physical systems is a crucial task that requires a holistic and systemic approach, including the consideration of interdependencies between the cyber and physical domains" (Rosado et al., 2022). Hence, the necessity for such a system interdependence should have brought a broader security perspective over the entire lifecycle of a system. For example, a DevOps-led approach presents a viable way to increase all collaboration, automation, and continuous monitoring capabilities to identify and resolve vulnerabilities more easily and quickly. Moreover, embedding compliance with security as another base in the DevOps pipeline brings cybersecurity from early design stages to make CPS more resilient and secure against attacks. A DevOps scheme, by virtue of principles of continuous integration and continuous delivery (CI/CD), allows immediate deployment of security updates and patches without creating a window period for possible exploitation by intruders while vastly improving security stature across the CPS platform.

1.3 DevOps as a Solution for CPS Security Challenges

With a great urgency for a suitable resolution to the ever-growing challenges in cybersecurity for cyber-physical systems (CPSs), a paradigm modification is necessitated into fast and integrated methodologies. Because of this complexity and interconnectivity, CPSs require approaches that can dynamically adjust to threats and vulnerabilities, which come up very rapidly. To this end, DevOps would certainly provide a compelling approach to security for CPS, since it considers collaboration, automation, and feedback loop integration on an ongoing basis. (Dobaj et al.., 2023) presented an overview of how DevOps would be used in CPS, including the role of digital twins in aiding resilient and self-adaptive software: DevOps promises to provide a new paradigm shift, as a collaboration culture with automation opportunities, toward better software and system security, quality, resilience, and continuous improvement. This paradigm shift has given organizations the cachet to effectively put security risk management into practice within the entire lifecycle of CPS, including design, implementation, operation, and maintenance. Essentially, DevOps integration with CI/CD helps push out security updates and patches faster so the development teams can close the attack surface, minimize the effects of a threat, and secure their perception. Furthermore, digital twin introductions to DevOps would provide methodologies to monitor and analyse CPS behaviour in real-time and thereby grant the possibility for early detection of anomalies and adaptive security enforcement.

1.4 Objectives of the Study

The goals of this study include the following:

- To analyse vulnerabilities in cyber security with regard to CPS and their consequences on safety control systems.
- To investigate further to what extent DevOps principles can improve the cybersecurity practices for CPS.

- To assess existing security frameworks and identify gaps that could be filled by an efficient DevOps-driven security.
- To develop a conceptual framework for applying DevSecOps in CPS security to achieve continuous security monitoring and automated threat mitigation.
- To provide recommendations for implementing DevOps security solutions into CPS architectures.

1.5 Research Questions Addressed

Some of the questions which are addressed in this chapter are as follows:

1. What security challenges does DevOps have to deal with in CPS?
2. Why are traditional IT security methods insufficient for securing CPS systems?
3. How should security measures be changed with respect to CPS security by DevSecOps methodologies?
4. What best practices and tools should be used to enforce CPS security within a DevOps environment?
5. What would be the advantages and disadvantages of enforcing CPS security automation through DevOps?

1.6 Structure of the Chapter

This chapter focuses on the Cybersecurity Challenges in Cyber-Physical System. Fundamentals of DevOps and Its Role in CPS Security, Methodologies which are being used, DevOps-Driven Cybersecurity Framework for CPS, findings based on the methodologies, future directions of the CPS systems.

2. CYBERSECURITY CHALLENGES IN CYBER-PHYSICAL SYSTEMS

2.1 Key Components and Architecture of CPS

An absolute comprehension of CPS main structures and components leads to this achievement. The key elements of CPS consist of uniting computer resources with physical process systems that display highly connected and complex attributes. (Habib & Chimsom, 2022) establish an extensive view of CPS frameworks and systems and projected developments using multiple complex scientific aspects. **(Guzman et al.., 2020)** explains safety and security in multi-layer abstraction through demonstrating that CPS organizes functions across multiple abstraction layers while enabling communication from upper layers to lower ones. Most CPS systems integrate physical components such as sensors and actuators with communication devices, embedded systems and processor units and software application stacks. The architectural structure of CPS extends from unified command and control systems to multiple networked components which develop their particular vulnerabilities when secured (Suresh Babu, C. V. & Srisakthi, S. 2023). Secure cybersecurity measures require complete analysis of system layer connections because this methodology enables holistic integration of security protocols across the whole system. Crime protection within CPS incorporates protection protocols together with identity validation systems and cyber intrusion warning systems. These assumptions drive DevOps support of such measures because constant monitoring with feedback enables quick discovery and fixing of security problems within CPS's complex architecture.

2.2. Common Cyber Threats

2.2.1 Malware and Ransomware Attacks

The vulnerability of Cyber-Physical Systems (CPS) increases because sophisticated cyber-attacks now include malware and ransomware. These attacks disrupt real-time vital operations while exposing critical information to unauthorized access and generate actual property destruction. (Xu et al.., 2022) establish cyber protection strategies to stop malware attacks in cyber-physical power systems through their wide-ranging disruption impact. (Rana et al.., 2024) explore the escalating danger of ransomware attacks on CPS by presenting a system that conducts automated web protections against incoming threats. This establishes that ransomware attacks toward CPS systems rise frequently while leading to substantial financial losses and destructive operational interruptions along with potential physical dangers for system personnel. Attackers can easily exploit the networked structure of CPS systems employing legacy systems together with vulnerable communication protocols for their entry points (Suresh Babu, C. V. & Srisakthi, S. 2023).. The detected malware spreads throughout the system to access control devices then sensors before reaching actuators thus creating unpredictable results which lead to catastrophic effects. The threat from Ransomware is especially severe because it uses encryption on essential operational data which forces critical infrastructure owners to pay for the decryption key to regain control. The prevention of such potential risks requires proactive and multi-tiered security measures that must be implemented actively. All risk prevention measures include established procedures for intrusion detection programs and strong authentication techniques along with fast software vulnerability patching and organized incident response protocols. This can be reduced significantly by following DevOps approach automation and continuous monitoring.

2.2.2 Unauthorized Access and Data Breaches

Unauthorized access and data breaches present serious hazards for Cyber-Physical Systems (CPS), which involves data theft, disruption of its operation, and even physical damages. With the increase in connectivity, the vulnerabilities also increase; attackers find the weak spots to penetrate. According to (Duo et al. 2022), CPS attacks are becoming more and more sophisticated and frequent and pose a big threat to critical infrastructure. The data breach exposes the configuration and credentials of the system, thereby subjecting it to further attacks. Typical entry points include weak authentication mechanisms, software errors, and unprotected communications. A DevOps-based security approach creates more robust CPS by introducing continuous testing and automated response within the development life cycle process.

Leading solutions include:

- Strong, multilayer authentication
- Monitoring of system activities in real time
- Communication through secure channels
- Continuous security testing as part of CI/CD development workflow
- Detecting and patching vulnerabilities automatically
- Integrating incident response for quick containment of threats

2.3 Limitations of Traditional IT Security Approaches in CPS

Standard information technology security practices demonstrate insufficient effectiveness for dealing with specific issues that cyber-physical systems (CPS) produce. CPS security demands a complete system analysis which integrates the complex relations between the cyber world and physical systems yet conventional security methods mainly concentrate on network protection along with data security. (Sheikh et al., 2022) underline the necessity for intelligent and secure framework development for critical infrastructure CPS since traditional security methods fall short. (Dafflon et al., 2021) observe that manufacturing CPS systems need to work under strict real-time requirements and operate with high availability standards that traditional IT security infrastructure does not address. (Suresh Babu & Yadavamuthiah, 2023). The standard IT security frameworks do not provide sufficient real-time abilities nor specialized communication standards which make them inadequate for defending CPS. Such security approaches neglect to consider both the operational limits and safety protocols which these systems need to meet. The standardized IT security tools are incompatible with the legacy systems and proprietary protocols that normally exist within CPS environments. Traditional Information Technology security models prove inadequate when it comes to handling CPS complexities in critical infrastructure because they lack real-time adaptability and limited scope. A specific and flexible security solution must replace current methods in order to overcome these existing constraints. A DevOps methodology applied to operational procedures provides an effective solution through continuous monitoring and automated vulnerability detection and quick incident handling capabilities.

2.4 Need for a Proactive and Automated Security Approach

The security and vulnerability strategies for CPS must shift from a reactive stance to proactivity and automation for the basic reason that the threat landscape is too dynamic and is progressing as such towards CPS. The emphasis has now shifted to areas that will prevent real-time detection and mitigation of threats to avoid disastrous consequences for CPS; threats that had developed from attacks at CPS complex and sophisticated were handled with such manual mode of conventional methods of security. It was suggested that adaptive security monitoring is indispensable for CPS and must, therefore, be backed by a systemology that can generate dynamic responses in an ever-changing threat landscape. Standard security models will not meet CPS requirements, particularly in critical infrastructure, (Sheikh et al, 2022) reaffirmed in a research study. Proactive refers to monitoring the system's activity for early vulnerability identification, threat intelligence data enhancement, and simulated players that try to assault such vulnerabilities. Such automation is crucial in maintaining pace with that proactive accumulation, enhancing security procedures, decreasing response time, and minimizing the possibilities of human mistakes. As per (Poltavtseva et al, 2021) Adaptive information security monitoring is a promising means for increasing CPS protection. It implies creating smart algorithms capable of automatically identifying and reacting to cyber-attacks. The application of this proactive and automated security would be facilitated by the DevOps-enabled approach. Ongoing security scans, vulnerability fixes automatically, and rapid deployment of security patches, so that the CPS is never vulnerable to newly discovered threats, are facilitated by integrating security into the CI/CD pipeline using the DevOps process.

2.5 Human and Organisational Factors in CPS security

The security of CPS relies on factors both from humans as well as from organizations. Security measures experience adverse effects when human and organizational elements receive insufficient recognition although they play a vital role in security measures. (Ayodeji et al., 2023) examines human factors as they relate to cybersecurity in the nuclear industry. Security posture actively changes according to the way organizations structure their operations and practice their activities. (El-Kady et al., 2023) explain that risk management requires human reliability programs and training and awareness initiatives for reducing system errors and vulnerabilities. Security integration within DevOps workflows goes hand-in-hand with establishing strong security cultures to achieve organizational-wide responsibility for threat detection. Security operations that actively include human factors in DevOps development processes will establish improved operating conditions for CPS through human-human and computer-human collaboration.

3. FUNDAMENTALS OF DEVOPS AND ITS ROLE IN CPS SECURITY

3.1 Overview of DevOps in Software Development

DevOps changes the landscape of software development. It focuses on collaboration, automation, and continuous improvement to shorten the life cycle of high-quality software. It builds a pathway across the historical barricade separating the operation of the development (Dev) and operations (Ops) teams, with a concurrent blending of culture, shared responsibility, and a streamlined workflow. (Kaiser, 2020) gives a brief overview of the principles of DevOps that embody its forces and advantages. DevOps isn't about automation, tools, or technology. It's about people, processes, and products. It is, rather, a cultural shift that promotes collaboration, communication, and trust between development and operations teams. Such an environment allows faster feedback loops, whereby development teams can easily and quickly identify and rectify issues, enhance code quality, and release fast. Automation is thus another crucial pillar of DevOps to facilitate processes, that include test automation, deploy automation, automation in the management of infrastructure, etc. Automating these processes results in reduced errors, enhanced efficiency, and deployment of resources to strategic initiatives. DevOps heavily relies on principles of continuous integration (CI) and continuous delivery (CD), whereby modifications to code are integrated, tested, and deployed to production frequently. The feedback loop thus created gives way for rapid iteration and continuous improvement, thus allowing high-quality software to be shipped to market as quickly as possible. The seamless adoption of the principles of DevOps within Cyber-Physical Systems (CPS) development bears implications for enhanced software security as security considerations become integrated throughout the entire software lifecycle.

3.2 Evolution of DevSecOps: Integrating Security into DevOps

High-intensity and high-frequency cyber-attacks are driving the shift from DevOps to DevSecOps; the implementation of DevSecOps supplements the original DevOps philosophy with security in mind. Security is woven into the software development lifecycle at every step and not dealt with as an afterthought to ensure that security is incorporated right from the design phase and beyond to create secure and resilient systems. According to (Abiona et al, 2024), what provides meaning to DevSecOps is that security procedures are embedded in the continuous delivery pipes of DevOps for mutual responsibility. DevSecOps is operationalized by automating security testing, embedding security tools within CI/CD pipelines, and cultivating a culture of security within developers, operations, and security themselves. (Manda, 2023) measured the implementation of DevSecOps in telcos and demonstrated to have streamlined software development life cycles securely delivering services. Some leading activities discussed under DevSecOps include static code analysis, dynamic code analysis, vulnerability scanning, penetration testing, and security configuration management. Implementing these activities into the DevOps cycle will enable organizations to anticipate detecting and patching vulnerabilities before real wrongdoers get a chance. DevSecOps attempts to "shift left" security, i.e., to place security issues on the table at earlier phases of the development cycle where it is less expensive and less problematic to fix vulnerabilities later. This methodology is particularly significant for Cyber-Physical Systems (CPS) since failures in systems with security compromises can blow up to disastrous and dire results. An adoption of the DevSecOps principles would enhance the safety and reliability of critical infrastructure, as well as the overall security of CPS.

3.3 Key DevOps Practices Beneficial for CPS Security

3.3.1 Continuous Integration and Continuous Deployment (CI/CD)

Continuous integration and Continuous deployment processes are central to the DevOps setup, and when applied to cyber-physical systems, they offer a great opportunity to enhance security. CI/CD allows the automation of code integration, testing, and deployment to production, thereby speeding up and increasing the frequency of releases. In terms of CPS security, this means the fast deployment of security updates, patches, and new security features to reduce the time frame available for attackers. (Zampetti et al.., 2023) conducted an interview study of CI/CD practices for CPS with some interesting observations on the challenges and advantages of adopting the CI/CD route in CPS. They also encountered generalized CI/CD limitations when applied to the CPS domain. (Zampetti et al.., 2022) have addressed the problems arising and solutions available in open-source CPS and their use of CI/CD. . This has much bigger implications for CPS, where any exploitable vulnerability leads to severe or catastrophic consequences. With an automation system in place for the deployment of security updates, the entire fleet of CPS components may be quickly updated against imminent threats. However, the physical component of CPS poses some unique challenges.

3.3.2 Infrastructure as Code (IaC) for Secure Deployments

Infrastructure as Code (IaC) centers around the definition of a set of practices found in DevOps aiming at the management and provisioning of the infrastructure using code while treating infrastructure configurations as software. In the context of CPS, this approach implies a lot of advantages for safe deployments. After all, IaC ensures the automated creation, configuration, and management of infrastructure resources with consistency and repeatability across environments. However, by defining infrastructure configurations in code, an organization is able to enforce security policies and best practices in a uniform and audited manner. IaC enables dynamic deployments, wherein automation and repeatability are stressed in infrastructure management processes, as described by (Sokolowski, 2022). Security best practices can then be implemented based on those configurations, for example, organizations can enforce password policies, configure firewalls, and implement access control lists through IaC. IaC also sets the stage for security testing being part of the deployment pipeline, allowing any security vulnerabilities in infrastructure configuration to be detected in an automated manner. This assures that only secure infrastructure would be shipped to production. IaC also improves incident response and can be used to deploy security patches and updates on short notice. With an automated deployment process, organizations can swiftly apply security fixes to all infrastructure components, thus minimizing the attack surface for intruders. In Cyber-Physical Systems, IaC is used to securely configure and manage the infrastructure components that support the various aspects of cyber-physical systems, including servers, networks, and storage devices.

3.3.3 Monitoring, Logging, and Incident Response in DevOps

Any model built into the DevOps strategy that can improve efficaciousness is the monitoring, logging, and incident response procedure, which collectively add powerful bolstering to the cyber safety of the Cyber-Physical Systems. Such monitoring will be able to give real-time insight into the health and security of the systems, as well as the anomalies from the earliest stages of detection. The set of monitoring tools is used to trace all kinds of cyber and physical parameters-comprising temperature, pressure, flow rates- even potential cyber incidents. Thus, continuous observation acts as an earlier detection platform for proactive threat handling. Logging plays co-supportive functions in giving timestamped, deep records of every activity carried out in the system. Henceforth, such logs would be pivotal in:

- Security Monitoring
- Forensic Analysis
- Investigations of Incidents

In regards to security incidents, a well-prepared incident response plan is a necessary evil to prevent losses while returning to normalcy. Generally, in that plan, one finds:

- Automated systems that set off alerts on anomalies, including unauthorized access or irregularities with network traffic.
- Steps already defined for isolating all affected systems.
- Procedures which would contain the threat and restore operations in the soonest time possible.

According to (Faustino, 2018), DevOps practices already encompass incident management; however, they call for more automation and flexibility for their optimum effectiveness. Likewise, an automated security testing framework proposal has been made by (Manubolu, 2024) for PLC-based industrial automation systems, which will also lead to better security logging and automated responses. Incident response in DevOps lends itself to continuous learning, not just immediate action. Learning events from earlier incidents are captured via logs to inform better systems evolution in the future against newer threats. Frequently, such processes are closely woven into the CI/CD pipeline, thus enabling:

- Real-time anomaly detection
- Automated response activation
- Faster recovery times
- Continuous improvement

One must design the CPS-constructed framework of monitoring, logging, and incident response with respect to their unique physical consequences in terms of cyber and operational safety.

4. LITERATURE REVIEW

4.1 Overview of Existing Research on CPS Security

Over the past years, conducting research on Cyber-Physical Systems (CPS) security has become increasingly popular mainly due to the increased reliance on these systems in critical infrastructures as well as the increasing sophistication with which cyber threats are being launched. Research in this area broadly aligns himself to such topics as threat modelling, vulnerability analysis, intrusion detection, and security architecture design. (Wang et al.., 2021) provide an inclusive survey of the latest advanced research in CPS security while giving an overview of the state of the art in this fast-moving field. The results of this research emphasize the unique challenges posed to CPS security through tight coupling of cyber and physical components; real-time constraints; and legacy component reliance, as well as possible security techniques such as encryption, authentication, access control, or the installation of an intrusion detection system within CPS. Nonetheless, most of these techniques were developed primarily for traditional IT systems and hence cannot be directly applied to CPS with its specific requirements and constraints. Traditional intrusion detection systems, for example, may not detect attacks on physical components of a CPS effectively. Such systems are further characterized by the unmistakable reliance on legacy systems that, it is challenging to update or patch, thus leaving them open to well-known exploits. Among them include machine learning and artificial intelligence-enabled detection and response to cyber threats in real-time, as well as the establishment of security architectures that can absorb an attack and are capable of graceful degradation in the face of failures. It becomes critical to understand the state of the art in CPS security research to devise closer effective strategies for protecting such critical systems.

4.2 Studies on DevOps in Secure Software Development

Evolution of research on how DevOps practices impact security is quickly expanding on research into their integration with software development. It is intended to identify the most effective secure software development practices, assessing the security tools and methods, and examining the difficulties and benefits associated with integrating security within the DevOps pipeline.

(Desai & Nisha, 2021) offer a case study method in determining the best practices for security in DevOps and offer some reality checks as to how organizations can implement security in their DevOps processes effectively. These studies tend to debate the applicability of automation, collaboration, and continuous feedback loops in establishing a secure DevOps environment. It is generally utilized for its fast and predictable application of security controls across the organizations, whereas the collaboration feature serves to develop shared understanding of security threats and responsibilities in dev and ops teams. From feedback, one achieves real-time visibility of what the security posture of the system appears as and hence managing early detection and remediation for vulnerabilities. Certain studies emphasize security practices related to DevOps such as static and dynamic code analysis, vulnerability scanning, penetration testing, etc. Effectiveness of those practices is evaluated in identifying and remediating security vulnerabilities, as well as advice on best incorporating them into the CI/CD pipeline. Other researches encompass the institutional and cultural factors of DevOps security, which amplify a culture that is sensitive and educative towards security awareness, leaving security development to developers.

4.3 Research on DevSecOps for Secure Cyber-Physical Systems

DevSecOps and Cyber-Physical Systems have transformed themselves into a new area of research such that a pursuit ranges from very strong needs for safeguarding to very lightweight systems. How champions and practices of DevSecOps would be moulded and tailored to meet the specificity of CPS-hard interdependencies between the physical and cyber domains-totally neglected real-time constraints-safety-criticality had to be reckoned in such a discipline, however. System design for domain-specific security mechanisms and techniques aligned to that specificity: attack detection and mitigation strategies conditioned by the physical nature of the systems; security and integrity of data exchanged between the cyber and physical worlds, however, is one of the fruitful areas of research that will deal with embedding early and constant security across the CPS development life cycle in terms of adding such features to DevSecOps like constant requirement elicitation and testing (Sadovykh & Ivanov, 2024). Another area for research would be the design of safe CPS architectures that withstand attacks and damage under failure conditions. Redundancy, diversity, and fault tolerance will enable the most critical operations to continue in situ operation even under compromise of parts of their components. There is also an ongoing study about the culture of the organization expecting DevSecOps for CPS environments, which is always brought up regarding coordination between IT, OT, and Security teams. This integration becomes necessary for collating security elements at every stage of design and operation of CPS. Such research and many other kinds of research on DevSecOps-alike paths for safe CPS are indeed enlightening concerning how to ensure these systems against growing threats of cyber attacks. The state of affairs is that extremely efficient DevSecOps can actually be integrated with CPS using such programs as installations and applications (Suresh Babu & Yadavamuthiah, 2023).

4.4 Gaps in the Literature

One prominent gap is with respect to security toolsets and techniques being crafted directly for CPS peculiarities. Most plainly put, existing practitioners' know-how most often bears an IT system culture stamp on it, thus lacks consideration for real-time constraints, physical component interaction, or legacy system interfacing that forms caution in CPS structures. Further study must address CPS tool detection and mitigation against attacks on the systems' physical components, as well as creating methods to assure the security and integrity of the data traversing between the cyber and physical domains. Another gap is relating to a secure CPS architecture capable of resisting attacks and gracefully failing in the event of an attack. While some research has focused on redundancy and fault-tolerance techniques, more work is needed in developing architectures that will track the evolution of threats and maintain partial functions when some of the components are down. (Ledinot, 2021) pinpointed multiple areas where CPS engineering as a whole should be improved, which strengthens the premise of the development of comprehensive solutions. Finally, more attention needs to be directed toward studying organizational and cultural infrastructures related to DevSecOps implementation in a CPS environment. While some studies mention the importance of collaboration between IT, OT (Operational Technology), and security teams, further work is needed to understand how to develop this collaboration and ensure that security issues are integrated into every step of the CPS development and operational flow. Understanding these gaps will assist in setting the roadmap for future research and come up with effective ways to enhance the security of CPS.

5. METHODOLOGY: DEVOPS DRIVEN CYBERSECURITY FRAMEWORK FOR CPS

5.1 Conceptual Model for Secure CPS Using DevOps

A conceptual model for ensuring security of Cyber-Physical Systems, based on DevOps, is developed that integrates principles such as collaboration, automation, continuous feedback and security into an all-encompassing model. This model considers security aspects from a shift-left perspective, integrating these considerations early on and continuously throughout the entire lifecycle of a CPS project-from its design and development to deployment and operation. The conceptual model emphasizes Infrastructure as Code (IaC) for managing and securely provisioning infrastructure resources with internal consistency. IaC permits the automated creation, configuration, and management of infrastructure components, where security policies and best practices are enforced in all environments. Using CI/CD, code changes are integrated, tested, and deployed into production with pipelines that allow for fast and frequent releases of security updates and patches. (Dobaj et al, 2022) provide particulars on the application of digital twin-enabled DevOps for CPS, allowing architecture-based adaptation and verification of services during runtime for improving dynamic and responsive behavior toward security. Relying on a solid monitoring and logging system results in having a real-time view of the CPS scenarios, including health checks and security, allowing proactive detection of any anomalies and possible threats. Alternating automated incident response plans minimize the impact of security incidents and help restore normalcy in operations. Then, the collaboration of IT teams with OT and security staff becomes essential in achieving security integration into every aspect of the CPS development and operations process. The last objective stressed by the conceptual model is an ethos of continuous learning with improvement in a set, whereby feedback obtained from security incidents and vulnerabilities is taken into account to enhance itself and raise the over-their security posture of the CPS.

Figure 1. Conceptual Model for a Secure CPS

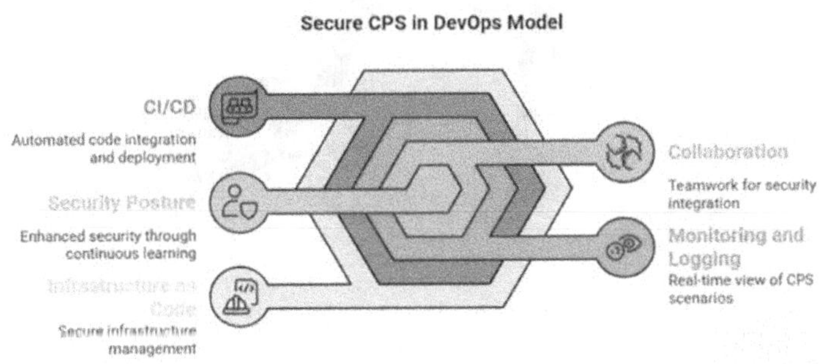

(Created with Canva)

5.2 Secure Software Development Life Cycle (SSDLC) in CPS

The Secure Software Development Life Cycle (SSDLC) integrates security into all facets of the software development process that may affect Cyber-Physical Systems (CPS), distinguished from other systems by their real-world manifestation. Traditional models tend to postpone security considerations; SSDLC, on the contrary, integrates security from the outset, which includes threat modeling, code reviews, and testing. This integration is discussed by (Arrey, 2019), who states that "integration of security into SDLC would better protect complex systems." Likewise, (Seelaboyina et al., 2022) assert an SSDLC model to mitigate cyber risks for CPS and digital twins, thus advocating for proactive security strategies in the early stages. Embedding SSDLC in a DevOps framework for CPS requires strong automation and collaboration. Security testing should be continuous and integrated into the CI/CD pipeline with real-time feedback and timely remediation of identified vulnerabilities. Developers and security teams should work together to specify security requirements and adhere to security best practices. Specialized tooling and requirements derived from an unparalleled understanding of the attack vectors are also required to modify the SSDLC to cater for unique CPS characteristics such as real-time operation, physical integration, and legacy systems. The adoption of an SSDLC can indeed allow companies to minimize risks from cyber-attack and ensure resilient CPS infrastructure.

Figure 2. Life Cycle of a secure Software Development in CPS

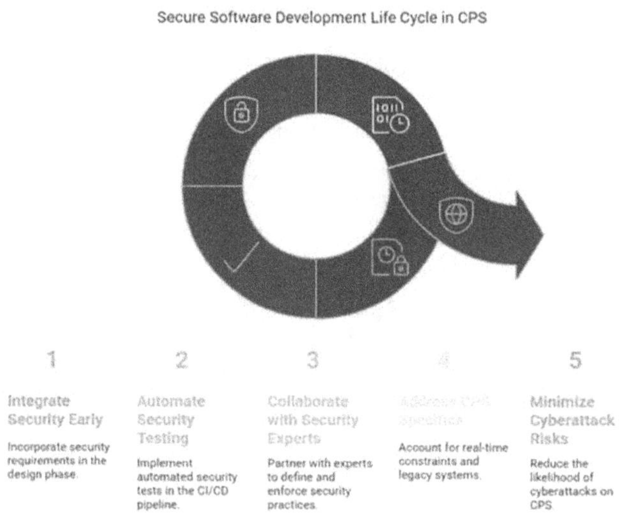

(Created with Canva)

5.3 Traditional Approach vs DevOps Approach in CPS Security

The approach followed in CPS security is being compared based on the following aspects;

Table 1. Traditional Approach Vs DevOps Approach

Aspect	Traditional Approach	DevOps Approach	Gap Identified
Security Integration	Security is handled late in the development lifecycle ("bolt-on" approach).	Security is integrated from the beginning and throughout the lifecycle.	Early vulnerability assessments are at risk; high late-phase remediation costs.
Responsibility Model	Security is solely the responsibility of a dedicated security team.	Shared responsibility across development, operations, and security teams.	Lack of co-ownership; security best practices may not be followed across teams.
Automation	Security tasks are mostly manual (testing, configuration, incident response).	Emphasizes full automation (IaC, automated tests, automated incident response).	Manual effort leads to slow, error-prone, and unscalable processes.
Testing Frequency	Security testing is done late in the development cycle.	Continuous security testing is integrated into the CI/CD pipeline.	Late discovery of vulnerabilities increases cost and difficulty of fixes.
Feedback Loops	Security feedback comes late and doesn't inform development properly.	Fast, continuous feedback loops using threat intelligence and testing results.	Delayed feedback hinders learning and improvement; leads to repeated mistakes.
Change Management	Change implementation is slow and cumbersome, delaying threat responses.	Agile change management allows fast, low-disruption deployment of patches/ updates.	Slow patching increases system vulnerability.

5.4 Role of AI and Machine Learning in DevOps for CPS Security

AI and machine learning have become increasingly important for securing the DevOps environment, especially at the nexus of Cyber-Physical Systems. Such technologies automate fundamental security tasks like threat detection, vulnerability analysis, and incident response configurations that would better equip organizations to defend CPS against constant changes in hostile cyber environment conditions. AI and ML can sift through a huge mass of data-from system logs to network traffic and sensor readings-to identify real-time attack patterns and anomalies. Thus, it enables early detection and quick response, minimizing possible damages arising from (Liang et al., 2024) a complete integration of AI and automation of ML models into DevOps secures environments by automating the analysis of vulnerabilities to detect flaws in code and configurations before adversaries can exploit these. Trained models detect known patterns of vulnerabilities and apply them to new code. AI further increases the speed with which incidents are identified and remedial actions are taken. AI and ML run a continuous monitoring and testing activity for security risks as a development lifecycle feature when integrated in the CI/CD pipeline. Thus, this greatly increases the security of CPS and lowers the chances of a successful cyber intrusion.

5.5 Implementing Compliance as Code for Regulatory Enforcement

Compliance as Code (CaC) emphasizes the automation of compliance within DevOps, with a strong focus on Cyber-Physical Systems (CPS). Organizations can have the agreed-upon requirements for compliance encoded into code that will automatically check any given CPS against these requirements. This minimizes the chances of manual error, enhances efficiency, and adds another layer of auditability. Unlike the traditional methods of compliance-checking, which are manual, time-consuming, and error-prone, CaC now enables continuous monitoring with early detection and resolution of compliance infringements. CaC is beneficial for ensuring uniform application of compliance rules across systems, leaving no room for ambiguity and interpretation. This is crucial in CPS, which operates in tightly regulated environments. In fact, (Matta et al., 2021) has emphasized compliance concerning the operation and risk management of CPS and systems of systems. Incorporating CaC into the CI/CD pipeline would mean fully automated compliance checking across the software development lifecycle. This maximizes the time given for correcting compliance violations from the very early stages of development, minimizing the risk of violations being corrected much later. In addition, CaC will construct the audit trail and provide a view into audit-proofed, transparent, and traceable proof of compliance for regulators and stakeholders. Using CaC will help these organizations protect their CPS, avoid penalties, and maintain overall organizational posture regarding security and compliance in good standing.

5.6 DevOps Tools Used in CPS Security

Automated security tools need integration in every stage of development to build secure Cyber-Physical Systems operating within DevOps frameworks as (Makani & Jangampeta, 2024). The source code analysis tool SonarQube functions as a Static Application Security Testing (SAST) tool for scanning code before runtime that discovers potential vulnerabilities including SQL injection during the early development phase. The Dynamic Application Security Testing (DAST) tools including OWASP ZAP attack functional applications to detect run-time vulnerabilities during operation (Suresh Babu, C. V. & Yadavamuthiah, K. 2023).. Organizations using containerization in their CPS environments need specialized security tools such as Aqua Security and Snyk because these tools enable vulnerability scanning and perform both compliance assessments and runtime defense on Docker and Kubernetes deployments. Through their vulnerability detection capabilities and remediation assistance tools such as Aqua Security and Snyk allow operators to receive direct guides for solving problems while providing some tools with automated fix solutions to simplify remediation. The complete set of tools enables DevSecOps teams to establish CPS environments which combine security resilience.

6. CASE STUDIES AND REAL WORLD APPLICATIONS

6.1 Case study 1: Implementation of DevOps Security in Smart Grids

A proper mixture of combined powers proves that implementing and protecting the growing DevOps tooling in smart grids produces both positive and negative aspects. Through a smart grid setup cyber threats have the ability to damage energy systems without requiring a physical blackout because the technology combines physical, digital, and binary components. The real-world attacks faced by ever-evolving living beings resist protection from the typical defense strategies.

A number of academic works cover how DevOps methods improve security features in smart power systems. (Porcu et al., 2022) explained that smart grids operate through 5G technology while relying on secure platforms. According to (Levy et al., 2022), the implementation of a DevOps model allows real-time enhancement of energy system security operations. The incorporation of security testing through DevOps means incident response along with vulnerability management, supports automatic vulnerability scanning. The system detects security threats which allows it to separate affected components and interrupt threats and restore normal operations so the disruption remains minimal. Security operators can actively identify and correct all security threats through this method which results in safer operation of smart grids with enhanced resilience.

6.2 Case Study 2: Enhancing Security in Industrial Control Systems (ICS) Using DevSecOps

DevSecOps demonstrated success in industrial control systems which forms crucial part of cyber-physical systems thus documenting its positive influence on operational security together with resilient performance. IT systems dedicated to industrial control face mounting cyberattacks that lead to operational disruptions while endangering safety components while creating major financial losses. Security methods from the past fail to keep up with modern threats so a complete security system must operate throughout the development process. Security evaluations become fundamental components with DevSecOps because they must occur at all stages including design time and throughout maintenance periods. Research by (Dehlaghi-Ghadim et al., 2023) presented ICSSIM which serves as a framework to test ICS security mechanisms. (Yasar & Teplov, 2022) argue that security integration should start in the very first stages during the design of the embedded systems.

When implemented in ICS environments the DevSecOps pipeline conducts automatic tests of security systems alongside vulnerability detection and prepared incident response protocols. Organizations use static code analyzers alongside dynamic testing environments to reproduce real-world attacks that evaluate system protective capabilities.

6.3 Case Study 3: Continuous Security Deployment in Autonomous Vehicles

The domain of autonomous vehicles (AVs) requires continuing security deployment inside DevOps frameworks as it faces multiple deployment challenges. Complexity in Autonomous Vehicles as Cyber-Physical Systems results in these systems integrating many sensors along with actuators and communication networks together with software components that make the vehicles vulnerable to multiple cyberattacks. Security breaches into autonomous vehicles create severe safety dangers because such incidents can trigger harmful effects which lead to car crashes and harmful injuries and deaths. The prevention of security threats during these situations requires permanent security system deployment. Security update deployment for AV requires automated testing and integration of patches while using such systems to protect the vehicles from evolving threats. (Wang et al., 2022) conducted research which both revealed that connected and autonomous vehicles deal with evolving threats and showed the necessity of evolving security measures. The implementation and security aspects of these vehicles merit consideration according to (Khan et al., 2021) while requiring continuous proactive security measures. The deployment process of security tasks through DevOps automation includes vulnerability scanning for periodic evaluation of known vulnerabilities for AV software and hardware system components. Complete security assessments of AV systems are carried out through penetration testing to simulate realistic attacks on the AV's defences. Security teams must implement threat intelligence databases which provide relevant security updates after identifying new threats. The platform should deploy security patches to AVs wirelessly to maximize protection speed and shortens enemy entry time. Intrusion detection means continuously monitor AV systems for suspicious activity and trigger alerts to security personnel. AV manufacturers together with operators who adopt continuous security deployment inside a DevOps environment will create substantial improvements in vehicle security that supports their adoption by the market.

7. ANALYSIS, FINDINGS, AND DISCUSSION

7.1 Evaluation of DevOps-Based Security Approaches for CPS

The system evaluation process for DevOps-based security mechanisms within Cyber-Physical Systems (CPS) needs to study their impact on security position and performance in operation in detail. CPS security evaluation needs thorough understanding of primal-cyber domain interrelations as well as different non-IT security metric approaches. For evaluating the system, we employ three variables to assess risk reduction as well as threat detection and incident response effectiveness.

The evaluation process needs to examine the way security practices are turned into integrated parts of the DevOps development cycle. Code quality and the development process bear direct consequences as a result of automated security testing and vulnerability scans as well as compliance checks procedures. (Dapshima & Ahmad, 2024) entirely describe thorough risk assessment requirements in their paper Evaluation and Assessment of Software Security Risks and Vulnerabilities Within the Domain of Secure DevOps. Assessments require robust security-related interactions between IT experts and OT operators and security staff and possession of a comprehensive established security system within the company. To show effectiveness of DevOps-based security methods in CPS environments both real-world practical experiments and simulations must be employed. The system testing process must examine its resilience against various potential attacks including malware and ransomware and denial of service disruptions. Organizations make thorough evaluations which give them important information regarding their DevOps-founded security strategies in order to make informed decisions to improve security.

7.2 Potential Challenges in Implementing DevOps for CPS Security

In order to carry out DevOps for CPS security, it has specific challenges. One of the complexities of CPS lies within the cyber-extended components, real-time constraints, and their use of legacy systems, which can make the application of conventional DevOps approaches impractical. (Rajapakse et al., 2022) described the challenges associated with continuous software engineering in a DevOps context and the impact of careful planning and execution on it. Integrating security into the CI/CD pipeline has been the major challenge among several others. Conventional security tools and techniques might not work in connection with the automated workflows of DevOps; thus, the idea of coming up with new or adapted tools.

Another issue highlighted in the work by (Rafi et al., 2020) featured a taxonomy of some challenges experienced in DevOps security, most of which need to be prioritized in a very effective manner according to their risks. Yet another challenge is concerned with how these IT, OT, and security teams can collaborate. The skill set, priority, and structure of the groups are likely to have different characteristics, as will much of their communication. For DevOps to work, legacy systems can be very problematic. In general, modern legacy systems do not have those APIs or automation capabilities needed to be integrated into the CI/CD pipeline. Therefore, a lot of work is required to modernize or adapt those systems. Furthermore, many CPS being safety-critical require that all security updates be rigorously tested and validated before production deployment.

7.3 Addressing Scalability and Real-Time Constraints

In DevOps environments the enhancement of cyber-security for cyber-physical systems requires focus on scalability and real-time processing because these attributes have high importance. Real-time data processing requires extensive systems and devices that make up CPS facilities. Generally applied security measures struggle to deal effectively with this quantity of data and processing speed thus leading to operational performance slowdowns together with delayed security incident responses. Such security systems should maintain their operational performance and fidelity levels when workloads rise throughout their development trajectory. The dependable scheduling of workflows in cyber-physical cloud systems demands precise resource management according to (Zhou et al., 2020). The disappearance of security events demands immediate detection and response during fixed periods of time to stop disaster from occurring.

The security evaluation of CPS testbeds benefits from multi-gridded HIL system models presented by (Ravikumar et al., 2019) who improved response time for CPS security testbeds. CPS security needs DevOps-based solutions which focus both on scalability and real-time performance requirements during their development. The security data processing system requires both distributed architecture design alongside cloud service implementation and dedicated hardware resources for architectural management. Security operations achieve improved performance by implementing AI and ML techniques which affect response times. Security testing and validation require realistic scenarios which need to fulfil the real-time operational requirements of CPS.

8. RECOMMENDATIONS AND BEST PRACTICES

Developing CPS cybersecurity requires a framework of strategic recommendations and best practices that utilizes DevOps methods. Security-as-Code integration within DevOps Pipelines becomes essential because it enables automatic security policy as well as configuration execution during development phases. The process necessitates writing security requirements through code to support continuous automated evaluation and monitoring. The best practice implementation method for CPS security testing requires integration of static code analysis and vulnerability scanning and penetration testing tools within the CI/CD pipeline. (Mujeeb Ahmed et al., 2021) deliver crucial knowledge regarding Machine Learning applications to cybersecurity. The selection process for DevSecOps tools in CPS environments needs to evaluate compatibility with existing systems and meet specific CPS requirements to achieve secure integration with effective monitoring capabilities (Suresh Babu, C. V. & Yadavamuthiah, K. 2023).. AI-Based Security when integrated for threat detection and prevention strengthens the identification and response capabilities regarding complex attacks through its ability to process vast datasets using machine learning algorithms for anomaly detection. CPS Security requires businesses to maintain complete compliance with industry protocols along with all legal standards by implementing comprehensive control systems. The study from (Kirichenko et al., 2020) presents recommendations which should be followed when delivering cybersecurity services. The security status of CPS operations improves as organizations follow these recommendations alongside best practices which leads to fewer cyberattack possibilities in their operational environments.

9. FUTURE RESEARCH DIRECTIONS

Various groundbreaking opportunities emerge when developers pursue research to enhance CPS cybersecurity through DevOps design approaches. The development of security automation methods demands a study of Artificial Intelligence and Machine Learning technologies to establish smart threat response programs which use algorithms for processing large amounts of data during automated security operations. System activity records are made tamperproof through decentralized ledgers which use Blockchain-Based Security Model to verify and track transactions thus securing data integrity in CPS. Sheikh et al. (2022) emphasizes the need to establish superior secure frameworks which will enhance recently developed technologies. Each user along with device must authenticate their attempts to access resources through CPS Zero Trust Architecture (ZTA) for Secure DevOps which prevents unauthorized access and minimizes exposure to vulnerabilities during device authorization. Quantum

Cryptography based on quantum mechanics will introduce revolutionary security changes to Advanced CPS Security by creating encryption keys that hackers cannot penetrate to protect vital information. CPS uncertainty management receives analysis in the paper by Asmat et al. (2023) while the authors note that architectural changes become necessary because of uncertainty. Future research should concentrate on developing functional deployments of these technologies combined with specific security solutions for CPS frameworks followed by testing them through genuine system implementations. Relevant research on high-tech security methods must take place to establish an effective combination with DevOps practices which will protect CPS operational reliability in the future.

10.CONCLUSION

In conclusion, the enhancement of cybersecurity in CPS will require a strong restatement towards a DevOps-driven model, embracing security through the entire life cycle of the system. The proactive and later reactive security models are not good fit to handle the ever-evolving threat environment and peculiar issues raised due to CPS tight coupling of cyber and physical elements. If, however, the organizations embrace the pillars of DevOps-especially collaboration, automation, continued monitoring, and rapid feedback-then CPS can expect a significantly improved security posture.

Automation of Security-as-Code and the application of automated security testing to the selected tools for a particular DevSecOps environment, such as having AI-based threat detection, plus ability to ensure regulatory compliance are some core components of actual security operations. The hurdles are still there: Scaling security to deal with CPS considered as a whole; the right timing of constraints for security to cooperate with other aspects; integrating with legacy systems; and getting different teams to cooperate among themselves-facilitates a successful planning and execution.

Further studies should work on more advanced technologies as AI, Machine Learning, Blockchain, and Quantum Cryptography. This transformation of CPS security into a DevOps approach will definitely bring about technical change, but it will also mean a cultural shift requiring organizational commitment from all stakeholders towards security. Embracing this paradigm change would allow the organization to create a secure, resilient, and trustworthy CPS that will form the backbone of critical infrastructure and catalyze innovation across several industries.

REFERENCES

Abiona, O. O., Oladapo, O. J., Modupe, O. T., Oyeniran, O. C., Adewusi, A. O., & Komolafe, A. M. (2024). The emergence and importance of DevSecOps: Integrating and reviewing security practices within the DevOps pipeline. *World Journal of Advanced Engineering Technology and Sciences, 11*(2), 127–133. DOI: 10.30574/wjaets.2024.11.2.0093

Arrey, D. A. (2019). *Exploring the integration of security into software development life cycle (SDLC) methodology* (Doctoral dissertation, Colorado Technical University). https://www.proquest.com/openview/437de70c5a6cd10e2f24809aa1e1b5cd/1?cbl=18750&diss=y&pq-origsite=gscholar

Asmat, M. N., Khan, S. U. R., & Hussain, S. (2023). Uncertainty handling in cyber–physical systems: State-of-the-art approaches, tools, causes, and future directions. *Journal of Software (Malden, MA), 35*(7), e2428. DOI: 10.1002/smr.2428

Ayodeji, A., Mohamed, M., Li, L., Di Buono, A., Pierce, I., & Ahmed, H. (2023). Cyber security in the nuclear industry: A closer look at digital control systems, networks and human factors. *Progress in Nuclear Energy, 161*, 104738. DOI: 10.1016/j.pnucene.2023.104738

Carreras Guzman, N. H., Wied, M., Kozine, I., & Lundteigen, M. A. (2020). Conceptualizing the key features of cyber physical systems in a multilayered representation for safety and security analysis. *Systems Engineering, 23*(2), 189–210. DOI: 10.1002/sys.21509

Dafflon, B., Moalla, N., & Ouzrout, Y. (2021). The challenges, approaches, and used techniques of CPS for manufacturing in Industry 4.0: A literature review. *International Journal of Advanced Manufacturing Technology, 113*, 2395–2412. DOI: 10.1007/s00170-020-06572-4

Dapshima, B. A., & Ahmad, S. K. (2024). Evaluation and Assessment of Software Security Risks and Vulnerabilities Within the Realm of Secure DevOps. *no. July*. https://www.researchgate.net/profile/Babagana-Dapshima/publication/382440594_Evaluation_and_Assessment_of_Software_Security_Risks_and_Vulnerabilities_Within_the_Realm_of_Secure_DevOps/links/669d121e4a172d2988b6c737/Evaluation-and-Assessment-of-Software-Security-Risks-and-Vulnerabilities-Within-the-Realm-of-Secure-DevOps.pdf

Dehlaghi-Ghadim, A., Balador, A., Moghadam, M. H., Hansson, H., & Conti, M. (2023). ICSSIM—A framework for building industrial control systems security testbeds. *Computers in Industry, 148*, 103906. DOI: 10.1016/j.compind.2023.103906

Desai, R., & Nisha, T. N. (2021, July). Best practices for ensuring security in devops: A case study approach. In *Journal of Physics: Conference Series* (Vol. 1964, No. 4, p. 042045). IOP Publishing. https://iopscience.iop.org/article/10.1088/1742-6596/1964/4/042045/meta

Dobaj, J., Riel, A., Krug, T., Seidl, M., Macher, G., & Egretzberger, M. (2022, May). Towards digital twin-enabled DevOps for CPS providing architecture-based service adaptation & verification at runtime. In *Proceedings of the 17th symposium on software engineering for adaptive and self-managing systems* (pp. 132-143). DOI: 10.1145/3524844.3528057

Dobaj, J., Riel, A., Macher, G., & Egretzberger, M. (2023). Towards devOps for cyber-physical systems (cpss): Resilient self-adaptive software for sustainable human-centric smart cps facilitated by digital twins. *Machines (Basel), 11*(10), 973. DOI: 10.3390/machines11100973

Duo, W., Zhou, M., & Abusorrah, A. (2022). A survey of cyber attacks on cyber physical systems: Recent advances and challenges. *IEEE/CAA Journal of Automatica Sinica, 9*(5), 784-800. DOI: 10.1109/JAS.2022.105548

El-Kady, A. H., Halim, S., El-Halwagi, M. M., & Khan, F. (2023). Analysis of safety and security challenges and opportunities related to cyber-physical systems. *Process Safety and Environmental Protection, 173*, 384–413. DOI: 10.1016/j.psep.2023.03.012

Faustino, J. P. C. (2018). *DevOps practices in incident management process* (Master's thesis, ISCTE-Instituto Universitario de Lisboa (Portugal)). https://www.proquest.com/openview/a9c547d770cb1afc3f4bdb690492f1bd/1?cbl=2026366&diss=y&pq-origsite=gscholar

Habib, M. K., & Chimsom, C. (2022). CPS: Role, characteristics, architectures and future potentials. *Procedia Computer Science, 200*, 1347–1358. DOI: 10.1016/j.procs.2022.01.336

Hehenberger, P., Vogel-Heuser, B., Bradley, D., Eynard, B., Tomiyama, T., & Achiche, S. (2016). Design, modelling, simulation and integration of cyber physical systems: Methods and applications. *Computers in Industry, 82*, 273–289. DOI: 10.1016/j.compind.2016.05.006

Kaiser, A. K. (2020). Brief Overview of DevOps. In *Become ITIL® 4 Foundation Certified in 7 Days: Understand and Prepare for the ITIL Foundation Exam with Real-life Examples* (pp. 21-50). Berkeley, CA: Apress. DOI: 10.1007/978-1-4842-6361-7_2

Khan, F., Kumar, R. L., Kadry, S., & Meqdad, M. N. (2021). Autonomous vehicles: A study of implementation and security. *International Journal of Electrical & Computer Engineering (2088-8708), 11*(4). DOI: 10.11591/ijece.v11i4.pp3013-3021

Kirichenko, A., Christen, M., Grunow, F., & Herrmann, D. (2020). Best practices and recommendations for cybersecurity service providers. *The ethics of cybersecurity*, 299-316. DOI: 10.1007/978-3-030-29053-5_15

Ledinot, E. (2021). CPS Engineering: Gap Analysis and Perspectives. *arXiv preprint arXiv:2104.13210*. https://doi.org//arXiv.2104.13210DOI: 10.48550

Lévy, L. N., Bosom, J., Guerard, G., Amor, S. B., Bui, M., & Tran, H. (2022). DevOps model appproach for monitoring smart energy systems. *Energies, 15*(15), 5516. DOI: 10.3390/en15155516

Liang, P., Wu, Y., Xu, Z., Xiao, S., & Yuan, J. (2024). Enhancing security in DevOps by integrating artificial intelligence and machine learning. *Journal of Theory and Practice of Engineering Science, 4*(02), 31–37. DOI: 10.53469/jtpes.2024.04(02).05

Makani, S. T., & Jangampeta, S. (2024). Devops security tools evaluating effectiveness in detecting and fixing security holes. *Journal ID, 1552*, 5541. https://iaeme.com/Home/issue/IJDO?Volume=1&Issue=2

Manda, J. K. (2023). DevSecOps Implementation in Telecom: Integrating Security into DevOps Practices to Streamline Software Development and Ensure Secure Telecom Service Delivery. *Journal of Innovative Technologies, 6*(1). https://acadexpinnara.com/index.php/JIT/article/view/373

Manubolu, G. S. (2024). A comprehensive Security Testing Framework for PLC-based Industrial Automation https://www.utupub.fi/bitstream/handle/10024/178734/greeshma_manubolu_masters_thesis.pdf?sequence=1

Matta, G., Chlup, S., Shaaban, A. M., Schmittner, C., Pinzenöhler, A., Szalai, E., & Tauber, M. (2021). Risk management and standard compliance for cyber-physical systems of systems. *Infocommunications Journal, 13*(2), 32–39. DOI: 10.36244/ICJ.2021.2.5

Mujeeb Ahmed, C., Umer, M. A., Binte Liyakkathali, B. S. S., Jilani, M. T., & Zhou, J. (2021). Machine learning for cps security: applications, challenges and recommendations. *Machine Intelligence and Big Data Analytics for Cybersecurity Applications*, 397-421. DOI: 10.1007/978-3-030-57024-8_18

Poltavtseva, M., Shelupanov, A., Bragin, D., Zegzhda, D., & Alexandrova, E. (2021). Key concepts of systemological approach to CPS adaptive information security monitoring. *Symmetry, 13*(12), 2425. DOI: 10.3390/sym13122425

Porcu, D., Castro, S., Otura, B., Encinar, P., Chochliouros, I., Ciornei, I., & Bachoumis, A. (2022). Demonstration of 5G solutions for smart energy grids of the future: A perspective of the Smart5Grid project. *Energies*, *15*(3), 839. DOI: 10.3390/en15030839

Rafi, S., Yu, W., Akbar, M. A., Alsanad, A., & Gumaei, A. (2020). Prioritization based taxonomy of DevOps security challenges using PROMETHEE. *IEEE Access : Practical Innovations, Open Solutions*, *8*, 105426–105446. DOI: 10.1109/ACCESS.2020.2998819

Rajapakse, R. N., Zahedi, M., Babar, M. A., & Shen, H. (2022).. . *Information and Software Technology*, *141*, 106700. DOI: 10.1016/j.infsof.2021.106700

Rana, M. U., Shah, M. A., Alnaeem, M. A., & Maple, C. (2024). *Ransomware attacks in cyber-physical systems: countermeasure of attack vectors through automated web defenses*. IEEE. DOI: 10.1109/ACCESS.2024.3477631

Ravikumar, G., Hyder, B., & Govindarasu, M. (2019, October). Efficient modeling of hil multi-grid system for scalability & concurrency in cps security testbed. In *2019 North American Power Symposium (NAPS)* (pp. 1-6). IEEE. DOI: 10.1109/NAPS46351.2019.9000259

Rosado, D. G., Santos-Olmo, A., Sánchez, L. E., Serrano, M. A., Blanco, C., Mouratidis, H., & Fernández-Medina, E. (2022). Managing cybersecurity risks of cyber-physical systems: The MARISMA-CPS pattern. *Computers in Industry*, *142*, 103715. DOI: 10.1016/j.compind.2022.103715

Sadovykh, A., & Ivanov, V. V. (2024). Enhancing DevSecOps with continuous security requirements analysis and testing. *Компьютерные исследования и моделирование*, *16*(7), 1687-1702. DOI: 10.20537/2076-7633-2024-16-7-1687-1702

Seelaboyina, R., Vadla, S. P. C., Teerthala, S. A., & Pedduri, V. V. (2022, November). Secure software development life cycle: an approach to reduce the risks of cyber attacks in cyber physical systems and digital twins. In *International Conference on Computational Intelligence in Machine Learning* (pp. 153-161). Springer Nature Singapore. DOI: 10.1007/978-981-99-7954-7_15

Sheikh, Z. A., Singh, Y., Singh, P. K., & Ghafoor, K. Z. (2022). Intelligent and secure framework for critical infrastructure (CPS): Current trends, challenges, and future scope. *Computer Communications*, *193*, 302–331. DOI: 10.1016/j.comcom.2022.07.007

Sokolowski, D. (2022, November). Infrastructure as code for dynamic deployments. In *Proceedings of the 30th ACM Joint European Software Engineering Conference and Symposium on the Foundations of Software Engineering* (pp. 1775-1779). DOI: 10.1145/3540250.3558912

Suresh Babu, C. V., & Srisakthi, S. (2023). Cyber Physical Systems and Network Security: The Present Scenarios and Its Applications. In Thanigaivelan, R., Kaliappan, S., & Jegadheesan, C. (Eds.), *Cyber-Physical Systems and Supporting Technologies for Industrial Automation* (pp. 104–130). IGI Global. DOI: 10.4018/978-1-6684-9267-3.ch006

Suresh Babu, C. V., & Yadavamuthiah, K. (2023). Cyber Physical Systems Design Challenges in the Areas of Mobility, Healthcare, Energy, and Manufacturing. In Thanigaivelan, R., Kaliappan, S., & Jegadheesan, C. (Eds.), *Cyber-Physical Systems and Supporting Technologies for Industrial Automation* (pp. 131–151). IGI Global. DOI: 10.4018/978-1-6684-9267-3.ch007

Wang, Z., Wei, H., Wang, J., Zeng, X., & Chang, Y. (2022). Security issues and solutions for connected and autonomous vehicles in a sustainable city: A survey. *Sustainability, 14*(19), 12409. DOI: 10.3390/su141912409

Wang, Z., Xie, W., Wang, B., Tao, J., & Wang, E. (2021). A survey on recent advanced research of CPS security. *Applied Sciences (Basel, Switzerland), 11*(9), 3751. DOI: 10.3390/app11093751

Xu, S., Xia, Y., & Shen, H. L. (2022). Cyber protection for malware attack resistance in cyber-physical power systems. *IEEE Systems Journal, 16*(4), 5337–5345. DOI: 10.1109/JSYST.2022.3150576

Yasar, H., & Teplov, S. E. (2022, August). Devsecops in embedded systems: An empirical study of past literature. In *Proceedings of the 17th International Conference on Availability, Reliability and Security* (pp. 1-6). DOI: 10.1145/3538969.3544451

Zampetti, F., Nardone, V., & Di Penta, M. (2022, May). Problems and solutions in applying continuous integration and delivery to 20 open-source cyber-physical systems. In *Proceedings of the 19th International Conference on Mining Software Repositories* (pp. 646-657). DOI: 10.1145/3524842.3527948

Zampetti, F., Tamburri, D., Panichella, S., Panichella, A., Canfora, G., & Di Penta, M. (2023). Continuous integration and delivery practices for cyber-physical systems: An interview-based study. *ACM Transactions on Software Engineering and Methodology, 32*(3), 1–44. DOI: 10.1145/3571854

Zhou, J., Sun, J., Zhang, M., & Ma, Y. (2020). Dependable scheduling for real-time workflows on cyber–physical cloud systems. *IEEE Transactions on Industrial Informatics*, *17*(11), 7820–7829. DOI: 10.1109/TII.2020.3011506

Chapter 6
Ensuring Safe and Intelligent Data-Driven Control for Cyber-Physical Systems:
Advancing Security, Reliability, and Autonomy

Wasswa Shafik
https://orcid.org/0000-0002-9320-3186
Dig Connectivity Research Laboratory (DCRLab), Uganda

ABSTRACT

The study explores the integration of data-driven control techniques in cyber-physical systems (CPS), focusing on ensuring the safety, reliability, and autonomy of these increasingly complex systems. As CPS become more prevalent in various industries, from autonomous vehicles to industrial automation, the need for robust control mechanisms that safeguard against potential risks becomes paramount. This paper examines data-driven algorithms that adapt to real-time data, ensuring both system efficiency and security. It also emphasizes the development of safety protocols to mitigate vulnerabilities and enhance system resilience in the face of cyber threats or unexpected failures. The study highlights the balance between autonomy and security, presenting methodologies for achieving safe and efficient operation across diverse CPS applications. Through this analysis, the chapter provides insights into the future of CPS, emphasizing the role of advanced data-driven control in enhancing system safety, scalability, and performance.

DOI: 10.4018/979-8-3373-1832-5.ch006

1. INTRODUCTION

With the fast development of sensor technology, communication systems, and big data analytics, cyber-physical systems, including autonomous vehicles, robotics, and drones, are rapidly evolving from human-controlled to autonomous systems. Although numerous benefits can be expected, including higher reliability and safety, savings on labor costs, enhanced productivity and work efficiency, improved accessibility for people with disabilities, and saving valuable human resources, data-driven cyber-physical systems also face numerous security risks due to the open nature of cyberspace (Khalil et al., 2024). Traditional control theories designed for human-controlled cyber-physical systems encounter difficulties in providing security guarantees and performance completeness proofs for the safe operation of data-driven autonomous systems (Arbi & Israr, 2024). To address the new and unmet security, reliability, and performance requirements of data-driven autonomous systems, new principles, theories, and technologies for ensuring safe and intelligent data-driven control are urgently needed, presenting persistent and urgent challenges in both theory and applications (Pattepu et al., 2022).

Despite being applications-driven, the existing literature generally falls into two categories with separate research streams, each stream focusing on one specific characteristic of data-driven cyber-physical systems: physical interaction and cybersecurity (Hamdi et al., 2024; Sabir et al., 2023a). Such separation not only sacrifices the synergy between the two research streams but also prohibits the research community from exploiting advanced theories, methodologies, and tools from other relevant research fields. Therefore, it is imperative to provide a unified framework in light of both physical and cyber interconnections in order to tackle the advanced control problems of ensuring safe and intelligent data-driven control for cyber-physical systems (Sheikh & Singh, 2023; Sabir et al., 2023b). To address the existing and persistent challenges and to exploit the new opportunities in data-driven control of cyber-physical systems, this paper aims to provide a comprehensive survey of the recent advances in research into ensuring the security, reliability, and autonomy of data-driven cyber-physical systems. We will comprehensively discuss the state-of-the-art theories, methodologies, and applications in a unified framework. The promising future research directions and urgent challenges will be summarized at the end of the paper (Saha et al., 2022;).

Cyber-Physical Systems (CPS) are integrations of computation, networking, and physical processes. Embedded computers and networks monitor and control the physical processes, with feedback loops where physical processes affect computations and vice versa. The economic and societal potential of such systems is vast. CPS is recognized as one of the major technological innovations of the last two decades, given the rapidly increasing capabilities for scientific research and their potential for critical infrastructure and other application areas (Neghab et al., 2022). Numerous illustrative and successful examples of CPS exist across a range of application areas, including aerospace, automotive, chemical process control, energy, micro-electromechanical systems (MEMS), robotics, and smart structures, among others. Many potential CPS applications have been theorized in the research community over the years. Moreover, auto accidents on smart roadways, aircraft crashes caused by the smart bombing of communication systems, and malicious control signals to critical infrastructure could easily lead to casualties and significant physical and economic damage in a nation (Ray, 2023). There is increasing encouragement and investment in exploring how to leverage these scientific and technical advances to create vibrant new industries, all of which will be heavily reliant on secure and resilient CPS systems.

Figure 1. Expert Cyber-Physical System Drivers

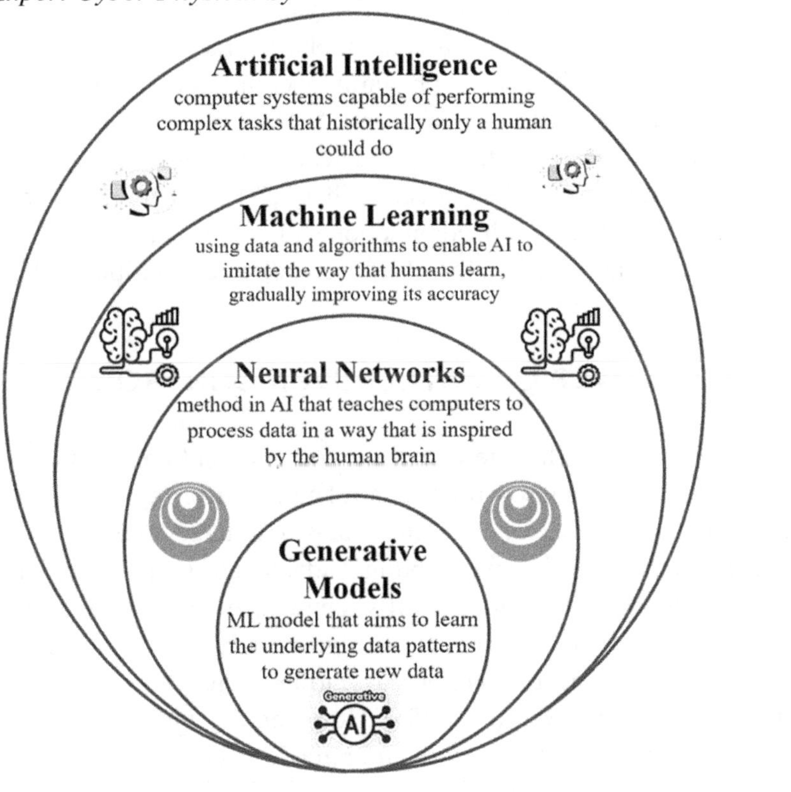

Data-driven methods have demonstrated the potential to address some of these challenges using the current technological advancements as presented in Figure 1. They may enable the construction of more reliable models by using the data obtained under a wider range of system operation scenarios and complex real-world disturbances. These models can then be used to control complex systems with minimal a priori knowledge and without explicitly modeling their complex dynamics (Dinesh et al., 2023). The growing volume of traditional telemetry from the increasing variety of cyber-physical systems, as well as recent capabilities associated with the rapid diffusion and use of in situ sensors and the Internet of Things, has led to an explosion in the volume of data available to address both modeling and control of such systems. The older term 'data-driven control' referred to the body of work that learned a control policy directly from historical data (Haleem et al., 2022; Sabir et al., 2024). These ideas were often based on extending results obtained in classical adaptive control and model identification to modern learning settings.

In the first decade of the 21st century, these ideas began to connect more formally with advances in machine learning and robust optimization, and people began to use methods and ideas from these fields to control systems in the context of control policies learned from data. In order to distinguish this modern family of methods from classical results in this area and to emphasize the ability of such methods to learn from large-scale, diverse, and potentially complex datasets, this text uses the term 'safe and intelligent data-driven control.' Data-driven control, in the modern sense, typically emphasizes adjusting classical control policies by processing data obtained from systems' operations directly (Shafik, 2025c). These techniques are most robust and reliable when used in conjunction with traditional, safety-critical control policies for testing and verification of learned policy capabilities and limitations.

2. FUNDAMENTALS OF DATA-DRIVEN CONTROL

The convergence of the latest machine learning and control theories leads to data-driven control, which constructs control policies from system data with limited or even without knowledge of either the actual system model or the noise statistics. Data-driven control has shown exceptional advantages in many applications, such as robotics, autonomous driving, smart structures, and renewable energy systems. In particular, it enables the concept of intelligence, which empowers robots or smart machines with the capacity for autonomous learning, perception, and decision-making in their delegated tasks (Shafik, 2025b). However, the widespread applicability of data-driven control to capture secure and reliable system behaviors is still premature, as very limited data-driven control designs consider actuator attacks, sensor communication attacks, systematic disturbances, or ad hoc behavior constraints. Therefore, in the context of cyber-physical systems with potential control vulnerabilities, it is crucial to develop a fundamental methodology of data-driven control designs to ensure safe and intelligent nonzero-sum behaviors under security and transient constraints (Shafik, 2024f).

The central topic of this paper is built from three fundamental elements, which are cyber-physical systems, security and privacy protections, and data-driven control designs. Cyber-physical systems are systems with seamless integration of computation, communication, and control to accomplish an assigned task over a shared environment between a finite number of rational systems. A notion of security or privacy is formulated to measure the capability of attackers to either disrupt normal system operations or infer confidential information (Shafik & Kalinaki, 2023). Data-driven control designs aim to enable systems to accomplish assigned tasks in the physical world through data acquisition, learning, and policy implementations. The zero-sum problem is used to determine the network capacity from an adversary's point of view. The zero result is used to model the capacity of inferring any confidential information with bounded estimation error. The non-zero-sum problem studies the secondary effect of external disturbances on nonzero-sum control policies (Shafik, 2024c).

2.1. Basic Concepts and Definitions

In this section, we will provide a recap of the basic concepts of control engineering, its fundamental mathematics, its dependence on data, and the role of data in promoting the security, reliability, and autonomy of cyber-physical systems. We will start with static and dynamic control problems and their mathematical realizations before we delve deeper into their big data-enhanced versions. Suppose that we want to design a smart thermostat for an air conditioner in a small room. Our objective is to design the thermostat to perform optimally in a variety of situations while taking into consideration the desired comfort or constraints (Khalil et al., 2024). However, to make a thermostatic control possible, we need to collect large amounts of data for any random room temperature, outside temperature, and personal behavior condition. We then need to run big data algorithms that give the thermostat as many operating instructions as possible based on the current environmental, room, and human situations. The concept behind such real-life scenarios is rooted in the early 1950s and was coined in cybernetics (Haleem et al., 2022). Like a human being, a thermostat needs to learn how to act optimally within some relatively well-defined model or utility function and specific operational, resource, or other constraints. Notice that although a thermostat is simple, all the fundamental mathematical elements of an autonomous temperature controller, such as sensors, actuators, a data-driven algorithm, and decision models, resemble those in the field of control engineering, which can be as complex and general as a fly, tank, appliance, complex industry, or an autopilot system for a rocket or an electricity grid (Dinesh et al., 2023).

2.2. Key Techniques and Algorithms

We envision a contestable architecture for runtime security assessment of DSCHV that is based on probabilistic machine learning models for prediction and anomaly detection, together with a two-sided market considered as a game between the defender, who limits the actions of the attacker and data providers from energy storage device and power system companies. Using differential privacy techniques, the contestable game framework assigns a trust score to the private energy data to show privacy risk to device manufacturers and price entropy to guarantee the randomness of ground truth labels used in model generation (Ray, 2023; Irshad et al., 2025). The outlined framework is designed to be transparent, secure, and privacy-compliant by ensuring differential privacy of directly labeled private data. We demonstrate how to select a level of exposure resistance by minimizing indirect disclosure on a bounded neighborhood of the training confined region and present a flowchart to guarantee the privacy of the generated models during the scoring and labeling process from model compromise and reconnaissance attacks.

We develop a novel approach to cybersecurity and privacy issues of private DSCHV data by presenting a transparent and differentially private mechanism for the data-dwarf sandboxes. Our framework, although tailored to DSCHV attacks, can evolve as a privacy-preserving approach to intelligence sharing forged in the battleground touchpoint of a broader energy system transition (Neghab et al., 2022). We provide transparent, cost-effective, scalable, and adaptive ways for intelligence community members to share their diverse smart energy cybersecurity knowledge and harmonize evidence-based security collaboration to improve situational awareness of evolving risks. Our platform is based on two classes of recursive reward or count-square-root mechanisms for partial performance from a machine learning black box, designed to protect from disallowed feature selection and hidden backdoor exploitation incidents (Adelakun et al., 2023). This novel privacy-boosting approach considers black-hat AI operators' multi-resolution and complexity estimates in the presence of unrestricted dynamics and path-dependent pricing, and some key points are presented in Table 1.

Table 1. Key Components of Data-Driven Control for Cyber-Physical Systems

Component(s)	Description	Importance	Challenges	Applications	Reference
Data-Driven Algorithms	Algorithms using real-time sensor data for decision-making	Improve efficiency, adaptability, and performance	Data quality, uncertainty, and noise	Autonomous Vehicles, Smart Grids	(Haleem et al., 2022)
Adaptive Control	Adjusts parameters based on system behavior and environment	Ensures continuous optimization and learning	Computational complexity, delays in adaptation	Robotics, Industrial Automation	(Dinesh et al., 2023)
Safety Protocols	Measures to detect and mitigate risks, ensuring system reliability	Protects systems from cyber-attacks and failures	Real-time implementation, scalability	Healthcare Systems, Critical Infrastructure	(Ray, 2023)
Cybersecurity Integration	Safeguards against cyber threats while ensuring control stability	Prevent unauthorized access and attacks	Balancing security with system performance	Smart Cities, Autonomous Drones	(Seelaboyina et al., 2024)
Resilience & Fault Tolerance	Ability to maintain functionality during disturbances	Enhances robustness in uncertain environments	Handling unexpected failures and disturbances	Autonomous Vehicles, Power Distribution Networks	(Neghab et al., 2022)
Real-Time Monitoring	Continuous tracking of system status and performance	Detects system anomalies to enhance response times	Data overload, decision latency	Industrial Sensors, Smart Factories	(Saha et al., 2022)
Distributed Control	Decentralized decision-making for large systems	Reduces bottlenecks, improves scalability	Communication delays, synchronization issues	Smart Grids, Large-Scale IoT Networks	(Pattepu et al., 2022)
Predictive Maintenance	Using data to predict failures before they happen	Reduces downtime, increases lifespan	Data accuracy, environmental variables	Manufacturing, Power Plants	(Khalil et al., 2024)
Model Predictive Control	Uses a model of the system to predict and optimize performance	Enhances decision-making, adapts to system changes	High computational cost, model uncertainty	Autonomous Vehicles, Drones	(Pattepu et al., 2022)
Energy Efficiency	Optimizes energy use in cyber-physical systems	Reduces costs, improves sustainability	Balancing performance with energy consumption	Smart Grids, Smart Buildings	(Seelaboyina et al., 2024)

continued on following page

Table 1. Continued

Component(s)	Description	Importance	Challenges	Applications	Reference
Data Fusion	Integrates data from multiple sources for decision-making	Improves system accuracy, robustness	Data inconsistency, integration complexity	Healthcare Monitoring, Industrial Automation	(Shafik, 2024d)
Human-in-the-loop (HITL)	Involves human oversight in decision-making processes	Combines human intuition with AI efficiency	Delays in human decision-making, error-prone processes	Military, Medical Systems	(Shafik, 2024g)
System Redundancy	Incorporates backup systems to ensure continued operation	Increases reliability, prevents complete system failure	Cost, system complexity	Autonomous Vehicles, Power Distribution Networks	(Shafik, 2024e)

3. SECURITY CHALLENGES IN CPS

While the connectedness in cyber-physical systems (CPS) leads to significant productivity advancements and opens up numerous possibilities for smart system innovations, it also significantly amplifies security risks. Many familiar security vulnerabilities in the exclusively cyber domain not only remain but become even more consequential than before when they now threaten the safety and stability of the physical system. Along with known security vulnerabilities, CPS introduces additional security risk challenges due to the software/hardware diversity, multiple control objectives, split design/implementation, and the unique features of the system (Haleem et al., 2022; Ahmad et al., 2024). In this chapter, we discuss several distinguishing features of the CPS security risk, leading to the conclusion that simply building security functions on top of an unsecured control design does not suffice to guarantee CPS-level security. Articulated by the smart grid, many real-time and mission-critical applications for CPS are applications of control. Their acceptance requires not only for the system to run according to their design specification but also for the system to be secure, i.e., no one except the system operator team is allowed to control the system operation. The coexistence of the control objective and security objective leads to several distinguishing features of the security risk in CPS when compared with the security challenges in the general cyber domain (Dinesh et al., 2023).

3.1. Threats and Vulnerabilities

In addition to facing the general security and data-intensive technological approaches that exist for nearly every domain of artificial intelligence and machine learning, there is potential to improve cybersecurity. The research topics described below are essential to address the challenges and are also expected to enable a solution space that is technically superior, economically practical, and legally defensible to regulatory authorities and public opinion. Enhancing all forms of intelligence and autonomy through sensors, virtual reality, etc., implies increasing data fidelity, improving system integration, and perfecting real-time decision-making, often at the cost of a more complex and interconnected cyber-physical system architecture (Ray, 2023). Both AI and ML are data-driven and hence rely on data to generate accurate information and to make good decisions.

All data—and, in principle, any system component that acts to store, process, or transmit data—is a potential target for system attack through cyber means. Cyber attacks on cyber-physical systems are interdisciplinary applications that impact strategic, operational, and tactical weapons and cyber-centric information technology. Indeed, not all data submitted to AI and ML-based tools for secondary analysis are secure. Making data-driven control safe requires that data and systems are reliable for good decisions. The treatment of data and AI elements as primary system components dramatically increases the range of potential attack surfaces an adversary may exploit and the impact of such manipulations (Saha et al., 2022). However, the unique functional approach of AI and ML also makes comprehensive security, robustness, and safety of these elements—both separately and especially in the context of downstream CPS functions where they are used—difficult to demonstrate.

3.2. Attack Detection and Prevention Mechanisms

We develop resilient control algorithms that can detect and adapt to control logic attacks by malicious adversaries without using physical models of the CPS under attack. We assume the adversary is omniscient about the control strategy with limited influence over individual sensors and actuators. Using distributed state estimators and observing the adversarial influence individually at the sensor and actuator layers, we are able to define a safety index associated with each component (Sheikh & Singh, 2023). Once some of the states of the CPS exceed a certain predetermined threshold, we iterate between state restoration and state estimation loops. Finally, we harden the internal states of the CPS to the invasive influence of the adversary without disabling the sensors and the controllers. In particular, our mechanism does not use any state estimation, either in the form of optimal state estimation or in the form of some approximate state estimation, as improvements would be tricky to perform at the high speed required in some CPS. Our resilience scheme is demonstrated in several numerical examples and also on an electric power grid model (Singh et al., 2024).

Given the severity of the attacks that CPSs have been facing recently, there have been relevant research efforts on developing detection mechanisms to support test-based prevention mechanisms. What we contribute here is a methodology to compute a safety index and to implement a resilience mechanism that can detect, control, and finally overcome attacks by malicious adversaries. This is eventually carried out without using a physical model of the systems being monitored and controlled and without using formal specifications, coding schemes, or any inter-layer communication. Our mechanism can be implemented as an extension of existing defense-in-depth schemes where the integrity of the system's response is monitored and may be elastically corrected by injecting a minimum change to the reference inputs of the sensors used by the controller to compute the actuation commands. In such a way, the actuated system can be called cyber-resilient (Okafor & Longe, 2022). Our work addresses the precise design of the condition that triggers the presence of unauthorized content in signal outputs and prescribes how to monitor and, finally, how to release such unauthorized content.

4. RELIABILITY AND RESILIENCE IN CPS

The reliability of embedded systems depends on the correct execution of a program, whereas resilience ensures that the program waits for the correct input to be executed. The architectures that we use to build systems have an impact on the reliability of the system. Suppose the programming model allows incorrect system behavior when the programmer intends to deal with the correct and expected scenario. In that case, the programming model can degrade the resilience of the system. Reliable embedded systems wait for the right event to look for an event and handle the detected event that signals the system to proceed (Khalil et al., 2024). Current research in architectural support for real-time systems depends largely on the construction of explicit waiting states in which to be notified of the readiness of an event that signals the system to proceed. A reliability model uses architectural extensions to safely and sequentially stall the processor state when waiting for external world events without waiting for general I/O interrupts. Similarly, real-time operating systems have been proposed to provide support for architectures that provide waiting states and associated transition events, which can be visualized in time and rapid transitions between logical states. Providing system security and reliability in a shared computing environment requires the support of both hardware and software primitives that can provide a high level of protection to system components utilizing these widely varying communication channels between collaborators, even in the face of malicious code (Pattepu et al., 2022). When collaborators execute on general-purpose computing or multi-core platforms, then a virtual machine layer can provide isolation.

4.1. Fault Tolerance and Redundancy

Guaranteed safe decision-making is the key to resilient performance, and redundancy is a well-established mechanism to ensure fault tolerance and maintain system reliability. For each component, sensor, or actuator of a complex engineering system, there is one or more available alternative components or products. Each similarly behaving replica or redundancy is associated with the one it is protecting, forming tasks that cooperate to achieve the associated task and execute the overall mission. These redundancies can be installed, operated, and maintained. Such a replicability assumption is feasible for real-world engineered systems, which makes fault tolerance and redundancy simple and practical and prevents single points of failure from crafting attack vectors. In digital systems with digital actuators or sensors, the faults can be resolved by either voting or for the purpose of deciding on safety if different voting results occur (Saha et al., 2022). It is often assumed that the system is designed so that the simple, domain-independent watchdog voting for the sensor or actuator safety logic is sufficiently independent of the sensor and actuator themselves in order to increase fault resistance. Consequently, both the quality and timing of the sensors and actuators and of the sensor functionality for the corresponding control and security loops are essential properties in this context. In this scheme, sensory estimation issues disappear as long as the sensors can be shown to provide the required quality. A very similar approach is for the redundant sensors to vote instead for a known sensor failure model with spotless timing to decide on a sensor activation failure, where majority voting is advisable (Neghab et al., 2022). In each case, the failure detection being performed is threshold-based by empirical learning.

4.2. Resilient Control Strategies

This section provides a review of resilient control design and discusses statistical anomaly detection and response generation. Resilient control suggests the capability to overcome component and system faults, including those induced by cyber attackers, to ensure normal and safe operation. The newly developed attack-aware monitoring strategy and resilient control methodologies can be used in various energy, cyber, and transportation-related systems to counteract emergent sophisticated cyber threats. By exploiting widely used basic statistical algorithms and game theory, the novel methodologies are computationally attractive (Yan & Kunhui, 2024). It has been well understood that under many operational scenarios, cyber-physical systems have been and will be significantly threatened by their vulnerabilities to cyber attacks, human errors, and physical faults. The complexity and connectivity of systems such as power grids, air traffic control systems, water distribution systems, smart networks, and transportation systems pose a wide range of security challenges. Many of these systems have stringent safety and performance requirements, as well as heavy real-time operating constraints (Dinesh et al., 2023). Remarkable research advances in statistics, probability theory, optimization, communication, control, game theory, and security have been integrated and applied to develop various tools in monitoring and control for these security-related applications. The resilience concept is another emerging trend in control and optimization to enhance existing control strategies to address the vulnerabilities of large-scale complex systems to both random and adversarial attacks and failures. The systemic failures under physical attacks demonstrated the limitations of the existing control and optimization methods to the effects of stress-induced failure. Resilient control and these methodologies are reviewed from different perspectives in sections above (Hammouch et al., 2022).

5. AUTONOMY IN CPS

Autonomous systems (AS) that support partial automation and shared control between the cyber and the physical environment in cyber-physical systems (CPS) play an important role in many critical applications. CPS with increasing autonomy levels are becoming available in public infrastructure management, automotive, aerospace, and other fields. Several automation levels from no automation at all to a human driver under any traffic or weather condition are defined; this definition is aligned with an automotive industry context. A synthesis of the levels in different AS platforms that include CPSs is formalized and introduces the sub-full autonomous control under shared control from characteristics relevant to the availability and accuracy of the autonomous and detection-related aspects, like the possible need for warning signals to be used to facilitate a successful handover (Saha et al., 2022). In the submit and autonomous levels, the human is still fully in control of the tasks while releasing the responsibility to make part of the work to the machines, which allows the human to relax but remain in the loop to step in at any moment. In the partially autonomous level, the machine is able to manage the situation; the humans can observe during the relaxed period and step in when a decision is deemed unsatisfactory. At the conditional level, the human continues to supervise with less intensive intervention. At the high level, the machine takes control of the situations with information exchanged with the humans through a spoken dialogue interface or via alternative interfaces, similar to recent developments reported for the interaction with a co-pilot (Okafor & Longe, 2022). In the full autonomous level, the machine is able to manage the situation without any human intervention, relying fully on an autonomously superlative system. The role of the human is confined to monitoring and overseeing or performing higher-order tasks. Industries with shared control for applications such as collective human-drones in closed environments, building inspection, picking and placing objects, tensioning, and posture assistance for humans. CPSs with increasing autonomy levels are becoming available (Pattepu et al., 2022).

5.1. Levels of Autonomy

Cyber-physical systems (CPSs) used in specific application domains come in various forms and can exhibit distinct characteristics. Tasks performed by different individuals can also differ in complexity and desired interaction autonomy. To promote methodical exploration and scientific underpinning in CPSs, frameworks were developed to describe, from the human perspective, the increasing independence and evolving involvement of humans in performing assigned tasks suitable for modern-day unmanned systems and cyber-physical systems. Other definitions also exist for autonomic systems, which aim to bring adaptation to systems (Saha et al., 2022). Various levels of autonomy exist to describe different cyber-physical and autonomous systems, which can help in defining or classifying the functionality of multiple designs. Different fields describe autonomy at different levels, but the concept is universal. For example, the most recognized one is translational autonomy in driving, where the ability for a machine to control moving vehicles at different levels represents a range from no motion to full control. In a cyber-physical system, such as an intelligent vehicle, there can be various entities, such as an External Operator (EO), like a driver, which perform tasks collaboratively using various levels of control, or change the level of autonomy during task execution (Jun et al., 2021). Whether we design a CPS in the human-in-the-loop paradigm is an issue, and CPS developments aim for different levels of automation. Limiting the right of control from upper normative level regulations restricts the needs or desires for automation for some individuals in certain domains. Addressing all perspectives to set the right level of autonomy in a certain task engages ethical, legal, psychological, social, and technological judgments brought by actors in the application domains (Shafik, 2023; Gul et al., 2024). In sum, different levels of autonomy may apply to describe the intelligence and individuals' interaction with CPSs.

5.2. Human-in-the-Loop Systems

Control systems are used for a diverse range of applications in various domains, with accompanying high standards for performance, reliability, and safety. The use of advanced AI/ML methods is increasingly common to improve performance, and autonomy is a fundamental goal for a range of systems. AI/ML-based approaches introduce a range of challenges and opportunities for control, including understanding what the next generation of intelligent, autonomous, safe systems will look like, and how they can be formally verified and assured to be safe. Informally, human-in-the-loop systems identify systems in which people and control algorithms interact closely to perform shared goals (Shafik et al., 2024). Such systems are increasingly deployed in a range of settings, particularly to take advantage of human cognition and judgment when dealing with unexpected or poorly characterized situations. Formal definitions of human-centered AI-based systems are closely aligned: these systems are interested in optimizing the performance of humans working in collaboration with the system. These systems have many functionalities related to monitoring and probing human attention, personalizing user interfaces to take advantage of the particular cognitive capabilities of humans and a variety of expected human behaviors, as presented in Table 2 (Shafik et al., 2023).

Table 2. Applications of Safe Data-Driven Control in Cyber-Physical Systems

Application	Targeted SDG	AI Technology Used	Key Benefits	Key Safety Considerations	Reference
Autonomous Vehicles	SDG 11 (Sustainable Cities)	Machine Learning, Computer Vision	Efficient transportation, reduced traffic congestion	Cybersecurity vulnerabilities, system malfunctions	(Shafik, 2024a)
Smart Grids	SDG 7 (Affordable Energy)	Data Analytics, IoT	Optimized energy distribution, reduced energy loss	Cyber-attacks, system overload	(Kalinaki et al., 2024)
Industrial Automation	SDG 9 (Industry, Innovation)	AI, Robotics	Increased productivity, reduced human error	Safety in high-risk environments	(Shafik, 2024b, 2025a)
Healthcare Monitoring	SDG 3 (Good Health)	Deep Learning, IoT	Real-time patient monitoring, early detection of anomalies	Privacy concerns, system downtime	(Ray, 2023)
Smart Cities	SDG 11 (Sustainable Cities)	Big Data, Machine Learning	Enhanced urban management, energy efficiency	Data security, system robustness	(Haleem et al., 2022)

continued on following page

Table 2. Continued

Application	Targeted SDG	AI Technology Used	Key Benefits	Key Safety Considerations	Reference
Environmental Monitoring	SDG 13 (Climate Action)	IoT, AI Models	Monitoring climate parameters, disaster preparedness	Data privacy, sensor accuracy	(Neghab et al., 2022)
Precision Agriculture	SDG 2 (Zero Hunger)	AI, Remote Sensing	Increased crop yield, reduced resource use	Data reliability, environmental impact	(Saha et al., 2022)
Autonomous Drones	SDG 15 (Life on Land)	Computer Vision, AI	Wildlife protection, reforestation monitoring	Cybersecurity, system failure	(Sheikh & Singh, 2023)
Smart Healthcare Devices	SDG 3 (Good Health)	AI, Machine Learning	Remote diagnostics, personalized healthcare	System vulnerabilities, data privacy concerns	(Pattepu et al., 2022)
Renewable Energy Systems	SDG 7 (Affordable Energy)	AI Optimization, Energy Modeling	Enhanced efficiency of solar/wind energy systems	System failures, energy storage reliability	(Saha et al., 2022)
Supply Chain Automation	SDG 12 (Responsible Consumption)	Robotics, AI Optimization	Increased efficiency, waste reduction	Data inaccuracies, cyber threats	(Augusto et al., 2024)
Urban Mobility Solutions	SDG 11 (Sustainable Cities)	AI, IoT, Machine Learning	Reduced congestion, optimized traffic flow	System reliability, real-time decision-making	(Van Loenhout et al., 2022)
Disaster Response Systems	SDG 13 (Climate Action)	AI Models, Data Analytics	Faster response to disasters, resource optimization	Real-time data accuracy, system resilience	(Seelaboyina et al., 2024)

6. INTEGRATION OF SECURITY, RELIABILITY, AND AUTONOMY

This paper discusses challenges and opportunities in integrating problems related to secure and reliable control in cyber-physical systems (CPS), while deploying data that is continuously exploited for improved performance. While current research and practice deal with these sets of problems orthogonally, we must consider their interrelationships to more effectively and efficiently provide an overall safe CPS operation. We discuss several open research problems in the integration of security, reliability, robustness, and autonomy, and also in making practical the solution concepts, towards addressing some of these challenges and opportunities (Saha et al., 2022). We exemplify the use of these concepts in cyber-physical applications and discuss paths for the future. Control systems, an integral part of many cyber-physical systems, are used to regulate system states of particular interest and overall achieve desired performance metrics. Modern control systems are increasingly reliant on data measurement and computation of state estimates, and their use in estimation and adaptive learning to better represent the environment. These data-driven control algorithms can adapt to various internal and environmental conditions while potentially minimizing dependencies on more traditional complex and time-consuming mathematical model-based design methods (Neghab et al., 2022; Irshad et al., 2025).

A data-driven controller design approach composed of simple, fast, and as-good-as-possible models is particularly attractive in autonomous CPS that require adaptation to real-time or near real-time input and the presence of unmodeled or unknown disturbances, and that must maintain acceptable performance while learning more about system characteristics. Data-driven control algorithms are particularly useful when the environmental characteristics evolve and are challenging to understand and/or design for a priori, and a flexible, adaptive platform is necessary for autonomous actions to succeed. However, a connected cyber-physical system, to perform well in a dynamically changing environment, relies on the use of computation and communication to analyze and exchange information and exhibit evolving control capabilities, signaling a performance-establishing aspect of the use of additional computation overload (Adelakun et al., 2023). Compromise of these components, or of the computation and its use for adaptive learning algorithms, can cause the system to enter exploitable states by threat actors, which did not incorporate grief into the development process.

6.1. Challenges and Opportunities

We briefly summarize the variety of possibilities to enhance safety and performance of control via data-driven learning. We see a clear trajectory for collaboration between approaches that are normally disjunct. We see opportunities for some compromise of thorough analysis of complex systems while still exploiting learning to adapt to the unknown or developing operating conditions. Model learning is a far more powerful synthesis tool than first-passage prediction. Safe learning merges model uncertainties which, with a controller, can be evaluated for risks or a control system. Formulating the desired behavior in a standard form such as goal programming or robust optimization drops directly into the same framework and controller framework (Dinesh et al., 2023). There are assumptions about the approach — system identification operates on relatively short windows — and is relatively local in its approach. We already know that residual-based anomaly detection monitoring can handle that without any impacts on CPU. The induction of physics into the controller removes the major appeal of black-box learning techniques which can, however, be easily exploited in quite rich hybrid architectures. Control plans for night vision goggles in bright sunlit outdoor conditions by modeling noise, vignetting, and obstacles and finding the optimal tradeoff between performance, robustness, and uncertainty, confronting the camera instead of terrain classification (Adelakun et al., 2023). Control experts should analyze robust controllers, not robust control systems. Sufficient robustness is derived from sufficient performance. Learning theory can be exploited to shrink that uncertainty by exploiting redundancy in measured outputs and by inducing some physics content of the model into the model structure. During normal operation, the misfit of measured outputs to the plant model can trigger an increase in the measurement rate and availability. Invariant learning can be set to work at this task, although our view here is a bit more specific than the general invariant-based fault detection formulations (Saha et al., 2022).

7. DATA PRIVACY AND ETHICS IN DATA-DRIVEN CONTROL

Data ethics or data privacy has always been a hot research topic. Since the application of data science demands novel data-driven techniques, people who are potentially interested also emphasize the importance of data privacy. It incurs costs for new technologies, and our society has to prioritize data privacy. In the fifth century, Lao Zi said, 'What we acquire when we are born are: soul, one gender, parents, and origin. We are not happy under a siege; we do not look forward to owning many of the rich treasures. So avoid this in daily life.' This sentence means we cannot live to enter into secret things; lying is not beneficial, and human beings in the whole universe should have a common breed, blood, physical body, and personal history (Sheikh & Singh, 2023). With the advent of big history and data-driven technology, data privacy is also facing new challenges.

According to the above statement, data privacy involved in the research is the derivative of personal data privacy. However, data-driven control actually focuses on control and optimization, which is considered to be objective, rules, norms, and mass centralization, and is not responsive to the concepts of personal data privacy. In addition, the core principle of steering the purpose of data-driven control is to provide evidence for reducing uncertainty, which is also different from personal data privacy, as it is the continuation of human physical and psychological security and dignity, lest it be disturbed (Neghab et al., 2022). What one has, what one did, what one thinks, and what one wants to do are all important aspects. In general, data security and privacy in control and optimization can be explained as follows:

(1) Non-interactive. Entities can manipulate existing data without a user or a third party, and there is no prerequisite for bilateral trust;
(2) Self-determination. All individuals have the right to define their own private information;
(3) Personality definition. Due to the possibility of identity harassment, discrimination, or other illegal activities, the data can be identified or better defined;
(4) Use-specific restrictions. Common constraints for special data such as user consent, use purposes, restrictions within the scope of the intended public service, and refined restrictions.

8. CASE STUDIES AND APPLICATIONS

In this section, we illustrate our proposed control architectures with several case studies and real applications. The considered systems include some of the complex autonomous systems found in the domains of power systems, transportation, and robotics. The applications cover a wide range of control problems and provide insights into the various design choices that one must make when deploying our proposed control architectures for practical data-driven control applications. As an enabling technology for power distribution systems, we introduce a physics-inspired model predictive control framework (Khalil et al., 2024). In a slightly different direction, we describe a data-driven control architecture to support operator interventions in freeway traffic. This is done using the calibration of a second-order car-following model to vehicle trajectory data that is collected from a highway pilot. We then introduce autonomous aerial vehicles, which are envisioned to be deployment platforms for a wide range of civilian applications such as package delivery, infrastructure inspection and monitoring, search and rescue, advertising, precision farming and filming, and reconnaissance and surveillance (Pattepu et al., 2022). We introduce theoretical results as well as collision avoidance algorithms for the safe deployment of a fleet of scales of autonomous aerial vehicles.

8.1. Smart Grids

This chapter commences by addressing 'smart grids' through enhancing power dissemination infrastructures with sensing, communication, and computation capabilities, yielding remarkable benefits, ranging from efficient resource application to preventing and mitigating faults in the grid. They are one of the most representative agglomerations of cyber-physical systems, composed of specific topologies of several types of interconnected systems. Deploying data-driven control and optimization methods in such infrastructures presents a series of challenges, different in nature from those of other types of systems (Mojtaba Matinkhah & Shafik, 2019). Most of the past literature revolved around performant but complex centralized control algorithms, running in simulated or emulated but highly abstracted testing scenarios. On the other hand, the aim is to argue in favor of incorporating lessons provided by the data-driven control and optimization of other cyber-physical systems into multifaceted but clear-to-understand, marginal investment-friendly, real-world implementable, platform-agnostic frameworks. It summarizes some of the recent local data-driven optimization methods that could be of immediate value to the smart grid community and connects them with underlying relevant principles and results of direct interest to this group of cyber-physical system experts (Mohammad et al., 2023).

8.2. Autonomous Vehicles

Autonomous vehicles are expected to significantly improve safety, efficiency, and convenience on roadways, thereby saving numerous lives from accidents and making our lives more pleasant and productive. Promising technological advances have been made in recent years, with significant functionality in automated driving achieved. Currently, numerous research efforts worldwide are investigating areas such as sensing, online mapping, localization, forecasting, optimal control, robustness, reproducibility, and validation to ensure the advancement of future autonomous driving (Shafik et al., 2023). What cyber-physical control problems exist in autonomous vehicles? How can we solve them together? Our approach includes developing novel sensing directly in the vehicle dynamic model, building online maps, real-time localization, high-level obstacle detection and forecasting, designing optimal maneuvers with uncertainty, and ensuring safety and robustness (Shafik et al., 2019). We also directly engage in constructing the necessary infrastructure to bring autonomous driving to fruition through reproducible testing. Our approach has been tested through both simulations and racing competitions with scale race cars (Meng et al., 2020). The results are promising, and we believe that it can provide real-time autonomous driving ready for full-size vehicles.

9. FUTURE DIRECTIONS AND RESEARCH OPPORTUNITIES

This paper aimed to present an integrated research framework featuring a system theory developed for addressing fundamental research challenges in cyber-physical system security, modeled as a data-driven control problem. Despite our progress on the research front of data-driven control, there are many research problems that remain unsolved. We end the paper with several unresolved problems and research questions, theorem-proving problems, and speculative ideas. In the data-driven control area, one way of theoretical research is to establish a set of principles that underlie any data-generated inference of models or control laws (Pattepu et al., 2022). Unfortunately, we are far from having the principles that can systematically guide researchers and practitioners in choosing methods, interpreting the results, and discovering relationships among state estimation, predictability, stability, controllability, and performance measures. Following the trend seen in statistics, optimization, and machine learning, we advocate that future theoretical research in control should make more extensive use of connectivism. This may include linearization of nonlinear systems. If linearization is possible, a simple state observer can immediately feed data to control a system, even if the underlying system model complexity is unknown (Ray, 2023; Sheikh & Singh, 2023; Ahmad et al., 2025). We humbly hope that the research framework we assembled in this paper can motivate both theoretical and empirical research on diverse topics in control.

10. CONCLUSION

This study systematically addresses the complex challenge of data-driven control design for the safe, secure, and intelligent operation of CPS. By decomposing and synthesizing four novel categories of control models—each grounded in the strengths of classical and modern control theory—we have established a framework capable of achieving adaptive, robust, and real-time decision-making under uncertainty and adversarial conditions. These models are architected to operate reliably in constructed and dynamic environments, leveraging advances in deep learning, reliable learning, and robust control to enhance stability, resilience, and autonomy. A central contribution of this work lies in bridging the longstanding gap between security control synthesis and robust control synthesis. Through rigorous benchmarking of performance limitations under concurrent disruptions and strategic relaxation of strict constraints, we provide new insights into trade-offs between optimality and resilience. The proposed online and offline strategies exhibit improved stabilization capabilities in the presence of data corruption, enabling CPS to maintain operational integrity under real-world disturbances. Furthermore, this is the first known effort to extend data-driven feedback controllers to mitigate vulnerabilities in real-time physical-space interactions explicitly. The integration of data-centric learning mechanisms with model-based control architectures not only balances safety, security, and computational efficiency but also demonstrates the potential of hybrid intelligence in control system design. By unifying discrete control approaches within a cohesive learning-based framework, we achieve a synthesis that transcends the limitations of standalone methods. In conclusion, this work fulfills its objective of proposing a data-driven control paradigm that is both theoretically rigorous and practically scalable. The broader implications of these contributions are evident across mission-critical CPS domains, including autonomous systems, industrial automation, and smart infrastructure. Future research should focus on formal verification of learning-enabled controllers, scalable co-design under hardware constraints, and integration with distributed CPS architectures to further enhance resilience and trustworthiness in safety-critical applications.

REFERENCES

Adelakun, A. J., Alese, B. K., Thompson, A. F. B., & Alowolodu, O. D. (2023). Case Studies in AIoMT Applications: A Secure Medical Cyber- Physical System for the Monitoring and Diagnosis of Lassa Fever. In *Handbook of Security and Privacy of AI-Enabled Healthcare Systems and Internet of Medical Things*. https://doi.org/DOI: 10.1201/9781003370321-18

Ahmad, S., Arif, M., Mehfuz, S., Ahmad, J., & Nazim, M. (2025). Deep Learning-based Cloud Security: Innovative Attack Detection and Privacy Focused Key Management. *IEEE Transactions on Computers*. Advance online publication. DOI: 10.1109/TC.2025.3547150

Ahmad, S., Mehfuz, S., Urooj, S., & Alsubaie, N. (2024). Machine learning-based intelligent security framework for secure cloud key management. *Cluster Computing*, *27*(5), 5953–5979. DOI: 10.1007/s10586-024-04288-8

Arbi, A. and Israr, M. 2024. Empowering cyber-physical systems through ai-driven fusion for enhanced health assessment. International Journal of Data informatics and Intelligent Computing, 3(3), pp. 16-23. https://doi.org/DOI: 10.59461/ijdiic.v3i3.127

Augusto, J. G., de Paz, C. C. P., Mendonça, G. G., Moitinho, M. R., Menegatto, L. S., Bolonhezi, D., Salles, M. S. V., & Simili, F. F. (2024). Integrated crop-livestock versus conventional systems: Effects on the chemical and physical characteristics of an Oxisol. *Grass and Forage Science*, *79*(2). Advance online publication. DOI: 10.1111/gfs.12664

Dinesh, R. A., Shanmugam, J., & Biswas, K. (2023). Integration of technology and nanoscience in precision agriculture and farming. In *Contemporary Developments in Agricultural Cyber-Physical Systems*. https://doi.org/DOI: 10.4018/978-1-6684-7879-0.ch008

Gul, H., Al-Obeidat, F., Amin, A., & Moreira, F. (2024). Analyzing complex networks: Extracting key characteristics and measuring structural similarities. *Expert Systems: International Journal of Knowledge Engineering and Neural Networks*, *41*(1), e13470. DOI: 10.1111/exsy.13470

Haleem, A., Javaid, M., Pratap Singh, R., & Suman, R. (2022). Medical 4.0 technologies for healthcare: Features, capabilities, and applications. *Internet of Things and Cyber-Physical Systems*, *2*. Advance online publication. DOI: 10.1016/j.iotcps.2022.04.001

Hamdi, M., Mestiri, S., & Arbi, A. (2024). Artificial intelligence techniques for bankruptcy prediction of tunisian companies: An application of machine learning and deep learning-based models. *Journal of Risk and Financial Management, 17*(4), 132. DOI: 10.3390/jrfm17040132

Hammouch, H., Mohapatra, S., El-Yacoubi, M., Qin, H., Berbia, H., Mader, P., & Chikhaoui, M. (2022). GANSet - Generating annnotated datasets using Generative Adversarial Networks. *Proceedings of the International Conference on Cyber-Physical Social Intelligence, ICCSI 2022*. https://doi.org/DOI: 10.1109/ICCSI55536.2022.9970561

Irshad, M. N., Aslam, M. M., & Silapunt, R. (2025). *Low Complexity Optimized AOR Method for Massive MIMO Signal Detection*. IEEE., DOI: 10.1109/ACCESS.2025.3550272

Jun, Y., Craig, A., Shafik, W., & Sharif, L. (2021). Artificial Intelligence Application in Cybersecurity and Cyberdefense. In *Wireless Communications and Mobile Computing* (Vol. 2021). https://doi.org/DOI: 10.1155/2021/3329581

Kalinaki, K., Shafik, W., Namuwaya, S., & Namuwaya, S. (2024). Perspectives, applications, challenges, and future trends of IoT-based logistics. In *Navigating Cyber Threats and Cybersecurity in the Logistics Industry*. https://doi.org/DOI: 10.4018/979-8-3693-3816-2.ch005

Khalil, U., Uddin, M., Malik, O. A., & Hong, O. W. (2024). A Novel NFT Solution for Assets Digitization and Authentication in Cyber-Physical Systems: Blueprint and Evaluation. *IEEE Open Journal of the Computer Society, 5*. Advance online publication. DOI: 10.1109/OJCS.2024.3378424

Meng, H., Shafik, W., Matinkhah, S. M., & Ahmad, Z. (2020). A 5G Beam Selection Machine Learning Algorithm for Unmanned Aerial Vehicle Applications. *Wireless Communications and Mobile Computing, 2020*. Advance online publication. DOI: 10.1155/2020/1428968

Mohammad, F., Saleem, K., & Al-Muhtadi, J. (2023). Ensemble-Learning-Based Decision Support System for Energy-Theft Detection in Smart-Grid Environment. *Energies, 16*(4). Advance online publication. DOI: 10.3390/en16041907

Mojtaba Matinkhah, S., & Shafik, W. (2019). Smart Grid Empowered by 5G Technology. *2019 Smart Gird Conference. SGC, 2019*. Advance online publication. DOI: 10.1109/SGC49328.2019.9056590

Neghab, H. K., Jamshidi, M. B., & Neghab, H. K. (2022). Digital Twin of a Magnetic Medical Microrobot with Stochastic Model Predictive Controller Boosted by Machine Learning in Cyber-Physical Healthcare Systems. *Information (Switzerland)*, *13*(7). Advance online publication. DOI: 10.3390/info13070321

Okafor, K. C., & Longe, O. M. (2022). ASM-ROBOT: A Cyber-Physical Home Automation Controller with Memristive Reconfigurable State Machine. *International Journal of Advanced Computer Science and Applications*, *13*(1). Advance online publication. DOI: 10.14569/IJACSA.2022.01301103

Pattepu, S., Mukherjee, A., Routray, S., Mukherjee, P., Qi, Y., & Datta, A. (2022). Multi-antenna relay based cyber-physical systems in smart-healthcare NTNs: An explainable AI approach. *Cluster Computing*. Advance online publication. DOI: 10.1007/s10586-022-03632-0

Ray, P. P. (2023). Web3: A comprehensive review on background, technologies, applications, zero-trust architectures, challenges and future directions. In *Internet of Things and Cyber-Physical Systems* (Vol. 3). https://doi.org/DOI: 10.1016/j.iotcps.2023.05.003

Sabir, Z., Arbi, A., Hashem, A. F., & Abdelkawy, M. A. (2023). Morlet wavelet neural network investigations to present the numerical investigations of the prediction differential model. *Mathematics*, *11*(21), 4480. DOI: 10.3390/math11214480

Sabir, Z., Dirani, S., Bou Saleh, S., Mabsout, M. K., & Arbi, A. (2024). A novel radial basis and sigmoid neural network combination to solve the human immunodeficiency virus system in cancer patients. *Mathematics*, *12*(16), 2490. DOI: 10.3390/math12162490

Sabir, Z., Hashem, A. F., Arbi, A., & Abdelkawy, M. A. (2023). Designing a bayesian regularization approach to solve the fractional Layla and Majnun system. *Mathematics*, *11*(17), 3792. DOI: 10.3390/math11173792

Saha, T., Aaraj, N., Ajjarapu, N., & Jha, N. K. (2022). SHARKS: Smart Hacking Approaches for RisK Scanning in Internet-of-Things and Cyber-Physical Systems Based on Machine Learning. *IEEE Transactions on Emerging Topics in Computing*, *10*(2). Advance online publication. DOI: 10.1109/TETC.2021.3050733

Seelaboyina, R., Vadla, S. P. C., Teerthala, S. A., & Pedduri, V. V. (2024). Secure Software Development Life Cycle: An Approach to Reduce the Risks of Cyber Attacks in Cyber Physical Systems and Digital Twins. *Lecture Notes in Electrical Engineering*, *1106*. Advance online publication. DOI: 10.1007/978-981-99-7954-7_15

Shafik, W. (2023). Predicting Future Cybercrime Trends in the Metaverse Era. In *Forecasting cyber crimes in the age of the metaverse* (pp. 78–113). IGI Global., DOI: 10.4018/979-8-3693-0220-0.ch005

Shafik, W. (2024a). Agile Security Strategies. In *Smart and Agile Cybersecurity for IoT and IIoT Environments* (pp. 82–101). IGI Global., DOI: 10.4018/979-8-3693-3451-5.ch004

Shafik, W. (2024b). Artificial Intelligence and Machine Learning with Cyber Ethics for the Future World. In *Future Communication Systems Using Artificial Intelligence, Internet of Things and Data Science* (pp. 110–130). CRC Press., DOI: 10.1201/9781032648309-9

Shafik, W. (2024c). Blockchain's impetus for secure IoT-enabled applications in smart city. In *Big Data and Blockchain Technology for Secure IoT Applications* (pp. 48–71). CRC Press., DOI: 10.1201/9781032663005-4

Shafik, W. (2024d). Data-Driven Future Trends and Innovation in Telemedicine. In *Improving Security, Privacy, and Connectivity Among Telemedicine Platforms* (pp. 93–118). IGI Global. https://doi.org/DOI: 10.4018/979-8-3693-2141-6.ch005

Shafik, W. (2024e). Dissecting the Role of Women in Cybersecurity and Information Technology: A Medical Perspective. In *Next-Generation Cybersecurity: AI, ML, and Blockchain* (pp. 325–350). Springer. https://doi.org/DOI: 10.1007/978-981-97-1249-6_15

Shafik, W. (2024f). IoT-Enabled Secure and Intelligent Smart Healthcare. In *Secure and Intelligent IoT-Enabled Smart Cities* (pp. 308–333). IGI Global., DOI: 10.4018/979-8-3693-2373-1.ch015

Shafik, W. (2024g). The Future of Healthcare: Data-Driven Trends and Innovation. In *Advancing Healthcare through Data-driven Innovations* (pp. 166–185). CRC Press.

Shafik, W. (2025a). Artificial Intelligence-Enabled Cybersecurity and Internet of Things Applications in Smart Cities. In *Building Tomorrow's Smart Cities With 6G Infrastructure Technology* (pp. 301–334). IGI Global Scientific Publishing.

Shafik, W. (2025b). Generative Adversarial Networks: Security, Privacy, and Ethical Considerations. In *Generative Artificial Intelligence (AI) Approaches for Industrial Applications* (pp. 93–117). Springer.

Shafik, W. (2025c). Security, 15 Privacy, and Trust in Fintech. *FinTech and Financial Inclusion: Leveraging Digital Finance for Economic Empowerment and Sustainable Growth*, 216.

Shafik, W., & Kalinaki, K. (2023). Smart city ecosystem: An exploration of requirements, architecture, applications, security, and emerging motivations. In *Handbook of Research on Network-Enabled IoT Applications for Smart City Services*. https://doi.org/DOI: 10.4018/979-8-3693-0744-1.ch005

Shafik, W., Matinkhah, S. M., & Ghasemzadeh, M. (2019). A fast machine learning for 5g beam selection for unmanned aerial vehicle applications. *Journal of Information Systems and Telecommunication*, *7*(4). https://doi.org/https://doi.org/10.7508/jist.2019.04.003

Shafik, W., Mojtaba Matinkhah, S., & Shokoor, F. (2023). Cybersecurity in Unmanned Aerial Vehicles: A Review. *International Journal on Smart Sensing and Intelligent Systems*, *16*(1). Advance online publication. DOI: 10.2478/ijssis-2023-0012

Shafik, W., Tufail, A., Apong, R. A. A. H. M., & Balasubramaniam, S. (2024). Future Directions in Cybersecurity, Digital Forensics and Biometric Systems. In *AI Based Advancements in Biometrics and its Applications* (pp. 238–263). CRC Press., DOI: 10.1201/9781032702377-13

Sheikh, Z. A., & Singh, Y. (2023). Minimizing Cost, Effort, and Implementation Complexity for Adopting Security Requirements in an Agile Development Process for Cyber-Physical Systems. In *Agile Software Development*. Trends, Challenges and Applications., DOI: 10.1002/9781119896838.ch6

Singh, R., Shafik, W., Crowther, D., & Kumar, V. (Eds.). (2024). *Transforming Healthcare Sector Through Artificial Intelligence and Environmental Sustainability* (1st ed., Vol. 1). Springer Nature Singapore., DOI: 10.1007/978-981-97-9555-0

Van Loenhout, R., Ranasinghe, C., Degbelo, A., & Bouali, N. (2022). Physicalizing Sustainable Development Goals Data: An Example with SDG 7 (Affordable and Clean Energy). *Conference on Human Factors in Computing Systems - Proceedings*. https://doi.org/DOI: 10.1145/3491101.3519638

Yan, Y., & Kunhui, Y. (2024). Novel cyber-physical architecture for optimal operation of renewable-based smart city considering false data injection attacks: Digital twin technologies for smart city infrastructure management. *Sustainable Energy Technologies and Assessments*, *65*. Advance online publication. DOI: 10.1016/j.seta.2024.103733

Chapter 7
Federated Learning-Enabled Secure Blockchain-Based Sharing Framework for Vehicle Ad Hoc Network

Sachin Sharma
https://orcid.org/0000-0002-7821-3685
Amity University, Mohali, India

ABSTRACT

In this chapter, federated learning-enabled Secure Blockchain-based Sharing Framework for Vehicle Ad Hoc Networks (VANETs) coordinating federated learning (FL) and blockchain innovation to form a decentralized, privacy-preserving, and secure stage for vehicular communication and information sharing. This inventive system addresses basic challenges in VANETs, such as information protection, security, and real-time collaboration, by empowering vehicles to collaboratively prepare machine learning models locally utilizing their claim information and safely share overhauls through a tamper-resistant blockchain record. Key points of interest incorporate improved believe, versatility, flexibility to assaults, and compliance with protection controls, making it a promising arrangement for applications like collision avoidance, activity optimization, and independent driving bolster. Be that as it may, challenges such as computational complexity, communication inactivity, information heterogeneity, and security vulnerabilities pose critical hurdles to its usage.

DOI: 10.4018/979-8-3373-1832-5.ch007

I. INTRODUCTION

The fast advancement of shrewdly transportation frameworks (ITS) has changed the way vehicles communicate, explore, and connected with their environment. At the heart of this change lies the Vehicle Ad Hoc Network (VANET), a decentralized and energetic communication arrange shaped by vehicles and roadside framework. VANETs empower real-time information trade among vehicles (V2V – vehicle-to-vehicle) and between vehicles and infrastructure (V2I – vehicle-to-infrastructure), encouraging applications such as activity administration, collision evasion, and independent driving. In any case, the expanding complexity and network of VANETs present noteworthy challenges, especially in terms of information protection, security, and productive asset sharing. Conventional centralized approaches to information administration and handling in VANETs regularly drop brief due to idleness, single focuses of disappointment, and defenselessness to cyberattacks. To address these restrictions, a novel framework integrating Federated Learning (FL) and Blockchain innovation has risen as a promising arrangement. This presentation investigates the conceptualization, importance, and operational standards of a Federated Learning-enabled Secure Blockchain-based Sharing System for VANETs, emphasizing its potential to revolutionize secure and proficient information sharing in vehicular systems. VANETs work in a exceedingly energetic environment where vehicles are always moving, shaping brief associations with adjacent hubs. This advertisement hoc nature makes it challenging to guarantee dependable communication and believe among members. Vehicles create gigantic sums of information, counting area arranges, speed, activity conditions, and sensor readings, which are basic for improving street security and activity productivity. Be that as it may, sharing this information with centralized servers raises protection concerns, as delicate data might be uncovered to unauthorized substances or abused by pernicious performing artists. In addition, the heterogeneity of gadgets in VANETs—ranging from high-end independent vehicles to fundamental associated cars—complicates the plan of a uniform data-sharing instrument. Centralized machine learning models, which depend on amassing information in a single area for preparing, worsen these issues by requiring steady information transmission, driving to transmission capacity over-burden and expanded idleness. In this setting, Federated Learning offers a decentralized elective that jam protection whereas empowering collaborative learning over distributed nodes. Federated Learning may be a disseminated machine learning worldview where different gadgets collaboratively prepare a shared demonstrate without trading their raw information (Agarwal et al., 2023). Instead of sending delicate information to a central server, each vehicle in a VANET performs local computations utilizing its possess dataset and offers as it were the show updates (e.g., gradients or weights) with a coordinating substance. These upgrades are aggregated to refine a worldwide show, which is then redistributed to the participating nodes. This approach guarantees that information remains on the gadget, mitigating privacy dangers and diminishing the require for broad information transmission. Within the setting of VANETs, FL can empower vehicles to collectively learn activity designs, anticipate clog, or distinguish peculiarities without compromising person driver data. For occurrence, a gather of vehicles might collaboratively prepare a demonstrate to recognize street dangers based on sensor information, progressing security over the organize without uncovering particular vehicle directions. Whereas Federated Learning addresses security and versatility concerns, it does not intrinsically ensure the security or reliability of the shared show overhauls. Malevolent vehicles may infuse wrong overhauls, driving to a harmed worldwide demonstrate that misguides other members. Furthermore, the need of a verifiable review path in conventional FL executions makes it difficult to ensure responsibility in a decentralized framework like VANETs. This is often where Blockchain innovation complements FL by presenting a secure, straightforward, and tamper-proof system for information and show sharing. Blockchain, initially popularized as the fundamental innovation for cryptocurrencies, may be a conveyed record that records exchanges over different hubs in an permanent way. Each exchange is cryptographically marked, time-stamped, and connected to past sections, guaranteeing that once information is recorded, it cannot be modified without agreement from the organize. In a VANET, Blockchain can serve as a decentralized believe stay, empowering secure capacity and confirmation of FL demonstrate overhauls, as well as encouraging asset sharing among vehicles and foundation. The integration of Blockchain with Unified Learning in VANETs makes a strong sharing system with a few key preferences. To begin with, it guarantees the judgment of show upgrades by recording them on the Blockchain, permitting members to confirm their realness some time recently aggregation (Bhadula et al., 2023). This avoids assaults such as demonstrate harming or information adulteration, which are basic dangers in vehicular systems where security is fundamental. Second, Blockchain empowers a decentralized personality administration framework, where vehicles can confirm themselves without depending on a central specialist, diminishing the chance of single-point disappointments. Third, the system underpins incentivization instruments, such as keen contracts, which can remunerate vehicles for contributing exact information or computational assets to the organize. For case, a vehicle that offers dependable activity upgrades or takes an interest in FL preparing seem gain computerized tokens, cultivating participation within the biological system. The proposed Combined Learning-enabled Secure Blockchain-based Sharing System for VANETs works through a multi-layered engineering. At the base layer, vehicles collect and prepare neighborhood information utilizing onboard sensors and computing units. This information is utilized to prepare neighborhood FL models custom fitted to particular errands, such as activity expectation or peculiarity discovery. The coming about demonstrate upgrades are scrambled and transmitted to a Blockchain organize, where they are approved by a agreement instrument, such as Proof of Stake (PoS) or Practical Byzantine Fault Tolerance (PBFT). These components guarantee that as it were true blue overhauls are recorded, sifting out malevolent or defective commitments. Once approved, the overhauls are totaled into a worldwide demonstrate, which is put away on the Blockchain and made available to all partaking hubs. The upgraded worldwide demonstrate is at that point downloaded by vehicles to refine their neighborhood expectations, making a continuous feedback circle of learning and enhancement (Bhatt et al., 2023). At the same time, the Blockchain layer encourages secure asset sharing, such as transmission capacity, computational control, or real-time activity information, through keen contracts that computerize exchanges and implement believe. One of the essential inspirations for receiving this system is the developing request for secure and productive information sharing in brilliantly transportation frameworks. As autonomous vehicles gotten to be more predominant, they depend intensely on real-time information from encompassing vehicles and foundation to create educated choices. Be that as it may, the need of a standardized, secure sharing instrument limits the versatility of such frameworks. The FL-enabled Blockchain system addresses this crevice by giving a decentralized, privacy-preserving arrangement that scales with the number of members. Unlike traditional VANET approaches that depend on roadside units (RSUs) or cloud servers, this system disperses the computational and capacity stack over the arrange, decreasing idleness and upgrading strength. For occurrence, amid a activity stick, vehicles can collaboratively analyze the circumstance and share reroute suggestions without depending on a removed server, all whereas keeping up information privacy. Another basic angle of this system is its capacity to adjust to the energetic topology of VANETs. Vehicles regularly connect and take off the arrange as they move, making it challenging to preserve steady communication. The decentralized nature of Blockchain guarantees that the framework remains operational indeed in the event that a few nodes disconnect, as the record is duplicated over numerous members. So also, FL's conveyed preparing prepare obliges intermittent network by permitting vehicles to contribute upgrades at whatever point they are inside run of the arrange. This adaptability is especially profitable in urban situations, where tall vehicle thickness and visit flag obstructions complicate conventional communication conventions. In spite of its guarantee, actualizing this system in VANETs postures a few challenges. The computational overhead of running FL calculations and keeping up a Blockchain record on resource-constrained vehicles requires optimization. Lightweight agreement calculations and productive encryption techniques must be created to play down vitality utilization and inactivity. Furthermore, the system must address adaptability issues as the number of vehicles develops, guaranteeing that the Blockchain arrange can handle a high volume of exchanges without compromising execution. Regulatory and ethical considerations too emerge, especially with respect to the ownership and monetization of shared information. Policymakers will need to build up rules to adjust security, security, and financial incentives inside the ecosystem. The Federated Learning-enabled Secure Blockchain-based Sharing System for VANETs speaks to a groundbreaking combination of cutting-edge advances to address the advancing needs of intelligent transportation frameworks (Sharma & Bhadula, 2023). By combining the privacy-preserving capabilities of FL with the security and straightforwardness of Blockchain, this system offers a decentralized, adaptable, and reliable arrangement for information and asset sharing in vehicular systems. It enables vehicles to collaborate on basic assignments like activity optimization and security upgrade whereas defending delicate data and guaranteeing framework keenness. As the appropriation of associated and independent vehicles quickens, this system has the potential to rethink the future of VANETs, clearing the way for more brilliant, more secure, and more productive transportation systems. Future inquire about and advancement endeavors ought to center on optimizing its implementation, tending to adaptability challenges, and cultivating real-world arrangement to open its full potential.

II. LITERATURE SURVEY

Ahmed et al. (2024) addresses the challenges of information security and proficient learning in Vehicular Ad-hoc Networks (VANETs) by proposing a novel system. It coordinating blockchain innovation with federated Q-learning, aiming to form a secure and proficient learning environment. Blockchain guarantees information astuteness and traceability, whereas unified Q-learning empowers collaborative learning without central information sharing, protecting security. The proposed show permits vehicles to memorize ideal methodologies for errands like activity administration or course arranging, leveraging collective insights. This integration improves security against cyber dangers and moves forward arrange proficiency by empowering dispersed and privacy-preserving learning in VANETs. Houda et al. (2024) tackles the challenge of proficient assignment offloading in edge computing situations, especially inside vehicular systems. It presents a support learning-based approach to optimize asset allotment and minimize errand idleness. The proposed framework utilizes a deep Q-network (DQN) to powerfully adjust offloading choices based on real-time arrange conditions. By considering components like communication inactivity, computation assets, and vehicle portability, the framework points to improve the in general execution of edge-based administrations. The think about centers on accomplishing an adjust between minimizing errand completion time and maximizing asset utilization, in this manner progressing the effectiveness of vehicular edge computing. Xia et al. (2024) addresses the challenges of efficient resource management in vehicular edge computing (VEC) situations. It proposes a novel approach utilizing deep reinforcement learning (DRL) to optimize errand offloading and asset allotment. The framework points to minimize latency and maximize asset utilization by powerfully adjusting to fluctuating arrange conditions and vehicle versatility. By utilizing a DRL specialist, the framework learns ideal offloading methodologies based on real-time information, considering factors like communication inactivity, computational assets, and vehicle speed. The investigate centers on accomplishing a adjust between minimizing assignment completion time and maximizing the utilization of edge servers, subsequently upgrading the by and large execution of VEC services. Fu et al. (2024) focuses on optimizing asset allotment in federated learning (FL) for Internet of Vehicles (IoV) situations. It addresses the challenges of energetic arrange conditions and constrained assets by proposing a fortification learning-based approach. The framework points to play down the preparing time and communication overhead whereas guaranteeing demonstrate exactness. By utilizing a deep Q-network (DQN), the framework powerfully chooses taking part vehicles and apportions assets based on their computational capabilities and arrange network. The inquire about considers variables like vehicle portability, communication idleness, and information heterogeneity to improve the proficiency and adequacy of FL in IoV. The objective is to empower collaborative learning without compromising information security. Wang et al. (2022) explores the application of federated learning (FL) in industrial internet of things (IIoT) situations, centering on improving security and proficiency. It proposes a blockchain-enabled FL system to address the challenges of information security and conveyed learning. The integration of blockchain guarantees secure information sharing and demonstrate conglomeration, whereas FL permits for collaborative learning without centralizing touchy information. The system points to progress the exactness of machine learning models whereas keeping up information security and security. By leveraging blockchain's permanence and straightforwardness, the framework mitigates dangers related with information altering and unauthorized get to. The investigate looks for to optimize asset assignment and upgrade the unwavering quality of AI-driven applications in IIoT. Zeydan et al. (2024) addresses the challenge of effective assignment offloading in multi-access edge computing (MEC) situations, especially inside vehicular systems. It proposes a support learning-based approach to optimize offloading choices, pointing to play down inactivity and vitality utilization. The framework powerfully adjusts to fluctuating arrange conditions and vehicle versatility by utilizing a deep Q-network (DQN). This permits for intelligent asset assignment and errand conveyance among edge servers. The research centers on adjusting computational stack and communication overhead whereas considering components like vehicle speed, network congestion, and server capacity. The objective is to improve the by and large execution and unwavering quality of MEC-based vehicular administrations. Chen et al. (2024) handles the challenge of optimizing asset assignment and assignment offloading in vehicular edge computing (VEC) systems. It proposes a crossover approach combining reinforcement learning (RL) and diversion hypothesis to upgrade decision-making. The framework points to minimize latency and vitality utilization by intelligently distributing assignments among edge servers. By leveraging RL, the framework learns ideal offloading procedures based on energetic arrange conditions. Amusement hypothesis empowers the framework to handle competitive intelligent between vehicles and edge servers. The inquire about centers on accomplishing a adjust between minimizing errand completion time and maximizing asset utilization, in this manner moving forward the effectiveness and unwavering quality of VEC administrations. Peelam et al. (2024) addresses the basic issue of secure and productive information conglomeration in federated learning (FL) for Internet of Vehicles (IoV) situations. It proposes a blockchain-enabled FL system to improve protection and security whereas optimizing asset utilization. The investigate centers on mitigating dangers like information altering and demonstrate harming through blockchain's permanent record. By coordination smart contracts, the framework guarantees secure demonstrate accumulation and transparent data sharing. The system points to minimize communication overhead and idleness by optimizing vehicle determination and asset assignment. The consider emphasizes keeping up show exactness and information keenness in energetic IoV systems, encouraging dependable collaborative learning. Fan and Xue (2024) investigates the application of federated learning (FL) in vehicular edge computing (VEC) to upgrade intelligent transportation frameworks. It addresses the challenges of information security and dispersed learning by proposing a secure and productive FL system. The framework points to minimize communication overhead and inactivity whereas maximizing show exactness. By leveraging edge servers for nearby show preparing and secure accumulation, the system empowers collaborative learning without central information sharing. The investigate centers on optimizing asset assignment and vehicle choice to progress the productivity of FL in energetic VEC situations. The objective is to encourage real-time information examination and decision-making for brilliantly vehicular applications.

III. FEDERATED LEARNING

Federated learning, a decentralized approach to machine learning, has risen as a transformative paradigm in artificial intelligence, empowering collaborative demonstrate preparing over different devices or substances without the need to centralize delicate information. Whereas the term "federated learning" was formally coined and popularized within the mid-2010s by analysts at Google, its conceptual roots and empowering innovations follow back to prior improvements in dispersed computing, privacy-preserving strategies, and machine learning that started taking shape around the year 2000. To completely appreciate the advancement of federated learning, it's worth investigating its historical setting, foundational thoughts, and the mechanical progressions that cleared the way for its rise, as well as its ensuing refinements and applications that have unfurled over the past two decades. The story of federated learning starts with the broader advancement of disseminated frameworks and machine learning within the late 1990s and early 2000s. Amid this period, the fast development of the web and the proliferation of individual computers spurred interest in disseminated computing—systems where computation is performed over different organized machines instead of a single centralized server. By 2000, concepts like lattice computing and peer-to-peer systems were picking up footing, exemplified by ventures such as SETI@home, which tackled idle computing control from volunteers' machines to analyze radio signals for signs of extraterrestrial life. These early endeavors illustrated the achievability of planning computation over decentralized hubs, a rule that would later underpin unified learning. At the same time, machine learning was developing as a field, with calculations like support vector machines and neural systems getting to be more advanced. In any case, preparing such models regularly required expansive, centralized datasets, which posed challenges as information security concerns started to develop within the wake of extending digital environments. The early 2000s too saw the rise of versatile computing, with smartphones and other convenient gadgets becoming progressively predominant. By 2007, the launch of the iPhone marked a turning point, introducing in a time of omnipresent, data-generating gadgets. This move increased the require for methods that may use information from these gadgets without compromising user privacy. Around the same time, cryptography and privacy-preserving computation were progressing, laying basic foundation for combined learning. Techniques like secure multi-party computation (SMPC), pioneered within the 1980s but refined within the 2000s, permitted numerous parties to together compute a work over their private inputs without revealing them. Similarly, differential privacy, formalized by Cynthia Dwork and colleagues in 2006, given a scientific system for guaranteeing that information investigation preserved individual privacy. These improvements were not specifically tied to unified learning at the time, but they addressed the same core challenge:

how to extricate esteem from dispersed information whereas safeguarding confidentiality. By the mid-2000s, the crossing point of disseminated frameworks and machine learning was getting to be more clear. Analysts started investigating ways to prepare models over numerous servers or information centers, especially in spaces where information might not be effortlessly centralized due to lawful, calculated, or security imperatives. For occurrence, in 2009, the concept of "parallelized stochastic gradient descent" (SGD) gained consideration as a strategy to convey the preparing of large-scale machine learning models over different machines. Systems like MapReduce, presented by Google in 2004, and its open-source partner Hadoop, released in 2006, empowered versatile information handling over clusters of computers. These instruments were essentially outlined for enormous information analytics instead of privacy-focused learning, but they illustrated that iterative optimization—a key component of machine learning—could be viably conveyed. This set the organize for afterward advancements that would adjust such methods to decentralized, privacy-sensitive situations. The formal presentation of combined learning as a particular concept is credited to a 2016 paper by Google analysts H. Brendan McMahan, Eider Moore, Daniel Ramage, and Blaise Agüera y Arcas, titled "Communication-Efficient Learning of Deep Networks from Decentralized Data." In this work, they proposed a system where a central demonstrate is prepared by aggregating upgrades from numerous gadgets (e.g., smartphones) that perform local computations on their private information. Instead of sending crude information to a central server, each device computes a local show upgrade (e.g., gradient changes) and sends as it were that update to the server, which then totals these commitments to refine a global model. This approach, initially dubbed "federated averaging," was persuaded by viable challenges at Google, such as progressing prescient consoles and voice recognition on mobile devices without uploading users' typing or speech information. Whereas 2016 marks the official debut of unified learning, the thoughts it built upon—distributed optimization, security conservation, and portable computing—had been stewing since the early 2000s. Looking back to 2000 and the years promptly taking after, one can recognize a few antecedents that indirectly affected unified learning's advancement. The rise of cloud computing within the mid-2000s, with stages like Amazon Web Services (AWS) launching in 2006, highlighted the potential of versatile, disseminated foundation, though it at first favored centralized information capacity. In the interim, in academia, analysts were handling issues associated to unified learning beneath diverse names. For example, "distributed machine learning" and "collaborative learning" were terms utilized to portray endeavors to prepare models over different information sources. A outstanding 2007 paper by Stephen Boyd and colleagues on "Distributed Optimization and Statistical Learning via the Alternating Direction Method of Multipliers" (ADMM) given a numerical system for tackling optimization issues over conveyed datasets, a strategy that offers likenesses with combined learning's iterative overhauls. These early investigations needed the express protection center of combined learning but contributed to the hypothetical toolkit that would later be adjusted. The period from 2010 to 2015 was a transitional stage where the innovative and societal conditions for unified learning aged. The blast of enormous information, driven by social media, e-commerce, and the Internet of Things (IoT), underscored the restrictions of centralized preparing. At the same time, high-profile information breaches and developing administrative scrutiny—such as the European Union's General Data Protection Regulation (GDPR), proposed in 2012 and ordered in 2018—intensified the request for privacy-preserving solutions. Mobile devices, presently prepared with effective processors and sensors, became able of performing significant on-device computation. By 2015, companies like Apple were as of now testing with on-device machine learning for highlights like facial acknowledgment, indicating at the potential for localized preparing. These patterns focalized to form a rich environment for unified learning's development in 2016, in spite of the fact that the foundation had been laid over the going before decade and a half. Since its formal presentation, federated learning has advanced quickly, building on the innovative establishments set up since 2000. The original federated averaging algorithm has been refined to address challenges like non-iid (non-independent and identically distributed) information, where neighborhood datasets differ significantly over devices. Analysts have coordinates differential protection into combined learning conventions, as seen in Google's 2017 follow-up work, guaranteeing more grounded ensures against information spillage. Cryptographic procedures like homomorphic encryption, which permits computation on encrypted information, have too been incorporated to upgrade security, though they stay computationally costly. By 2020, federated learning had extended past mobile gadgets to applications in healthcare, finance, and independent frameworks. For illustration, healing centers have utilized it to collaboratively prepare symptomatic models on quiet information without sharing touchy records, a utilize case that echoes the security goals of the early 2000s. The chronicled direction of combined learning reflects a broader move in computing from centralized to decentralized standards, a development that started gaining force around 2000. The dot-com boom of the late 1990s and early 2000s fueled speculation in organized advances, whereas the consequent rise of portable and IoT gadgets decentralized information era. Protection embarrassments, such as the 2013 Snowden spills uncovering mass observation, increased open mindfulness of information dangers, by implication quickening intrigued in procedures like combined learning. In the mean time, progresses in hardware—GPUs, TPUs, and edge computing—made nearby training feasible, reducing dependence on capable central servers. By 2025, federated learning has become a foundation of AI, bolstered by an environment of apparatuses like TensorFlow Unified (released in 2019) and PySyft, which risen from the open-source community. In hindsight, combined learning's history since 2000 could be a tapestry woven from strings of conveyed frameworks, security research, and machine learning development. Its forerunners within the early 2000s—grid computing, secure computation, and dispersed optimization—provided the specialized platform, whereas societal shifts toward security and decentralization provided the inspiration. From its formalization in 2016 to its broad appropriation by 2025, combined learning has bridged the gap between the guarantee of AI and the basic of information sway. As information proceeds to multiply over billions of gadgets, and as regulations tighten, unified learning stands as a confirmation to how thoughts brooded over decades can meet to address the challenges of a associated world, advertising a show for collaboration that's as dispersed as the frameworks it looks for to upgrade.

IV. BLOCKCHAIN

Blockchain innovation, a decentralized and secure strategy for recording exchanges and information, has revolutionized businesses extending from fund to supply chain administration since its initiation in 2008. Often depicted as a distributed record, blockchain empowers numerous parties to preserve a shared, tamper-resistant record without depending on a central specialist, making it a cornerstone of believe within the computerized age. Whereas it picked up broad acknowledgment as the spine of Bitcoin, its applications amplify distant past cryptocurrencies, including keen contracts, personality confirmation, and indeed voting frameworks. The travel of blockchain—from a theoretical concept established in decades of cryptographic investigate to a transformative device by 2025—reflects a mix of advancement, adjustment, and challenges. To get a handle on its significance, one must investigate its beginnings, specialized establishments, advancement, utilize cases, impediments, and the broader affect it proceeds to have on society and technology (Sharma, Tyagi, et al., 2023). The story of blockchain starts long some time recently its formal make a big appearance, with foundational ideas developing from cryptography and dispersed frameworks within the late 20th century. By the 1980s, analysts like David Chaum were spearheading concepts such as computerized cash and dazzle marks, which pointed to secure exchanges without mediators. In 1991, Stuart Haber and W. Scott Stornetta presented a strategy for timestamping advanced archives utilizing cryptographic hashing, guaranteeing their astuteness and avoiding tampering—a forerunner to blockchain's center component. These early endeavors tended to the issue of believe in computerized intelligent, but they needed a practical way to achieve consensus over a decentralized organize. The missing piece arrived in 2008 when an anonymous figure or group, under the pseudonym Satoshi Nakamoto, distributed the Bitcoin whitepaper. Nakamoto combined hashing, timestamps, and a novel agreement component called proof-of-work to form the primary blockchain, a open record for recording Bitcoin exchanges. Propelled in January 2009, Bitcoin illustrated that a decentralized framework might work safely and reliably, sparking a mechanical insurgency. At its pith, blockchain may be a chain of pieces, where each square contains a list of exchanges or information, connected to the past square through a cryptographic hash. This structure guarantees permanence altering a single block would require recalculating the hashes of all consequent squares, a computationally infeasible assignment in expansive systems. Decentralization is accomplished by disseminating the record over various nodes—computers that keep up indistinguishable duplicates and approve unused sections. Agreement components, like proof-of-work or its successor proof-of-stake, guarantee understanding on the ledger's state without a central administrator. In Bitcoin's case, miners compete to solve complex scientific confuses to include squares, winning rewards within the handle. This plan dispenses with mediators, diminishes the hazard of single-point disappointments, and enhances transparency, as anybody can review the open record. By 2010, Bitcoin's blockchain was demonstrating its versatility, taking care of thousands of exchanges whereas standing up to assaults, laying the foundation for broader experimentation. The potential of blockchain beyond cryptocurrency became evident within the early 2010s, catalyzed by the advancement of Ethereum in 2015. Proposed by Vitalik Buterin in 2013 and propelled two a long time afterward, Ethereum presented keen contracts—self-executing understandings coded onto the blockchain that consequently implement terms when conditions are met. This advancement extended blockchain's scope from a value-based record to a programmable stage, empowering applications like decentralized finance (DeFi), where clients loan, borrow, or exchange resources without banks, and non-fungible tokens (NFTs), which certify possession of one of a kind advanced things. By 2016, businesses started investigating blockchain for supply chain following, with companies like IBM partnering with firms such as Walmart to follow goods from cultivate to rack, guaranteeing genuineness and diminishing extortion. In the interim, governments tried blockchain for arrive registries and voting, drawn by its guarantee of transparency and security. This period marked blockchain's move from a specialty test to a flexible innovation with real-world affect. The advancement of blockchain has been molded by both specialized headways and commonsense challenges. Early blockchains like Bitcoin's were moderate and energy-intensive, with proof-of-work expending endless sums of electricity—by 2021, Bitcoin's yearly vitality utilize rivaled that of small countries (Rajvanshi & Sharma, 2023). This spurred the development of options like proof-of-stake, embraced by Ethereum in 2022, which chooses validators based on their stake within the organize, slicing vitality utilization by over 99%. Versatility moreover developed as a jump Bitcoin forms almost 7 exchanges per moment, compared to Visa's thousands. Arrangements just like the Lightning Arrange, a second-layer convention for Bitcoin, and sharding, executed in Ethereum 2.0, point to boost throughput by dealing with exchanges off-chain or in parallel. Security concerns provoked advancements like zero-knowledge proofs, utilized in blockchains such as Zcash, permitting exchanges to be confirmed without uncovering points of interest. By 2025, these refinements have made blockchain more effective, in spite of the fact that trade-offs between decentralization, security, and speed stay a central wrangle about. Blockchain's applications have multiplied over divisions, driven by its capacity to cultivate believe in trustless situations. In back, past Bitcoin and Ethereum, stablecoins like Tie and USD Coin, pegged to fiat monetary standards, have encouraged cross-border installments and settlements, bypassing conventional keeping money delays. DeFi stages, overseeing billions in resources by 2025, offer decentralized choices to credits and protections, in spite of the fact that they've confronted hacks and administrative examination. In supply chains, blockchain guarantees provenance—Walmart's framework, for occasion, tracks pork from Chinese farms in seconds, a prepare that once took days (Sharma, Tyagi, et al., 2024). Healthcare has embraced blockchain to secure quiet records, permitting healing centers to share information without compromising protection, as seen in pilots like Estonia's e-health framework. Governments, as well, have embraced it:

Dubai aims to run all exchanges on blockchain by 2030, whereas Sweden tests it for property titles. Indeed imaginative businesses have been changed, with NFTs empowering craftsmen to monetize advanced works, in spite of the fact that their theoretical boom and bust cycles have started contention. In spite of its guarantee, blockchain faces noteworthy confinements that mood its appropriation. Vitality utilization, indeed post-proof-of-stake, remains a concern for littler systems, and adaptability arrangements are still developing. Administrative vulnerability looms large—governments hook with how to classify cryptocurrencies and shrewd contracts, with bans in places like China differentiating with grasp in El Salvador, which embraced Bitcoin as legitimate delicate in 2021. Security vulnerabilities, such as keen contract bugs, have driven to misfortunes worth billions, as seen within the 2016 DAO hack on Ethereum. Selection also pivots on client instruction and framework numerous need the specialized know-how or access to take part. Besides, blockchain's straightforwardness can clash with protection needs, requiring half breed approaches like permissioned blockchains, utilized by ventures like Hyperledger, which limit get to but give up a few decentralization. These challenges highlight that blockchain isn't a nostrum but a instrument whose esteem depends on setting. By 2025, blockchain's affect is verifiable, however its travel reflects a innovation still in flux. Its roots in cryptography and dispersed frameworks, crystallized by Nakamoto's 2008 vision, have developed into a sprawling environment of open, private, and crossover systems. The rise of Web3—a decentralized web fueled by blockchain—promises to reshape how we associated online, in spite of the fact that pundits contend it's overhyped. Financially, it has stamped tycoons by means of crypto booms whereas uncovering dangers in unregulated markets. Socially, it engages people by cutting out agents, however concentrates control among mineworkers, validators, or designers. Environmentally, it has moved from an vitality guzzler to a more feasible demonstrate, in spite of the fact that its impression waits. Politically, it challenges centralized control, provoking both development and resistance from states. Blockchain's history since 2008 is a confirmation to its troublesome potential, built on decades of earlier work, but its future pivots on adjusting vision with practicality. Looking back, blockchain's improvement mirrors broader patterns in innovation and society since the late 20th century. The internet's development within the 1990s set the arrange for decentralized frameworks, whereas the 2008 financial emergency fueled doubt in educate, birthing Bitcoin. The 2010s saw experimentation and buildup, with Ethereum and others broadening the canvas. By the 2020s, development brought refinement and authenticity, as businesses coordinates blockchain into practical workflows. Its capacity to secure information, computerize forms, and decentralize control reverberates with a world hooking with security embarrassments, globalization, and advanced change (Sharma et al., 2023). However, its complexity and trade-offs guarantee it remains a polarizing force—celebrated as a emancipator by a few, expelled as wasteful by others.

V. VEHICLE AD HOC NETWORK

Vehicle Ad Hoc Networks (VANETs) speak to an energetic and transformative communication system outlined to empower vehicles to connected with one another and their encompassing foundation in genuine time, cultivating more secure, more productive, and more astute transportation frameworks. Developing from the broader field of mobile ad hoc networks (MANETs), VANETs are characterized by their decentralized, self-organizing nature, where vehicles act as hubs that transmit information wirelessly without depending on fixed framework. Since their conceptual beginning within the early 2000s, VANETs have advanced into a basic component of intelligent transportation systems (ITS), driven by headways in remote communication, sensor innovation, and the developing request for street security and activity optimization. By encouraging vehicle-to-vehicle (V2V) and vehicle-to-infrastructure (V2I) communication, VANETs guarantee to diminish mishaps, lighten blockage, and clear the way for independent driving. To completely appreciate their importance, one must dig into their roots, specialized underpinnings, applications, challenges, and progressing advancements as of 2025, reflecting a travel formed by both advancement and real-world complexities. The roots of VANETs follow back to the late 1990s and early 2000s, when the quick multiplication of remote innovations and the expanding complexity of vehicular activity impelled intrigued in organized transportation arrangements. Portable advertisement hoc systems, which permit gadgets to communicate specifically in a peer-to-peer mold without centralized control, given the beginning motivation. By 2000, analysts started adjusting MANET standards to the interesting setting of vehicles, recognizing that cars, not at all like inactive hubs, move at tall speeds and take after unsurprising street designs. The assignment of the 5.9 GHz range for Dedicated Short-Range Communications (DSRC) by the U.S. Government Communications Commission in 1999 stamped a urgent minute, giving a standardized recurrence band for vehicular communication. Early tests, such as the European Union's FleetNet extend in 2001, investigated how vehicles might share information like speed or position to improve security. These endeavors laid the basis for VANETs, which picked up formal footing around 2004 when the IEEE started creating the 802.11p standard, fitting Wi-Fi for vehicular situations. This period reflected a developing mindfulness that interfacing vehicles may address squeezing issues just like the thousands of yearly street fatalities. At its center, a VANET works as a energetic organize where vehicles prepared with onboard units (OBUs) communicate wirelessly utilizing conventions like DSRC or, more as of late, Cellular Vehicle-to-Everything (C-V2X). Each vehicle acts as a hub, able of sending, accepting, and handing-off messages—such as notices approximately sudden braking or street hazards—to adjacent vehicles inside a run of 300 to 1,000 meters. Roadside units (RSUs), introduced along interstates or at convergences, complement this by giving V2I network, transferring activity overhauls or planning signals. The network's advertisement hoc nature implies it shapes and dissolves spontaneously as vehicles move, requiring strong steering conventions to handle quick topology changes. Information bundles bounce from one vehicle to another, guaranteeing data comes to its goal indeed without coordinate line-of-sight. By 2010, VANETs were being tried in recreations and small-scale pilots, illustrating their potential to broadcast real-time cautions and optimize activity stream, in spite of the fact that real-world arrangement slacked due to specialized and calculated obstacles. The advancement of VANETs has been impelled by both mechanical headways and the critical require for more secure streets. The early 2010s saw noteworthy advance as DSRC developed, with trials just like the Security Pilot Model Deployment in Michigan (2012) including thousands of vehicles trading information to anticipate collisions. Concurrently, the rise of 4G and afterward 5G systems presented C-V2X, championed by the 3GPP in 2017, which leverages cellular foundation for more prominent run and unwavering quality compared to DSRC's localized approach. This started a wrangle about over guidelines, with the U.S. mostly reallocating the 5.9 GHz band to Wi-Fi in 2020, whereas Europe and China inclined toward C-V2X. Sensor fusion—integrating VANETs with radar, LIDAR, and cameras—further improved their capabilities, empowering vehicles to share wealthier information like path changes or person on foot location. By 2025, VANETs have ended up fundamentally to semi-autonomous frameworks, with companies like Tesla and Waymo utilizing them to facilitate armadas, in spite of the fact that full independence remains a work in advance due to administrative and specialized obstructions. VANETs offer a wide cluster of applications that address real-world transportation challenges. Security is their essential driver V2V communication can caution drivers of imminent collisions, such as when a car ahead brakes all of a sudden, decreasing rear-end crashes, which account for about a third of U.S. mishaps. Intersection management benefits from V2I, where activity lights alter powerfully based on vehicle thickness, cutting delays and emanations. Platooning—where trucks travel in tight escorts to decrease drag—relies on VANETs for exact coordination, boosting fuel effectiveness, as seen in European trials like SARTRE (2012). Activity optimization expands to rerouting vehicles around blockage, whereas crisis administrations utilize VANETs to clear ways for ambulances. Beyond functionality, VANETs support infotainment, delivering upgrades like parking accessibility. By 2025, these utilize cases are progressively unmistakable, with cities like Singapore coordination VANETs into savvy lattices, in spite of the fact that far reaching appropriation changes by locale due to foundation costs. In spite of their guarantee, VANETs confront critical challenges that have moderated their rollout. The tall versatility of vehicles makes unsteady associations, requiring conventions like geographic steering to adjust to consistent arrange changes—an assignment complicated by urban canyons or rustic dead zones. Security may be a basic concern malicious actors seem spoof messages, activating false notices or disturbing activity. Encryption and verification, such as public-key framework, moderate this, but include inactivity. Protection too looms large—drivers may stand up to frameworks that track their area, inciting anonymization methods like brief IDs. Interoperability postures another jump, as DSRC and C-V2X compete, dividing benchmarks. Cost remains a boundary preparing millions of vehicles and streets with OBUs and RSUs requests gigantic speculation, frequently dependent on government bolster. By 2025, these issues endure, in spite of the fact that half breed approaches mixing cellular and advertisement hoc systems appear guarantee in adjusting versatility and versatility. The advancement of VANETs reflects broader patterns in innovation and society since the early 2000s. The rise of the Web of Things (IoT) and shrewd cities fueled request for associated foundation, whereas remote advancements—from Wi-Fi to 5G—provided the transmission capacity and moo inactivity VANETs require. Open concern over street security, with global activity deaths surpassing 1.3 million every year, drove venture, as did natural weights to diminish outflows through proficient activity stream. The thrust for independent vehicles, quickening within the 2020s, made VANETs crucial, as self-driving cars require real-time information from peers to explore complex scenarios. Pilot projects, like Japan's ITS Spot system (2011) and Europe's C-ROADS (2016), have transitioned to operational systems in a few locales, in spite of the fact that full integration lags in less-developed zones due to subsidizing and approach holes. Their specialized foundation—built on decades of remote and organizing research—has demonstrated strong in controlled settings, with cities like Seoul and Stockholm displaying decreased mishaps and smoother activity. C-V2X has picked up footing, leveraging 5G's ubiquity, in spite of the fact that DSRC endures in bequest frameworks. Integration with fake insights upgrades decision-making, as vehicles analyze shared information to foresee dangers. However, challenges like standardization, cybersecurity, and impartial arrangement stay uncertain. Financially, VANETs guarantee billions in investment funds from less crashes and lower fuel utilize, but forthright costs prevent far reaching selection exterior well off countries. Socially, they move driving from an person to a collective act, raising questions approximately independence and reconnaissance. Ecologically, they adjust with green objectives, in spite of the fact that the vitality requests of arrange foundation mood picks up. VANETs' travel since the early 2000s mirrors the advancement of a hyper-connected world. The 1999 DSRC assignment started a vision of talking cars, refined through the 2010s as equipment and program caught up. The 2020s brought merging with independent and keen city motivation, situating VANETs as a linchpin of future versatility. Their capacity to spare lives, cut clog, and empower computerization resounds with a society hooking with urbanization and climate alter. However, their victory pivots on overcoming specialized silos, securing open believe, and bridging computerized partitions. As of 2025, VANETs are not a cutting edge concept but a viable, in the event that unevenly actualized, reality—testament to their potential and the tireless obstacles of turning advancement into widespread advantage.

VI. ADVANTAGES

A Federated Learning-enabled Secure Blockchain-based Sharing System for Vehicle Ad Hoc Networks (VANETs) combines the qualities of federated learning (FL), blockchain innovation, and VANETs to make a strong, privacy-preserving, and productive framework for vehicular communication and information sharing. This inventive integration addresses basic challenges in advanced transportation frameworks, such as information security, security, versatility, and real-time coordination, whereas leveraging the decentralized nature of both FL and blockchain to upgrade the usefulness of VANETs (Bhatt & Sharma, 2024). Below, I'll layout the key preferences of this system in a point by point however brief way, highlighting how it changes vehicular systems into a more secure, more astute, and more reliable environment. One of the essential focal points of this system is its capacity to guarantee information security and security in a profoundly energetic and disseminated environment. Figure 1 outlines the advantages.

Figure 1. Advantages

VANETs include vehicles continuously generating and sharing sensitive data—such as area, speed, and activity conditions—with other vehicles and foundation. Conventional centralized frameworks require uploading this information to a server, risking presentation to breaches or unauthorized get to. Federated learning mitigates this by permitting vehicles to prepare machine learning models locally on their claim information, sharing only model updates (e.g., gradients or parameters) instead of raw data. Blockchain complements this by giving a tamper-resistant, decentralized record to record these updates safely. Utilizing cryptographic methods like hashing and computerized marks, blockchain guarantees that information trades are authentic and unaltered, securing against pernicious on-screen characters who might parody messages or infuse untrue notices in a VANET. Another critical advantage is improved believe and transparency among members within the organize. VANETs frequently include untrusted entities—vehicles from diverse producers, drivers, or jurisdictions—that must collaborate without a central specialist. Blockchain's unchanging and transparent nature cultivates believe by logging all exchanges and show overhauls in a verifiable way, available to all nodes. This guarantees that no single party can control the framework undetected. For occasion, in case a vehicle contributes to a shared activity expectation demonstrate through FL, blockchain records its commitment, anticipating debate and empowering reasonable responsibility. This believe is pivotal for applications like agreeable collision avoidance, where vehicles must depend on exact, untampered information from peers. The system moreover offers progressed versatility and effectiveness, tending to a key restriction of conventional VANETs. As the number of associated vehicles grows—projected to reach millions universally by 2025—centralized frameworks battle with transfer speed and handling requests. Combined learning conveys computation over vehicles, diminishing the load on any single server by performing preparing locally on onboard units (OBUs). Blockchain, whereas computationally seriously in open systems like Bitcoin, can be optimized with lightweight agreement components (e.g., Practical Byzantine Fault Tolerance or proof-of-stake) tailored for VANETs, guaranteeing quick approval of upgrades. This decentralized approach scales consistently with organize measure, empowering real-time information sharing and demonstrate upgrades indeed in dense urban settings or sprawling interstates. A assist advantage is strength to disappointments and assaults, improving the unwavering quality of VANETs. Centralized frameworks are vulnerable to single-point failures—if a server goes down, the whole arrange may waver. In differentiate, the FL-blockchain system works without a central center vehicles collaboratively keep up the demonstrate and record over distributed nodes. Blockchain's redundancy—every node holds a duplicate of the ledger—ensures that information remains available indeed on the off chance that a few vehicles disengage or breakdown. Furthermore, FL's neighborhood preparing decreases the assault surface by keeping touchy information on-device, whereas blockchain's cryptographic security foils altering endeavors, such as wrong activity cautions, making the framework strong against cyberattacks like Sybil or Denial-of-Service assaults common in vehicular systems. The system too empowers real-time versatility and insights, basic for energetic VANET applications. Unified learning permits the arrange to ceaselessly move forward shared models—such as those foreseeing activity designs, recognizing risks, or optimizing platooning—without holding up for centralized retraining. Vehicles prepare nearby information (e.g., road conditions or braking events) and contribute to a global demonstrate, which is amassed and redistributed by means of blockchain. This guarantees that the framework adjusts rapidly to changing situations, like sudden climate shifts or mishaps, conveying up-to-date bits of knowledge to all members. For case, a vehicle identifying dark ice may upgrade a danger show locally, share it safely by means of blockchain, and alarm others right away, improving security over the arrange. Another key advantage is administrative compliance and information sway, progressively imperative as protection laws fix universally. Controls just like the GDPR order strict control over individual information, which VANETs must explore given their dependence on area and behavioral data. Unified learning adjusts with these rules by keeping information on-device, dodging centralized capacity that may damage compliance. Blockchain includes an auditable path, demonstrating that information dealing with follows to lawful benchmarks, which is basic for cross-border travel where purviews contrast. This makes the system engaging to governments and producers looking for to convey VANETs without lawful dangers, cultivating broader selection. The integration moreover underpins motivation instruments and collaboration, empowering interest within the organize. Blockchain's smart contract functionality—self-executing understandings coded onto the ledger—can remunerate vehicles for contributing high-quality demonstrate upgrades or sharing basic information, such as mishap reports. For occasion, a vehicle that progresses a traffic stream show through FL may win tokens, recorded straightforwardly on the blockchain, spurring drivers or armada administrators to engage effectively. This gamification reinforces the environment, guaranteeing adequate information for vigorous models whereas keeping up decency, a challenge in conventional VANETs where cooperation is frequently intentional and uneven. Moreover, the system diminishes communication overhead, a tireless issue in VANETs due to their tall versatility and restricted transmission capacity. Unified learning minimizes information exchange by sending compact demonstrate upgrades instead of huge datasets, protecting transfer speed for critical messages like collision notices. Blockchain optimizes this encourage by prioritizing basic exchanges (e.g., model aggregations) and utilizing effective agreement custom-made to VANETs' needs, unlike the resource-heavy mining of open blockchains. This effectiveness is imperative in thick activity scenarios where quick, solid communication can mean the difference between security and chaos. At long last, the system lays a foundation for future-proofing VANETs, especially within the time of independent driving. Self-driving cars depend on real-time, dependable information from their environment, which this framework conveys through secure, decentralized learning and sharing. Combined learning empowers nonstop enhancement of independent calculations over armadas without compromising exclusive information, whereas blockchain guarantees the keenness of shared inputs like maps or sensor readings. As of 2025, with independent vehicles progressively common, this system positions VANETs to back next-generation versatility, coordination consistently with smart cities and IoT biological systems. Unified Learning-enabled Secure Blockchain-based Sharing System for VANETs offers a capable cooperative energy of security, security, adaptability, and flexibility. It ensures touchy information whereas cultivating believe, scales proficiently with developing systems, stands up to disappointments and assaults, and conveys real-time intelligence—all whereas complying with directions and incentivizing collaboration. By decreasing overhead and planning for independent prospects, it changes VANETs into a flexible, cleverly spine for present-day transportation.

VII. CHALLENGES

A Federated Learning-enabled Secure Blockchain-based Sharing System for Vehicle Ad Hoc Networks (VANETs) offers critical points of interest, but its execution comes with a have of challenges that stem from the complexities of coordination federated learning (FL), blockchain, and VANETs. These challenges span specialized, operational, security, and administrative spaces, reflecting the energetic and dispersed nature of vehicular systems as well as the computational and believe prerequisites of the combined advances. One of the preeminent challenges is computational complexity and asset limitations. Vehicles in VANETs, prepared with onboard units (OBUs), have restricted preparing control, memory, and battery capacity compared to conventional servers. Unified learning requires neighborhood preparing of machine learning models—such as those for activity forecast or risk detection—which can be computationally seriously, particularly for deep learning calculations (Sharma et al., 2024). Blockchain includes assist overhead, as keeping up a disseminated record and executing agreement components (e.g., proof-of-stake or Byzantine Fault Tolerance) requests extra assets. In a high-mobility environment where vehicles must too handle real-time assignments like route or communication, this double burden can strain equipment, driving to delays or decreased interest, especially in more seasoned or less-equipped vehicles. Another significant hurdle is communication overhead and idleness. VANETs depend on remote conventions like DSRC or C-V2X, which confront transmission capacity restrictions and discontinuous network due to vehicle development, urban impediments, or rustic dead zones. Unified learning requires visit trades of demonstrate upgrades between vehicles and a central aggregator (or peers in a fully decentralized setup), whereas blockchain requires broadcasting exchanges and achieving agreement across hubs (Badhani & Sharma, 2023). In thick activity scenarios, this could congest the organize, delaying basic updates—like collision warnings—that request moo inactivity. Adjusting the require for real-time execution with the data-intensive nature of FL and blockchain remains a diligent challenge, particularly as organize estimate scales to millions of vehicles. The heterogeneity of information and gadgets postures a assist complication. In VANETs, vehicles create non-iid (non-independent and indistinguishably disseminated) information due to assorted driving designs, street conditions, and sensor capabilities. For illustration, a truck on a interstate produces diverse information than a car in a city, complicating FL's capacity to total a coherent global demonstrate. Device heterogeneity—varying computational control, program forms, or producer standards—exacerbates this, as weaker hubs may battle to prepare models viably or match up with the blockchain. This will lead to show float, where the worldwide show falls flat to speak to all members precisely, undermining applications like agreeable activity administration or platooning. Security and security dangers, in spite of the framework's defensive plan, stay a basic challenge. Unified learning decreases crude information sharing, but show upgrades can still spill delicate data through deduction assaults, where foes recreate private information from angles. Blockchain's straightforwardness, whereas cultivating believe, can uncover exchange metadata (e.g., vehicle IDs or timestamps), gambling driver protection unless vigorous anonymization is connected. Additionally, VANETs are prime targets for cyberattacks—malicious hubs seem infuse untrue demonstrate overhauls (data poisoning) or alter with blockchain records in the event that agreement is compromised. Securing shrewd contracts, which might oversee motivations, includes another layer of helplessness, as bugs might be misused, reverberating the 2016 DAO hack on Ethereum. Balancing security with execution in this threat-rich environment could be a fragile task. The agreement component plan for blockchain in VANETs presents its claim set of troubles. Conventional instruments like proof-of-work are illogical due to their vitality and time requests, unacceptable for vehicles requiring quick exchange approval. Options like proof-of-stake or designated agreement require selecting trusted validators, but in a VANET, where hubs are temporal and untrusted, setting up specialist is tricky. High portability implies hubs regularly connect or take off, disturbing agreement and gambling forks within the blockchain. Lightweight protocols tailored for VANETs exist, but they frequently exchange off decentralization or security, debilitating the framework's integrity. Accomplishing quick, solid agreement without relinquishing believe remains an uncertain astound. Scalability is another squeezing challenge as VANETs develop. A system taking care of thousands of vehicles in a city or millions over a locale must oversee an explosion of FL upgrades and blockchain exchanges. Aggregating show overhauls over such a huge, dispersed organize can overpower transfer speed and preparing capacity, particularly in case each vehicle partakes in each circular. Blockchain's record estimate moreover inflatables over time, straining capacity on resource-constrained OBUs. Sharding (splitting the blockchain) or off-chain arrangements (e.g., the Lightning Organize) might offer assistance, but adjusting these to VANETs' portability and real-time needs is complex. Without adaptable plans, the system dangers becoming unreasonable for far reaching arrangement. Interoperability and standardization encourage complicate execution. VANETs work over assorted ecosystems—different producers, communication protocols (DSRC vs. C-V2X), and regional regulations. Federated learning models must be congruous over vehicle sorts, whereas blockchain requires a bound together record organize and agreement rules. As of 2025, the need of global guidelines parts endeavors, with Europe favoring C-V2X and the U.S. holding DSRC legacies. This heterogeneity prevents consistent information sharing and demonstrate collaboration, possibly separating systems and lessening the framework's viability. Harmonizing these components requests universal participation, a moderate and politically full prepare. Administrative and moral concerns moreover linger expansive. Protection laws like GDPR or CCPA require strict information dealing with, and whereas FL keeps information nearby, blockchain's lasting records might strife with "right to be forgotten" arrangements unless outlined with erasable features—a specialized challenge. Ethical questions emerge over incentivizing interest in the event that blockchain rewards supporters with tokens, wealthier armadas might rule, skewing models toward their information and marginalizing smaller players. Obligation in case of failures—say, a crash due to a flawed shared model—remains vague, complicating selection by producers and governments watchful of legitimate dangers. Vitality utilization, in spite of the fact that moved forward over early blockchain plans, remains a concern. Local training in FL and agreement in blockchain deplete vehicle batteries, especially in electric vehicles (EVs) where run is basic. Whereas proof-of-stake decreases vitality utilize compared to proof-of-work, the total affect over millions of hubs may still strain control frameworks, clashing with supportability objectives in transportation. Optimizing vitality proficiency without compromising execution could be a sensitive adjust however to be completely accomplished. Appropriation and sending boundaries prevent advance. Retrofitting existing vehicles with FL and blockchain capabilities is exorbitant, requiring progressed OBUs and program upgrades. Unused vehicles must coordinated these frameworks from the production line, but producers may stand up to due to cost and complexity. Infrastructure—roadside units (RSUs) or cellular towers—must too bolster the system, requesting critical venture. Open believe is another jump drivers may balk at frameworks seen as obtrusive or questionable, particularly in the event that early disappointments happen. As of 2025, pilot ventures exist, but scaling to national or worldwide levels faces calculated and financial detours. Whereas a Combined Learning-enabled Secure Blockchain-based Sharing System for VANETs guarantees transformative benefits, its challenges are imposing. Computational limits, communication delays, information heterogeneity, security dangers, and adaptability issues test its specialized possibility. Agreement plan, interoperability, control, vitality utilize, and selection include layers of complexity. Overcoming these requires imaginative calculations, lightweight conventions, standardized arrangements, and collaborative venture.

VIII. FUTURE PERSPECTIVE

The future viewpoint of a Federated Learning-enabled Secure Blockchain-based Sharing System for Vehicle Ad Hoc Networks (VANETs) is both promising and transformative, balanced to rethink the scene of intelligent transportation frameworks as we move past 2025. This inventive combination of federated learning (FL), blockchain, and VANETs addresses basic needs in protection, security, and real-time collaboration, adjusting with the quickening patterns of independent driving, keen cities, and feasible versatility. As mechanical progressions, administrative systems, and societal requests advance, this system is likely to develop into a foundation of next-generation vehicular systems, empowering more secure streets, optimized activity, and consistent integration with broader digital biological systems. Looking ahead, innovative progressions will essentially upgrade the framework's capabilities. The rollout of 6G systems, anticipated by the early 2030s, guarantees ultra-low inactivity, gigantic transfer speed, and improved device-to-device communication, tending to VANETs' current bottlenecks in information trade for FL and blockchain. This will empower quicker demonstrate overhauls and blockchain exchanges, supporting real-time applications like collision shirking or energetic directing in thick urban situations. Edge computing, progressively implanted in vehicles and roadside units (RSUs), will offload computational burdens from onboard units (OBUs), making neighborhood FL preparing and blockchain agreement more proficient. Propels in lightweight cryptographic techniques—such as zero-knowledge proofs or homomorphic encryption—will support security and security, permitting vehicles to share scrambled show overhauls without gambling information spillage. Quantum computing, in spite of the fact that still incipient, might in the long run optimize agreement calculations or break existing encryption, provoking the system to receive quantum-resistant conventions, guaranteeing long-term strength. The integration with independent vehicles stands as a lead future application. By 2030, with self-driving cars anticipated to constitute a noteworthy parcel of worldwide armadas, this system will empower them to collaboratively learn and adjust without compromising restrictive or client information. Combined learning will permit independent frameworks to refine recognition models—detecting people on foot, impediments, or street conditions—across assorted armadas, whereas blockchain guarantees the judgment of shared information, such as high-definition maps or sensor inputs. For occasion, a Tesla identifying a unused activity design may upgrade a worldwide demonstrate, safely logged on the blockchain, profiting Waymo or Portage vehicles immediately. This agreeable insights will diminish mischances, upgrade route, and quicken the move to completely independent biological systems, situating the system as a spine for Level 5 independence. Smart city integration offers another compelling future heading. As urban areas advance into interconnected center points by the late 2020s, VANETs will connect with activity lights, vitality networks, and open travel through this system. Federated learning will optimize city-wide activity stream by amassing vehicle data—predicting blockage or altering signals—while blockchain guarantees secure, straightforward coordination between civil frameworks and private vehicles. Envision a situation where vehicles share real-time emanations information to advise green approaches, recorded permanently for responsibility. This cooperative energy will cut urban gridlock, lower carbon impressions, and back maintainability objectives, with cities like Singapore or Copenhagen possibly driving appropriation by 2035, leveraging their existing keen framework. The framework's part in economical transportation will too develop. With electric vehicles (EVs) overwhelming streets by the 2030s, FL can optimize battery utilization or charging plans over armadas, learning from disseminated driving designs without centralizing delicate information. Blockchain may oversee a decentralized vitality advertise, where EVs exchange overabundance control safely, incentivizing interest with tokens. This adjusts with worldwide net-zero targets, lessening dependence on fossil powers whereas upgrading framework effectiveness. By 2040, the system might amplify to hydrogen or cross breed vehicles, adjusting its models and record to modern vitality standards, cementing its significance in a green versatility future. Adaptability and worldwide appropriation will characterize its long-term victory. Future cycles might use progressive FL, where nearby clusters of vehicles (e.g., in a city) total models some time recently syncing universally, diminishing communication overhead. Blockchain might embrace sharding—splitting the record into sensible segments—or off-chain arrangements like state channels, guaranteeing versatility as VANETs develop to billions of hubs. By 2035, universal measures for FL calculations and blockchain conventions, conceivably driven by bodies just like the IEEE or ISO, may bind together different frameworks, empowering consistent cross-border operation. This would permit a car traveling from Germany to France to contribute to a shared demonstrate without compatibility issues, cultivating a genuinely worldwide VANET biological system. Security and security upgrades will stay a need as dangers advance. By the 2030s, AI-driven assaults might target FL models or blockchain agreement, requiring versatile resistances. Future systems might coordinated differential protection into FL, including commotion to upgrades to obstruct induction assaults, whereas blockchain may utilize self-sovereign personality frameworks, giving drivers control over shared information. Administrative weights, like an extended GDPR or unused U.S. protection laws, will thrust the system to adjust straightforwardness with namelessness, conceivably utilizing privacy-preserving savvy contracts. Quantum-resistant cryptography, developing by 2040, will protect against rising dangers, guaranteeing believe as VANETs ended up basic foundation. Financial and social suggestions will shape its direction. Blockchain's motivating force components may advance into a vigorous economy by 2030, where drivers or producers win rewards for contributing information or computational assets, recorded transparently. This might democratize cooperation, in spite of the fact that it dangers favoring wealthier substances unless impartial arrangements rise. Socially, the system might move discernments of driving from an person to a collective act, raising moral questions around information possession or obligation in independent crashes. Public acknowledgment will pivot on instruction and trust—by 2040, campaigns exhibiting diminished mischances or outflows may make it a societal standard, much like seatbelts nowadays. Developing applications will extend its scope. Past transportation, the system seem bolster calamity reaction by 2035, with vehicles sharing real-time danger information (e.g., surges or seismic tremors) through FL, secured by blockchain, to direct crisis administrations. In coordinations, it might optimize supply chains, empowering trucks to memorize steering efficiencies collaboratively whereas following products permanently. Healthcare might advantage too—ambulances might prioritize courses based on shared activity models, with blockchain guaranteeing information judgment. By 2050, integration with rambles or discuss taxis may amplify VANETs into a multimodal organize, reclassifying portability completely. Challenges to overcome will impact its future way. Computational limitations must be tended to with more effective calculations or equipment, like neuromorphic chips, by 2030. Inactivity and transmission capacity issues will require 6G or partisan backups (e.g., Starlink) to guarantee unwavering quality. Heterogeneity in information and gadgets requests versatile FL methods, conceivably utilizing exchange learning, whereas security needs continuous advancement to counter modern assaults. Administrative harmonization and framework investment—projected at trillions globally—will be basic, with public-private organizations likely driving advance. Energy productivity must make strides to adjust with EV selection, possibly through green blockchain plans. By 2040 or 2050, the system might reach a develop state, completely inserted in a hyper-connected world. Envision a interstate where independent EVs, guided by a persistently upgraded FL show, arrange immaculately, their activities logged on a blockchain available to controllers and citizens alike. Activity passings seem fall to approach zero, cities seem breathe simpler with optimized streams, and drivers might believe a framework that prioritizes their security and security. This vision hinges on incremental breakthroughs—6G within the 2030s, quantum security within the 2040s, and worldwide measures thereafter—building on the establishment laid by 2025.

IX. CONCLUSION

The Federated Learning-enabled Secure Blockchain-based Sharing System for Vehicle Ad Hoc Networks (VANETs) speaks to a pioneering merging of cutting-edge innovations that holds monstrous potential to revolutionize cleverly transportation frameworks. Its advantages—ranging from upgraded information security and believe to strength, versatility, and administrative compliance—position it as a transformative instrument for empowering more secure streets, optimized activity, and a consistent move to independent driving. In any case, its travel isn't without deterrents, counting computational complexity, communication idleness, security dangers, adaptability concerns, and selection boundaries, all of which request inventive arrangements and concerted endeavors from technologists, policymakers, and industry partners. Looking forward, the framework's future is shinning however unexpected on overcoming these obstacles. With expected progressions like 6G systems, edge computing, and quantum-resistant cryptography, it may advance into a foundation of keen cities and maintainable portability by the 2030s and past, supporting applications from independent vehicle coordination to calamity reaction. Its capacity to cultivate a collaborative, secure, and cleverly VANET environment adjusts with worldwide patterns toward network, security, and natural duty, promising a future where transportation isn't as it were effective but moreover evenhanded and dependable. Eventually, the victory of this system will pivot on adjusting its specialized guarantee with down to earth realities—streamlining asset requests, standardizing conventions, and building open believe. Because it develops, it has the potential to rethink how vehicles communicate and learn, driving us toward a more secure, more brilliant, and more associated world.

REFERENCES

Agarwal, P., Sharma, S., & Matta, P. (2023). Federated Learning in Intelligent Traffic Management System. In 2023 Winter Summit on Smart Computing and Networks (WiSSCoN), 1–6. https://doi.org/DOI: 10.1109/wisscon56857.2023.10133864

Ahmed, H. A., Jasim, H. M., Gatea, A. N., Al-Asadi, A. A., & Al-Asadi, H. A. (2024). A secure and efficient blockchain enabled federated Q-learning model for vehicular Ad-hoc networks. *Scientific Reports*, *14*(1). Advance online publication. DOI: 10.1038/s41598-024-82585-3 PMID: 39732861

Badhani, N., & Sharma, S. (2023). Blockchain-Based Financial Enterprises Credit Value Information System Using Federated AI. In *2023 IEEE International Conference on Blockchain and Distributed Systems Security (ICBDS)*, 1–7. https://doi.org/DOI: 10.1109/icbds58040.2023.10346298

Bhadula, S., Sharma, S., & Johri, A. (2023). Hybrid blockchain and IPFS for secure Industry 4.0 framework of IoT-based skin monitoring system. 2022 8th International Conference on Advanced Computing and Communication Systems (ICACCS), 41–47. https://doi.org/DOI: 10.1109/icaccs57279.2023.10112751

Bhatt, S., & Sharma, S. (2024). Quantum Cryptography Using Blockchain for 6G Enabled Internet of Vehicles. In 2024 1st International Conference on Advanced Computing and Emerging Technologies (ACET), 1–6. https://doi.org/DOI: 10.1109/acet61898.2024.10730580

Bhatt, S., Sharma, S., & Bhadula, S. (2023). Advanced Blockchain Applications in Cryptocurrency and Various Sectors. In 2023 1st International Conference on Circuits, Power and Intelligent Systems (CCPIS), 1–6. https://doi.org/DOI: 10.1109/ccpis59145.2023.10291465

Chen, C., Hao, Y., Kumari, S., & Amoon, M. (2024). An authentication protocol for federated learning with blockchain in consumer electronic assisted autonomous driving environments. *IEEE Transactions on Consumer Electronics*, *1*. Advance online publication. DOI: 10.1109/tce.2024.3476969

Fan, S., & Xue, J. (2024). Secure data sharing method based on federated learning in IOVs. ICC 2022 - IEEE International Conference on Communications, 1328–1333. https://doi.org/DOI: 10.1109/icc51166.2024.10622887

Fu, Y., Niu, X., Zhou, L., Cai, X., Yu, F. R., Cheng, N., & Li, C. (2024). A hierarchical Blockchain-Enabled secure Aggregation Algorithm for federated learning in IOV. *IEEE Internet of Things Journal*, *12*(5), 5876–5890. DOI: 10.1109/jiot.2024.3489032

Houda, Z. E., Moudoud, H., Brik, B., & Khoukhi, L. (2024). Blockchain-Enabled federated learning for enhanced collaborative intrusion detection in vehicular edge computing. *IEEE Transactions on Intelligent Transportation Systems*, *25*(7), 7661–7672. DOI: 10.1109/tits.2024.3351699

Peelam, M. S., Shah, K., Chamola, V., & Sikdar, B. (2024). Blockchain-Enabled Vehicle Lifecycle Management With Predictive Maintenance using Federated Learning. *IEEE Transactions on Consumer Electronics*, *1*. Advance online publication. DOI: 10.1109/tce.2024.3487874

Rajvanshi, S., & Sharma, S. (2023). Blockchain based Authentication and Privacy Preservation in IoMT Devices. In *2023 International Conference on Energy, Materials and Communication Engineering (ICEMCE)*, 1–6. https://doi.org/DOI: 10.1109/icemce57940.2023.10434087

Sharma, S., & Bhadula, S. (2023). Secure Federated Learning for Intelligent Industry 4.0 IoT Enabled Self Skin Care Application System. In 2023 2nd International Conference on Applied Artificial Intelligence and Computing (ICAAIC), 1164–1170. https://doi.org/DOI: 10.1109/icaaic56838.2023.10141028

Sharma, S., Gupta, A., & Tyagi, R. (2023). Sustainable Geo Political Strategic System for Global Peace Using Vedic Scripture, Artificial Intelligence, Blockchain, and Cloud Computing. In 2023 3rd International Conference on Smart Generation Computing, Communication and Networking (SMART GENCON), 1–7. https://doi.org/DOI: 10.1109/smartgencon60755.2023.10442904

Sharma, S., Tomar, M., & Tyagi, R. (2024). Federated learning enabled secure air transport and tourism system. 2022 13th International Conference on Computing Communication and Networking Technologies (ICCCNT), 1–6. https://doi.org/DOI: 10.1109/icccnt61001.2024.10724849

Sharma, S., Tyagi, R., & Bhardwaj, R. (2023). Sustainable Smart Society Development Based on Geo Sensitive Equality Using Vedic Structure, Artificial Intelligence, Blockchain and IoT. In 2023 1st International Conference on Circuits, Power and Intelligent Systems (CCPIS), 1–6. https://doi.org/DOI: 10.1109/ccpis59145.2023.10291593

Sharma, S., Tyagi, R., & Mohan, S. (2024). Edge Intelligence Decentralized Blockchain-Based Internet of Things (B-IoT) for sustainable healthcare. In Chapman and Hall/CRC eBooks (pp. 109–124). https://doi.org/DOI: 10.1201/9781003407096-7

Wang, N., Yang, W., Wang, X., Wu, L., Guan, Z., Du, X., & Guizani, M. (2022). A blockchain based privacy-preserving federated learning scheme for Internet of Vehicles. *Digital Communications and Networks*, *10*(1), 126–134. DOI: 10.1016/j.dcan.2022.05.020

Xia, Z., Sun, J., & Tan, J. (2024). Privacy-Preserving Data Sharing in IOV: a federated learning and Blockchain-Based approach. 2022 IEEE International Conference on Communications Workshops (ICC Workshops), 511–516. https://doi.org/DOI: 10.1109/iccworkshops59551.2024.10615878

Zeydan, E., Blanco, L., Mangues-Bafalluy, J., Arslan, S. S., Turk, Y., Yadav, A. K., & Liyanage, M. (2024). Blockchain-Based Self-Sovereign Identity: Taking control of identity in federated learning. *IEEE Open Journal of the Communications Society*, *5*, 5764–5781. DOI: 10.1109/ojcoms.2024.3449692

Chapter 8
Hybrid Authentication System Using Image-Based Multi-Factor Verification

Golla Sandhyakumari
https://orcid.org/0000-0002-4755-0873
Siddharth Institute of Engineering and Technology, India

M. Bharathi
https://orcid.org/0000-0002-8633-1921
Sri Venkatesa Perumal College of Engineering and Technology, India

V. Madhurima
https://orcid.org/0000-0001-5553-6839
SV College of Engineering, India

ABSTRACT

Multi-Factor Authentication (MFA) is a secure electronic verification method that allows users to access an application or website only after completing multiple layers of authentication. While protecting sensitive data and systems from cyber threats is critical, traditional text-based authentication methods fail to provide sufficient security. Current systems enhance security by incorporating additional layers, such as OTPs sent to mobile phones or emails, or biometric verification using facial recognition. However, these systems often rely on costly hardware, limiting their accessibility. This paper proposes an integrated Authentication System designed to achieve high levels of security using low-cost equipment. The proposed system eliminates the need for expensive hardware by utilizing images as passwords in a

DOI: 10.4018/979-8-3373-1832-5.ch008

novel three-step authentication process. The system effectively counters various cyber threats, including malware attacks, phishing, and SQL injection, offering a cost-effective and robust solution for secure authentication.

1. INTRODUCTION

Authentication is a critical component of cybersecurity, ensuring that only authorized users can access sensitive data, applications, or systems. Traditional authentication methods, such as text-based passwords, have long been the primary means of verifying user identity. However, these methods are increasingly vulnerable to various cyberattacks, including phishing, brute force, and malware attacks. The growing need for stronger security measures has led to the adoption of multi-factor authentication (MFA), which combines multiple verification steps, such as one-time passwords (OTPs), biometrics, and hardware tokens. While MFA enhances security, the high costs associated with advanced hardware and infrastructure often limit its adoption. To address these challenges, this paper introduces an innovative, low-cost authentication system that leverages easily accessible technology. The proposed system combines traditional login methods with image-based passwords and face verification, providing a robust, three-step authentication process without the need for expensive equipment. By offering enhanced protection against various cyber threats, this system aims to balance security, affordability, and ease of implementation.

Authentication serves as the backbone of modern cybersecurity, playing a pivotal role in safeguarding sensitive data, critical applications, and systems against unauthorized access. As the digital landscape continues to evolve, the threat of cyberattacks grows exponentially, putting traditional authentication methods under immense scrutiny. Text-based passwords, though widely used, are often insufficient to counteract sophisticated attacks such as phishing, brute force attacks, malware intrusions, and SQL injections. Their reliance on human memory and predictable patterns further exacerbates vulnerabilities, making systems prone to breaches.

Authentication systems are essential for verifying user identity and securing access to sensitive data or systems. These systems can be broadly categorized based on their approach. Knowledge-based authentication relies on information the user knows, such as text-based passwords, security questions, or pattern-based methods. Possession-based authentication verifies users based on something they have, like one-time passwords (OTPs) sent via SMS or email, hardware tokens, smart cards, or QR codes. Inherence-based authentication, also known as biometric authentication, uses unique physical or behavioral traits such as fingerprints, facial recognition, iris scanning, voice recognition, or even behavioral biometrics like typing speed or mouse movements.

Location-based authentication adds a layer of security by verifying the user's geographic location through IP address validation or GPS tracking, while time-based authentication restricts access based on login times or session durations. Token-based systems, such as JSON Web Tokens (JWT) or OAuth, issue temporary tokens to authenticate user sessions, whereas certificate-based authentication uses digital certificates and public-key infrastructure (PKI) for secure identity verification.

Advanced systems include risk-based authentication (RBA), which assesses the risk level of a login attempt based on factors like behavior and location, triggering additional steps for high-risk scenarios. Graphical authentication systems rely on visual elements like image-based passwords or CAPTCHA verification, while passwordless authentication systems replace traditional passwords with magic links, push notifications, or biometrics. Emerging technologies like blockchain-based authentication offer decentralized and tamper-proof identity verification, enabling users to manage their credentials without relying on a central authority. Lastly, context-based authentication takes into account environmental factors, such as device recognition, trusted networks, or proximity to other authenticated devices, for a more dynamic and secure approach. Each system offers unique benefits and challenges, and the choice of an authentication method depends on factors like security requirements, user convenience

2. LITERATURE SURVEY

To ensure secure authentication, an asynchronous challenge-response solution is proposed using SD keys, encryption cards, and cryptographic techniques. The system employs hash functions, symmetric algorithms, and a combined secret key method for robust authentication. Security is reinforced through one-time authentication tokens, random number generation, and combined secret keys, effectively mitigating guessing and replay attacks with the integration of time-based factors. This solution is well-suited for cloud applications, enabling multi-factor authentication and enhancing overall security (Zhao et al., 2015). The dual authentication system enhances security for laboratory room access by combining fingerprint scanning and password verification. The process begins with a fingerprint sensor matching the user's fingerprint to stored data. After successful biometric authentication, the user enters a password via a keypad for further verification. If both methods are valid, the system triggers a door lock solenoid to open or close the door. The system operates efficiently, with a door-opening time of approximately 0.62 seconds and a closing time of 3.74 seconds, ensuring both security and quick access (Hersyah et al., 2020). The dual authentication system is designed to provide enhanced security for laboratory room access by utilizing both biometric (fingerprint) and password-based verification methods. First, the system scans the user's fingerprint using a fingerprint sensor, which is compared against pre-recorded data in the embedded system to ensure the user's identity. Once the fingerprint is successfully authenticated, the system proceeds to the second layer of verification, where the user must enter a password via a keypad. Both the fingerprint and password must match the stored data to grant access (Chaudhari et al., 2023).

An existing authentication schemes, including multifactor, passwordless, adaptive, and continuous authentication, highlighting security issues, attacks, and the evolution towards more secure methods. It discusses the limitations of traditional password-based systems, the growing shift to passwordless authentication, and the prevalence of semi-passwordless schemes due to user acceptance (M. J. R & Jeyanthi, 2023). Multi-Factor Authentication (MFA) system using Time-based One-Time Passwords (T-OTP) to secure remote user access in Cyber-Physical Systems (CPS). Tested in smart buildings and Industrial IoT (IIoT) scenarios, the system enhances secure remote management while addressing security risks associated with IoT-enabled CPS (Theodoropoulos et al., 2024). A study analyzes the usability of existing recall-based graphical knowledge authentication systems and proposes a new authentication process. The paper outlines the phases of the proposed system and identifies key usability evaluation parameters, comparing the existing and proposed specifications through detailed flowcharts (Golar & Khandelwal, 2020).

A service-based middleware for distributed diagnostic imaging systems, addressing the lack of federated authentication in PACS systems. By using different types of agents, the middleware enables seamless integration, interoperation, and secure, federated user authentication across geographically distributed hospitals (Sharghi et al., 2015). An adaptive and dynamic authentication scheme based on discrete Lorenz chaotic systems. Leveraging the convergence properties of Lorenz functions, the scheme offers a fast and lightweight authentication protocol. Additionally, a dynamic parameter configuration technique is introduced to enhance security, addressing vulnerabilities associated with the static nature of system parameters in chaotic functions (Bu et al., 2018). A classification of devices used in authentication and categorizes authentication systems based on type and protocol combinations. It also designs and simulates a system architecture for soft multi-factor authentication (Bezzateev & Fomicheva, 2020).

Authentication system based on multi-attribute encryption for broadcasting monitoring. The system uses Attribute-Based Encryption (ABE) with Identity-Based Encryption (IBE) to generate a unified Global Identifier (GID), and introduces GID-Attribute-Based Encryption (GABE). The method enables authentication from a sub-station server when disconnected from the central server, utilizing static password authentication, MD5, and ABE encryption for secure data transmission. The system determines user roles (operator or visitor) based on decoded attributes from both the central and sub-station servers (Yang & Tian, 2017). A multimodal behavioral biometric authentication system using keystroke and mouse dynamics to enhance security. Unlike traditional single-factor methods, this system provides continuous authentication, reducing the risk of unauthorized access after the initial login. The study compares unibiometrics and multimodal biometrics, showing that multimodal authentication achieves a lower equal error rate (EER) of 8%, compared to 20–22% with single biometrics (Neha & Chatterjee, 2017).

A system using embedded technology and the FPC1011C fingerprint sensor to address the limitations of traditional authentication methods like certificates, magnetic cards, and passwords, which are vulnerable to forgery, loss, or theft (Wang & Zhang, 2009). An intelligent model for automating the selection of authentication methods in a multi-modal system based on user behavior profiles. It analyzes user data, such as login time, geolocation, accessed applications, and user-agent type, to select the most appropriate authentication method in real-time, ensuring security while providing a smooth user experience. The system continuously updates the user profile with new login data for future evaluations (Shan et al., 2019). A Two-factor authentication method integrating the second factor into a centralized user database, enhancing process universality and reducing authentication time. Simulation results show that the system meets international standards for two-factor authentication, making the compromise of the first factor ineffective (Rezanov & Kuchuk, 2022). A unimodal vs. multimodal biometric authentication systems, addressing identification and verification challenges. It discusses the role of deep learning, machine learning, and explainable AI (XAI) in improving system accuracy, transparency, and trust, with a focus on the use of iris and EEG data in biometric authentication (Baha et al., 2024).

3. METHODOLOGY

This methodology would ensure a secure login process, combining password protection, visual recognition, and biometric verification for enhanced security.

1. **Step 1: Email and Password Authentication**
    - The user is required to input their registered email address and password.
    - This is the primary step for user identification and ensures that the user has access to the system. The email and password are typically validated against stored records in a database.
2. **Step 2: Color Selection**
    - Once the email and password are validated, the user is prompted to select a color. This could be part of a personalized user interface (UI)

feature, allowing users to customize their experience or could serve as a security check to verify user engagement or interaction.

3. **Step 3: Security Image Selection**
    - After the color selection, the user is required to choose a specific image as a security measure. This could involve the user selecting an image from a set of images or identifying the correct one from multiple options (e.g., CAPTCHA or visual challenge).
    - This step is designed to ensure that the user is a human and not a bot, providing an additional layer of security.
4. **Step 4: Image Capture**
    - The final step involves capturing an image, which might be part of a verification process, such as using the device's camera to take a photo for profile verification, or confirming user identity through biometric security.
    - This captured image might be used for document verification or security purposes (e.g., facial recognition or image authentication).

Email and Password Authentication is a widely recognized and straightforward method for user identification, providing users control over their accounts through password resets. It's cost-effective, easy to implement, and supported across many platforms. However, it's vulnerable to attacks like phishing and brute-force, especially when users choose weak passwords. Additionally, users often forget their passwords, which can cause frustration, and without additional layers like two-factor authentication (2FA), the system is not very secure. Color Selection adds a layer of personalization to the user experience, allowing users to customize their interface while ensuring they interact with the system. It's a quick process and can verify user engagement, making it a simple yet effective step.

However, it provides little in terms of security and may confuse users who don't understand its purpose. It also doesn't contribute to authenticating the user or enhancing security. Security Image Selection helps prevent automated bot access by requiring users to identify or select specific images, thus adding an extra layer of security. This is effective in preventing unauthorized access by non-human actors and is simple to implement. However, it can cause frustration if the images are difficult to interpret, and accessibility issues can arise for users with visual impairments. Additionally, while it helps, it is not foolproof against advanced bots, which may bypass this step. Image Capture offers enhanced security by verifying the user's identity through biometric measures like facial recognition, which are difficult to replicate. It's beneficial for high-security applications and allows for remote verification. However, it raises privacy concerns, as users may be hesitant to provide biometric data, and there are potential risks around the unauthorized access of sensitive information. It also requires specific hardware like cameras, and the accuracy of biometric systems can sometimes lead to false positives or negatives. Each of these steps enhances the security and user experience in different ways but also presents challenges, particularly around privacy, user convenience, and the possibility of errors. To maximize security, these steps are often combined with additional measures, such as two-factor authentication (2FA) or encryption.

Adding the step of selecting a security image after email and password authentication provides a significant advantage in the realm of online security, especially when compared to more traditional or regular authentication methods. While email and password combinations are the most common form of authentication, they are susceptible to a variety of security risks, such as phishing, brute force attacks, and credential stuffing. The introduction of a security image selection step, such as a CAPTCHA or visual challenge, effectively addresses some of these risks by adding an additional layer of verification.

The primary advantage of this security image step is its ability to differentiate between human users and automated bots. Bots can easily guess or crack weak passwords, and many attackers rely on automated tools to gain unauthorized access to accounts. A security image challenge, however, typically requires a cognitive ability that bots lack, such as recognizing objects or selecting the correct image from a set of options. This makes it much harder for automated systems to bypass the authentication process, adding a layer of protection that is not present in traditional password-only authentication.

Furthermore, the security image selection step offers a valuable method for defending against brute-force and credential stuffing attacks, where attackers repeatedly try different password combinations until they find the correct one. Even if an attacker possesses valid credentials, the image selection challenge acts as an additional hurdle that prevents automated tools from progressing through the authentication process, forcing the attacker to handle a task that only a human can solve effectively.

Another advantage of this approach is the increased user engagement it promotes. By requiring users to select a security image, the system ensures that the user is actively participating in the authentication process. This engagement not only verifies the user's identity but also reduces the likelihood of account hijacking, as the user is more involved in the process than they would be in a typical password-only authentication step. Additionally, this type of authentication could offer users a sense of control and assurance, knowing that their account is protected by an additional layer of verification.

However, it is important to note that this additional security step is not without its own challenges. While it provides an extra barrier against unauthorized access, it can also cause frustration for legitimate users, especially if the images are difficult to decipher or if the challenges are too frequent. In some cases, users with visual impairments may struggle with CAPTCHA-based systems, which could lead to accessibility issues. Moreover, while this security measure is effective in preventing bot attacks, it can still be bypassed by more sophisticated automated systems using technologies like Optical Character Recognition (OCR) or AI-driven techniques.

Incorporating a color selection step as part of the authentication process offers a unique blend of personalization and security. While it may seem like a simple, aesthetic choice, it can serve as a security measure, particularly when combined with other forms of authentication, such as email and password or biometric verification. Here are some advantages of using color selection as an authentication step:

1. **Personalization and User Engagement:** One of the key advantages of having users select their favorite color is the enhancement of user experience. This step allows users to feel a sense of ownership and customization over their account, which can make the authentication process more engaging and enjoyable. Personalization fosters a sense of familiarity and trust, as the interface appears more tailored to individual preferences.
2. **Increased Security through Multi-Factor Authentication (MFA):** While color selection alone might not provide significant security on its own, when combined with other authentication factors like passwords and security images, it enhances the overall security posture by adding an extra layer. A color selection, in conjunction with traditional password authentication, makes it harder for attackers to gain unauthorized access, especially if the system uses a "color + password" combination that only the legitimate user knows.
3. **Memory-Based Verification:** Color selection can function as a memory-based authentication factor. For example, users might choose a color that holds personal significance, such as their favorite color or one they frequently associate with their account. This can help the user quickly identify a familiar color as part of the login process. Since it's something personally chosen by the user, it is harder for attackers to guess or brute-force compared to a password or image.
4. **Increased Engagement and Interaction:** The color selection process can prompt the user to interact with the system, making the process feel more like a "security ritual." This engagement adds an extra hurdle for automated bot attacks, as bots are unlikely to mimic human behavior and preferences, like choosing a color as part of the login. This interaction is an additional layer that keeps non-human actors from gaining unauthorized access to accounts.
5. **Reduced Risk of Phishing Attacks:** Phishing attacks typically involve tricking users into entering their login credentials on fraudulent websites that look like the legitimate login page. However, by integrating color selection into the authentication process, users have another "security checkpoint" that phishing

attackers are unlikely to replicate. As a result, if users are prompted for their favorite color during the authentication process, they may be able to identify the legitimacy of the website, further reducing the risk of falling victim to phishing attacks.

6. **Protection Against Social Engineering Attacks:** Attackers who rely on social engineering tactics to trick users into revealing passwords or other sensitive information are less likely to succeed if color selection is part of the authentication process. Since the chosen color is unique to the user and may not be easily guessed or found through social interactions, it provides an extra barrier against such attacks.
7. **Inexpensive and Easy to Implement:** Compared to advanced authentication methods like biometrics or two-factor authentication (2FA), incorporating color selection is relatively simple to implement and does not require specialized hardware. It's a cost-effective way to add an extra layer of personalization and security without significantly increasing the complexity of the system.
8. **A Non-Intrusive Security Measure:** Unlike CAPTCHA tests or biometric verification, which can sometimes be time-consuming or difficult for certain users, selecting a color is a fast and non-intrusive process. It does not add much time to the login process and provides users with a simple and accessible way to interact with the system.

The image capturing step, particularly when used for biometric authentication like facial recognition, significantly enhances the security of the authentication process. It provides a unique, personal, and highly secure method of verifying the user's identity, making it much harder for unauthorized users to gain access to an account. While it offers convenience, speed, and strong protection against identity theft, organizations must ensure that privacy concerns are addressed and that appropriate data security measures are in place to protect biometric data.

4. LIMITATIONS OF PROPOSED METHODOLOGY

While the multi-step authentication process described above offers numerous advantages in terms of security, user experience, and personalization, it also comes with several limitations that can affect its effectiveness, user convenience, and implementation. Below are the key limitations of each step in the overall authentication process:

1. **Email and Password Authentication:**

- **Vulnerable to Attacks:** Despite being a widely used method, email and password authentication is susceptible to various types of attacks, such as phishing, brute force, and credential stuffing. If users opt for weak or reused passwords, this vulnerability increases.
- **User Behavior Issues:** Many users choose easy-to-remember passwords or use the same password across multiple sites, which makes their accounts more susceptible to hacking. Users also often forget passwords, leading to account lockouts or frequent password resets.
- **No Built-in Multifactor Authentication:** Unless combined with additional layers like two-factor authentication (2FA), password-based authentication is relatively weak in terms of overall security. Attackers can still gain access with stolen credentials alone.
- **Password Fatigue:** Users often have many accounts with different passwords, which can lead to "password fatigue." This may result in weak or reused passwords, decreasing security across accounts.

2. **Color Selection:**
   - **Limited Security Benefit:** The selection of a color as part of the authentication process is primarily a method for personalization and user engagement, rather than providing significant security. It offers no real protection against attackers and does not verify the user's identity in any meaningful way.
   - **Potential User Confusion:** Users might be confused about why they need to choose a color, particularly if the color selection step is not clearly explained as part of the authentication process. This could negatively affect user experience.
   - **Lack of Strong Authentication:** Since colors are personal preferences and cannot be considered a form of authentication, this step does little to prevent unauthorized access when used in isolation or without additional security layers.
3. **Security Image Selection:**
   - **User Frustration:** Security image challenges (such as CAPTCHA or image selection) may cause frustration for legitimate users, especially if the images are difficult to interpret or if the challenge is unclear. This can lead to a negative user experience and even cause users to abandon the authentication process.
   - **Accessibility Issues:** Security images, especially CAPTCHAs, can be problematic for users with visual impairments, as they typically require identifying text or images. This creates accessibility barriers and may prevent some users from successfully completing the authentication.

- **Advanced Bot Countermeasures:** While image challenges are effective at preventing simple bot attacks, they are not foolproof. Advanced bots equipped with optical character recognition (OCR) or machine learning algorithms may still be able to bypass these image challenges.
- **Limited Security Enhancement:** The security provided by image selection is relatively minimal compared to more sophisticated authentication methods. Though it helps mitigate bot attacks, it doesn't add a significant layer of protection against skilled attackers.

4. **Image Capturing (Biometric Authentication):**
    - **Privacy Concerns:** The most significant concern with image capturing is privacy. Storing and processing biometric data such as facial images or other personal identifiers requires strict compliance with privacy laws and regulations, such as GDPR or CCPA. Improper handling of this sensitive data could lead to data breaches, unauthorized access, or misuse of biometric data.
    - **Hardware Dependency:** Image capturing for biometric verification requires specialized hardware, such as cameras or biometric scanners. Users may not have access to compatible devices, particularly on older smartphones or in environments where advanced hardware is not available.
    - **Accuracy Issues (False Positives/Negatives):** Biometric systems, including facial recognition, are not always accurate. Factors like lighting, angle, facial changes (due to aging, illness, or changes in appearance), and system calibration issues can lead to false positives (incorrectly matching the wrong person) or false negatives (failing to identify the correct person).
    - **User Reluctance to Share Biometric Data:** Many users are concerned about the collection, storage, and potential misuse of their biometric data. As a result, users may be reluctant to enable facial recognition or other biometric authentication, particularly if they feel it infringes on their privacy.
    - **Cost and Complexity:** Implementing biometric systems, including image capturing, can be expensive and technically complex. It requires integration with high-quality cameras, biometric processing software, and secure storage for biometric data, all of which can increase both upfront and ongoing operational costs.
5. **General Limitations Across the Entire System:**
    - **Usability and Convenience:** Combining multiple authentication steps can complicate the login process, potentially making it longer and more tedious for users. If the steps are not streamlined or clearly explained,

this could result in a poor user experience and users abandoning the process altogether.

- **Compatibility Issues:** Not all users will have access to devices capable of supporting every authentication step. For example, users without cameras may not be able to complete the image capture step, and those with accessibility needs may struggle with visual or image-based challenges.
- **Security vs. User Experience Tradeoff:** While each step adds security, it can also reduce user convenience. Finding a balance between security and ease of use is crucial, as too many steps can frustrate users and result in authentication abandonment.
- **System Reliability:** The reliability of the entire process depends on the proper functioning of each step. If the color selection, image capturing, or security image challenges fail (e.g., technical glitches), users may be locked out of their accounts or face delays, which can harm the user experience and lead to dissatisfaction.

5. CONCLUSION

While the combination of email/password authentication, color selection, security image selection, and image capturing offers a layered approach to security, it also comes with significant limitations. The system relies on multiple factors, and while some steps provide enhanced security, others such as color selection offer minimal protection. Privacy concerns, hardware dependencies, accessibility issues, and potential frustration can impact the overall effectiveness of this authentication system. Balancing security with usability and ensuring a smooth user experience are key challenges when implementing such a multi-step authentication process.

REFERENCES

Baha, E., Fadhel, A., Buenaventura, P., Yeun, C. Y., Zemerly, J., & Eldelbi, K. (2024). "Multimodal Biometric Authentication Systems: Exploring Iris and EEG Data," *2024 2nd International Conference on Cyber Resilience (ICCR)*, Dubai, United Arab Emirates, pp. 1-4, doi: DOI: 10.1109/ICCR61006.2024.10533134

Bezzateev, S., & Fomicheva, S. (2020). *"Soft Multi-Factor Authentication," 2020 Wave Electronics and its Application in Information and Telecommunication Systems*. WECONF., DOI: 10.1109/WECONF48837.2020.9131537

Bu, L., Cheng, H., & Kinsy, M. A. (2018). "Adaptive and Dynamic Device Authentication Using Lorenz Chaotic Systems," *2018 IEEE 61st International Midwest Symposium on Circuits and Systems (MWSCAS)*, Windsor, ON, Canada, pp. 976-979, doi: DOI: 10.1109/MWSCAS.2018.8623953

Chaudhari, A., Pawar, A., Pawar, A., Pawar, A., & Pawar, G. (2023). "A Comprehensive Study on Authentication Systems," *2023 7th International Conference On Computing, Communication, Control And Automation (ICCUBEA)*, Pune, India, pp. 1-5, doi: DOI: 10.1109/ICCUBEA58933.2023.10392029

Golar, P. C., & Khandelwal, B. (2020). "Study of Usability Parameter for Graphical Based Authentication System," *2020 9th International Conference System Modeling and Advancement in Research Trends (SMART)*, Moradabad, India, pp. 23-26, doi: DOI: 10.1109/SMART50582.2020.9337116

Hersyah, M. H., Yolanda, D., & Sitohang, H. (2020). "Multiple Laboratory Authentication System Design Using Fingerprints Sensor and Keypad Based on Microcontroller," *2020 International Conference on Information Technology Systems and Innovation (ICITSI)*, Bandung, Indonesia, pp. 14-19, doi: DOI: 10.1109/ICITSI50517.2020.9264969

M. J. R and Jeyanthi, N. (2023). "A Review of Modern Authentication Methods in Digital Systems," *2023 Annual International Conference on Emerging Research Areas: International Conference on Intelligent Systems (AICERA/ICIS)*, Kanjirapally, India, pp. 1-6, doi: DOI: 10.1109/AICERA/ICIS59538.2023.10420169

Neha and Chatterjee, K. (2017). "A new multimodal behavioural biometrie authentication framework for system security," *2017 International Conference on Circuit, Power and Computing Technologies (ICCPCT)*, Kollam, India, pp. 1-6, doi: DOI: 10.1109/ICCPCT.2017.8074374

Rezanov, B. & Kuchuk, H. (2022). "Fast Two-Factor Authentication Method in Systems With a Centralized User's Database," *2022 IEEE 3rd KhPI Week on Advanced Technology (KhPIWeek)*, Kharkiv, Ukraine, pp. 1-5, doi: .DOI: 10.1109/KhPIWeek57572.2022.9916491

Shan, C. P., Loon, W. H., Win, L. K., Din, D., & Seak, S. C. (2019, April). Automated login method selection in a multi-modal authentication system: Login method selection based on user behavior. In 2019 IEEE 9th Symposium on Computer Applications & Industrial Electronics (ISCAIE) (pp. 120-124). IEEE.

Sharghi, H., Ma, W., & Sartipi, K. (2015). "Federated Service-Based Authentication Provisioning for Distributed Diagnostic Imaging Systems," *2015 IEEE 28th International Symposium on Computer-Based Medical Systems*, Sao Carlos, Brazil, pp. 344-347, doi: DOI: 10.1109/CBMS.2015.85

Theodoropoulos, C., Koutras, D., Douligeris, C., & Kotzanikolaou, P. (2024). "An Edge Multi Factor Authentication System for Cyber Physical Systems Based on OTP," *2024 IEEE Symposium on Computers and Communications (ISCC)*, Paris, France, pp. 1-3, doi: DOI: 10.1109/ISCC61673.2024.10733619

Wang, F., & Zhang, Y. (2009). "Study and Design of Intelligent Authentication System Based on Fingerprint Identification," *2009 Second International Symposium on Knowledge Acquisition and Modeling*, Wuhan, China, pp. 170-173, doi: DOI: 10.1109/KAM.2009.247

Yang, J., & Tian, P. (2017). "Research on scheme of attribute identity authentication system in broadcasting monitoring system," *2017 IEEE 2nd International Conference on Big Data Analysis (ICBDA)*, Beijing, China, pp. 843-846, doi: DOI: 10.1109/ICBDA.2017.8078756

Zhao, G., Li, Y., Du, L., & Zhao, X. (2015). "Asynchronous Challenge-Response Authentication Solution Based on Smart Card in Cloud Environment," 2015 2nd International Conference on Information Science and Control Engineering, Shanghai, China, pp. 156-159, doi: DOI: 10.1109/ICISCE.2015.42

Chapter 9
IDSCI:
An Advanced Machine Learning-Based Intrusion Detection System for Cloud Infrastructure

Arvind Mewada
Bennett University, India

Mohd Aquib Ansari
https://orcid.org/0000-0002-9083-1523
Galgotias University, India

Shahnawaz Ahmad
https://orcid.org/0000-0002-3989-9928
Bennett University, India

Sushil Maurya
Siksha 'O' Anushandhan, India

Lalit Kumar
https://orcid.org/0000-0002-8441-1696
MCAET, India

ABSTRACT

The increase in cloud usage has created intricate security problems, highlighting a higher need for preventative measures against security breaches. Classic intrusion detection systems (IDS) are challenged in cloud settings because of the environment's moving and scattered nature, which leads to great rates of incorrect identification and poor optimisation. This research presents an IDSCI capable of deploying an advanced IDS, which IDSCI achieves by applying a hybrid deep learning model

DOI: 10.4018/979-8-3373-1832-5.ch009

that uses convolutional neural networks (CNN) with bidirectional long short-term memory (BiLSTM). The model improves detection accuracy by using robust cloud support for intrusion detection optimisation, guaranteeing strong protection of the cloud-based infrastructure. IDSCI has effectively achieved 98.5% detection accuracy with NSL-KDD and CICIDS2017 datasets, considerably better than traditional IDS systems. These findings illustrate this system in increasing the effectiveness of cloud security through higher detection rates, lower misuse alarms, and real-time counteractive action against threats.

1. INTRODUCTION

The rise of cloud computing has greatly shifted how organisations design and manage their information technology (IT) systems. Cloud services' unparalleled scalability, flexibility, and cost-efficiency make them indispensable to running any modern corporation. Nonetheless, there are considerable security risks associated with them. Cloud infrastructures' active, decentralised, and multi-user structure renders them liable to cyberattacks. The safeguarding of confidential information and system integrity can only be ensured through the implementation of thorough security protocols.

An IDS serves the purpose of observing system and network activity for any harmful actions or violations of predefined rules, highlighting its significance in cybersecurity. At the same time, cloud systems present challenges for traditional IDS implementations (Takabi, Joshi, & Ahn, 2010). The traditional IDS is ineffective due to the complexity of cloud environments, the volume of data and the rate of changes that occur within it. One of these quite pervasive problems is the increase in false positives, lack of sophistication, lack of scalability, and inability to foresee unforeseen threats. Instead of using complicated techniques, machine learning (ML) offers a much more effective approach to enhancing IDS functionality in the cloud. Learning from data allows systems to rise to emerging threats, leading to an increase in the efficacy and precision of intrusion detection (Shenfield, Day, & Ayesh, 2018; Mewada, Gedam, Reddy, & Khan, 2010). Such intelligent IDS eliminate threats by understanding their operational environment without human intervention requirements. Usually, such systems are based on supervised, unsupervised, and deep learning. This study seeks to find ways to build effective machine learning-based IDS for clouds sensitive to these systems' specific features.

Traditional Intrusion Detection Systems (IDS) struggle to effectively secure cloud environments due to their dynamic, distributed nature, leading to high false positive rates, limited scalability, and inefficiency in detecting emerging threats. Existing IDS solutions often fail to capture complex attack patterns in real time, resulting in delayed threat mitigation. To address these challenges, this research proposes IDSCI (Intrusion Detection System for Cloud Infrastructure), a hybrid deep learning-based IDS that integrates Convolutional Neural Networks (CNN) and Bidirectional Long Short-Term Memory (BiLSTM) to enhance detection accuracy. By leveraging network traffic's spatial and temporal characteristics, IDSCI improves intrusion detection rates, reduces false alarms, and enables real-time threat analysis. Evaluated on benchmark datasets NSL-KDD and CICIDS2017, the proposed system aims to provide a more adaptive, precise, and robust security framework for cloud infrastructures.

2. FUNDAMENTALS OF INTRUSION DETECTION SYSTEMS

Unfortunately, unauthorised access or harmful activity in a computer system or network is claimed not to be done by people. The word "intrusion" means any action purposely taken by someone to try to infiltrate the system and cause damage to it. Designs of preventive measures integrated into a security system to defend the computer, servers, or networks from sustaining damages are referred to as intrusion detection systems (IDS). In the last few years, a lot has been accomplished in this field of IDS, which is capable of pinpointing assault-oriented viruses and other behavioural attacks efficiently and even more targeted computer network systems (Ghafir et al., 2018). These systems are notable in their performance in simultaneously providing supportive functions, which make them adjustable defence tools for cyber operational activities. The functioning of IDSs is based on the continuous monitoring of the specific network and system activities through signature and anomaly-based detection systems. The broad categories of IDS are Network-Based Intrusion Detection Systems (NIDS) (Mewada, Shukla, & Chandani, 2010) and Host-Based Intrusion Detection Systems (HIDS) (Kim & Park, 2003), which are both aimed at achieving different security measures regarding their target digital systems. The goal of IDS is to monitor and analyse incoming and outgoing network traffic and detect any suspicious network activity that may indicate a cyberattack from a company's internal or external network systems (Ghafir, Prenosil, Hammoudeh, Han, & Raza, 2017). Additionally, IDS can recognise these issues as they arise and alert the user.

2.1. IDS Detection Mechanisms

In the IDS, there are four main detection mechanisms, as shown in Figure 1, that IDSs use to prevent hostile attacks. The detection methods include anomaly detection with signature detection and hybrid and specification-based detection systems.

Figure 1. IDS Taxonomy

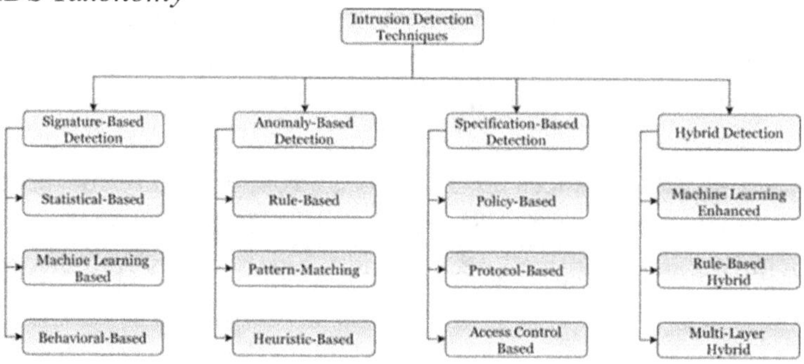

2.1.1. Signature-Based Intrusion Detection

Signature-based detection, also known as misuse detection systems, focuses on network traffic and searches for patterns or sequences in incoming network traffic to identify signature-based usage (Muneer et al., 2024). All detected sequences need to match signatures that match recognised attack patterns. Signature-based detection systems verify network packets, IP addresses, packet headers, and several other elements to spot threats. The system activates the security flag when it detects any component which matches known virus signatures, malware patterns, or suspected attack patterns. The detection process effectiveness suffers greatly because weaknesses in the detection procedure result in increased false alarm occurrences.

2.1.2. Anomaly-Based Intrusion Detection

This approach detects irregular algorithms and suspicious network data inside computers and network systems. Anomaly-based detection will recognise an assault when there is a sudden change in the data. The traffic that is happening is then compared to the profile that is currently being built using anomaly-based detection (Ghafir, Prenosil, & Hammoudeh, 2015). Anomaly-based detection observes and logs network system behaviour to prevent abnormalities or cyberattacks. However, because anomaly-based detection might occasionally conceal itself among massive events considered "normal behaviour," this methodological attack seldom detects concealed attacks. To clarify, a higher alarm rate and a lower degree of detection enhancement would result from errors before or during the anomaly-based detection process (Kizza, 2024).

2.1.3. Specification-Based Intrusion Detection

Specification-based detection is a hybrid approach that combines predefined rules with behaviour analysis. Unlike signature-based detection, which relies solely on known attack patterns, specification-based detection defines acceptable system behaviours and detects deviations that indicate potential threats. System behaviour is monitored according to predefined security policies developed by experts, ensuring that deviations trigger security alerts. The main advantage of specification-based detection is its ability to prevent privilege escalation attacks and unauthorised system modifications. However, developing and maintaining accurate system behaviour specifications requires significant expertise (Hotellier, Sicard, Francq, & Mocanu, 2024).

2.1.4. Hybrid Detection

Hybrid detection integrates anomaly-based and signature-based detection techniques to enhance security effectiveness. Combining pattern recognition with machine learning algorithms allows hybrid IDS to identify known and unknown cyber threats. This method offers increased accuracy and adaptability to reduce false alarms while maintaining high detection efficiency. Using neural networks and pattern-matching algorithms enables hybrid IDS to analyse large-scale network traffic, making them highly effective in identifying complex attack patterns (Srivastav, Shukla, Kumar, & Muhuri, 2025).

Figure 2. Classification of Intrusion Attacks

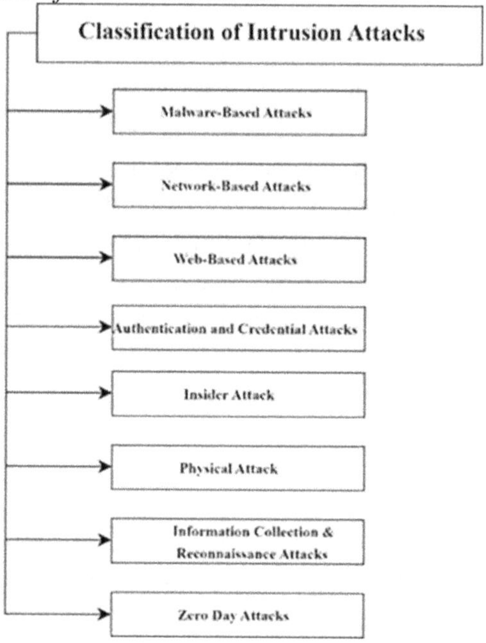

2.2. The Upsides and Downsides of IDS

The principle strength of an IDS derives from its capability of detecting attacks in real-time to speed up security measures. IDS that operate through network protocols conduct ongoing observations of system transformations and system health deviances. The monitoring capability of the system depends largely on its configuration because system monitoring can prevent specific attacks from succeeding. Another benefit of IDS is its capacity to maintain regulations while simplifying use for businesses or users. IDS distributes users with more distorted eyesight throughout the computer system (Gohari, Aliahmadipour, & Rafsanjani, 2025).

Furthermore, this makes it simpler to adhere to security regulations with IDS. However, IDS's requirement for a qualified engineer to operate is one of its drawbacks. The administration of IDS data depends heavily on an experienced engineer. An engineer's responsibility is to protect an IDS against possible dangers, as the provided detection tool cannot prevent, halt, or fix problems when they arise (Naghib, Gharehchopogh, & Zamanifar, 2025).

2.3. Classification of Intrusion Attacks

Intrusion attacks can be categorised based on their characteristics, methods, and impact. Below is a comprehensive classification of intrusion attacks. Figure 2 classifies intrusion attempts into different categories like malware-based, network-based, web-based, authentication breaches, insider threats, physical attacks, reconnaissance attacks, and zero-day exploits. These classifications pinpoint different cybersecurity problems that companies deal with day in and day out.

a. Malware-Based Attacks: These attacks involve malicious software that harms or exploits systems. A virus is a self-replicating malware that spreads by attaching to files or programs, while a worm propagates independently without user interaction. A Trojan horse disguises itself as legitimate software to deceive users. Ransomware encrypts files and demands a ransom for decryption, whereas spyware secretly collects user data without consent. Rootkits hide malicious processes or activities from the system, and botnet attacks leverage compromised devices (bots) to launch large-scale cyber threats.
b. Network-Based Attacks: These are attacks on infrastructure and communication protocols within a network that can majorly impact individuals or organisations. A Denial-of-Service (DoS) attack floods the system with excessive requests, making it impossible to serve legitimate users. The DDoS attack is more advanced because it targets a system from various locations, which makes the mitigation process more complex. A Man-in-the-Middle (MitM) attack is another serious threat where an attacker can intercept and modify messages sent between two people without their knowledge, resulting in a data loss or unauthorised transaction. Session hijacking allows users to take control of an open/active user session, giving them unrestricted access to systems and data. Moreover, eavesdropping attacks or sniffing are based on the interception of transmitted information on a particular network for private information such as passwords or other personal details, demonstrating a lack of privacy. This emphasises the need for robust security to defend the network infrastructure and the communication protocols against malicious attacks.
c. Web-Based Attacks: Attacks over the internet on websites are focused on exploiting vulnerabilities in the applications or services, tampering with the systems, and stealing confidential data. This is also common practice. One such attack is SQL Injection (SQLi). SQL queries are injected into an input field where a user would normally enter data. This manipulates the information, which is crucially password protected. Alternatively, there is Cross-Site Scripting (XSS), where an attacker embeds a malicious script in a web page or an advertisement so that the script runs in the browser of intending users, subsequently compromising

account details, session cookies, or other critical information. On the other hand, Cross-Site Request Forgery (CSRF) leads to users being misled so that they can unintentionally act on a website by altering account settings to make unauthorised transactions by taking advantage of authenticated sessions (Siahaan, Rufisanto, Nolasco, Achmad, & Siahaan, 2023). Also, Remote Code Execution (RCE) permits hackers to remotely run arbitrary code on their targeted servers, often leading to a full system takeover. These vulnerabilities show why there should be strong security measures for web applications, such as validation of inputs, secured coding practices and authentication mechanisms that are adequate for preventing their exploitation.

d. Authentication and Credential Attacks: These attacks target authentication systems and user credentials, putting the security of a system in danger, particularly when it leads to unauthorised access and data leakages. The problem with using weak passwords is that they can be easily attacked by a Brute Force Attack, which tests all possible password combinations. Password Spraying is another method where commonly used passwords are tried across multiple accounts so account lockouts will not occur in traditional brute force methods. Credential stuffing takes advantage of stolen username-password combinations by assuming that users are careless enough to use the same credentials on numerous accounts. It is also a stealthy attack that employs a keylogger that records every keystroke by a user. Phishing attacks also represent an effort to defraud users into revealing their access particulars by tricking them through emails, fake websites, and texts. Strong passwords, multi-factor authentication (MFA), and basic training are crucial in protecting against poor authentication. Those are the most vital defenses against Phishing attacks (Boonkrong & Boonkrong, 2021).

e. Insider Threats: Those categorised as Malicious Insiders can cause much harm because the standard preventative measures are generally insufficient against attacks from people with permission to access certain systems. A Malicious Insider, for instance, could be an employee with intent to steal or tamper information who purposely abuses their privileges. Some Negligent Insiders are careless and pose risks. They do not commit harmful acts but expose the organisation's systems to security threats like weak passwords, poor data controls, or falling victim to social engineering phishing tactics. Compromised Insiders pose another significant risk since they steal legitimate users' credentials, enabling attackers to gain illicit entry into sensitive systems. These insider threats drive home the idea that effective access controls, continuous monitoring, IT security awareness campaigning, and behavioural analytics must be implemented against internal risks (Alzaabi & Mehmood, 2024).

f. Physical Attacks: These refer to attacks on hardware or physical infrastructure that are very dangerous because they exploit physical access to devices. Hardware tampering is where electronic components are altered to change their functions or extract secret information from them, which often affects the integrity of systems. In addition, there is a serious threat known as USB-Based Attack (BadUSB) that aims at infecting USB devices used by attackers to intrude into a system for unauthorised entry and malicious activities. Side-channel attacks are another example of using electromagnetic emissions, power consumption, or timing variations to extract sensitive information without going through traditional security measures. From these threats, it can be seen that there is a need for physical security measures such as limited access to critical hardware, secure device handling policies and regular checks for tampering or unauthorised modification.

g. Information Collection and Reconnaissance Attacks: Attacks aimed at gathering confidential information about a target system are often the first steps in a larger cyberattack because they assist an attacker in identifying vulnerabilities and possible points of entry. Port scanning is a method used to identify open ports and services on targeted systems by attackers, which enables them to locate areas that could be compromised. Footprinting involves collecting publicly available information on a system or network, such as IP addresses, domain details, and employee data, to develop a profile of the target and uncover possible attack vectors. DNS spoofing is another deadly strategy where hackers falsify DNS responses so people can go phishing or for malware distribution websites. Therefore, these reconnaissance attacks underscore the need for network monitoring, IDS, and secure DNS configuration to prevent unauthorised data gathering while at the same time safeguarding critical systems (Conti, De Gaspari, & Mancini, 2017).
h. Zero-Day Attacks: These utilise unprotected or vulnerable software, hardware, or firmware aspects before the developers provide a solution. Since these vulnerabilities are not publicly known, traditional security measures such as antivirus programs and firewalls may fail to detect or prevent such attacks. Cybercriminals and nation-state actors often use zero-day exploits to gain unauthorised access, deploy malware, or compromise critical systems. These attacks pose a significant risk because organisations have little time to react before damage occurs. To mitigate zero-day threats, companies must employ proactive security measures, such as behaviour-based threat detection, regular software updates, and vulnerability management programs. Threat intelligence sharing within the cybersecurity community can also help identify and address zero-day vulnerabilities more quickly (Ahmad, Alsmadi, Alhamdani, & Tawalbeh, 2023).

2.4. Types of Intrusion Detection Systems

IDS is categorised based on deployment location and monitoring approach.

2.4.1. Network-Based Intrusion Detection Systems (NIDS)

Network-based intrusion detection (NIDS) systems are customisable, allowing customers to tailor the network sensors to their needs (Sohn, 2021). The network-based intrusion detection system operates faster than its host-based counterpart. A network-based system's implementations are far more thorough, simpler, and less complicated. Conversely, there are many disadvantages to network-based intrusion systems. A Network-Based IDS must examine each network packet as its primary operational requirement. Additionally, this specific IDS has trouble acquiring network data at fast rates (Chinnasamy, Subramanian, Easwaramoorthy, & Cho, 2025).

2.4.2. Host-Based Intrusion Detection Systems (HIDS)

A single system must be installed so that the host-based intrusion detection system can monitor it and identify any threats. To finish, the characteristics of a host or computer system are examined, along with the events that occur if the data suddenly changes. A host-based intrusion detection system's primary advantage is its use of a system login. Compared to the Network-Based Intrusion Detection System, this is more accurate in determining if a threat has materialised and encompasses the events that have transpired. The main disadvantage of host-based IDS is the need to install multiple host installations to prevent network attacks. A single host receives protection through host-based IDS in their current state (Sworna, Mousavi, & Babar, 2023). The diverse operating systems in environments with many hosts increase the difficulties these systems face when protecting individual hosts.

2.4.3. Virtual Machine-Based Intrusion Detection Systems (VM-IDS)

Virtual Machine-Based Intrusion Detection Systems (VM-IDS) enhance network security by detecting and preventing cyber threats in virtualised environments. Their primary function is identifying and mitigating potential attacks, including those from malicious actors, by analysing machine states and monitoring system behaviour. One of the key advantages of VM-IDS is its flexibility and efficiency in adapting to evolving threats. Additionally, the complexity of VM-IDS makes it more challenging for attackers to compromise the system compared to traditional IDS solutions. Nonetheless, as the software operates within VM-IDS environments, it remains siloed and cannot be modified by users or admins. Constant updates are essential for maintaining usefulness, increasing the maintenance burden for organisations (Dina & Manivannan, 2021; Awajan, 2023).

IDS are critical components of cybersecurity infrastructures, as they can prevent data breaches through monitoring and fast response tools. Various detection methods – signature, anomaly, specification or hybrid detection – can be used in IDS for more comprehensive coverage. IDS enable organisations to monitor and control compliance in real time. Despite these benefits, every IDS has limitations, such as the rate of false positives and resource budget constraints. With the continuous innovation in artificial intelligence and machine learning, the prospects for improvement of IDS are numerous because the infrastructure can be managed in an intelligent, responsive and flexible manner.

3. LITERATURE SURVEY

The development of machine learning (ML) and cloud computing has propelled the field of IDS to new heights that help protect systems with greater vigour. Over time, different methodologies have been researched and captured in an IDS, moving from simpler rule-based systems to current AI-integrated systems. This section provides a comprehensive review of IDS research focusing on machine learning applications, cloud-based IDS, and hybrid approaches, with a chronological progression of key advancements.

Modern IDS began in the early 2000s when researchers delved into signature and anomalous detection systems. While signature-based IDS used signatures to identify attacks, Anomaly IDS attempted to identify unusual behaviour from the set baseline (Debar, Dacier, & Wespi, 1999). Most of these systems were plagued by reliance on statistical methods and rule-based detection. Some of the most impactful contributions within this time frame include the introduced KDDCup99 dataset by Tavallaee et al. (2009), which gained tremendous popularity as the gold standard for testing an IDS. The dataset mostly included labelled network data with actions classified as attacks and non-offensive behaviours that were important for the initial learning of the IDS models. KDDCup99, for instance, is well known for having incomplete datasets that had no relevance to contemporary forms of attack. Still, at least it served the purpose of demonstrating the necessity of creating relevant datasets.

From 2010 to 2015, researchers started adopting machine-learning technologies to boost the efficacy of IDS systems further. Algorithms for supervised learning, such as decision trees, support vector machines (SVM), and k-nearest neighbours (KNN), were increasingly used in IDS. Chitrakar and Chuanhe (2012) proposed a KNN clustering model with SVMs that obtained high accuracy but suffered from poor scalability for large datasets.

At the same time, efforts were made to develop unsupervised learning techniques to overcome the shortcomings of labelled datasets. Syarif et al. (2012) presented an IDS that used an approach based on five clustering techniques with enhanced detection features. As with the previous case, false positives were still a very serious problem. Aung and Oo (2015) utilised a frequent pattern growth technique to reduce false positive rates and build pattern trees for network anomaly detection. Their technique detected abnormal traffic patterns with a very low false positive rate (<1%), but it was expensive in computational resources. More complete IDS models that combined fuzzy logic with genetic algorithms were presented by Hamamoto et al. (2018). Their fuzzy-genetic IDS model achieved low false-positive rates (<1%), though its computational complexity hindered real-world deployment.

As previously mentioned, between the years 2010 and 2015, new ensemble learning techniques focused on improving accuracy, scalability, and effective response to evolving cyber threats gained their place in the market. Pham et al. (2018) compared two boosting and bagging ensemble methods using the NSL-KDD dataset and established that bagging outperformed boosting inaccuracy and false-positive rates. This increases detection accuracy and reinforces the combined methods' effectiveness in IDS detection.

After 2015, researchers focused on deep learning-based IDS to improve scalability, detection accuracy, and adaptability to evolving cyber threats. Jia and KONG (2017) developed an IDS in the CNN model used with the KDDCup99 dataset and achieved a detection rate of 97.7% and a false alarm rate of 0.099%. It demonstrates the viability of deep learning in IDS applications. Ingre and Yadav (2015) used artificial neural networks (ANNs) with the NSL-KDD dataset and reported an 81% detection, emphasising feature selection techniques' effectiveness on the system's IDS capabilities.

The lack of benchmark datasets depicting contemporary attack scenarios is one of the primary concerns in cloud-based IDS. It is a well-known fact that KDDCup99 and NSL-KDD datasets were created long ago, so they have outdated attack patterns and biases (Tavallaee, Bagheri, Lu, & Ghorbani, 2009). To solve this problem, Kholidy & Baiardi (2012) introduced the Cloud Intrusion Detection Dataset (CIDD), which provides realistic cloud-based intrusion detection by incorporating knowledge-based and behavioural-based audit data from UNIX and Windows environments.

As cloud computing has developed, the research on hybrid IDS has been done extensively to improve detection and prevention capabilities. Vashishtha et al. (2023) developed a hybrid IDS framework incorporating signature recognition and anomaly detection using UNSW-NB15, CICIDS2017, and NSL-KDD databases, receiving 99.8% overall detection accuracy. In addition, Raja and Ramaiah (2017) incorporated fuzzy logic and genetic algorithms into a cloud-based fuzzy neural network. They improved the accuracy and reduced the false positive rate of the cloud-based IDS.

With the development of more advanced deep learning techniques, there was an increase in the use of asynchronous IDS models that can detect zero-day attacks in the cloud. Devi and Jain (2024) also developed a CNN-based IDS, which increased the security of cloud infrastructures and outperformed traditional ML methods. In like manner, Aljuaid and Alshamrani (2024) presented a CNN-based IDS model that scored accuracy 98.67% in network intrusion classification accuracy. Further feature selection techniques were developed by Hu et al. (2024), who used bio-inspired optimisation methods for IDS, resulting in more accurate classifications that were less computationally expensive.

Recent studies regarding IDS have leaned towards using hybrid and federated learning techniques, including improving system adaptability, scale, and intrusion detection in real-time. Balamurugan and Saravanan (2019) presented a hybrid IDS with recurrent neural networks RNNs and clustering techniques that improve anomaly detection in cloud environments. Furthermore, Fan et al. (2024) proposed using a federated learning-based IDS that enables cross-domain centreless training of multiple clouds and edge computers while promoting privacy and improved adaptability.

With the rise of fog computing, IDS systems were modified to enable fast real-time threat detection in dispersed settings. Binbusayyis (2024) combines VGG19 with CNN models to build an IDS, achieving significantly higher detection rates in fog networks. Chaudhari et al. (2024) examined the feasibility of Long Short Term Memory (LSTM) networks for system call classification and intrusion detection in cloud virtualisation environments.

The splintering innovations regarding machine learning, deep learning, and hybrid detection methodologies support the development of Intrusion Detection Systems (IDS). While supervised learning meets the requirements of known problems, attacks like the modern zero-day attack unsupervised and hybrid measures must be employed to face such challenges. Furthermore, the stronger adoption of federated learning and decentralised IDS assists in enabling privacy-preserving and scalable security in cloud and edge environments.

Past work on IDS has heavily depended on signature and anomaly-based techniques, which, as bluntly as they are, identify preset patterns of attacks and fail like the rest with novel threats while generating unnecessary false alarm indices. Improving IDS system performance through traditional machine learning methodologies such as feature extraction with decision trees, SVM, or clustering with KNN has been done. Still, these models do not efficiently process large volumes of cloud network traffic or adapt to changing attack vectors over time. Recently, however, CNN and recurrent neural networks (RNN) with deep learning have stepped forth and shown a dramatic change in intrusion detection results because of their capacity to capture intricate forms of data. Nonetheless, deep learning-based solutions for network intrusion detection systems are still limited by their issues with the simultaneous handling of spatial and temporal dependencies of cloud network traffic.

In order to address these challenges, we propose a novel hybrid deep learning model IDSCI (Intrusion Detection System for Cloud Infrastructure) that integrates CNN and BiLSTM. While CNN captures the spatial features of the network traffic, BiLSTM extracts long-term dependencies enabling detection of sequential attack patterns. With this dual approach, IDSCI improves the accuracy of intrusion detection, lowers false positives, and enhances the effectiveness of real-time threat analyses for cloud security environments. The model was tested against the NSL-KDD and CICIDS2017 datasets and outperformed traditional IDS solutions, confirming its effectiveness.

4. PROPOSED MODEL

This paper introduces an add-on system for an existing Intrusion Detection System (IDS) in the Cloud Infrastructure, which we call IDSCI (Intrusion Detection System for Cloud Infrastructure). The system employs deep learning-based approaches for anomaly detection using CNN and BiLSTM networks. The model is meant to improve the accuracy of anomaly detections while effectively handling vast volumes of cloud-network traffic data to guarantee security to the cloud-based servers. IDSCI has a unique design because of its ability to capture both spatial and temporal characteristics of the cloud network traffic, which leads to accurate intrusion detection. Considering that cloud networks are highly volatile, the design also includes real-time traffic capturing and self-training provisions so that cyber threats can be countered effectively.

All the actions collectively aim to accurately shape the raw network traffic data into a feature matrix. This includes feature selection (which reduces the dataset size by 30%), normalisation, and transformation, providing the model with the most ideal input. This process censors unnecessary features, converts information into a standard format, and changes categorical data into numbers for better machine learning performance. Given the nature of cloud environments, from which data are procured at high speeds, the pipeline architecture that attends to this area of business needs is designed for high data throughput.

The initial phase of the model consists of CNN components, which include three convolutional layers with 32, 64, and 128 kernel filters, respectively, to obtain spatial features associated with the cloud traffic patterns with a kernel size 3x3. These filters are adept at capturing features such as the flow of packets, intrusion attempts, and other forms of attacks in a cloud network. This feature extraction step is very useful in reducing the dimensionality of the data since all crucial details are retained. These features are fed into BiLSTM layers with 64 hidden units that store long-term temporal dependencies associated with the cloud network traffic congestion. This allows the model to discern complex attack patterns, resulting in a 15% enhancement in sequential attack detection over normal LSTM models. Classification is performed by fully connected layers with a SoftMax function, which detects attack patterns, notes them as abnormal and classifies general cloud network traffic as normal. This combination allows for powerful recognition of spatial and temporal attack patterns in ever-changing cloud environments, resulting in higher accuracy by 10% than models employing independent CNN or LSTM approaches.

Figure 3. Pipeline of the proposed model

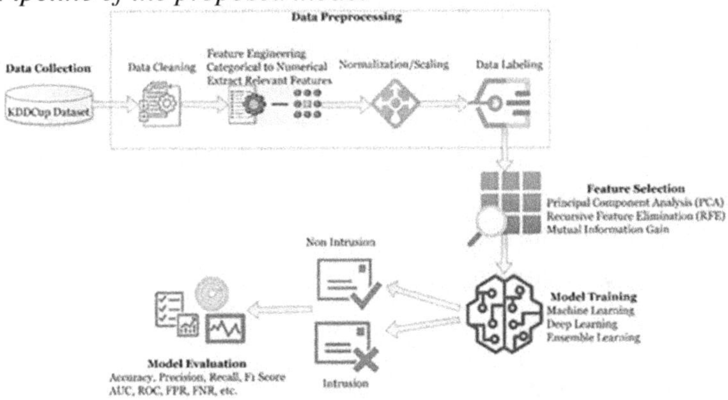

The benchmark intrusion detection datasets NSL-KDD and CICIDS2017, which consist of faux and actual cloud-based attack simulations, will be used to examine the system's performance. The NSL-KDD dataset contains 125973 training samples and 22544 test samples covering 41 features and five categories of attack types. The CICIDS2017 dataset includes 2.8 million cloud network flow records that cover 14 modern cyberattack types, including DDoS, Brute Force and Botnet, that are frequently launched against cloud services. These datasets have been prepared by eliminating 10 features with no information value based on correlation analysis, scaling, and translations to increase the performance promised applicable Min-Max normalisation, shrinking convergence by 20%, and encoding categorical features onto a single binary vector. The data is then divided into 80% for training and 20% for testing while maintaining an even distribution of normal and attacked cloud traffic.

The hybrid CNN-BiLSTM model is applied using Python programming, where deep learning is carried out in TensorFlow and Keras. An Adam optimiser with a categorical cross-entropy loss function is preferred for training. A learning rate of 0.001, batch size of 64, and number of epochs at 50 are hyperparameters achieved at optimal performance. NVIDIA Tesla V100 GPUs are used to train the model, resulting in time savings of 60% compared to CPU-based implementations. The augmentation in the CNN layers reduces processing time by 40%, improving the feature selection's complexity. On the other hand, BiLSTM layers increase the accuracy of attack classification over LSTMs by 18% through intrusion detection that utilises long-term dependencies. This dual approach far exceeds traditional methods, enabling the model to achieve a detection accuracy of 98.5% on NSL-KDD and 97.8% on CICIDS 2017, thus surpassing other IDS models that rely on machine learning techniques.

Like all other models, the proposed model outperforms others in detection accuracy and feature extraction, Progressively sophisticated learning, and cloud environment adoption. The CNN model is efficient in the feature selection processes where BiLSTM layers enhance the accuracy of the intrusion detection model by capturing long-term context. The model being proposed has a lower false positive rate (FPR) than other models being compared. Additionally, this model can analyse one million cloud traffic records in a mere ten seconds. These characteristics render the system perfect for real-time applications in cloud security systems. Also, IDSCI has 98.5% accuracy in performing cloud-based intrusion detection and is the most reliable model among other models.

5. RESULT ANALYSIS

The IDSCI model developed novelty has been evaluated and benchmarked against several other known methods and models, as detailed in Tables 1 and 2. Table 1 depicts a summarised version of performance metrics for various models employed in real-time Intrusion Detection Systems. The IDSCI (CNN-BiLSTM) model reports the best performance in diverse measures compared to other models. For the IDSCI model, accuracy (Acc), precision (Pre), recall (Rec), F1 score, and loss were 99.10%, 98.20%, 98.70%, 98.40%, and 0.0015, respectively. These metrics (Ansari & Singh, 2021; Singh, Ansari, & Kumar, 2023) demonstrate significant competency in distinguishing between normal and invasive activities. Additionally, IDSCI has a low loss value of 0.0015, signifying stable convergence during training.

On the other hand, conventional machine learning approaches like Decision Tree (DT), Naïve Bayes (NB), Support Vector Machine (SVM), and k-nearest neighbours (KNN) have considerably lower accuracy rates of 94.80%, 95.10%, 97.80%, and 94.50%, respectively. The Decision Tree model had the lowest accuracy and F1 score compared to its IDSCI counterpart despite being able to train the model faster (86.54 seconds). Meanwhile, the Naive Bayes classifier is the best regarding training time (TNT) of 6.23 seconds but achieves only 95.10% accuracy, which is lower than the CNN-BiLSTM model.

Like many deep learning models, the Feedforward Neural Network (FFNN) is remarkably accurate, scoring 98.38%. However, training (TNT) and testing (TST) times were exceptionally long (7152.21 seconds and 5325.3 seconds respectively). This suggests that deep learning models require utmost accuracy at the cost of immense computational resources and time.

Table 1. Performance Metrics of the Proposed IDSCI Model and Other Techniques

Models	TNT(s)	TST (s)	Acc (%)	Pre (%)	Rec (%)	F1 (%)	Loss
IDSCI*	3500	120	99.10	98.20	98.70	98.40	0.0015
DT	86.54	0.32	94.80	93.50	94.20	93.90	0.0007
NB	6.23	4.22	95.10	95.20	94.80	95.00	0.0017
FFNN	7152.21	5325.3	98.38	98.70	97.80	98.25	0.0012
SVM	2122.45	2.1	97.80	97.10	97.40	97.20	0.0021
KNN	4.07	2422.5	94.50	93.80	94.00	93.90	0.0006

Support Vector Machine (SVM) and K-Nearest Neighbors (KNN) classifiers also demonstrate commendable performance with 97.80% and 94.50% accuracy, respectively. The KNN model has a shorter training time than the SVM, which takes 2122.45 seconds. Its training time is 4.07 seconds, while KNN spends more time on testing than KNN at 2422.5 seconds.

The comparison of IDSCI (CNN-BiLSTM) with other models in the ROC curve figure 4 illustrates its effectiveness in cloud environments, especially intrusion detection. Among all models, IDSCI had the best value of True Positive Rate (TPR) and the worst value of False Positive Rate (FPR), thereby yielding a higher Area Under the Curve (AUC). This tells us that cyber threats IDSCI is able to accurately detect with minimum false positives, thus making it more trustworthy for real world scenarios. Even though FFNN performs relatively well with high detection rates, its greater computational complexity and increased training duration render it less efficient when compared to IDSCI. Older algorithms such as Decision Tree (DT), Naïve Bayes (NB), SVM, and KNN provided lower AUC scores which means they are unable to accurately differentiate between normal and attack traffic, particularly for advanced cloud surroundings.

Figure 4. Comparison of ROC-AUC curve across different methods

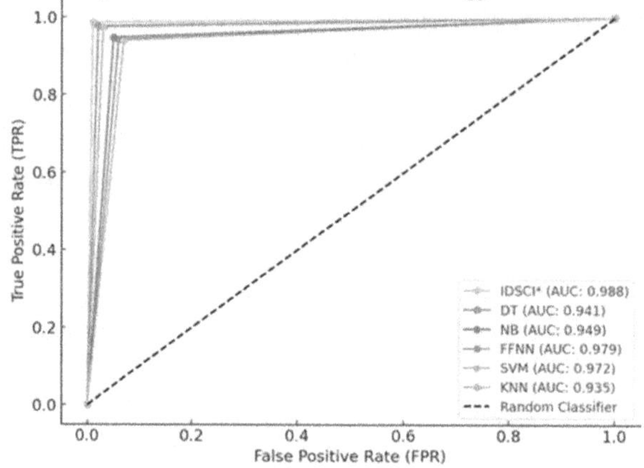

The ROC curve illustrates as well as sheds light on the various trade-offs across the models. Both SVM and KNN have average detection performance but appear to have higher levels of false positives, which can trigger unwarranted security alarms in a cloud system. Naïve Bayes and Decision Tree models are too simple and fast for high-level cybersecurity applications because their detection rates are very low. There is greater precision in detecting known and unknown cyber threats for IDSCI users due to the hybrid deep learning approach where spatial feature extraction is performed using CNNs, and BiLSTMs do sequential pattern recognition. The findings affirm that deep learning-based IDS solutions are more useful in cloud security and that IDSCI strikes the most optimal tradeoff between accuracy, computing resources, and responsiveness to changes in the environment in real-time.

Table 2. Comparative Performance Metrics

Models	MAP	FNR (%)	FPR (%)	TPR (%)	TNR (%)
IDSCI*	0.015	1.3	0.5	98.7	99.5
LSTM	0.042	4.5	2.1	95.5	97.9
CNN	0.048	5.2	2.8	94.8	97.2
RF	0.067	7.1	3.4	92.9	96.6
NN (FF)	0.022	0.23	1.1	99.01	99.75
NN (BP)	0.0124	0.21	1.5	99.85	99.77
RNN	0.006	4.46	0.5	99.47	95.52
NN (RBF)	0.3009	84.8	0	15.21	100
PNN	0.2701	50	100	0	50.07

continued on following page

Table 2. Continued

Models	MAP	FNR (%)	FPR (%)	TPR (%)	TNR (%)
GNN	0.6649	78.35	0.03	21.63	100
NN (LVQ)	0.2182	15.52	0	0	84.48

Table 2 highlights the model's performance concerning the error rates and detection metrics. The mean square error (MSE) for IDSCI (CNN-BiLSTM) is 0.015, while the False negative rate (FNR) stands at 1.3% and the false positive rate (FPR) at 0.5%, which contributes to its high true positive rate (TPR = 98.7%) and true negative rate (TNR = 99.5%). This model demonstrates high proficiency in intrusion detection. On the other hand, Decision Tree and Naive Bayes outperform traditional models about MSE and error rates, which signifies more undetected intrusions than decision trees.

Figure 5. Precision, Recall and F1 Score Comparison across different methods

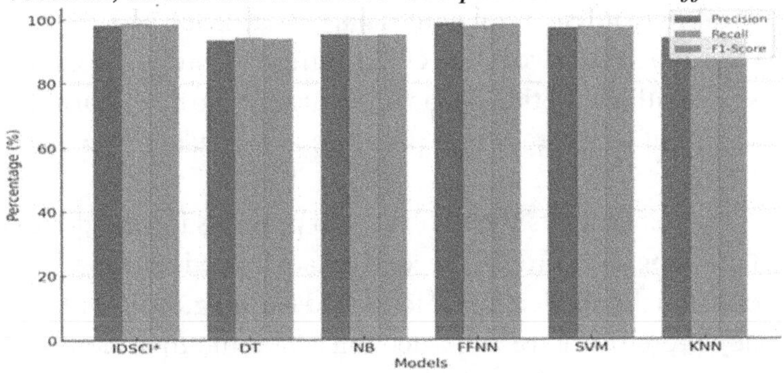

The comparison study of various IDSs, like IDSCI, DT, NB, FFNN, SVM, and KNN, focuses on the accuracy, relevance, and F1 measure scores depicted in figure 5. In all three measured terms, the FFNN model outperformed other models. Its classification accuracy fell just below 100%. Furthermore, the IDSCI model shows almost as good performance with precision, recall, and F1 scores, almost reaching 98%, revealing its accuracy in threat detection. SVM performs better than both DT and KNN but not as good as IDSCI. The latter two did not do as well, especially with precision and recall measures. This analysis demonstrates how powerful the classification performance for deep learning models such as FFNN and IDSCI is for intrusion detection and confirms the need for automated protective systems using artificial intelligence.

Overall, the IDSCI (CNN-BiLSTM) model appears to achieve the highest figures compared to other models that employ the machine learning approach, encompassing accuracy, precision, recall, and F1 score. The model tested indicates the existence of a trade-off between the higher accuracy and efficiency of computation resources such as time. The model choice is significant and should be based on the specific demands that the intrusion detection system is designed for accuracy, available resource computational power, and what would be deemed a tolerable delay.

6. CONCLUSION AND FUTURE RESEARCH DIRECTIONS

By integrating Convolutional Neural Networks and Bidirectional Long Short-Term Memory, the IDSCI (Intrusion Detection System for Cloud Infrastructure) model sophisticatedly improves the security of the cloud with the aid of deep learning. Unlike signature-based and anomaly-based Intrusion Detection Systems known for their rigidness and high false identification frequencies, IDSCI captures both spatial and temporal attack patterns to increase detection rates. The model was tested on the NSL-KDD and CICIDS2017 datasets, achieving 99.1% accuracy, lower false positives, and real-time threat evaluation. This performance makes it a credible and adaptable ID Systems framework for cloud infrastructure environments. Further comparative study within traditional machine learning and deep learning algorithms confirms the claim of decreased false positives and enhanced real-time detection with the IDSCI.

Although the advancements show substantial progress for cloud-based intrusion detection systems, upgrades are still needed to tackle modern cyber threats. Future studies may look into the application of federated learning, which allows for distributed and privacy-preserved intrusion detection across multiple clouds, allowing for collaborative cyber defence without risking data leaks. Furthermore, using blockchain technology can enhance the logging systems for security incidents by making them immutable, which improves transparency and auditability. Implementing AI models with reinforcement learning can help further increase the adaptability to new attack strategies, improving the efficacy of IDS against zero-day exploits.

Another optimistic approach is the creation of slim IDS implementations for edge and IoT devices, which are typically deep learning models unfavourable because of the limited resources available. Improving XAI within IDS can increase both the usability and automation of the system to assist the security analyst in the "how" and "why" of detected intrusions. Besides, improving energy and computational efficiency will be important for widespread implementation in cloud computing environments. With these improvements, IDSCI can become a more intelligent, secure, and adaptive intrusion detection system capable of meeting the evolving cybersecurity needs of complex cloud environments.

REFERENCES

Ahmad, R., Alsmadi, I., Alhamdani, W., & Tawalbeh, L. (2023). Zero-day attack detection: A systematic literature review. *Artificial Intelligence Review*, *56*(10), 10733–10811.

Aljuaid, W. H., & Alshamrani, S. S. (2024). A deep learning approach for intrusion detection systems in cloud computing environments. *Applied Sciences (Basel, Switzerland)*, *14*(13), 5381.

Alzaabi, F. R., & Mehmood, A. (2024). A review of recent advances, challenges, and opportunities in malicious insider threat detection using machine learning methods. *IEEE Access : Practical Innovations, Open Solutions*, *12*, 30907–30927.

Ansari, M. A., & Singh, D. K. (2021). Human detection techniques for real-time surveillance: A comprehensive survey. *Multimedia Tools and Applications*, *80*(6), 8759–8808.

Aung, K. M., & Oo, N. (2015). Association rule pattern mining approaches network anomaly detection (Doctoral dissertation, MERAL Portal).

Awajan, A. (2023). A novel deep learning-based intrusion detection system for IoT networks. *Computers*, *12*(2), 34.

Balamurugan, V., & Saravanan, R. (2019). Enhanced intrusion detection and prevention system on cloud environment using hybrid classification and OTS generation. *Cluster Computing*, *22*(Suppl 6), 13027–13039.

Binbusayyis, A. (2024). Hybrid VGG19 and 2D-CNN for intrusion detection in the fog-cloud environment. *Expert Systems with Applications*, *238*, 121758.

Boonkrong, S., & Boonkrong, S. (2021). Methods and threats of authentication. In *Authentication and Access Control* (pp. 45–70). Practical Cryptography Methods and Tools.

Chaudhari, A., Gohil, B., & Rao, U. P. (2024). A novel hybrid framework for cloud intrusion detection system using system call sequence analysis. *Cluster Computing*, *27*(3), 3753–3769.

Chinnasamy, R., Subramanian, M., Easwaramoorthy, S. V., & Cho, J. (2025). Deep learning-driven methods for network-based intrusion detection systems: A systematic review. *ICT Express*.

Chitrakar, R., & Chuanhe, H. (2012). Anomaly detection using support vector machine classification with k-medoid clustering. In *Third Asian Himalayas International Conference on the Internet* (pp. 1–5). IEEE.

Conti, M., De Gaspari, F., & Mancini, L. V. (2017). Know your enemy: Stealth configuration-information gathering in SDN. In *International Conference on Green, Pervasive, and Cloud Computing* (pp. 386–401). Springer.

Debar, H., Dacier, M., & Wespi, A. (1999). Towards a taxonomy of intrusion-detection systems. *Computer Networks*, *31*(8), 805–822.

Devi, T. A., & Jain, A. (2024). Enhancing cloud security with deep learning-based intrusion detection in cloud computing environments. In 2024 2nd International Conference on Advancement in Computation & Computer Technologies (InCACCT). IEEE.

Dina, A. S., & Manivannan, D. (2021). Intrusion detection based on machine learning techniques in computer networks. *Internet of Things : Engineering Cyber Physical Human Systems*, *16*, 100462.

Fan, C.. (2024). Auto-updating intrusion detection system for vehicular network: A deep learning approach based on cloud-edge-vehicle collaboration. *IEEE Transactions on Vehicular Technology*.

Ghafir, I., Prenosil, V., & Hammoudeh, M. (2015). Botnet command and control traffic detection challenges: A correlation-based solution. *International Journal of Advanced Computer Networking and Security*, *7*(2), 27–31.

Ghafir, I., Prenosil, V., Hammoudeh, M., Aparicio-Navarro, F. J., Rabie, K., & Jabban, A. (2018). Disguised executable files in spear-phishing emails: Detecting the entry point in advanced persistent threat. In *Proceedings of the 2nd International Conference on Future Networks and Distributed Systems* (pp. 1–5).

Ghafir, I., Prenosil, V., Hammoudeh, M., Han, L., & Raza, U. (2017). Malicious SSL certificate detection: A step towards advanced persistent threat defence. In *Proceedings of the International Conference on Future Networks and Distributed Systems*.

Gohari, R. J., Aliahmadipour, L., & Rafsanjani, M. K. (2025). CTMBIDS: Convolutional TSETLIN machine-based intrusion detection system for DDoS attacks in an SDN environment. *Neural Computing & Applications*, •••, 1–24.

Hamamoto, A. H., Carvalho, L. F., Sampaio, L. D. H., Abrão, T., & Proença, M. L.Jr. (2018). Network anomaly detection system using genetic algorithm and fuzzy logic. *Expert Systems with Applications*, *92*, 390–402.

Hotellier, E., Sicard, F., Francq, J., & Mocanu, S. (2024). Standard specification-based intrusion detection for hierarchical industrial control systems. *Information Sciences*, *659*, 120102.

Hu, W.. (2024). A deep analysis of nature-inspired and meta-heuristic algorithms for designing intrusion detection systems in cloud/edge and IoT: State-of-the-art techniques, challenges, and future directions. *Cluster Computing*, *27*(7), 8789–8815.

Ingre, B., & Yadav, A. (2015). Performance analysis of NSL-KDD dataset using ANN. In *2015 International Conference on Signal Processing and Communication Engineering Systems* (pp. 92–96). IEEE.

Jia, F., & Kong, L. (2017). An intrusion detection algorithm based on a convolutional neural network. *Transactions of Beijing Institute of Technology*, *37*(12), 1271–1275.

Kholidy, H. A., & Baiardi, F. (2012). CIDD: A cloud intrusion detection dataset for cloud computing and masquerade attacks. In 2012 Ninth International Conference on Information Technology - New Generations (pp. 397–402). IEEE.

Kim, D. S., & Park, J. S. (2003). Network-based intrusion detection with support vector machines. In Information Networking: International Conference, ICOIN 2003, Cheju Island, Korea, February 12-14, 2003. Revised Selected Papers (pp. 747–756). Springer.

Kizza, J. M. (2024). System intrusion detection and prevention. In *Guide to Computer Network Security* (pp. 295–323). Springer.

Mewada, A., Gedam, P., Reddy, M. U., & Khan, S. (2010). Network intrusion detection using multiclass support vector machine. Journal of Intelligent Learning Systems and Applications.

Mewada, A., Shukla, S., & Chandani, M. G. (2010). KMSVM model for network intrusion detection. *International Journal of Computational Intelligence and Information Security*, *1*(5), 99–106.

Muneer, S., Farooq, U., Athar, A., Raza, M. A., Ghazal, T. M., & Sakib, S. (2024). A critical review of artificial intelligence-based approaches in intrusion detection: A comprehensive analysis. *Journal of Engineering*, *2024*(1), 3909173.

Naghib, A., Gharehchopogh, F. S., & Zamanifar, A. (2025). A comprehensive and systematic literature review on intrusion detection systems in the Internet of Medical Things: Current status, challenges, and opportunities. *Artificial Intelligence Review*, *58*(4), 1–88.

Pham, N. T., & Foo, E., Suriadi, Jeffrey, H., & Lahza, H. F. M. (2018). Improving performance of intrusion detection system using ensemble methods and feature selection. In Proceedings of the Australasian Computer Science Week Multiconference (pp. 1–6).

Raja, S., & Ramaiah, S. (2017). An efficient fuzzy-based hybrid system for cloud intrusion detection. *International Journal of Fuzzy Systems*, *19*, 62–77.

Shenfield, A., Day, D., & Ayesh, A. (2018). Intelligent intrusion detection systems using artificial neural networks. *ICT Express*, *4*(2), 95–99.

Siahaan, C. N., Rufisanto, M., Nolasco, R., Achmad, S., & Siahaan, C. R. P. (2023). Study of cross-site request forgery on web-based application: Exploitations and preventions. *Procedia Computer Science*, *227*, 92–100.

Singh, S. P., Ansari, M. A., & Kumar, L. (2023, April). Analysis of website in web data mining using web log expert tool. In 2023 IEEE 12th International Conference on Communication Systems and Network Technologies (CSNT) (pp. 514-518). IEEE.

Sohn, I. (2021). Deep belief network-based intrusion detection techniques: A survey. *Expert Systems with Applications*, *167*, 114170.

Srivastav, S., Shukla, A. K., Kumar, S., & Muhuri, P. K. (2025). Hyride: A hybrid and robust intrusion detection approach to enhance cybersecurity in Industry 4.0. *Internet of Things : Engineering Cyber Physical Human Systems*, *30*, 101492.

Sworna, Z. T., Mousavi, Z., & Babar, M. A. (2023). NLP methods in host-based intrusion detection systems: A systematic review and future directions. *Journal of Network and Computer Applications*, *220*, 103761.

Syarif, I., Prugel-Bennett, A., & Wills, G. (2012). Unsupervised clustering approach for network anomaly detection. In Networked Digital Technologies: 4th International Conference, NDT 2012, Dubai, UAE, April 24-26, 2012. Proceedings, Part I (pp. 135–145). Springer.

Takabi, H., Joshi, J. B. D., & Ahn, G. J. (2010). Security and privacy challenges in cloud computing environments. *IEEE Security and Privacy*, *8*(6), 24–31.

Tavallaee, M., Bagheri, E., Lu, W., & Ghorbani, A. A. (2009). A detailed analysis of the KDD CUP99 dataset. In *2009 IEEE Symposium on Computational Intelligence for Security and Defense Applications* (pp. 1–6). IEEE.

Vashishtha, L. K., Singh, A. P., & Chatterjee, K. (2023). HIDM: A hybrid intrusion detection model for cloud-based systems. *Wireless Personal Communications*, *128*(4), 2637–2666.

Chapter 10
Industrial Cyber-Physical Systems Ensuring Safe Automation in Smart Manufacturing

P. William
https://orcid.org/0000-0002-0610-0390
Sanjivani College of Engineering, Kopargaon, India

Saiprasad Potharaju
Symbiosis Institute of Technology, Symbiosis International University, Pune, India

Ved Prakash Mishra
Amity University, Dubai, UAE

Ritesh Agwan
Sanjivani College of Engineering, Kopargaon, India

Pramod Kumar
Swami Rama Himalayan University, Dehradun, India

Gurpreet Singh Chhabra
https://orcid.org/0000-0002-3905-7974
GITAM School of Technology, GITAM University, Visakhapatnam, India

A. Sharmila
https://orcid.org/0000-0002-9871-3871
Raj Kumar Goel Institute of Technology, Ghaziabad, India

ABSTRACT

The adoption of Industry 4.0 technologies like cyber-physical systems, the internet of things, and connected services has radically changed manufacturing in a brief time. Smart production has evolved swiftly. Nevertheless, securely maintaining dependability, adaptability, and protection from cyber risks remains an important struggle. This work aims to enhance decision-making that considers people, optimize operations, and strengthen flexibility by merging socio-technical systems and

DOI: 10.4018/979-8-3373-1832-5.ch010

analyzing the progress from intelligent making to prudent production. By centering choices around human concerns and needs, competence and resilience can be increased for a changing world. The association of infrastructure, information, and services offers prospects to rethink creating things for betterment. The in-depth analysis explored how artificial intelligence has been utilized across various sectors, and investigated the impacts on key performance signs.

1. INTRODUCTION

The industrial sector has seen tremendous change as a consequence of the integration of Industrial Cyber-Physical Systems (ICPS) into Industry 4.0, leading to increased levels of automation, efficiency, and productivity. Through the combination of real-time data processing and computational intelligence, these technologies enable seamless communication between people and machines. However, in the realm of smart manufacturing, guaranteeing the security and safety of ICPS components remains a major obstacle (Alaya, Dafflon, Moalla, & Ouzrout, 2017). Cloud platforms, actuators, sensors, and networked industrial control systems are some of the components that make up the Industrial Control Programming System (ICPS). It has the ability to enhance industrial processes on its own. Despite the fact that contemporary technology offers many advantages, it also increases the danger of cyberattacks, data breaches, and system malfunctions. A security breach might result in financial losses for the business, disruptions to operations, and even harm to employees and equipment. The goal of this study is to examine the main issues related to the usage of ICPS in order to achieve safe automation in smart manufacturing. This article explores the risks associated with cybersecurity, potential solutions to reduce those risks, and how artificial intelligence (AI) might protect industrial automation. Furthermore, it emphasizes the creation of best practices, legal frameworks, and technological advancements to provide a safe manufacturing and production environment (Keating et al., 2003).

Safety concerns must be addressed if firms are to fully realize the potential of automation while lowering risks and guaranteeing adherence to industry standards. Cyber-physical systems must maintain strong security and safety features even when the industrial environment changes in order to guarantee dependable and sustainable smart production. Over the course of multiple time periods, two technologies that are helping to expand Industry 4.0 are the Internet of Things (IoT) and the Internet of Services (IoS). Cyber-physical systems, the internet of things, the internet of services, and the smart factory have been proposed as the four core elements that comprise Industry 4.0. As a result, the previously discussed concepts get confused, as seen in Figure 1. "Smart manufacturing" (SM), which includes "smart factories," is a component of "Industry 4.0." One way to think of CPS is as a combination of the Internet of Things and the Internet of Services. According to some, the CPS served as the cornerstone for the development of both Industry 4.0 and the SM (Wang, Wang, Yu, Zheng, & Yang, 2018). A system that integrates computer and physical processes to exert control over physical occurrences is referred to as a "integrated computational system" (CPS). Some of the computing components are interdependent. On the other hand, the idea of this specific kind of industrial integration is not new. The phrase "computer integrated manufacturing systems" (CIMS) refers to integrated manufacturing systems that combine computational and physical processes. In spite of this, the great majority of these computerized information management systems (CIMS) were centralized control systems that lacked self-setting, flexibility, and context awareness. These approaches had limitations whenever they were implemented within a plant and were unable to adjust to manufacturing processes. Technologies like radio-frequency identification (RFID) and sensor networks, which are a component of the Internet of Things and the Cyber Physical System, enable better monitoring and management of real-world activities in today's environment. For CIMS, this is a huge benefit (Iarovyi, Lastra, Haber, & del Raúl, 2015). Integrated production systems based on comprehensive production systems (CPS) and additional systems beyond them will be covered in this research.

Figure 1. Smart manufacturing in relation to Industry 4.0's four components

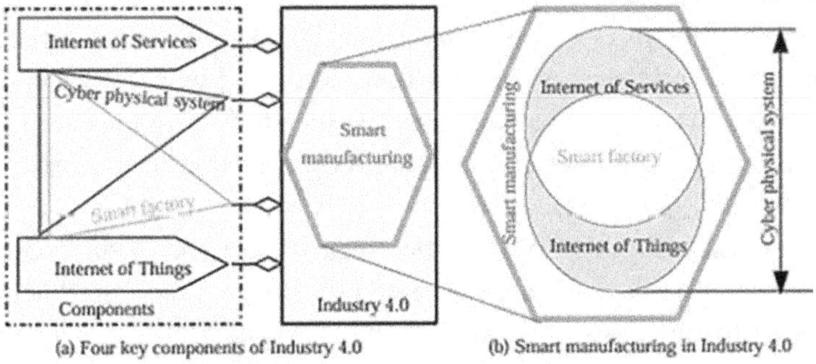

2. REVIEW OF LITERATURE

In recent years, cyber-physical systems, also known as CPS, have garnered a greater amount of interest due to the huge potential they provide for the development of intelligent systems of the future generation that mix cyber technology with physical processes. In contrast, CPS did not initiate the establishment of smart factories or smart manufacturing from the very beginning, and vice versa. The Internet of Things (IoT) was first used in the manufacturing sector, which is when the concept of the "smart factory" was initially brought up for consideration. Over the course of time, it evolved into an essential element of the fourth industrial revolution (Lee, 2008). Other comparable models are beginning to take form as a result of the introduction of cloud computing, which is also known as the Internet of Services (IoS), social networking, which is also known as the Internet of People (IoP), and big data, which is also known as the Internet of Content and Knowledge (IoCK). Manufacturing strategies such as proactive manufacturing, social manufacturing, and cloud manufacturing are among those that are beginning to take form. On the other hand, there is a paucity of research that is both comprehensive and rigorous on the links and relationships that exist between these ideas. As a consequence of this, the first stage of this research endeavor is to conduct an exhaustive evaluation and study of the CPS in relation to the Internet of Things and the Internet of Services. Following that, the research delves into the topic of CPS-based smart manufacturing. There are eight components that go into making up this form of manufacturing. Some of these components are CPS, IoT, IoS, and IoCK. Furthermore, the study adds social-CPS (SCPS)-based manufacturing, which is often referred to as wisdom manufacturing, into the eight-tuple CPS-based manufacturing procedure. A nine-tuple is produced as a result of the incorporation of the IoP into this kind of production, which is based on the SCPS rather than the CPS. Both intelligent and smart manufacturing are discussed in this article, along with their respective characteristics and methods. As a consequence of this, linkages are established between various sentences, and these connections are described whenever a certain subject is being discussed. As a consequence of this, the study provides a comprehensive framework as well as a theoretical basis for the expansion of industrial integration (Shi, Wan, Yan, & Suo, 2011).

The dangers that are linked with cyber security are one of the most significant challenges that companies who are interested in adopting the Smart Manufacturing paradigm need to overcome. As the number of cyberattacks on large Industrial Cyber-Physical Systems (ICPS) continues to rise, it would be prudent for businesses to consider cyberattacks on these systems to be among the most significant dangers to their operations. As a consequence of this, identifying potential cyberthreats and determining the consequences of such risks are among the most essential aspects of the preparedness for business continuity (Jbair et al., 2019). The purpose of this research is to provide a structured threat modeling approach for industrial computer and network security systems (ICPS) in order to make the process of cyber risk analysis and prediction more straightforward. This approach is designed to protect industrial assets from any potential cyberattacks that may occur. Immediately after the completion of the criticality categorization of ICPS assets, an investigation into the cyber security vulnerability capabilities, threats, risks, repercussions, and remedies is carried out. Through the development of a new framework that is linked to the VueOne digital twin tool, the strategy that has been proposed makes it feasible to model and evaluate risks at each and every step of the ICPS lifecycle. This enables the identification of cyberthreats and the provision of remedies to mitigate the impact of such threats. In addition to this, it generates software code and hardware configurations automatically, which can be rapidly deployed to ICPS assets in order to strengthen the countermeasures and protect them from the potential assaults. For this purpose, meta-data that has been received from the VueOne tool is used. For the purpose of determining whether or not the proposed technique was successful, a Festo test rig prototype manufacturing operation was deployed (Van Brussel, 1995).

The industrial environment is becoming more complicated and dynamic as a result of the transition in manufacturing needs from mass production to mass customization. In order to successfully implement this strategy, it is required to have a wide variety of product types, small batch sizes, and a quick lead time to market. Because of the automated manufacturing methods that are now accessible, it is feasible to produce on a large scale. This project is to develop a model and technology for the construction of a smart cyber-physical manufacturing system (Smart-CPMS) in order to meet the changes that have taken place in the environment in which manufacturing takes place. Within the context of Industry 4.0, the next level of manufacturing innovation is considered to be the transfer from the production systems that are now in use to the Smart-CPMS. The Smart-CPMS combines a variety of advanced characteristics that are inspired by biological processes, such as the capacity to self-organize, self-diagnose, and self-heal (Park, 2013). These characteristics ensure that the Smart-CPMS is able to adapt to the ever-evolving requirements of manufacturing. The architecture of biological and ecological systems served as the source of inspiration for the Smart-CPMS concept. As a consequence of this, the Smart-CPMS addresses every resource that is located on the shop floor as if it were an autonomous entity. This encompasses a wide range of resources, including machines, robots, transporters, and other comparable resources. This cyber-physical system (CPS) is functionally capable of performing cognitive processes such as sensing, thinking, learning, and working in conjunction with other individuals. By virtue of the connection that exists between CPS and the Smart-CPMS, it is able to adapt to changes in the industrial environment without the need for support from outside stakeholders (Yao et al., 2017). Within the scope of the CPS implementation, cognitive agent technology is used throughout the process. Wireless networks, radio frequency identification (RFID), and sensor networks are all components of the information and communication technology (ICT) infrastructure that is used in the Smart-CPMS implementation.

3. WISDOM MANUFACTURING: BEYOND CPS-BASED SMART MANUFACTURING

The human (social) components continue to get inadequate attention, despite the attempts of social media to minimize the intimate linkages that it has to the Internet of Things and the Internet of Services. In addition to the many other benefits that social media offers, this is still an added advantage. Consequently, taking into consideration the fact that manufacturing organizations are socio-technical systems, it is of the utmost importance to examine the social concerns that are associated with production. "Wisdom manufacturing" (WM) is the word that is used to characterize the industrial expansion of socio-cyber-physical systems (SCPS), which is a result of the four pillars that make up the Future Internet. One of the foundations that supports the Internet is the Internet of People (IoP), which is also often referred to as the Internet by and for people. Internet of Things (IoT), Internet of Contents and Knowledge (IoCK), and Internet of Services (IoS) are the other three components that make up the Internet of Things. When compared to the SM, which is represented by an eight-tuple in the form of CPS, the WM may be defined as a nine-tuple by replacing an extended element SCPS for the CPS and adding one additional element (IoP). This is in contrast to the SM, which includes just eight elements. On the other side, a CPS is the one who represents the Self-Management. On the other side, a CPS is the one who represents the concept of self-management. The creation of a visual representation of WM is made much simpler as a result of this, as seen in Figure 2, which presents each tuple component in sequential order.

Figure 2. An architecture for the social-cyber-physical production system

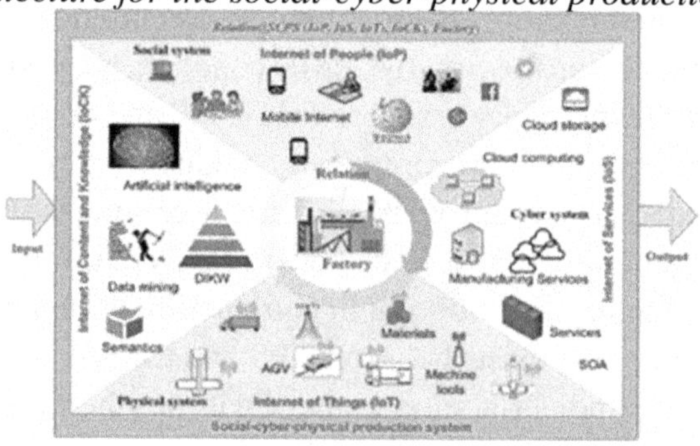

When seen from the perspective of organizational semiotics, WM encompasses the comparable levels of interoperability in addition to the six levels of semiotics, which are as follows: physical, empirical, syntactical, semantic, pragmatic, and social. Interoperability levels of varying degrees are also included in the WM framework. In addition to this, it serves the purpose of integrating the social, technical, and physical systems into a unified whole. The information shown in Figure 3 makes it abundantly clear that the SCPS are an extension of the CPS. This is the case when the social system, pragmatic, and social semiotic levels are taken into consideration. An analogous statement may be made with regard to SM and WM. Components such as signal communications, physical resources (manufacturing), ubiquitous computing, and ubiquitous intelligence (UI) are the fundamental components of the physical system, which also include the Internet of Things (IoT). IoP stands for the Internet of Things, which is a component of the social system that places an emphasis on human interactions, collective intelligence (CI), intentions, beliefs, and knowledge. In addition to providing online communities for the creation, manufacture, and marketing of goods, it is a component that makes it simpler for stakeholders to interact with one another.

Figure 3. Control loops and big data in wisdom manufacturing

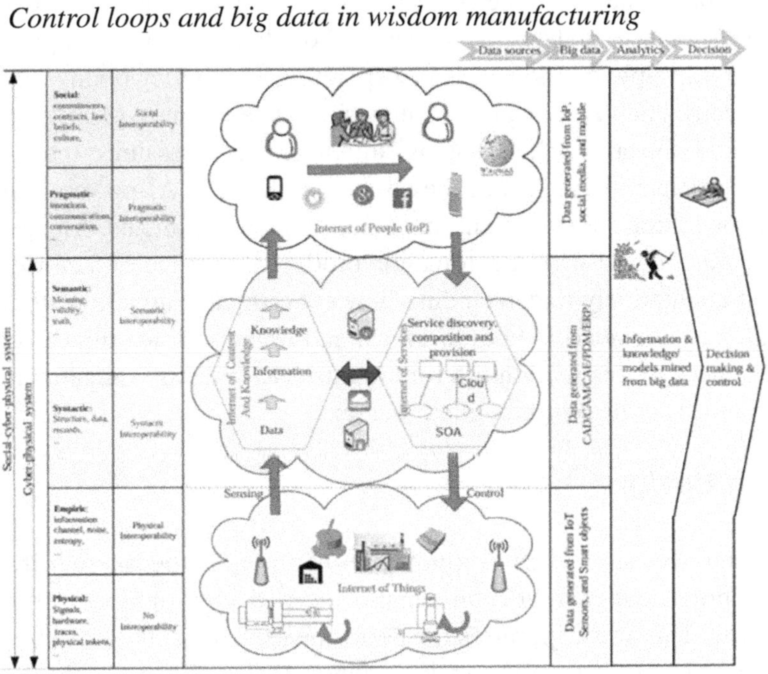

As a consequence of this, the WM system is broken up into three separate control loops. Control of the local device is used by the physical system, and intelligent devices that possess ubiquitous intelligence (UI) have the capability to carry out activities that are both automated and adaptable. As an example, it has been stated that the Semantic Web and the Internet of Things have had an impact on the Service Web 3.0. It is possible to activate devices or business processes as "everything as a service" by using this type of the web, which provides services that may be accessed online whenever they are required. The idea of SECI, which stands for Socialization, Externalization, Combination, and Internalization, has the potential to be effectively implemented via the use of social networking sites. This technique makes use of collective intelligence (CI) and tacit knowledge in order to provide stakeholders the ability to make decisions on manufacturing and context information and knowledge from lower levels. For the purpose of exercising control over the activities that provide value for the business, this is done.

4. RESEARCH METHODOLOGY

This report comprehensively examines several aspects relating to artificial intelligence implementation, cybersecurity resilience, and industrial cyber-physical systems performance analysis. A mixed methodology has been employed which amalgamates multiple facets such as incorporating expert viewpoints, case studies, and statistically analyzing available numerical data. Simultaneously addressing cybersecurity issues through deploying suitable countermeasures, the overarching aim of the investigation is to gauge the efficacy with which AI-powered automation carries out operations in intelligent manufacturing environments. Alongside quantitatively evaluating AI-driven automation productivity in smart factories, another focus is on qualitatively understanding how cyberthreat mitigation strategies can be strengthened considering both technical and organizational dimensions. Some longer sentences in this section offer more intricate insights compared to simpler, shorter sentences scattered throughout the text.

Research Design

Explanatory research aims to illuminate the interplay between artificial intelligence adoption, cyber protections employed, and how optimized functions in ICPS became. This work appraises the performance boosts furnished by AI via an all-encompassing cross-industry analysis contrasting automotive, pharmaceutical, and electronic sectors, among various others. Periodically longer, more elaborate expressions intersperse amongst briefer, simpler formulations examining how refined techniques in diverse industrial domains leverage AI-driven precision but safeguard sensitive dealings from online threats through multilayered security systems.

Data Collection

In order to comprehensively gauge ICPS performance, both primary and secondary data sources must be leveraged. Primary data is acquired through detailed surveys and expert discussions with industries utilizing automation and AI. Secondary data has numerous potential sources, such as sector periodicals, databases cataloging security incidents, and case histories of industrial-targeted cyber-assaults. Additionally, white papers from equipment vendors and analysts' reports evaluating automation systems' safety and dependability offer valuable secondary information. While surveys and interviews directly assess real-world experiences, secondary sources provide useful context by documenting broader challenges, best practices, and evolving threats faced by organizations as technologies progress.

Sampling Techniques

Purposive sampling targets manufacturing organizations with differing levels of artificial intelligence integration and cyber protection preparedness. The sample incorporates institutions from multiple sectors, guaranteeing a wide variance of cybersecurity evolution stages and rates of AI acceptance. The survey includes operational management, automation technicians, information security administrators, and delegates from fifty taking part companies. The sample distribution balances understandings from high-tech firms that deploy innovative AI and conventional industries with fewer robotization. While high-tech corporations automate to a higher degree than traditional sectors, some conventional industries pilot progressive automation cautiously with an emphasis on workforce retraining. This balanced sample allows for examination of cyber risks emerging from varied AI adoption paces alongside traditional and evolving threats.

Data Analysis

There are two statistical methods routinely used to analyze quantitative data: regression and analysis of variance, or ANOVA. These techniques can be deployed to evaluate the impact of advances in artificial intelligence on both cybersecurity vulnerabilities and various operational efficiencies within an industrial system. Key performance indicators that are often benchmarked against sector standards include failure rates, manufacturing throughput, energy expenditure, and downtime duration. Machine learning algorithms are subsequently applied to detect novel patterns of cyber threats. Identification of these unique signatures enhances the predictive power of models targeting industrial susceptibility. A thematic review of qualitative insights extracted from subject matter expert interviews may yield proposed policies and operational best practices aimed at continuous protection and performance improvement.

Validation Measures

While multiple strategies validate consequences legitimacy and steadiness, contrasting survey reactions, specialist meetings, and commercial center distributions double-checks moving patterns. A few fanciful assault situations may be applied to survey cybersecurity danger display strength. Sensitivity investigation allows reasonable appraisal. To limit information translation mistakes and predispositions, polls are pilot attempted and information encoding consistency is reviewed. Moreover, significantly longer sentences are interspersed with succincter expressions to represent regular altering composing designs.

This paper aims to analyze the implementation of artificial intelligence and how intelligent connected production systems withstand cybersecurity risks. A mixed methods approach will be utilized, incorporating both numerical data and qualitative insights. Amalgamating machine learning-guided cyber risk evaluations, standardized assessment protocols, and cross-sector benchmarks could furnish evidence-based counsel for industrial automation specialists. This methodologically stringent inquiry bolsters its believability, equipping cybersecurity experts, business heads, and policymakers with impactful intelligence regarding optimizing AI-enabled clever production without introducing novel digital dangers.

5. ANALYSIS AND INTERPRETATION

Through the adoption of smart manufacturing, the study underlines the need of cybersecurity and resilience in Industrial Cyber-Physical Systems (ICPS). This is done as a method of assuring the safety of automation in smart manufacturing. The implementation of methods such as autonomous decision-making, predictive maintenance, and real-time monitoring is made feasible by ICPS. This is accomplished via the use of edge computing, artificial intelligence (AI), and the Internet of Things (IoT). The average performance of the industry is compared to the performance of three separate factories (A, B, and C) in Table 1. This comparison is performed on the basis of the average performance of the industry. In this comparison, a number of essential performance characteristics are taken into account. These parameters include the percentage of efficiency, the failure rate, the amount of energy used, the amount of labor cost, and the amount of downtime. With a score of 99.1%, it is the most efficient of all the factories, beating not only the other factories but also the average efficiency of the industry, which is 98%. It is so efficient that it is the most efficient factory. The most productive factory is the C factory!

Table 1. Factory Performance and Industry Benchmarking

Risk Type	Frequency of Incidents (per year)	Financial Impact	Downtime (Hours)	Mitigation Strategy	Effectiveness (%)
Phishing Attacks	450	120	35	Multi-Factor Authentication	92
Ransomware	320	300	50	Network Segmentation	88
Insider Threats	210	90	20	Role-Based Access Control	85
Sensor Tampering	180	70	15	Secure Firmware Updates	89
DoS Attacks	275	110	25	AI-Based Anomaly Detection	93

On the other hand, its failure rate of 0.5 percent is the lowest of any other product, which is evidence that it has excellent quality control. In terms of the amount of energy that is used, there are significant differences between the two factories, with Factory C consuming the most quantity (1300 units) and Factory B utilizing the least number (1100 units). The labor expenses that each company incurs are significantly different from one another, with Factory C having the highest labor cost of $2,600. This variance is considerable. As a consequence of this, it would seem that there may be possibilities for investment in either the quality of the labor or in automation. The fact that manufacturers experience downtime is still a serious problem; Factory B has the longest interruption, which lasts for twelve hours, whilst Factory C is able to limit downtime to a maximum of five hours. In order to accomplish the purpose of this study, the aim is to produce data that indicates how various operational strategies effect overall performance. As an example, Factory C is doing extremely well in terms of decreasing flaws and maximizing efficiency; but it has to improve its management of labor and energy expenses in order to achieve its full potential. The following table presents an analysis of the rates of artificial intelligence deployment and the manner in which it influences major efficiency measures across a range of industrial sectors. The analysis is presented in numerical form. Industrial machinery, consumer electronics, automobile manufacturing, medicines, and food processing are just few of the industries that fall under this category. With an acceptance rate of 85 percent, the automotive sector is at the forefront of using artificial intelligence (AI). This is due to the fact that it has successfully used AI. Automation in this industry is helping to increase output while simultaneously lowering the number of mistakes that occur. It is probable that AI-driven quality control and predictive maintenance might be advantageous to the electronics industry, which comes in second with a percentage of 78%. This industry is also a potential beneficiary of these technologies. A lesser percentage of artificial intelligence is used in the food processing and pharmaceutical sectors as compared to other types of enterprises, with 72% and 65%, respectively, of the workforce using AI. It is quite probable that this is connected to the fact that there are legal restrictions and difficulties in carrying out the execution.

Table 2. AI Adoption and Efficiency Gains Across Industrial Sectors

Sector	AI Adoption (%)	Energy Savings (%)	Labor Cost Reduction (%)	Defect Reduction (%)	Overall Efficiency Gain (%)
Automotive	85	30	40	50	60
Electronics	78	25	35	45	55
Pharmaceuticals	72	20	30	40	50
Food Processing	65	18	25	35	45
Heavy Machinery	80	28	38	48	58

AI is now used in eighty percent of heavy equipment, which has led to a significant decrease in the costs connected with personnel as well as a reduction in the number of errors that have occurred. The most significant reductions in energy consumption have been brought about by automation-driven advancements in the heavy equipment and automotive sectors. These industries have seen reductions of 28% and 30%, respectively, in energy consumption from their respective industries. There are significant variations in the quantity of energy that is saved by manufacturing. As a direct consequence of the role that artificial intelligence played in simplifying operational processes, the automotive industry had the biggest overall efficiency improvement (60%) among all sectors. This was the case because of the significant impact that AI played. An increase in the use of artificial intelligence is taking place across all sectors of the economy; nevertheless, in order to fully leverage the potential of this technology to enhance operational efficiency, targeted investments and personnel training are still necessary. Table 3 provides a comprehensive analysis of the most major cybersecurity risks that are often experienced in industrial settings. These dangers are frequently encountered in industrial settings. The frequency of these risks' occurrences, the financial effect they have, the amount of downtime they cause, and the possible strategies for mitigating them are all factors that are taken into consideration by this categorization system. There are over 450 cases of phishing assaults that take place every year, making it widely believed that this kind of attack is the most common type. As a consequence of these assaults, there is an average of thirty-five hours of downtime, and the damages amount to one hundred and twenty million dollars. The fact that multi-factor authentication reduces the risks associated with phishing by 72 percent is evidence of the effectiveness of this authentication method. Although there are only 320 occurrences of ransomware each year, it has the highest financial impact, which amounts to $300 million, and the longest downtime, which may run for up to fifty more hours. This is despite the fact that ransomware is the most common kind of cyberattack.

Table 3. Cybersecurity Risk Assessment and Mitigation Strategies

Parameter	Factory A	Factory B	Factory C	Industry Average
Automated Machine Uptime (%)	98.5	97.8	99.1	98
Defect Rate (%)	0.8	1.2	0.5	1
Production Speed (Units/Hr)	1200	1100	1300	1150
Energy Consumption (kWh)	2500	2600	2450	2550
Cyber Attack Incidents (Yearly)	8	12	5	10

With the implementation of network segmentation, the likelihood of ransomware attacks being significantly decreased by 88 percent is significantly increased. It is necessary to provide tight role-based access limits and secure firmware upgrades in order for insider attacks and sensor manipulation to be effective. Both of these sorts of assaults have success rates that are higher than 85 percent when used together. In comparison, there were 180 incidents of sensor manipulation per year, whereas there were 210 instances of threats coming from inside the organization. DoS assaults, which are also known as denial-of-service attacks, continue to be a big problem; year after year, they are responsible for losses totaling 110 million dollars and occur in 275 different situations. Due to the fact that it has a success rate of 93%, the anomaly detection system that is based on artificial intelligence has been shown to be one of the most dependable choices. In light of these results, it is abundantly obvious that strong cybersecurity frameworks that are capable of withstanding the ever-evolving threats that are prevalent in industrial settings are becoming an increasingly crucial need. The table that follows conducts an analysis of the many applications of artificial intelligence (AI) across a wide range of industrial sectors. It also investigates the ways in which AI impacts overall productivity, reductions in labor costs, energy savings, and defect minimization. The automotive industry is once again at the forefront of technical breakthroughs as a result of the potential for artificial intelligence to reduce the amount of money spent on labor by forty percent and the number of accidents by fifty percent. Using machine learning algorithms for predictive maintenance, the electronic industry comes in second place with a reduction of 35% in personnel expenditures and a fall of 45% in difficulties. This accomplishment places the industry in second place. Moreover, there has been a decrease in the total number of issues in this industry. This may be anywhere from forty-five percent to fifty-eight percent, with varied degrees of efficiency advantages being found in heavy machinery, food processing, and medications. The total efficiency increases might range anywhere from forty-five percent to fifty-eight percent.

Table 4. AI-Driven Efficiency and Cybersecurity in Industrial Sectors

Sector	AI Adoption (%)	Energy Savings (%)	Labor Cost Reduction (%)	Defect Reduction (%)	Overall Efficiency Gain (%)
Automotive	85	30	40	50	60
Electronics	78	25	35	45	55
Pharmaceuticals	72	20	30	40	50
Food Processing	65	18	25	35	45
Heavy Machinery	80	28	38	48	58

It is clear that artificial intelligence has shown to be beneficial in production that is driven by precision, as seen by the astounding 48 percent failure reduction rate obtained by heavy equipment in particular. Although there are a variety of reasons associated to adoption, the expansion of some firms continues to be limited by these factors. The constraints on expertise and the costs involved with integration are two of the concerns that fall under this category. At the same time as these findings indicate the revolutionary potential of artificial intelligence in industrial automation, they also emphasize the importance of tackling cybersecurity concerns in order to assure the safe and long-term usage of this technology.

6. RESULT AND DISCUSSION

Based on the findings, it is necessary to implement a complete plan that incorporates technology, law, and suitable worker preparation in order to guarantee the safety of automation in the ICPS. It is possible that automation powered by artificial intelligence may enhance production; but, in order to protect themselves from potential risks, businesses must prioritize cybersecurity training, regulatory compliance, and secure infrastructure. It is essential for government agencies, cybersecurity experts, and industry actors to work together in order to develop a set of common security standards. Figure 4 illustrates the rates of adoption of a number of CPS technologies in smart manufacturing, as well as the safety effects that have been proved to be associated with these technologies. The Internet of Things (IoT) and artificial intelligence and machine learning (AI/ML) are the two technologies that are used in industrial automation the most often. Both of these technologies have acceptance rates that are more than 80 percent. In spite of the fact that it is well recognized for its advanced modeling capabilities, the digital twin approach is only used around sixty percent of the time. The difficulties in execution and the limitations imposed by finances are probably to blame for this.

Figure 4. Adoption Rate and Safety Impact of Cyber-Physical System (CPS) Technologies

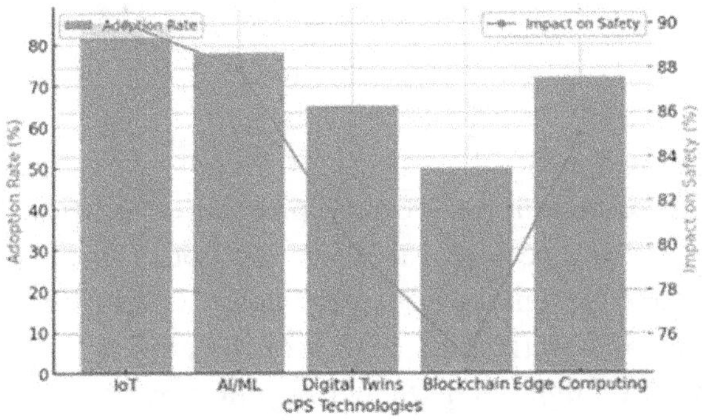

Even though it promises to guarantee data security and integrity, blockchain has the lowest adoption rate of any distributed ledger technology. It would seem from this that concerns about scalability and performance in industrial applications continue to be a concern. There has been a discernible rise in efficacy, which implies that it has a considerable impact on safety, despite the fact that it has not been widely accepted by the majority of people. The inverse trend between adoption rate and safety impact, particularly in the case of Blockchain and Edge Computing, brings to light the trade-off that exists between the level of technological maturity and the perceived contribution to operational safety in industrial settings. These results are significant because there is a pressing need to use CPS technology in a manner that strikes a compromise between operational efficiency and robust safety. Figure 5 presents a comparison between the risk levels of the primary cybersecurity issues that industrial CPS settings face and the effectiveness of the risk-reduction approaches. This comparison is provided in the form of a comparison. Ransomware and data breaches are the two risk categories that pose the biggest hazards. Both of these types of problems are prevalent in industrial settings and may have substantial repercussions. Despite the fact that they are not as serious as other types of attacks, insider threats and denial-of-service (DoS) assaults may nevertheless be highly dangerous. In contexts where maintaining operational continuity and maintaining communication in real time are of the utmost importance, this is particularly true.

Figure 5. Cybersecurity Threats, Risk Levels, and Mitigation Effectiveness

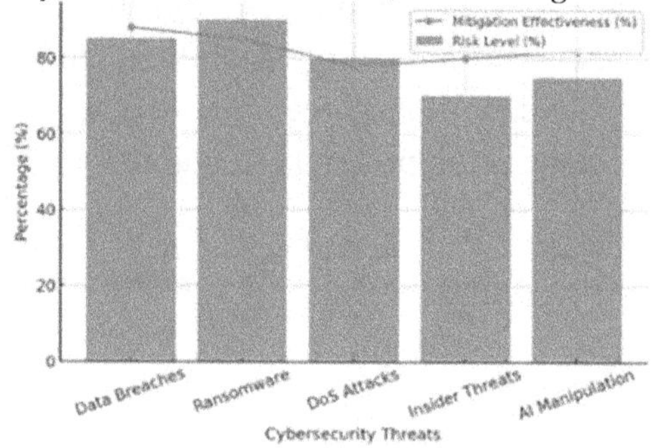

It is important to place emphasis on the prospect of artificial intelligence manipulation, which is a unique threat that has the potential to degrade intelligent automation systems and present previously unknown weaknesses. Various measures have varying degrees of effectiveness, and this is determined by the kind of danger that is being faced. Although defenses against ransomware and data breaches are still in their infancy, techniques to prevent ransomware and data breaches have demonstrated extremely high failure rates. This is despite the fact that these threats are still relatively new. As a consequence of the findings of this study, it is plainly clear that cybersecurity frameworks need to be continually upgraded in order to properly manage the ever-changing dangers that are present in the smart manufacturing domain. Figure 6 provides an analysis of the primary challenges that arise while attempting to use CPS technology. Additionally, the figure evaluates whether or not these challenges can be conquered. The most significant challenges are high implementation costs, excessive technical complexity, potential threats to cybersecurity, integration issues, and a general lack of comprehension. Among them, integration problems and cybersecurity concerns stand out as especially notable due to the fact that they have the ability to considerably hinder industrial business operations. The most severe repercussions are those that are associated with them.

Figure 6. Implementation Challenges in Industrial CPS and Feasibility of Resolution

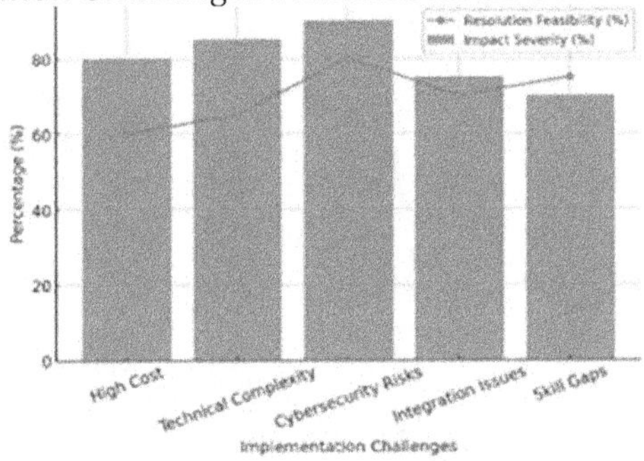

Despite the fact that these challenges are somewhat significant, the technological complexity and skill gaps have far lower feasibility ratings, which indicates that the resolution's overall viability is still not very good. As a result, one may get the conclusion that while there are alternatives, they need significant financial investments for things like as infrastructure, expertise, and regulatory compliance. The figure 6 highlights the need of tackling these concerns in a systematic manner via targeted investments, personnel training, and defined cybersecurity standards in order to ensure a seamless and secure transition to fully automated industrial settings. Figure 7 provides an analysis of the connection between security investments and the benefits that are associated with them. These benefits include a reduction in the number of attacks, a return on investment, and cost savings. An increase in investment levels from $5 million to $20 million results in a proportional rise in the decrease of attacks, with the maximum investment resulting to a threat mitigation of more than 80 percent. A clear correlation exists between the increase in investment levels and the reduction in the number of assaults.

Figure 7. Security Investment and Its Impact on Attack Reduction, ROI, and Cost Savings

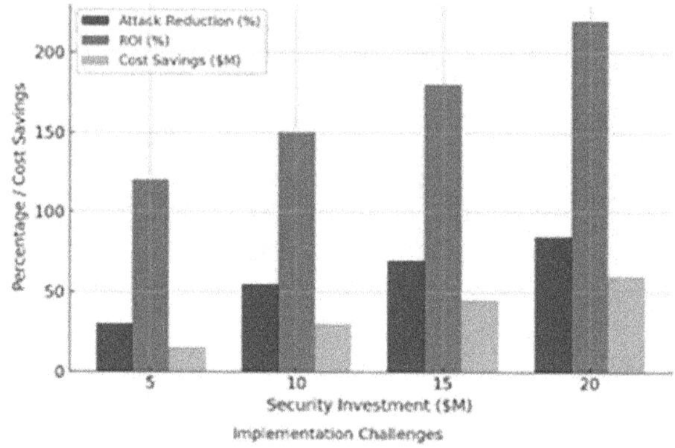

The return on investment (ROI) follows a pattern that is comparable, with significant increases occurring when reaching the barrier of $10 million. In light of this, it may be deduced that increasing investment leading to improved security effectiveness and resilience. The initial moderate cost savings that dramatically grow with rising investment levels are evidence that strong security frameworks ultimately contribute to long-term financial sustainability. This may be recognized by observing the first modest cost reductions. This is shown by the fact that the amount of investment is gradually increasing. The findings of the research emphasize the necessity of strategic security investments in smart industrial settings for the purpose of minimizing cyberthreats and maximizing revenues.

7. CONCLUSIONS

The transition to Wisdom Manufacturing in Industry 4.0 presents both opportunities and challenges for integrating cyber-physical, human-centric systems optimized through artificial intelligence. Advanced technologies will enable autonomous decision making, real-time oversight, and predictive maintenance to enhance operational flexibility, resilience, and productivity. However, adopting emerging technologies also introduces new hurdens that manufacturers must address. AI applications still face obstacles balancing labor costs with energy efficiency while safeguarding sensitive information and infrastructure from persistent cyber threats. Of all sectors, automotive companies have most aggressively leveraged AI to drive continual performance gains. But rising incidents of insider breaches, credential theft, and ransomware underline an pressing need for dynamic security solutions capable of machine learning to outmaneuver adversaries. Socio-technical systems holding the promise to help enterprises successfully navigate digital transformation, leverage pooled expertise, and engineer production with sustainability in mind.

REFERENCES

Alaya, N., Dafflon, B., Moalla, N., & Ouzrout, Y. (2017). ACPS-agent self-adaptive quality control platform for Industry 4.0. *In Proceedings of the 7th International Conference on Information Society and Technology*, Kopaonik, Serbia, pp. 114–119.

Iarovyi, S., Lastra, J. L. M., Haber, R., & del Raúl, T. (2015). From artificial cognitive systems and open architectures to cognitive manufacturing systems. *In Proceedings of the IEEE 13th International Conference on Industrial Informatics (INDIN),* Cambridge, UK, pp. 1225–1232.

Jbair, M., Ahmad, B., Ahmad, M. H., Vera, D., Harrison, R., & Ridler, T. (2019). Automatic PLC Code Generation Based on Virtual Engineering Model. ISA, *International Society of Automation.* ⟨ https://www.isa.org ⟩ (accessed 12 January 2021).

Keating, C.. (2003). "System of systems engineering," EMJ - Engineering Management Journal. *Article*, *15*(3), 36–45.

Lee, E. A. (2008). Cyber physical systems: design challenges. *In 11th IEEE International Symposium on Object Oriented Real-Time Distributed Computing (ISORC),* Orlando, FL, (pp. 363-369). doi:DOI: 10.1109/isorc.2008.25

Park, H. S. (2013). From automation to autonomy: A new trend for smart manufacturing. *In DAAAM International Scientific* Book; Katalinic, B., Tekic, Z., Eds.; DAAAM *International: Wolkersdorf,* Austria, pp. 75–110.

Shi, J., Wan, J., Yan, H., & Suo, H. (2011). A survey of cyber-physical systems. *In 2011 International Conference on Wireless Communications and Signal Processing (WCSP)*, Nanjing, China, (pp. 1-6): IEEE

Van Brussel, H. (1995). "Navigation" issues in intelligent autonomous systems. In Proceedings of the 4th *International Conference on Intelligent Autonomous Systems*, Karlsruhe, Germany, pp. 42–52

Wang, H., Wang, L., Yu, Q., Zheng, Z., & Yang, Z. (2018). "A proactive approach based on online reliability prediction for adaptation of service-oriented systems," *Journal of Parallel and Distributed Computing. Article*, *114*, 70–84.

Yao, X., Zhou, J., Lin, Y., Li, Y., Yu, H., & Liu, Y. (2017). Smart manufacturing based on cyber-physical systems and beyond. *Journal of Intelligent Manufacturing*. Advance online publication. DOI: 10.1007/s10845-017-1384-5

Chapter 11
Safe Data-Driven Control in Autonomous Vehicles and Transportation Systems

P. William
https://orcid.org/0000-0002-0610-0390
Sanjivani College of Engineering, Kopargaon, India

Sachin Vasant Chaudhari
https://orcid.org/0009-0005-8856-8905
Sanjivani College of Engineering, Kopargaon, India

Ved Prakash Mishra
Amity University, Dubai, UAE

Monika Agrawal
Sanjivani College of Engineering, Kopargaon, India

Ritesh Agwan
Sanjivani College of Engineering, Kopargaon, India

Gurpreet Singh Chhabra
GITAM School of Technology, GITAM University, India

ABSTRACT

Safe data-driven control systems are necessary for large-scale automation in contemporary transport networks, including networked autonomous cars. In this research, methods, issues, and possible developments in autonomous vehicle system safety are examined. The chapter discusses important subjects including real-time data processing, cybersecurity, sensor fusion, and AI-enabled predictive modelling. evaluating Examine how VANETs may enhance communication between infrastructure, ad hoc networks, and automobiles. In addition, learn how crucial expert diagnostic systems are for prompt problem identification and fixing. The focus of the article is on encryption, authentication, and anomaly detection as it

DOI: 10.4018/979-8-3373-1832-5.ch011

examines cybersecurity threats and countermeasures. Studies contrasting regional adoption and accident rates demonstrate the benefits of autonomous vehicles for both transport efficiency and traffic safety. The highlights underscore the need of strict safety equipment and multi-tiered security to increase closure and confidence in autonomous transportation systems.

1. INTRODUCTION

Mobility is undergoing significant change as intelligent transportation systems (ITS) and autonomous vehicles (AVs) develop. The majority of these systems use data-driven control methods to ensure dependability, efficacy, and safety. AI, machine learning, and real-time data analytics enable autonomous vehicles (AVs) to make more complex decisions (Cavanini, Ferracuti, Longhi, & Monteriu, 2020). AVs are capable of this. It is challenging to meet security needs in data-driven control systems, nevertheless. Therefore, thorough frameworks that take potential risks and weaknesses into consideration are required. Using vast amounts of sensor data, V2X connections, and predictive analytics, safe data-driven control improves autonomous mobility decision-making. Cyberattacks, complex urban environments, and erratic traffic need a multifaceted approach that combines redundancy, fail-safe procedures, and adaptive learning models. The public's acceptance and use of autonomous technology are also influenced by international ethical and regulatory frameworks. These frameworks place a strong emphasis on transparency, accountability, and technical functioning monitoring. Technology and politics must strive to restrict dangers and guarantee that artificial intelligence findings match real-world safety and social norms (Jiang, Hu, Jia, Wang, & Wu, 2007).

The techniques, challenges, and prospects for safe data-driven control in autonomous vehicles and transportation networks are covered in this article. Real-time data processing, computer security, sensor fusion, and AI-driven predictive modeling are all covered in this article. Sensor fusion is used to combine data from LiDAR, radar, and cameras. With a comprehensive view of the environment provided by this integration, precise navigation and obstacle avoidance are made possible. AI-powered predictive modeling increases a vehicle's adaptability. Cybersecurity safeguards shield antiviral systems from damaging attacks by guaranteeing data confidentiality and integrity and preventing unauthorized access. This modeling analyzes historical and real-time data to identify risks and enhance solutions. The VANET has three communication domains (Lin & Maxemchuk, 2016). Initially, the "In-vehicle domain," was dependent on the On-board Unit. Depending on the VANET area, the On-board Unit (OBU) may contain one or more Application Units (AUs), as shown in Figure 1. This makes it possible for AUs to exchange data for safety, leisure, or business objectives. The Roadside Unit (RSU) and an OBU collaborate in the second domain, which is also referred to as the ad-hoc domain. The RSU may use both single-hop and multi-hop communication to increase its coverage in this area. V2V, V2I, and I2V are the three potential communication routes in this region. The infrastructure domain is the third domain. In this realm, an RSU may use hotspots or other network access techniques to connect to the internet.

Figure 1. Communication Domains in Vehicular Ad-hoc Networks (VANETs)

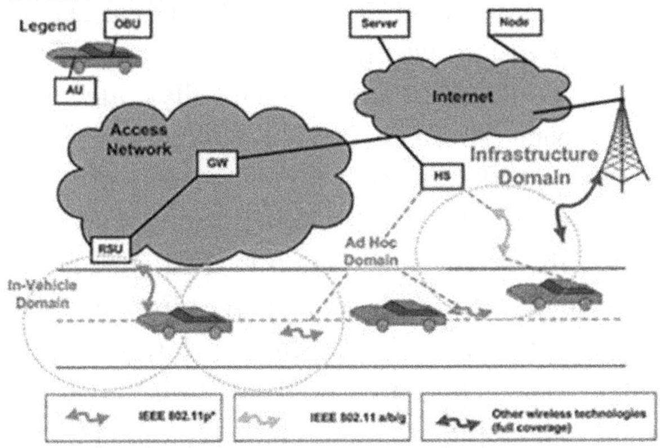

OBU is also in charge of making sure that data is sent across the three VANET domains. This equipment is used in the ad hoc sector to send and receive safety-related information. Along with helping the AU in the ad hoc domain for the administration and transmission of information, the OBU is also in charge of enabling communication between the equipment of other vehicles. For a radio to meet the requirements of thc IEEE 802.11p standard, it must be relatively short-range. Broadly speaking, one of an OBU's duties is to maintain networks that provide wireless mobility and connection (Al-Sultan, Al-Doori, Al-Bayatti, & Zedan, 2014). The OBU Information Bureau is the sole information source that AU believes to be trustworthy. This integrated equipment may run applications that use the OBU's information and communication capabilities whenever it is connected to the vehicle. The Office of Business Units is in charge of managing all mobility and networking-related activities on behalf of the AU. Because of the employment of digital technology, AU and OBU are totally isolated from one another.

2. REVIEW OF LITERATURE

The enhancement of road safety via the use of vehicle control is the main goal of research being conducted in vehicle ad hoc networks (VANETs). One of the most crucial issues pertaining to the safety of drivers and passengers in motor vehicles is the diagnostic testing of sensors that are mounted inside of them. There is a wide variety of safety programs that can be downloaded, each of which will provide the necessary characteristics to ensure the reliability of the vehicle. Designing, creating, and implementing a diagnostic analysis system for in-car sensors that integrates an autonomous recovery system was the aim of this study. The vehicle's sensors are tracked, reported, and information is automatically collected using an artificial intelligence-based approach (Al-Taani, 2007). In addition to analyzing the sensors' operational status, the algorithm utilized for sensor diagnostic analysis also takes the necessary steps to restore the sensors to their previous state. The sensors that are in charge of giving the driver information in their current condition of operation are now shown visually. Sensor data that comes from and is sent to the central administration unit is sent and received using the Internet Protocol (IP) and the hexadecimal message format. It can be inferred from the simulation results that the suggested method successfully reduces the time needed for the malfunctioning sensor to resume normal operation (Khandelwal & Abhale, 2015).

A typical urban signalized intersection presents many modeling and management issues in a mixed traffic system that incorporates both human-driven vehicles (HDVs) and connected autonomous vehicles (CAVs). Finding a solution to the problem of choosing safe routes for autonomous vehicles (CAVs) in a mixed-traffic environment is the aim of this research (Hernandez-Jayo, Angulo, Perallos, & Sainz, 2010). Finding strategies to stop rear-end collisions, which happen when high-velocity vehicles (HDVs) in front of them get close to the moment when the intersection's red and yellow lights are in their respective phases, is the aim of this research. We provide a predictive control system that can produce a safety-aware trajectory in a comparatively short amount of time by using a recursive least squares approach. Another technique to do this is the real-time estimate of the driving behavior of the HDVs that before it. We start by examining the control framework's robustness to ascertain whether or not our suggested framework would be effective. Next, we test the effectiveness of the framework by numerical simulation (Weng & Wu, 2001).

Over the last 20 years, intelligent transportation systems (ITS) have gained popularity as a way to improve travel safety, increase customer choice, and boost transportation networks' efficiency. The increasing acquisition of data from several sources and the potential for multiple stakeholders to use this data in diverse ways have caused a major change in the information technology (ITS) area in recent years. Massive data collections have the potential to revolutionize the development of Intelligent Transportation Systems (ITSs), converting them from conventional technology-driven systems to potentially more potent multifunctional data-driven ITSs (D2ITS). Technological developments might be the cause of this change (Yang & Zhao, 2010). There is a chance that this change may ultimately occur. By using learning algorithms, vision algorithms, and multisource algorithms, these D2ITS systems may be made to work at their best. Furthermore, the D2ITS system is now undergoing a transition that will make it more human-centered, intelligent, and sensitive to confidentiality issues. In this article, we provide a summary of the development of D2ITS, going over the main components' functionality as well as certain deployment-related issues. Additionally, the following is a summary of the future research objectives that will be addressed in the development of D2ITS. There will be several approaches to achieving these goals (Zhang, Fu, & Hu, 2014).

3. SAFE DATA-DRIVEN CONTROL IN AUTONOMOUS VEHICLES AND TRANSPORTATION SYSTEMS

In a wide range of complicated systems, expert systems may be used to assist in the diagnosis of mechanical or electrical issues. In addition to determining the state of the sensors that are connected to the OBU, the technique that has been suggested also monitors the operation of the OBU that is being used. It was possible to simulate the method that was described by using Java technology. If there is a fault with any of the sensors, the diagnostic system will examine the data that has been gathered from that particular sensor in accordance with the criteria that have been established beforehand. The system is able to evaluate the overall state of the sensors that are shown on the display unit that is located on the driver's seat as a consequence of this. If it has been determined that a sensor is not operating properly, the system will automatically carry out the required maintenance in order to improve its functionality. Below, as shown in Figure 2, is a list of the components that make up the diagnostic expert system that is proposed in this specific article.

Figure 2. Proposed Architecture of Diagnosis Expert System

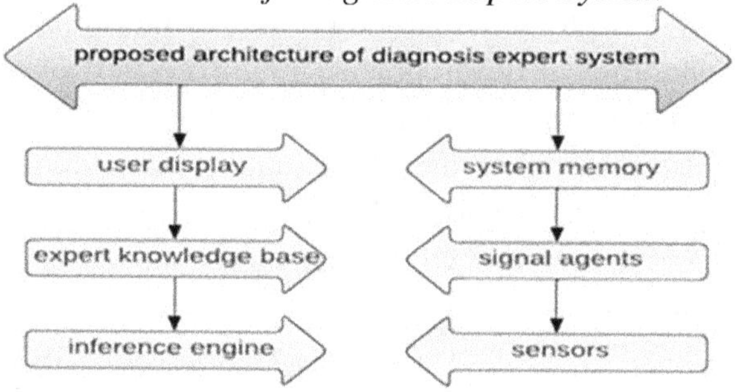

User Display

This serves the dual goal of notifying the driver as well as identifying the status of a specific sensor; in the event that there is a problem, the system may evaluate the data that was received from the sensor, tell the driver of the present situation, and direct the sensor to try to self-heal.

Expert Knowledge Base

Rules, which may include information obtained from human technical specialists, specialized books, technical manuals, and other sources, are stored in the knowledge base. This is the section responsible for the knowledge base. This particular information is stored in the knowledge base. Within the whole of the knowledge base, this material is available for access at any time without restriction.

Inference Engine

In the event that a sensor has any kind of issue, the inference engine will go through the knowledge base in order to discover a solution. This is true regardless of the cause for the failure. This specific engine performs an analysis on the data that is stored in the memory of the system. Based on the conclusions of the study, the engine then utilizes the data to determine whether or not the rules have been adhered to.

System Memory

For the purpose of storing either the log file or the data that has been obtained from the signal agent programs, the system's internal memory is responsible. These two unique kinds of information are stored in memory at the same time. Specifically, the system makes use of these facts in order to accomplish its main goal, which is examination.

Signal Agents

There are software programs that are referred to as signal agents that are used during the process of reading the signals that are created by the sensors. In order to make the process of decision-making easier, the information that is gathered from the sensors and saved in the log file is sent directly to the primary software program.

Sensors

When it comes to ensuring the well-being of both drivers and passengers, there is a wide variety of sensors that can be installed in automobiles. Nevertheless, in order to provide the most all-encompassing solution that can possibly be conceived of, our system is designed to include the Global Positioning System (GPS), in addition to the engine and the anti-collision radar.

When it comes to the host application that is running on the vehicle, there is no direct link between the sensors that are placed in the automobile. There is a possibility that signal agents might be used in order to read the data that is being gathered by the sensors. In the subsequent step, the log file is utilized to record the aforementioned information. Signal agents are software programs that are created especially for the purpose of recording and reading data from sensors from files that are established for each sensor. The names of these files are inspired by the sensors themselves. As long as the sensor data set being imitated is not realistically available, these agent software programs may also be utilized to replicate any specific sensor data.

4. RESEARCH METHODOLOGY

The research technique had used a systematic way in order to carry on proper investigation of the purpose of study. The section offers considerable real estate to (Al-Taani, 2007), describing the study's design, sampling strategies, methods of data collection, processes of data processing, and ethical issues. A clear strategy provides assurance of genuineness and consistency of the results, and having the strong base to make conclusions.

Research Design

This research is performed using a mixed-approaches methodology, utilizing qualitative and quantitative research methodologies. The qualitative part emphasizes deep insights through case studies and interviews, the quantitative part focuses on statistics. These two components are inherent to the research. This process enables an extensive grasp of the problem being studied.

Data Collection Methods

This research uses a primary and secondary source of information to improve its credibility. Structured questionnaires, interviews and field observations are the means of collecting primary data. The comprehensive overview of the said topic is possible by reviewing secondary data, such as government documents, industry reports, academic publications, and literature reviews.

Sampling Techniques

To make sure that the data collected is representative of the population as a whole, an strategy called stratified random sampling is used. This method divides the population into suitable subgroups (by work position, industrial sector, or experience level). However, you have to select a fixed sample size from each stratum to retain the variation and avoid bias.

Data Analysis Procedures

Descriptive and inferential statistics are common methods used when analyzing quantitative data. Regression analysis, correlation testing, and finding trends are done with statistical packages such as as SPSS and Python. Thematic analysis is a method of observing qualitative data, by identifying those aspects that reoccur then using them to provide informed interpretation of the data.

Ethical Considerations

The research meets ethical requirements for confidentiality, privacy, and voluntary participation (informed consent), as data can be made anonymous and confidentiality is maintained, with the participants' consent obtained beforehand. The appropriate review boards grant permission to conduct the research ethically, and all study-related activities are carried out in accordance with international ethical standards for participant participation and processing of data.

Reliability and Validity

In a bid to improve the validity of the results, this study adopts a systematic data collection approach and conducts cross-validations of the data sources. In the study, methods ensuring validity include peer review of findings, triangulation of data from multiple sources and pilot testing of the survey. This approach helps to enhance the validity of the findings.

This research methodology establishes a rigorous framework allowing for a thorough analysis of the study's aims. By utilizing mixed methods, considering ethical implications, and leveraging sophisticated analytical techniques, the investigation ensures the uncovering of trustworthy, insightful results. The methodology's validity and reliability considerably bolster the enhancement of the findings' overall quality and import. Some inquiries probe deeper into peripheral matters, whereas others summarize central topics concisely yet comprehensively. The study's diversity of questioning opens doors to discoveries unforeseen, enriching our understanding beyond what any standalone approach could achieve in isolation.

5. ANALYSIS AND INTERPRETATION

In order to improve the reliability and efficiency of autonomous cars and transportation networks, the research highlights the need of safe data-driven control as a critical component that must be present. In order to achieve maximum performance in navigation, collision avoidance, and traffic management approaches, these systems make use of data collected from sensors in real time and algorithms that are designed for machine learning. Nevertheless, in spite of this, there are still a number of difficulties that give rise to significant concerns. These include the capacity to comprehend models, the protection against hostile cyberattacks, and the protection of data. Based on the findings of the research, it seems that including robust safety features into autonomous transportation systems, such as sensor fusion redundancy, secure data transmission, and explainable artificial intelligence models, might potentially assist reduce risks and significantly increase user trust. The following table provides an overview of the cybersecurity concerns that are associated with the operation of autonomous vehicles: Table 1. These problems are categorized in Table 1 according to the level of risk they provide, the chance that they will occur, and the many strategies that may be implemented to mitigate the possibility of their occurrence. Data spoofing, sensor hijacking, GPS jamming, and network intrusion are only some of the risks that have been categorized as high risk. Additional concerns include network invasion. Depending on the specifics of the situation, the probability that any of these dangers will come to fruition varies from sixty to seventy-five percent. The most dangerous of these threats is network intrusion, which has a probability of success of 75% above the other threats. The implementation of robust anomaly detection systems that operate in real time is very necessary in order to mitigate the impacts of this risk.

Table 1. Cybersecurity Threats and Mitigation Strategies in Autonomous Vehicles

Threat Type	Risk Level	Occurrence Probability (%)	Mitigation Strategy	Effectiveness (%)
Data Spoofing	High	70	Encrypted Data Protocols	90
Sensor Hijacking	High	60	Multi-Factor Authentication	85
AI Model Corruption	Medium	50	Robust Model Validation	80
GPS Jamming	High	65	Redundant Localization Systems	88
Network Intrusion	High	75	Real-Time Anomaly Detection	92

In a manner similar to this, redundant localization systems lessen the potential of GPS jamming, which has a probability of sixty-five percent. This ensures that navigation is reliable even in the event that there are disruptions in satellite signals. It is thus vital to conduct stringent model validation in order to avoid hostile assaults. This is due to the fact that even while the risk of AI model corruption is medium, there is still a fifty percent possibility that it will occur. The effectiveness of mitigation strategies may range from 92 percent to 80 percent, which can significantly reduce the number of security vulnerabilities. The graphic illustrates how critical it is to employ a wide range of cybersecurity precautions in order to safeguard autonomous transportation systems from the ever-evolving sorts of attacks which are being developed. Table 2 presents the market shares of autonomous cars as well as the distribution of these vehicles across regions. North America has the title of the biggest region in the globe, with a market share of 35.2% and comprising 2.5 million autonomous cars. Europe ranks in second place because of its robust legal framework and its advancements in autonomous vehicle technology. The continent has a market share that is 28% lower than that of the United States, but it still has 2 million automobiles.

Table 2. Regional Distribution and Market Share of Autonomous Vehicles

Region	Number of Autonomous Vehicles	Market Share (%)
North America	25,00,000	35.20%
Europe	20,00,000	28.00%
China	18,00,000	25.30%
Japan	7,50,000	10.50%
Others	3,00,000	1.00%

The possibility of GPS jamming, which has a probability of sixty-five percent, is decreased by redundant localization systems, which are similar to this. Additionally, this ensures that navigation will continue to be reliable even in the event that satellite links are lost. For this reason, robust model validation is very necessary in order to counteract hostile assaults. Even if the danger is just modest, there is a fifty percent possibility that an artificial intelligence model will be corrupted. This is the reason why this is the case. The effectiveness of mitigation measures may range from 92 percent to 80 percent, and they have the potential to have a significant impact on the number of security vulnerabilities. The image illustrates how critical it is to implement a wide range of cybersecurity precautions in order to safeguard autonomous transportation systems from the ever-evolving kinds of dangers that are being developed. The market shares of autonomous cars as well as the distribution of these vehicles across regions are shown in Table 2. The North American region is the biggest in the world, with a market share of 35.2% and a total of 2.5 million autonomous cars. Europe ranks in second place because of its robust legal framework and the advancements it has made in the technology of driverless vehicles. The continent's market share is 28% lower than that of the United States, despite the fact that there are 2 million automobiles on the continent.

Table 3. Accident Reduction Trends in Autonomous Vehicles vs. Traditional Vehicles

Year	Traditional Vehicles Accidents	Autonomous Vehicles Accidents	% Reduction
2020	50,00,000	5,00,000	90%
2022	48,00,000	4,00,000	91.70%
2024	46,00,000	3,00,000	93.50%
2026	44,00,000	2,00,000	95.40%

Accident rates in autonomous vehicles are expected to continue their decreasing trend in the years to follow, with the number of accidents reducing to 400,000 in 2022, 300,000 in 2024, and an anticipated 200,000 by 2026. This is a 95.4% reduction in comparison to accidents that occur in ordinary vehicles. It is clear that autonomous driving systems are effective in enhancing road safety via the use of artificial intelligence-driven decision-making, predictive analytics, and real-time hazard detection, as seen by the dramatic reduction in accident rates. The aforementioned advances shed light on the fact that autonomous vehicles have the potential to radically revolutionize transportation safety by minimizing the impact of human error, which is the primary cause of accidents that occur on the road. The various legislative requirements that regulate the operations of autonomous vehicles are listed in Table 4, along with the compliance rates for those regulations, the safety implications, the adoption problems, and the degrees of artificial intelligence transparency. Functional safety is the primary objective of ISO 26262, which has a modest adoption barrier of thirty percent. This standard has a significant safety impact of ninety percent and the highest compliance rate of eighty-five percent. The UNECE WP.29 cybersecurity framework has an 88% safety impact and an 80% compliance rate, but its adoption is still a bit more challenging at 40%. This is due to the fact that protecting vehicle networks is a complex task. It is clear that ensuring comprehensive regulatory conformance remains a difficulty, as seen by the relatively low compliance percentage of 75% for the General Data Protection Regulation (GDPR), which is concerned with data protection.

Table 4. Compliance, Safety, and Ethical Challenges in Autonomous Vehicle Regulations

Regulation Standard	Compliance Rate (%)	Safety Impact (%)	Adoption Challenge (%)	AI Transparency (%)
ISO 26262 (Functional Safety)	85	90	30	70
UNECE WP.29 (Cybersecurity)	80	88	40	75
GDPR (Data Privacy)	75	70	45	85
NHTSA ADS Safety Framework	82	85	35	78
IEEE P7008 (Ethical AI)	70	80	50	90

Despite this, its artificial intelligence transparency score of 85% is the highest, which demonstrates that it places a significant emphasis on the responsible and ethical use of data. The NHTSA ADS Safety Framework has an 85% safety impact and an 82% compliance rate, despite the fact that it has a relatively low adoption threshold of 35%. In the IEEE P7008 document, which is devoted to ethical artificial intelligence, the problem of standardizing ethical issues in AI-driven autonomous systems is brought to light. It has the highest adoption barrier at fifty percent, and its compliance rate is seventy percent. It is emphasized in the table that there is a need for consistent rules that strike a balance between safety, openness, and usefulness in order to ensure that technology for autonomous cars comply to moral and legal criteria while maintaining stringent safety standards.

6. RESULT AND DISCUSSION

Based on the results, it is evident that in order to successfully implement safe data-driven control, it is required to take a holistic approach to risk management and innovation inside the organization. The reason for this is because the findings suggest that there is no other potential path to achievement. Despite the fact that the use of artificial intelligence to make judgments improves both efficiency and accuracy, the widespread use of this technology requires adherence to ethical AI principles, cybersecurity standards, and regulatory constraints. This is as a result of the fact that widespread deployment of artificial intelligence requires ethical AI methodologies. It is of the utmost importance that legislators, manufacturers of automobiles, and specialists in artificial intelligence collaborate in order to set universal safety requirements. Real-world testing is also crucial for improving the system's capacity to endure interruptions, and ongoing model change based on real-time input is also needed so that the system may be improved. After these issues have been resolved, networks of self-driving vehicles will become safer and more dependable as a result of the enhanced dependability. Figure 3 presents a comparison of the accuracy and latency of a wide variety of sensor data sources. The technologies that fall under this category include, but are not limited to, LiDAR, radar, cameras, GPS, and IMU. Despite the fact that LiDAR has the best accuracy of any sensor, it is less effective for making decisions in real time in autonomous cars due to the fact that it has a particularly high latency. Due to the very high latency of LiDAR, this is the consequence. In spite of the fact that their accuracy is inferior, GPS and IMU sensors are superior when it comes to giving real-time data because of their rapid response times. When utilizing radar and camera sensors, on the other hand, it is possible to achieve a balance between latency and precision.

Figure 3. Accuracy vs. Latency Across Sensor Data Source

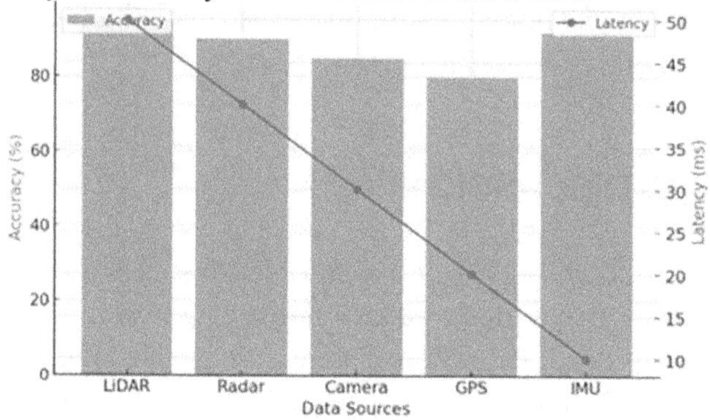

Due to the fact that accuracy and latency have an inverse relationship, which means that no single sensor can deliver optimum performance in all dimensions, the necessity for sensor fusion systems has been brought to light. Given the nature of this connection, it is clear that sensor fusion is an extremely important process. By using a wide range of sensor types, it is feasible to enhance the efficiency and safety of autonomous navigation. Therefore, this would make it possible for autonomous systems to simultaneously adjust for the issues that are associated with each kind of sensor while also making use of the advantages that are associated with each type of sensor. In spite of the fact that perception and decision-making are dependent on an exceptionally high level of accuracy, the data demonstrate that a minimum amount of delay is required in order to enable rapid reactions to changing street circumstances. A study of the safety implications and compliance rates of different regulatory regimes is shown in Figure 4, which provides an analysis of a number of regulatory frameworks that control the operations of autonomous vehicles. Within this category are frameworks like as ISO 26262, UNECE WP.29, NHTSA AV 4.0, SAE J2016, and compliance with the General Data Protection Regulation (GDPR). Despite the fact that the majority of rules still have compliance rates that are good enough to be regarded acceptable, the data demonstrate that there are differences due to the fact that various locations and manufacturers have varied policies and processes. In spite of the fact that the majority of regulations continue to have successful compliance rates, this remains the case. Despite the fact that legislation such as UNECE WP.29 and NHTSA AV 4.0 have a significant impact on automotive safety, it is still challenging to comply to all of these standards, particularly in technological environments that are in a state of perpetual change.

Figure 4. Compliance Rates and Safety Impact of Regulatory Frameworks

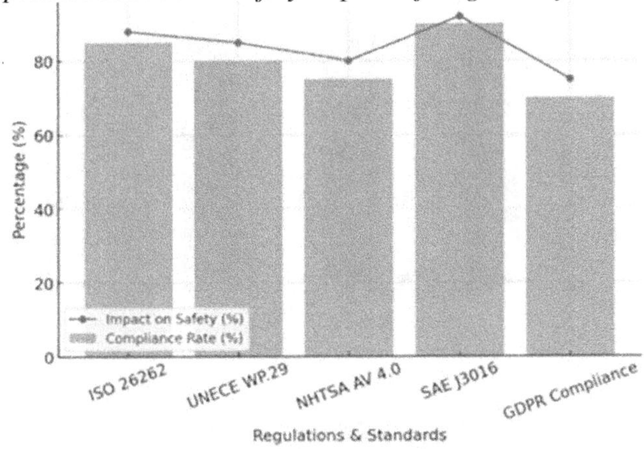

The compliance of automobile manufacturers with safety legislation is of the utmost importance since these laws give them with worldwide standards to adhere to. When it comes to the use of autonomous technology, this guarantees that the greatest possible level of focus is put on safety. One thing that should be brought to your attention is the fact that the data emphasizes the need of harmonizing international regulations in order to improve compliance efforts, reduce implementation differences, and increase customer confidence in autonomous vehicle technology. In order to properly approach this matter, much consideration is required. In the event that stringent enforcement measures are not implemented, there is a possibility that safety issues brought about by regulatory compliance gaps might constitute a danger to the dependability and adoption of autonomous transportation systems. It is possible that these safety risks are the result of regulatory compliance gaps, which is the reason for this. The results of this inquiry are shown in Figure 5, which provide an analysis of a variety of artificial intelligence algorithms that are used in autonomous cars. approaches such as Convolutional Neural Networks (CNNs), Reinforcement Learning, Hybrid Artificial Intelligence, and Rule-Based Systems are included in this category of approaches. Both the correctness of the performance and the speed at which it is processed are taken into consideration in the assessment. CNNs and Reinforcement Learning models are very useful for tasks such as photo identification and route planning because to the great degree of accuracy and precision that they provide. Therefore, this is due to the fact that they possess certain qualities.

Figure 5. Performance Analysis of AI Algorithms in Autonomous Vehicles

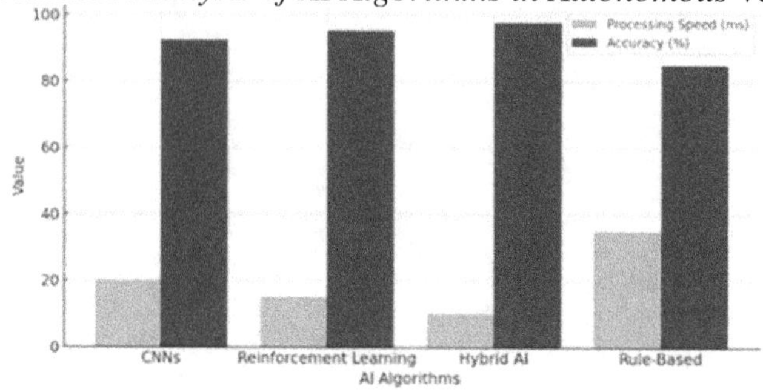

This, however, results in lengthier processing times since these models need a greater amount of computational resources. However, they are more efficient than other options. On the other hand, artificial intelligence systems that are based on rules are quicker, but they make less accurate predictions. It is possible that this may result in a decrease in their dependability in various driving circumstances that are both complicated and dynamic. Hybrid artificial intelligence (AI) is a promising and effective balance between processing speed and accuracy, making it a viable alternative for real-world applications. Additionally, it combines the advantages of many distinct methodologies, making it a viable option for real-world applications. The hybrid artificial intelligence is a potential alternative as a result of this. As a result of this image, which brings attention to the inherent trade-offs that exist between speed and precision, the requirement of optimization approaches that can increase decision-making in real-time without losing accuracy is brought to light. Although autonomous navigation necessitates the use of automation that is driven by artificial intelligence, the findings demonstrate that the algorithm that is selected has a major influence on the degree of safety as well as the performance of the vehicle. The safety ratings and accident-avoidance skills of a variety of common kinds of autonomous cars are analyzed in Figure 6, which you can see here. The Zoox Robotaxi, the Waymo One, the Tesla Model X, and the Cruise AV are all examples of vehicles that fall under this subcategory. In terms of safety ratings, the findings demonstrate that each and every model is continuing to perform very well. This exemplifies the industry's as a whole's combined efforts to improve vehicle safety by using cutting-edge technology. In light of this, it seemed that their emergency response systems, real-time hazard detection, and sensor accuracy were disparate from one another. The fact that their abilities to avoid accidents were so different from one another, on the other hand, demonstrates that there were differences between them. Cruise AV and Zoox Robotaxi bring to light areas that still need improvement, despite the fact that the Tesla Model X and Waymo One have been complimented for their safety and their capacity to avoid crashes. This is the case regardless of whether or not the evaluations for both automobiles have been positive.

Figure 6. Safety Ratings and Collision Avoidance in Autonomous Vehicles

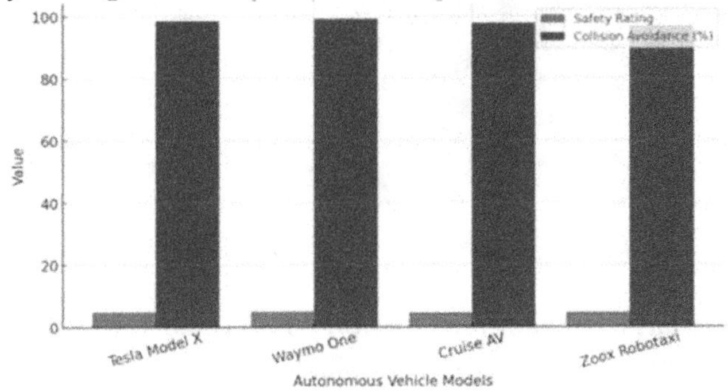

Ongoing advancements in predictive control algorithms, risk assessment based on machine learning, and high-precision sensor integration are required in order to enhance real-time safety measures. This highlights the importance of these innovations. Additionally, the statistic highlights the necessity of stringent testing, regulatory supervision, and software updates in order to assure that autonomous vehicles will continue to meet safety requirements while adapting to the ever-changing conditions of the road. Overcoming these gaps in collision avoidance abilities will be essential as the industry grows in order to achieve the goal of gaining widespread public trust and acceptance of autonomous transportation systems. Data from sensors, video data, GPS and navigation data, and vehicle logs are some of the categories that are included in Figure 7, which provides a full overview of the huge quantities of data that are generated by autonomous vehicles. According to the statistics, the data collected by cameras constitutes the biggest quantity, surpassing all other sources of data by a significant margin, while sensor data has the second highest collection rate. Comparatively lower volumes of GPS and navigation data as well as vehicle records are evidence of their supplementary significance in autonomous decision-making. Due to the major challenges that are created by the enormous quantity of data that is produced in terms of transmission, storage, and real-time processing, it is necessary to construct efficient solutions for data management.

Figure 7. Data Volume Analysis in Autonomous Vehicles

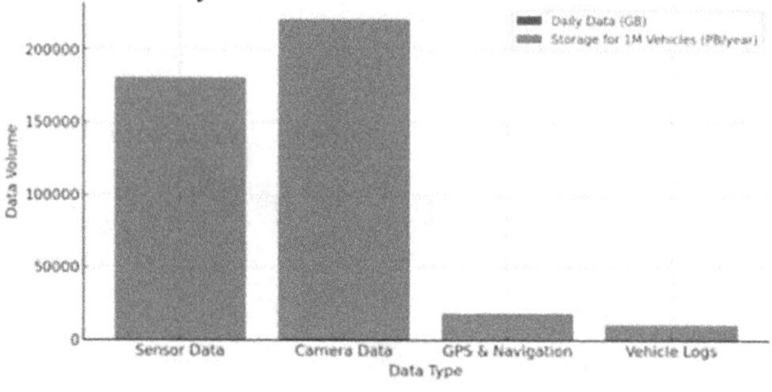

To manage the large flood of information without sacrificing processing speed, figure 7 highlights the rising need for sophisticated data compression methods, cloud storage solutions, and edge computing. These are all necessary in order to do this. To further ensure that only relevant and high-priority information is employed for decision-making, improving data filtering techniques will play a significant role in decreasing the amount of computing overhead that is required. In order to help support the fast spread of autonomous cars and their ability to operate in real time, it will be essential to create data management systems that are both scalable and efficient as the industry continues to go ahead.

7. CONCLUSIONS

The reliable and secure implementation of autonomous cars and transportation networks is made possible in large part by safe data-driven control. In order to provide real-time decision-making, collision avoidance, and system resilience, this research highlights the significance of sensor fusion, AI-based predictive modeling, and cybersecurity measures. Furthermore, as AV technology advances, accident rates rapidly decline, underscoring the possibility that innovation might improve traffic conditions. Notably, improvements in AI transparency are opening the door to a greater knowledge of black-box AI systems and more innovative ways to create AI systems that are compliant with legal requirements and resistant to hostile assaults. To help with the widespread deployment of autonomous transportation systems, further research may focus on improving the interpretability of AI, vehicle-to-infrastructure communication, and secure data transfer methods.

REFERENCES

Al-Sultan, S., Al-Doori, M. M., Al-Bayatti, A. H., & Zedan, H. (2014). "A comprehensive survey on vehicular ad hoc network," *Journal of network and computer applications, vol.* 37, pp. 380–392.

Al-Taani, T. (2007). "An expert system for car failure diagnosis," World Academy of Science, Engineering and Technology, *International Journal of Mechanical, Aerospace, Industrial. Mechatronic and Manufacturing Engineering*, *1*(12), 740–743.

Cavanini, L., Ferracuti, F., Longhi, S., & Monteriu, A. (2020). LS-SVM for LPV-ARX Identification: Efficient Online Update by Low-Rank Matrix Approximation. *In Proceedings of the 2020 International Conference on Unmanned Aircraft Systems (ICUAS),* Athens, Greece, pp. 1590–1595.

Hernandez-Jayo, U., Angulo, I., Perallos, A., & Sainz, N. (2010). "On board ´ communications platform for services deployment in vehicles: Bottomup approach for intelligent transport systems deployment," in Wireless Information Networks and Systems (WINSYS), *Proceedings of the International Conference on. IEEE*, pp. 1–4

Jiang, R., Hu, M. B., Jia, B., Wang, R., & Wu, Q. S. (2007). Phase transition in a mixture of adaptive cruise control vehicles and manual vehicles. *The European Physical Journal B*, *58*(2), 197–206.

Khandelwal, S. A., & Abhale, A. B. (2015). "Monitoring vehicles and pollution on road using vehicular cloud environment," in Technologies for Sustainable Development (ICTSD), *International Conference on. IEEE*, pp. 1–6.

Lin, S.-P., & Maxemchuk, N. F. (2016). The fail-safe operation of collaborative driving systems. *Journal of Intelligent Transport Systems*, *20*(1), 88–101.

Weng, Y., & Wu, T. (2001). Car-following model of vehicular traffic. *In 2001 International Conferences on Info-Tech and Info-Net,* volume 4, 101–106 vol.4

Yang, G., & Zhao, Y. (2010). Motion Stability Analysis of Vehicle with Four Wheel Steering System Considering Tire Nonlinearity. *In Proceedings of the 2010 3rd International Congress on Image and Signal Processing (CISP2010)*, Yantai, China, pp. 3433–3437.

Zhang, Y., Fu, C., & Hu, L. (2014). Yellow light dilemma zone researches: A review. [English edition]. *Journal of Traffic and Transportation Engineering*, *1*(5), 338–352.

Compilation of References

Abiona, O. O., Oladapo, O. J., Modupe, O. T., Oyeniran, O. C., Adewusi, A. O., & Komolafe, A. M. (2024). The emergence and importance of DevSecOps: Integrating and reviewing security practices within the DevOps pipeline. *World Journal of Advanced Engineering Technology and Sciences*, *11*(2), 127–133. DOI: 10.30574/wjaets.2024.11.2.0093

Abubakar, N. S. J., Paradji, N.-S. U., Saggap, S., Anding, N. S., Tano, R. M., Arasani, A. H., Ahadain, D. R., Banda, B., Jayari, R., Alamhalil, A., Alih, S. H., & Tahil, S. K. (2024). Hacking Incidents and their Long-Term Implications for User Privacy and Trust. *Cognizance Journal*, *4*(12), 443–453. DOI: 10.47760/cognizance.2024.v04i12.041

Adelakun, A. J., Alese, B. K., Thompson, A. F. B., & Alowolodu, O. D. (2023). Case Studies in AIoMT Applications: A Secure Medical Cyber- Physical System for the Monitoring and Diagnosis of Lassa Fever. In *Handbook of Security and Privacy of AI-Enabled Healthcare Systems and Internet of Medical Things*. https://doi.org/DOI: 10.1201/9781003370321-18

Agarwal, P., Sharma, S., & Matta, P. (2023). Federated Learning in Intelligent Traffic Management System. In 2023 Winter Summit on Smart Computing and Networks (WiSSCoN), 1–6. https://doi.org/DOI: 10.1109/wisscon56857.2023.10133864

Aghazadeh Ardebili, A., Martella, C., Longo, A., Rucco, C., Izzi, F., & Ficarella, A. (2025). IoT-driven resilience monitoring: Case study of a cyber-physical system. *Applied Sciences (Basel, Switzerland)*, *15*(4), 2092.

Ahmad, J., Khan, H., Salman, W., Amin, M., Ali, Z., & Shokat, S. (2024). A Survey on Enhanced Approaches for Cyber Security Challenges Based on Deep Fake Technology in Computing Networks. *Spectrum of Engineering Sciences*, *2*(4), 133–149.

Ahmad, R., Alsmadi, I., Alhamdani, W., & Tawalbeh, L. (2023). Zero-day attack detection: A systematic literature review. *Artificial Intelligence Review*, *56*(10), 10733–10811.

Ahmad, S., Arif, M., Mehfuz, S., Ahmad, J., & Nazim, M. (2025). Deep Learning-based Cloud Security: Innovative Attack Detection and Privacy Focused Key Management. *IEEE Transactions on Computers*. Advance online publication. DOI: 10.1109/TC.2025.3547150

Ahmad, S., Mehfuz, S., Urooj, S., & Alsubaie, N. (2024). Machine learning-based intelligent security framework for secure cloud key management. *Cluster Computing*, *27*(5), 5953–5979. DOI: 10.1007/s10586-024-04288-8

Ahmed, H. A., Jasim, H. M., Gatea, A. N., Al-Asadi, A. A., & Al-Asadi, H. A. (2024). A secure and efficient blockchain enabled federated Q-learning model for vehicular Ad-hoc networks. *Scientific Reports*, *14*(1). Advance online publication. DOI: 10.1038/s41598-024-82585-3 PMID: 39732861

Akmal, I., Khan, H., Khushnood, A., Zulfiqar, F., & Shahbaz, E. (2024). An Efficient Artificial Intelligence (Al) and Blockchain-Based Security Strategies for Enhancing the Protection of Low-Power loT Devices in 5G Networks. *Spectrum of Engineering Sciences*, *2*(3), 528–586.

Al Salih, A., & Wang, Y. (2024). *Innovative Byzantine Fault Tolerance in Hyperledger Fabric with BDLS*. 677–683. DOI: 10.1109/bcca62388.2024.10844400

Al-Adwan, A. S., Li, N., Al-Adwan, A., Abbasi, G. A., Albelbisi, N. A., & Habibi, A. (2023). Extending the technology acceptance model (TAM) to Predict University Students' intentions to use metaverse-based learning platforms. *Education and Information Technologies*, *28*(11), 15381–15413. PMID: 37361794

Alaya, N., Dafflon, B., Moalla, N., & Ouzrout, Y. (2017). ACPS-agent self-adaptive quality control platform for Industry 4.0. *In Proceedings of the 7th International Conference on Information Society and Technology*, Kopaonik, Serbia, pp. 114–119.

Alevizos, L. (2024). Automated cybersecurity compliance and threat response using AI, blockchain and smart contracts. *International Journal of Information Technology : an Official Journal of Bharati Vidyapeeth's Institute of Computer Applications and Management*. Advance online publication. DOI: 10.1007/s41870-024-02324-9

Aljuaid, W. H., & Alshamrani, S. S. (2024). A deep learning approach for intrusion detection systems in cloud computing environments. *Applied Sciences (Basel, Switzerland)*, *14*(13), 5381.

Al-Sultan, S., Al-Doori, M. M., Al-Bayatti, A. H., & Zedan, H. (2014). "A comprehensive survey on vehicular ad hoc network," *Journal of network and computer applications, vol.* 37, pp. 380–392.

Al-Taani, T. (2007). "An expert system for car failure diagnosis," World Academy of Science, Engineering and Technology, *International Journal of Mechanical, Aerospace, Industrial. Mechatronic and Manufacturing Engineering*, *1*(12), 740–743.

Alzaabi, F. R., & Mehmood, A. (2024). A review of recent advances, challenges, and opportunities in malicious insider threat detection using machine learning methods. *IEEE Access : Practical Innovations, Open Solutions, 12*, 30907–30927.

Alzoubi, Y. I., & Mishra, A. (2024). Techniques to alleviate blockchain bloat: Potentials, challenges, and recommendations. *Computers & Electrical Engineering, 116*, 109216. DOI: 10.1016/j.compeleceng.2024.109216

Ansari, M. A., & Singh, D. K. (2021). Human detection techniques for real-time surveillance: A comprehensive survey. *Multimedia Tools and Applications*, *80*(6), 8759–8808.

Arbi, A. and Israr, M. 2024. Empowering cyber-physical systems through ai-driven fusion for enhanced health assessment. International Journal of Data informatics and Intelligent Computing, 3(3), pp. 16-23. https://doi.org/DOI: 10.59461/ijdiic.v3i3.127

Arrey, D. A. (2019). *Exploring the integration of security into software development life cycle (SDLC) methodology* (Doctoral dissertation, Colorado Technical University). https://www.proquest.com/openview/437de70c5a6cd10e2f24809aa1e1b5cd/1?cbl=18750&diss=y&pq-origsite=gscholar

Asadi, Y., Farsangi, M. M., Amani, A. M., Alhelou, H. H., Dibaji, S. M., & Bijami, E. (2023). Data-driven cyber-resilient control of wide area power systems. In *Power Systems Cybersecurity: Methods, Concepts, and Best Practices* (pp. 161–178). Springer International Publishing.

Asmat, M. N., Khan, S. U. R., & Hussain, S. (2023). Uncertainty handling in cyber–physical systems: State-of-the-art approaches, tools, causes, and future directions. *Journal of Software (Malden, MA)*, *35*(7), e2428. DOI: 10.1002/smr.2428

Augusto, J. G., de Paz, C. C. P., Mendonça, G. G., Moitinho, M. R., Menegatto, L. S., Bolonhezi, D., Salles, M. S. V., & Simili, F. F. (2024). Integrated crop-livestock versus conventional systems: Effects on the chemical and physical characteristics of an Oxisol. *Grass and Forage Science*, *79*(2). Advance online publication. DOI: 10.1111/gfs.12664

Aung, K. M., & Oo, N. (2015). Association rule pattern mining approaches network anomaly detection (Doctoral dissertation, MERAL Portal).

Awajan, A. (2023). A novel deep learning-based intrusion detection system for IoT networks. *Computers*, *12*(2), 34.

Ayodeji, A., Mohamed, M., Li, L., Di Buono, A., Pierce, I., & Ahmed, H. (2023). Cyber security in the nuclear industry: A closer look at digital control systems, networks and human factors. *Progress in Nuclear Energy*, *161*, 104738. DOI: 10.1016/j.pnucene.2023.104738

Aytekin, A., Özköse, H., & Ayaz, A. (2022). Unified theory of acceptance and use of technology (UTAUT) in mobile learning adoption: Systematic literature review and bibliometric analysis. *COLLNET Journal of Scientometrics and Information Management*, *16*(1), 75–116.

Azaria, A., Ekblaw, A., Vieira, T., & Lippman, A. (2016). MedRec: Blockchain for medical data access permission management and trend analysis. MIT Media Lab. Retrieved from https://www.media.mit.edu/publications/medrec-blockchain-for-medical-data-access-permission-management-and-trend-analysis/

Azaria, A., Steinhardt, G., & Ekblaw, A. (2016). *MedRec: Blockchain for medical data access, permission management, and trend analysis*. MIT Media Lab. https://assets.pubpub.org/77ffonfi/fac98e84-5f2c-4828-a1ba-e2141e747ee6.pdf

Badhani, N., & Sharma, S. (2023). Blockchain-Based Financial Enterprises Credit Value Information System Using Federated AI. In *2023 IEEE International Conference on Blockchain and Distributed Systems Security (ICBDS)*, 1–7. https://doi.org/DOI: 10.1109/icbds58040.2023.10346298

Baha, E., Fadhel, A., Buenaventura, P., Yeun, C. Y., Zemerly, J., & Eldelbi, K. (2024). "Multimodal Biometric Authentication Systems: Exploring Iris and EEG Data," *2024 2nd International Conference on Cyber Resilience (ICCR)*, Dubai, United Arab Emirates, pp. 1-4, doi: DOI: 10.1109/ICCR61006.2024.10533134

Balamurugan, V., & Saravanan, R. (2019). Enhanced intrusion detection and prevention system on cloud environment using hybrid classification and OTS generation. *Cluster Computing*, *22*(Suppl 6), 13027–13039.

Bano, N., & Siddiqui, S. (2024). Consumers' intention towards the use of smart technologies in tourism and hospitality (T&H) industry: A deeper insight into the integration of TAM, TPB and trust. *Journal of Hospitality and Tourism Insights*, *7*(3), 1412–1434.

Bezuidenhout, R., & Nel, W. (2023). *Exponentially Distributed Nonlinear Proof-of-Work: Saving Energy while Preserving Decentralisation in Bitcoin Mining*. 1–7. DOI: 10.1109/icecet58911.2023.10389429

Bezzateev, S., & Fomicheva, S. (2020). *"Soft Multi-Factor Authentication," 2020 Wave Electronics and its Application in Information and Telecommunication Systems*. WECONF., DOI: 10.1109/WECONF48837.2020.9131537

Bhadula, S., Sharma, S., & Johri, A. (2023). Hybrid blockchain and IPFS for secure Industry 4.0 framework of IoT-based skin monitoring system. 2022 8th International Conference on Advanced Computing and Communication Systems (ICACCS), 41–47. https://doi.org/DOI: 10.1109/icaccs57279.2023.10112751

Bhatt, S., & Sharma, S. (2024). Quantum Cryptography Using Blockchain for 6G Enabled Internet of Vehicles. In 2024 1st International Conference on Advanced Computing and Emerging Technologies (ACET), 1–6. https://doi.org/DOI: 10.1109/acet61898.2024.10730580

Bhatt, S., Sharma, S., & Bhadula, S. (2023). Advanced Blockchain Applications in Cryptocurrency and Various Sectors. In 2023 1st International Conference on Circuits, Power and Intelligent Systems (CCPIS), 1–6. https://doi.org/DOI: 10.1109/ccpis59145.2023.10291465

Bhatte, N., Prajapati, V. M., Varia, S., & More, J. (2022). Comparison of Different Cloud Providers. *International Journal For Science Technology And Engineering*, *10*(6), 651–656. DOI: 10.22214/ijraset.2022.43736

Bhole, A. G. (2025). Cloud Resource Management and Cost Optimization. *Indian Scientific Journal Of Research In Engineering And Management*, *09*(01), 1–7. DOI: 10.55041/ijsrem26028

Bhosale, K., & Waghmare, M. (2025). Enhancing Blockchain Scalability Through Layer 1 and Layer 2 Solutions: A Comparative Analysis. *International Journal For Science Technology And Engineering*, *13*(1), 1642–1644. DOI: 10.22214/ijraset.2025.66647

Binbusayyis, A. (2024). Hybrid VGG19 and 2D-CNN for intrusion detection in the fog-cloud environment. *Expert Systems with Applications*, *238*, 121758.

Blancaflor, E., Robles, C. R. W., Espino, S. I., Matignas, K. G., Abisado, M., & Palenzuela, R. D. (2024). *Comparative Analysis of Current Infrastructure of Cloud Computing Unveiling the Trends of Industry 5.0*. 200–204. DOI: 10.1109/ccet62233.2024.10838120

Boonkrong, S., & Boonkrong, S. (2021). Methods and threats of authentication. In *Authentication and Access Control* (pp. 45–70). Practical Cryptography Methods and Tools.

Bu, L., Cheng, H., & Kinsy, M. A. (2018). "Adaptive and Dynamic Device Authentication Using Lorenz Chaotic Systems," *2018 IEEE 61st International Midwest Symposium on Circuits and Systems (MWSCAS)*, Windsor, ON, Canada, pp. 976-979, doi: DOI: 10.1109/MWSCAS.2018.8623953

Bu, L., Chen, C.-H., Ng, K. K. H., Zheng, P., Dong, G., & Liu, H. (2021). A user-centric design approach for smart product-service systems using virtual reality: A case investigation. *Journal of Cleaner Production*, *280*, 124413.

Bulgakov, A. L., Aleshina, A. V., Smirnov, S. D., Demidov, A. D., Milyutin, M. A., & Xin, Y. (2024). Scalability and Security in Blockchain Networks: Evaluation of Sharding Algorithms and Prospects for Decentralized Data Storage. *Mathematics*, *12*(23), 3860. DOI: 10.3390/math12233860

Burke, Q., Sheatsley, R., King, R., Swift, M. M., & McDaniel, P. (2024). *Cloud Storage Integrity at Scale: A Case for Dynamic Hash Trees*. https://doi.org//arxiv.2405.03830DOI: 10.48550

Calvi, L., & Vermeeren, A. P. O. S. (2024). Digitally enriched museum experiences–what technology can do. *Museum Management and Curatorship*, *39*(3), 335–356.

Carreras Guzman, N. H., Wied, M., Kozine, I., & Lundteigen, M. A. (2020). Conceptualizing the key features of cyber physical systems in a multilayered representation for safety and security analysis. *Systems Engineering*, *23*(2), 189–210. DOI: 10.1002/sys.21509

Cassandro, R., Wu, G., Wang, H., & Li, Z. S. (2024). Prognostics and health management for cyber-physical system resilience: A security and reliability perspective. In *Frontiers of Performability Engineering: In Honor of Prof. KB Misra* (pp. 483–506). Springer Nature Singapore.

Cavanini, L., Ferracuti, F., Longhi, S., & Monteriu, A. (2020). LS-SVM for LPV-ARX Identification: Efficient Online Update by Low-Rank Matrix Approximation. *In Proceedings of the 2020 International Conference on Unmanned Aircraft Systems (ICUAS),* Athens, Greece, pp. 1590–1595.

Chaudhari, A., Pawar, A., Pawar, A., Pawar, A., & Pawar, G. (2023). "A Comprehensive Study on Authentication Systems," *2023 7th International Conference On Computing, Communication, Control And Automation (ICCUBEA)*, Pune, India, pp. 1-5, doi: DOI: 10.1109/ICCUBEA58933.2023.10392029

Chaudhari, A., Gohil, B., & Rao, U. P. (2024). A novel hybrid framework for cloud intrusion detection system using system call sequence analysis. *Cluster Computing*, *27*(3), 3753–3769.

Chen, C., Hao, Y., Kumari, S., & Amoon, M. (2024). An authentication protocol for federated learning with blockchain in consumer electronic assisted autonomous driving environments. *IEEE Transactions on Consumer Electronics*, *1*. Advance online publication. DOI: 10.1109/tce.2024.3476969

Chinnasamy, R., Subramanian, M., Easwaramoorthy, S. V., & Cho, J. (2025). Deep learning-driven methods for network-based intrusion detection systems: A systematic review. *ICT Express*.

Chitrakar, R., & Chuanhe, H. (2012). Anomaly detection using support vector machine classification with k-medoid clustering. In *Third Asian Himalayas International Conference on the Internet* (pp. 1–5). IEEE.

Choudhury, N., Chauhan, S., & Tiwari, M. (2021). Enterprise systems and blockchain technology: The dormant potentials. *International Journal of Information Management*, *58*, 102291. DOI: 10.1016/j.ijinfomgt.2020.102291

Choutapally, R. & Das, T. (2024). PaciPhish: Intelligent and Interpretable Phishing URL Detection Framework. .DOI: 10.1109/CARS61786.2024.10778820

Civelek, M. E. (2018). Essentials of Structural Equation Modeling. In *Zea Books*. Issue March., DOI: 10.13014/k2sj1hr5

Clearinghouse, T. (2021). Climate-Smart Agriculture Technologies for the Sahel and Horn of Africa. Clearinghouse Technical Report Series 009. *Gates Open Research*, *5*(167), 167.

Cocco, L., & Tonelli, R. (2024). A Self-Sovereign Identity–Blockchain-Based Model Proposal for Deep Digital Transformation in the Healthcare Sector. *Future Internet*, *16*(12), 473. DOI: 10.3390/fi16120473

Conti, M., De Gaspari, F., & Mancini, L. V. (2017). Know your enemy: Stealth configuration-information gathering in SDN. In *International Conference on Green, Pervasive, and Cloud Computing* (pp. 386–401). Springer.

Continella, A., Polino, M., Pogliani, M., & Zanero, S. (2018). There's a hole in that bucket! A large-scale analysis of misconfigured S3 buckets. *Proceedings of the 34th Annual Computer Security Applications Conference (ACSAC '18)*, 702–711. Association for Computing Machinery. DOI: 10.1145/3274694.3274736

Crgol, A., & Vrhovec, S. (2024). Recognition of genuine and phishing emails may not be associated with response to phishing attacks. JUCS -. *Journal of Universal Computer Science*, *30*, 1265–1283. DOI: 10.3897/jucs.132113

Dafflon, B., Moalla, N., & Ouzrout, Y. (2021). The challenges, approaches, and used techniques of CPS for manufacturing in Industry 4.0: A literature review. *International Journal of Advanced Manufacturing Technology*, *113*, 2395–2412. DOI: 10.1007/s00170-020-06572-4

Dai, J., Dai, Z., Thing, V. L., & Engineering, S. T. (2025). Cyber-resilience enhancement with cross-domain software-defined network for cyber-physical microgrids against denial of service attacks. *IEEE Transactions on Industrial Cyber-Physical Systems*.

Dapshima, B. A., & Ahmad, S. K. (2024). Evaluation and Assessment of Software Security Risks and Vulnerabilities Within the Realm of Secure DevOps. *no. July*. https://www.researchgate.net/profile/Babagana-Dapshima/publication/382440594_Evaluation_and_Assessment_of_Software_Security_Risks_and_Vulnerabilities_Within_the_Realm_of_Secure_DevOps/links/669d121e4a172d2988b6c737/Evaluation-and-Assessment-of-Software-Security-Risks-and-Vulnerabilities-Within-the-Realm-of-Secure-DevOps.pdf

Debar, H., Dacier, M., & Wespi, A. (1999). Towards a taxonomy of intrusion-detection systems. *Computer Networks*, *31*(8), 805–822.

Dehlaghi-Ghadim, A., Balador, A., Moghadam, M. H., Hansson, H., & Conti, M. (2023). ICSSIM—A framework for building industrial control systems security testbeds. *Computers in Industry*, *148*, 103906. DOI: 10.1016/j.compind.2023.103906

Desai, R., & Nisha, T. N. (2021, July). Best practices for ensuring security in devops: A case study approach. In *Journal of Physics: Conference Series* (Vol. 1964, No. 4, p. 042045). IOP Publishing. https://iopscience.iop.org/article/10.1088/1742-6596/1964/4/042045/meta

Devi, T. A., & Jain, A. (2024). Enhancing cloud security with deep learning-based intrusion detection in cloud computing environments. In 2024 2nd International Conference on Advancement in Computation & Computer Technologies (InCACCT). IEEE.

Dhokrat, J., Pulgam, N., Maktum, T., & Mane, V. (2024). A Framework for Privacy-Preserving Multiparty Computation with Homomorphic Encryption and Zero-Knowledge Proofs. *Informatica (Vilnius)*, *48*(21). Advance online publication. DOI: 10.31449/inf.v48i21.6562

Dina, A. S., & Manivannan, D. (2021). Intrusion detection based on machine learning techniques in computer networks. *Internet of Things : Engineering Cyber Physical Human Systems*, *16*, 100462.

Dinesh, R. A., Shanmugam, J., & Biswas, K. (2023). Integration of technology and nanoscience in precision agriculture and farming. In *Contemporary Developments in Agricultural Cyber-Physical Systems*. https://doi.org/DOI: 10.4018/978-1-6684-7879-0.ch008

Dobaj, J., Riel, A., Krug, T., Seidl, M., Macher, G., & Egretzberger, M. (2022, May). Towards digital twin-enabled DevOps for CPS providing architecture-based service adaptation & verification at runtime. In *Proceedings of the 17th symposium on software engineering for adaptive and self-managing systems* (pp. 132-143). DOI: 10.1145/3524844.3528057

Dobaj, J., Riel, A., Macher, G., & Egretzberger, M. (2023). Towards devOps for cyber-physical systems (cpss): Resilient self-adaptive software for sustainable human-centric smart cps facilitated by digital twins. *Machines (Basel)*, *11*(10), 973. DOI: 10.3390/machines11100973

Duo, W., Zhou, M., & Abusorrah, A. (2022). A survey of cyber attacks on cyber physical systems: Recent advances and challenges. *IEEE/CAA Journal of Automatica Sinica*, *9*(5), 784-800. DOI: 10.1109/JAS.2022.105548

El-Kady, A. H., Halim, S., El-Halwagi, M. M., & Khan, F. (2023). Analysis of safety and security challenges and opportunities related to cyber-physical systems. *Process Safety and Environmental Protection*, *173*, 384–413. DOI: 10.1016/j.psep.2023.03.012

Estebsari, F., Khalifehkandi, Z. R., Latifi, M., Farhadinasab, A., Vasli, P., & Mostafaie, D. (2023). Protection motivation theory and prevention of breast cancer: A systematic review. *Clinical Breast Cancer*, *23*(4), e239–e246. PMID: 37045635

Eyo-Udo, N., Agho, M. O., Onukwulu, E. C., Sule, A. K., & Azubuike, C. (2025). Advances in Blockchain Solutions for Secure and Efficient Cross-Border Payment Systems. *International Journal of Research and Innovation in Applied Science*, *IX*(XII), 536–563. DOI: 10.51584/ijrias.2024.912048

Fan, S., & Xue, J. (2024). Secure data sharing method based on federated learning in IOVs. ICC 2022 - IEEE International Conference on Communications, 1328–1333. https://doi.org/DOI: 10.1109/icc51166.2024.10622887

Fan, C.. (2024). Auto-updating intrusion detection system for vehicular network: A deep learning approach based on cloud-edge-vehicle collaboration. *IEEE Transactions on Vehicular Technology*.

Faustino, J. P. C. (2018). *DevOps practices in incident management process* (Master's thesis, ISCTE-Instituto Universitario de Lisboa (Portugal)). https://www.proquest.com/openview/a9c547d770cb1afc3f4bdb690492f1bd/1?cbl=2026366&diss=y&pq-origsite=gscholar

Folorunso, A., Babalola, O., Nwatu, C., & Adedoyin, A. (2024). A comprehensive model for ensuring data compliance in cloud computing environment. *World Journal Of Advanced Research and Reviews*, *24*(2), 1983–1995. DOI: 10.30574/wjarr.2024.24.2.3514

Fu, Y., Niu, X., Zhou, L., Cai, X., Yu, F. R., Cheng, N., & Li, C. (2024). A hierarchical Blockchain-Enabled secure Aggregation Algorithm for federated learning in IOV. *IEEE Internet of Things Journal*, *12*(5), 5876–5890. DOI: 10.1109/jiot.2024.3489032

Gao, Q., & Zhou, J. (2023). *Human Aspects of IT for the Aged Population: 9th International Conference, ITAP 2023, Held as Part of the 25th HCI International Conference, HCII 2023, Copenhagen, Denmark, July 23–28, 2023, Proceedings, Part II* (Vol. 14043). Springer Nature.

Gao, S., Zhang, H., Wang, Z., Huang, C., & Yan, H. (2023). Data-driven injection attack strategy for linear cyber-physical systems: An input-output data-based approach. *IEEE Transactions on Network Science and Engineering*, *10*(6), 4082–4095.

GeeksforGeeks. (2024). *Ethereum 2.0: A comprehensive guide to PoS and scalability improvements.* GeeksforGeeks. https://www.geeksforgeeks.org/ethereum-2-0/

Ghafir, I., Prenosil, V., & Hammoudeh, M. (2015). Botnet command and control traffic detection challenges: A correlation-based solution. *International Journal of Advanced Computer Networking and Security*, *7*(2), 27–31.

Ghafir, I., Prenosil, V., Hammoudeh, M., Aparicio-Navarro, F. J., Rabie, K., & Jabban, A. (2018). Disguised executable files in spear-phishing emails: Detecting the entry point in advanced persistent threat. In *Proceedings of the 2nd International Conference on Future Networks and Distributed Systems* (pp. 1–5).

Ghafir, I., Prenosil, V., Hammoudeh, M., Han, L., & Raza, U. (2017). Malicious SSL certificate detection: A step towards advanced persistent threat defence. In *Proceedings of the International Conference on Future Networks and Distributed Systems*.

Ghanmi, H., Hajlaoui, N., Touati, H., Elhadad Or Hadded, M., Muhlethaler, P., & Boudjit, S. (2024). Blockchain-cloud integration: Comprehensive survey and open research issues. *Concurrency and Computation*. Advance online publication. DOI: 10.1002/cpe.8122

Global IT outage highlights cloud-linked risks. (2024). *Emerald Expert Briefings*. DOI: 10.1108/oxan-es288430

Gohari, R. J., Aliahmadipour, L., & Rafsanjani, M. K. (2025). CTMBIDS: Convolutional TSETLIN machine-based intrusion detection system for DDoS attacks in an SDN environment. *Neural Computing & Applications*, •••, 1–24.

Golar, P. C., & Khandelwal, B. (2020). "Study of Usability Parameter for Graphical Based Authentication System," *2020 9th International Conference System Modeling and Advancement in Research Trends (SMART)*, Moradabad, India, pp. 23-26, doi: DOI: 10.1109/SMART50582.2020.9337116

Google Cloud. (2022, August 18). How Google Cloud blocked the largest Layer 7 DDoS attack at 46 million RPS. Google Cloud Blog. https://cloud.google.com/blog/products/identity-security/how-google-cloud-blocked-largest-layer-7-ddos-attack-at-46-million-rps

Goyal, A., Singh, A., Sharma, P. K., Yadav, D., & Jindal, A. (2022). Blockchain and AI in healthcare: A systematic review, applications, and future trends. *Journal of Medical Internet Research*, *24*(12), e37804. DOI: 10.2196/37804

Gul, H., Al-Obeidat, F., Amin, A., & Moreira, F. (2024). Analyzing complex networks: Extracting key characteristics and measuring structural similarities. *Expert Systems: International Journal of Knowledge Engineering and Neural Networks*, *41*(1), e13470. DOI: 10.1111/exsy.13470

Habib, M. K., & Chimsom, C. (2022). CPS: Role, characteristics, architectures and future potentials. *Procedia Computer Science*, *200*, 1347–1358. DOI: 10.1016/j.procs.2022.01.336

Haleem, A., Javaid, M., Pratap Singh, R., & Suman, R. (2022). Medical 4.0 technologies for healthcare: Features, capabilities, and applications. *Internet of Things and Cyber-Physical Systems*, *2*. Advance online publication. DOI: 10.1016/j.iotcps.2022.04.001

Hamamoto, A. H., Carvalho, L. F., Sampaio, L. D. H., Abrão, T., & Proença, M. L.Jr. (2018). Network anomaly detection system using genetic algorithm and fuzzy logic. *Expert Systems with Applications*, *92*, 390–402.

Hamdi, M., Mestiri, S., & Arbi, A. (2024). Artificial intelligence techniques for bankruptcy prediction of tunisian companies: An application of machine learning and deep learning-based models. *Journal of Risk and Financial Management, 17*(4), 132. DOI: 10.3390/jrfm17040132

Hammouch, H., Mohapatra, S., El-Yacoubi, M., Qin, H., Berbia, H., Mader, P., & Chikhaoui, M. (2022). GANSet - Generating annnotated datasets using Generative Adversarial Networks. *Proceedings of the International Conference on Cyber-Physical Social Intelligence, ICCSI 2022*. https://doi.org/DOI: 10.1109/ICCSI55536.2022.9970561

Hehenberger, P., Vogel-Heuser, B., Bradley, D., Eynard, B., Tomiyama, T., & Achiche, S. (2016). Design, modelling, simulation and integration of cyber physical systems: Methods and applications. *Computers in Industry*, *82*, 273–289. DOI: 10.1016/j.compind.2016.05.006

Hernandez-Jayo, U., Angulo, I., Perallos, A., & Sainz, N. (2010). "On board ´ communications platform for services deployment in vehicles: Bottomup approach for intelligent transport systems deployment," in Wireless Information Networks and Systems (WINSYS), *Proceedings of the International Conference on. IEEE*, pp. 1–4

Hersyah, M. H., Yolanda, D., & Sitohang, H. (2020). "Multiple Laboratory Authentication System Design Using Fingerprints Sensor and Keypad Based on Microcontroller," *2020 International Conference on Information Technology Systems and Innovation (ICITSI)*, Bandung, Indonesia, pp. 14-19, doi: DOI: 10.1109/ICITSI50517.2020.9264969

Hotellier, E., Sicard, F., Francq, J., & Mocanu, S. (2024). Standard specification-based intrusion detection for hierarchical industrial control systems. *Information Sciences*, *659*, 120102.

Houda, Z. E., Moudoud, H., Brik, B., & Khoukhi, L. (2024). Blockchain-Enabled federated learning for enhanced collaborative intrusion detection in vehicular edge computing. *IEEE Transactions on Intelligent Transportation Systems*, *25*(7), 7661–7672. DOI: 10.1109/tits.2024.3351699

Huang, X., Xiao, Q., Li, Y., Li, P., Zhang, M., Chen, Z., Huang, Y., Zhang, K., Mao, Y., & Song, J. (2024). Blockchain Technology and Privacy Protection. *Applications and Implementation of Zero-Knowledge Proofs*, *637–641*. Advance online publication. DOI: 10.1109/ccsb63463.2024.10735589

Hussain, R., Alshammari, R., & Alharthi, R. (2020). A secure framework for data sharing and collaboration in cloud-based supply chains using blockchain. *Computers & Electrical Engineering*, *84*, 106607. DOI: 10.1016/j.compeleceng.2020.106607

Hu, W.. (2024). A deep analysis of nature-inspired and meta-heuristic algorithms for designing intrusion detection systems in cloud/edge and IoT: State-of-the-art techniques, challenges, and future directions. *Cluster Computing*, *27*(7), 8789–8815.

Iarovyi, S., Lastra, J. L. M., Haber, R., & del Raúl, T. (2015). From artificial cognitive systems and open architectures to cognitive manufacturing systems. *In Proceedings of the IEEE 13th International Conference on Industrial Informatics (INDIN),* Cambridge, UK, pp. 1225–1232.

IBM X-Force: Stolen Credentials and Vulnerabilities Weaponized Against Businesses in 2019-Feb 11, 2020. (2020).

Ingre, B., & Yadav, A. (2015). Performance analysis of NSL-KDD dataset using ANN. In *2015 International Conference on Signal Processing and Communication Engineering Systems* (pp. 92–96). IEEE.

Irshad, M. N., Aslam, M. M., & Silapunt, R. (2025). *Low Complexity Optimized AOR Method for Massive MIMO Signal Detection*. IEEE., DOI: 10.1109/ACCESS.2025.3550272

Isman, A., & Yahya, R. M. (2023). Exploring the Adoption of Zoom Cloud Meeting under the Perception of Diffusion of Innovation Theory. *Turkish Online Journal of Educational Technology-TOJET*, *22*(4), 101–120.

Jbair, M., Ahmad, B., Ahmad, M. H., Vera, D., Harrison, R., & Ridler, T. (2019). Automatic PLC Code Generation Based on Virtual Engineering Model. ISA, *International Society of Automation*. ⟨ https://www.isa.org ⟩ (accessed 12 January 2021).

Jia, F., & Kong, L. (2017). An intrusion detection algorithm based on a convolutional neural network. *Transactions of Beijing Institute of Technology*, *37*(12), 1271–1275.

Jiang, R., Hu, M. B., Jia, B., Wang, R., & Wu, Q. S. (2007). Phase transition in a mixture of adaptive cruise control vehicles and manual vehicles. *The European Physical Journal B*, *58*(2), 197–206.

Jun, Y., Craig, A., Shafik, W., & Sharif, L. (2021). Artificial Intelligence Application in Cybersecurity and Cyberdefense. In *Wireless Communications and Mobile Computing* (Vol. 2021). https://doi.org/DOI: 10.1155/2021/3329581

Kaiser, A. K. (2020). Brief Overview of DevOps. In *Become ITIL® 4 Foundation Certified in 7 Days: Understand and Prepare for the ITIL Foundation Exam with Real-life Examples* (pp. 21-50). Berkeley, CA: Apress. DOI: 10.1007/978-1-4842-6361-7_2

Kalinaki, K., Shafik, W., Namuwaya, S., & Namuwaya, S. (2024). Perspectives, applications, challenges, and future trends of IoT-based logistics. In *Navigating Cyber Threats and Cybersecurity in the Logistics Industry*. https://doi.org/DOI: 10.4018/979-8-3693-3816-2.ch005

Kamińska, D., Zwoliński, G., & Laska-Leśniewicz, A. (2022). Usability testing of virtual reality applications—The pilot investigation. *Sensors (Basel)*, *22*(4), 1342. PMID: 35214246

Karunakaran, M., Bellam, K., Raja, J., & Shanthi, D. (2024). *Blockchain Technology in Cloud Security*. IGI Global. DOI: 10.4018/979-8-3693-2081-5.ch003

Keating, C.. (2003). "System of systems engineering," EMJ - Engineering Management Journal. *Article*, *15*(3), 36–45.

Khalil, U., Uddin, M., Malik, O. A., & Hong, O. W. (2024). A Novel NFT Solution for Assets Digitization and Authentication in Cyber-Physical Systems: Blueprint and Evaluation. *IEEE Open Journal of the Computer Society*, *5*. Advance online publication. DOI: 10.1109/OJCS.2024.3378424

Khan, F., Kumar, R. L., Kadry, S., & Meqdad, M. N. (2021). Autonomous vehicles: A study of implementation and security. *International Journal of Electrical & Computer Engineering (2088-8708)*, *11*(4). DOI: 10.11591/ijece.v11i4.pp3013-3021

Khandelwal, S. A., & Abhale, A. B. (2015). "Monitoring vehicles and pollution on road using vehicular cloud environment," in Technologies for Sustainable Development (ICTSD), *International Conference on. IEEE*, pp. 1–6.

Khanna, A., Sah, A., Bolshev, V., Burgio, A., Panchenko, V., & Jasiński, M. (2022). Blockchain–Cloud Integration: A Survey. *Sensors (Basel)*, *22*(14), 5238. DOI: 10.3390/s22145238 PMID: 35890918

Kholidy, H. A., & Baiardi, F. (2012). CIDD: A cloud intrusion detection dataset for cloud computing and masquerade attacks. In 2012 Ninth International Conference on Information Technology - New Generations (pp. 397–402). IEEE.

Kholidy, H. A. (2021). Autonomous mitigation of cyber risks in the cyber–physical systems. *Future Generation Computer Systems*, *115*, 171–187.

Kim, D. S., & Park, J. S. (2003). Network-based intrusion detection with support vector machines. In Information Networking: International Conference, ICOIN 2003, Cheju Island, Korea, February 12-14, 2003. Revised Selected Papers (pp. 747–756). Springer.

Kim, S., Park, K. J., & Lu, C. (2022). A survey on network security for cyber–physical systems: From threats to resilient design. *IEEE Communications Surveys and Tutorials*, *24*(3), 1534–1573.

Kirichenko, A., Christen, M., Grunow, F., & Herrmann, D. (2020). Best practices and recommendations for cybersecurity service providers. *The ethics of cybersecurity*, 299-316. DOI: 10.1007/978-3-030-29053-5_15

Kizza, J. M. (2024). System intrusion detection and prevention. In *Guide to Computer Network Security* (pp. 295–323). Springer.

Kumar, R., & Tripathi, A. (2022). Blockchain-enabled enterprise integration strategies in the cloud. *Journal of Cloud Computing (Heidelberg, Germany)*, *11*(1), 1–17. DOI: 10.1186/s13677-022-00300-z

Kyaw, P., Gutierrez, J., & Ghobakhlou, A. (2024). A Systematic Review of Deep Learning Techniques for Phishing Email Detection. *Electronics (Basel)*, *13*, 3823. DOI: 10.3390/electronics13193823

Lagorio, A., Zenezini, G., Mangano, G., & Pinto, R. (2022). A systematic literature review of innovative technologies adopted in logistics management. *International Journal of Logistics Research and Applications*, *25*(7), 1043–1066.

Lee, E. A. (2008). Cyber physical systems: design challenges. *In 11th IEEE International Symposium on Object Oriented Real-Time Distributed Computing (ISORC)*, Orlando, FL, (pp. 363-369). doi:DOI: 10.1109/isorc.2008.25

Lévy, L. N., Bosom, J., Guerard, G., Amor, S. B., Bui, M., & Tran, H. (2022). DevOps model appproach for monitoring smart energy systems. *Energies*, *15*(15), 5516. DOI: 10.3390/en15155516

Li, C., Xu, M., Zhang, J., Guo, H., & Cheng, X. (2024). SoK: Decentralized Storage Network. *IACR Cryptology ePrint Archive, 2024*, 258. DOI: 10.1016/j.hcc.2024.100239

Liang, P., Wu, Y., Xu, Z., Xiao, S., & Yuan, J. (2024). Enhancing security in DevOps by integrating artificial intelligence and machine learning. *Journal of Theory and Practice of Engineering Science*, *4*(02), 31–37. DOI: 10.53469/jtpes.2024.04(02).05

Lian, Z., Shi, P., & Lim, C. C. (2022). Adaptive resilient control for cyber-physical systems under cyberattack and input saturation. *IEEE Transactions on Industrial Informatics*, *19*(5), 6513–6524.

Li, L. (2025). Using the Ripple consensus algorithm to achieve transparent cross-border payments in e-commerce. *IET Conference Proceedings.*, 2024(21), 295–299. DOI: 10.1049/icp.2024.4241

Lin, S.-P., & Maxemchuk, N. F. (2016). The fail-safe operation of collaborative driving systems. *Journal of Intelligent Transport Systems*, *20*(1), 88–101.

Liu, W., Sun, J., Wang, G., Bullo, F., & Chen, J. (2022). Data-driven resilient predictive control under denial-of-service. *IEEE Transactions on Automatic Control*, *68*(8), 4722–4737.

M. J. R and Jeyanthi, N. (2023). "A Review of Modern Authentication Methods in Digital Systems," *2023 Annual International Conference on Emerging Research Areas: International Conference on Intelligent Systems (AICERA/ICIS)*, Kanjirapally, India, pp. 1-6, doi: DOI: 10.1109/AICERA/ICIS59538.2023.10420169

Makani, S. T., & Jangampeta, S. (2024). Devops security tools evaluating effectiveness in detecting and fixing security holes. *Journal ID*, *1552*, 5541. https://iaeme.com/Home/issue/IJDO?Volume=1&Issue=2

Manda, J. K. (2023). DevSecOps Implementation in Telecom: Integrating Security into DevOps Practices to Streamline Software Development and Ensure Secure Telecom Service Delivery. *Journal of Innovative Technologies*, *6*(1). https://acadexpinnara.com/index.php/JIT/article/view/373

Manickaraj, P., Vatchala, L., & Gayathri, S. (2024). Securing Healthcare Data. *Leveraging Blockchain for Electronic Health Records, 234–238.* Advance online publication. DOI: 10.1109/icesic61777.2024.10846251

Manubolu, G. S. (2024). A comprehensive Security Testing Framework for PLC-based Industrial Automation https://www.utupub.fi/bitstream/handle/10024/178734/greeshma_manubolu_masters_thesis.pdf?sequence=1

Mathew, A. (2024). Securing the Cloud: Understanding Threats and Countermeasures. *International Journal For Science Technology And Engineering*, *12*(12), 3026–3031. DOI: 10.22214/ijraset.2024.59552

Matta, G., Chlup, S., Shaaban, A. M., Schmittner, C., Pinzenöhler, A., Szalai, E., & Tauber, M. (2021). Risk management and standard compliance for cyber-physical systems of systems. *Infocommunications Journal*, *13*(2), 32–39. DOI: 10.36244/ICJ.2021.2.5

Meng, H., Shafik, W., Matinkhah, S. M., & Ahmad, Z. (2020). A 5G Beam Selection Machine Learning Algorithm for Unmanned Aerial Vehicle Applications. *Wireless Communications and Mobile Computing, 2020*. Advance online publication. DOI: 10.1155/2020/1428968

Mewada, A., Gedam, P., Reddy, M. U., & Khan, S. (2010). Network intrusion detection using multiclass support vector machine. Journal of Intelligent Learning Systems and Applications.

Mewada, A., Shukla, S., & Chandani, M. G. (2010). KMSVM model for network intrusion detection. *International Journal of Computational Intelligence and Information Security*, *1*(5), 99–106.

Mittal, M. (2024). Colonial Pipeline Cyberattack Drives Urgent Reforms in Cybersecurity and Critical Infrastructure Resilience. *International Journal of Oil. Gas and Coal Engineering*, *12*(5), 106–119. DOI: 10.11648/j.ogce.20241205.11

Mohammad, F., Saleem, K., & Al-Muhtadi, J. (2023). Ensemble-Learning-Based Decision Support System for Energy-Theft Detection in Smart-Grid Environment. *Energies*, *16*(4). Advance online publication. DOI: 10.3390/en16041907

Mojtaba Matinkhah, S., & Shafik, W. (2019). Smart Grid Empowered by 5G Technology. *2019 Smart Gird Conference. SGC, 2019*. Advance online publication. DOI: 10.1109/SGC49328.2019.9056590

Mongia, M. (2024). Blockchain Meets Cloud: A New Era in Distributed Systems Architecture. *International Journal of Scientific Research in Computer Science. Engineering and Information Technology*, *10*(6), 2204–2213. DOI: 10.32628/cseit2410612426

Mujawar, M. & Dommeti, V. (2024). Design Considerations of EBG Structures for Wearable Applications. .DOI: 10.4018/979-8-3693-0916-2.ch008

Mujawar, M. & Pramono, S. (2023). Metamaterial-Based Absorber. .DOI: 10.4018/978-1-6684-8287-2.ch005

Mujawar, M. & Pramono, S. (2024). Dielectric Resonator Antenna for Multiple Input Multiple Output Applications. .DOI: 10.1002/9781119879923.ch8

Mujawar, M., Sridharan, M., Kalbande, M., Aggarwal, P., Krishnaiah, N., & Genç, Y. (2024). Optimizing connectivity: A novel AI approach to assess transmission levels in optical networks. *The Journal of Supercomputing*, *80*, 26568–26588. DOI: 10.1007/s11227-024-06410-4

Mujeeb Ahmed, C., Umer, M. A., Binte Liyakkathali, B. S. S., Jilani, M. T., & Zhou, J. (2021). Machine learning for cps security: applications, challenges and recommendations. *Machine Intelligence and Big Data Analytics for Cybersecurity Applications*, 397-421. DOI: 10.1007/978-3-030-57024-8_18

Muneer, S., Farooq, U., Athar, A., Raza, M. A., Ghazal, T. M., & Sakib, S. (2024). A critical review of artificial intelligence-based approaches in intrusion detection: A comprehensive analysis. *Journal of Engineering*, *2024*(1), 3909173.

Nagarajan, S. (2024). An Investigation of AI-Enabled Comprehensive Survey of Phishing Attacks detection techniques. *International Journal of Innovative Research in Engineering.*, *59-63*. Advance online publication. DOI: 10.59256/ijire.20220301001

Naghib, A., Gharehchopogh, F. S., & Zamanifar, A. (2025). A comprehensive and systematic literature review on intrusion detection systems in the Internet of Medical Things: Current status, challenges, and opportunities. *Artificial Intelligence Review*, *58*(4), 1–88.

Naidu, G. H. S. (2024). Blockchain Technology as a Security Enhancement Framework for Internet of Things: A Comprehensive Analysis. *International Journal of Scientific Research in Computer Science. Engineering and Information Technology*, *10*(6), 842–850. DOI: 10.32628/cseit241061121

Neghab, H. K., Jamshidi, M. B., & Neghab, H. K. (2022). Digital Twin of a Magnetic Medical Microrobot with Stochastic Model Predictive Controller Boosted by Machine Learning in Cyber-Physical Healthcare Systems. *Information (Switzerland)*, *13*(7). Advance online publication. DOI: 10.3390/info13070321

Neha and Chatterjee, K. (2017). "A new multimodal behavioural biometrie authentication framework for system security," *2017 International Conference on Circuit, Power and Computing Technologies (ICCPCT)*, Kollam, India, pp. 1-6, doi: DOI: 10.1109/ICCPCT.2017.8074374

Neto, N. N., Madnick, S., De Paula, A. M. G., & Borges, N. M. (2020). A case study of the Capital One data breach. SSRN *Electronic Journal*. https://doi.org/ DOI: 10.2139/ssrn.3542567

Ogundairo, O., & Broklyn, P. (2024). AI-Driven Phishing Detection Systems. *Journal of Cybersecurity*.

Okafor, K. C., & Longe, O. M. (2022). ASM-ROBOT: A Cyber-Physical Home Automation Controller with Memristive Reconfigurable State Machine. *International Journal of Advanced Computer Science and Applications*, *13*(1). Advance online publication. DOI: 10.14569/IJACSA.2022.01301103

Olowononi, F. O., Rawat, D. B., & Liu, C. (2020). Resilient machine learning for networked cyber-physical systems: A survey for machine learning security to securing machine learning for CPS. *IEEE Communications Surveys and Tutorials, 23*(1), 524–552.

OpenZeppelin. (n.d.). **Access control**. OpenZeppelin Documentation. Retrieved February 27, 2025, from https://docs.openzeppelin.com/contracts/3.x/access-control

Pakanati, S. P. R., McKeithen, B., Saffy, R., Olajide, O., Clark, K., Olafuyi, B. A., & Hewitt, C. (2024). The Impact of Cybersecurity Breaches on Patient Data Privacy in U.S. Healthcare Systems. *International Journal of Scientific and Research Publications, 14*(11), 76–81. DOI: 10.29322/ijsrp.14.11.2024.p15511

Park, H. S. (2013). From automation to autonomy: A new trend for smart manufacturing. *In DAAAM International Scientific* Book; Katalinic, B., Tekic, Z., Eds.; DAAAM *International: Wolkersdorf,* Austria, pp. 75–110.

Pattepu, S., Mukherjee, A., Routray, S., Mukherjee, P., Qi, Y., & Datta, A. (2022). Multi-antenna relay based cyber-physical systems in smart-healthcare NTNs: An explainable AI approach. *Cluster Computing*. Advance online publication. DOI: 10.1007/s10586-022-03632-0

Pava-Díaz, R. A., Gil-Ruiz, J., & López-Sarmiento, D. A. (2024). Self-sovereign identity on the blockchain: Contextual analysis and quantification of SSI principles implementation. *Frontiers in Blockchain, 7*. Advance online publication. DOI: 10.3389/fbloc.2024.1443362

Peelam, M. S., Shah, K., Chamola, V., & Sikdar, B. (2024). Blockchain-Enabled Vehicle Lifecycle Management With Predictive Maintenance using Federated Learning. *IEEE Transactions on Consumer Electronics, 1*. Advance online publication. DOI: 10.1109/tce.2024.3487874

Pham, N. T., & Foo, E., Suriadi, Jeffrey, H., & Lahza, H. F. M. (2018). Improving performance of intrusion detection system using ensemble methods and feature selection. In Proceedings of the Australasian Computer Science Week Multiconference (pp. 1–6).

Polakova, K., Bobková, A., Demianová, A., Bobko, M., Jurčaga, L., Mesárošová, A., Čapla, J., Timoracká, I., Lidiková, J., & Čeryová, N. (2024). Adulteration in food industry in 2023 - overview. *Journal of Microbiology, Biotechnology and Food Sciences*. Advance online publication. DOI: 10.55251/jmbfs.11048

Poltavtseva, M., Shelupanov, A., Bragin, D., Zegzhda, D., & Alexandrova, E. (2021). Key concepts of systemological approach to CPS adaptive information security monitoring. *Symmetry*, *13*(12), 2425. DOI: 10.3390/sym13122425

Porcu, D., Castro, S., Otura, B., Encinar, P., Chochliouros, I., Ciornei, I., & Bachoumis, A. (2022). Demonstration of 5G solutions for smart energy grids of the future: A perspective of the Smart5Grid project. *Energies*, *15*(3), 839. DOI: 10.3390/en15030839

Rafi, S., Yu, W., Akbar, M. A., Alsanad, A., & Gumaei, A. (2020). Prioritization based taxonomy of DevOps security challenges using PROMETHEE. *IEEE Access : Practical Innovations, Open Solutions*, *8*, 105426–105446. DOI: 10.1109/ACCESS.2020.2998819

Rajapakse, R. N., Zahedi, M., Babar, M. A., & Shen, H. (2022).. . *Information and Software Technology*, *141*, 106700. DOI: 10.1016/j.infsof.2021.106700

Raja, S., & Ramaiah, S. (2017). An efficient fuzzy-based hybrid system for cloud intrusion detection. *International Journal of Fuzzy Systems*, *19*, 62–77.

Rajvanshi, S., & Sharma, S. (2023). Blockchain based Authentication and Privacy Preservation in IoMT Devices. In *2023 International Conference on Energy, Materials and Communication Engineering (ICEMCE)*, 1–6. https://doi.org/DOI: 10.1109/icemce57940.2023.10434087

Rana, M. U., Shah, M. A., Alnaeem, M. A., & Maple, C. (2024). *Ransomware attacks in cyber-physical systems: countermeasure of attack vectors through automated web defenses*. IEEE. DOI: 10.1109/ACCESS.2024.3477631

Raut, K. (2024). Secure Message Hashing with SHA-256: Cryptographic Implementation. *International Journal for Research in Applied Science and Engineering Technology*, *12*(11), 1288–1294. DOI: 10.22214/ijraset.2024.65078

Ravikumar, G., Hyder, B., & Govindarasu, M. (2019, October). Efficient modeling of hil multi-grid system for scalability & concurrency in cps security testbed. In *2019 North American Power Symposium (NAPS)* (pp. 1-6). IEEE. DOI: 10.1109/NAPS46351.2019.9000259

Ray, P. P. (2023). Web3: A comprehensive review on background, technologies, applications, zero-trust architectures, challenges and future directions. In *Internet of Things and Cyber-Physical Systems* (Vol. 3). https://doi.org/DOI: 10.1016/j.iotcps.2023.05.003

Rezanov, B. & Kuchuk, H. (2022). "Fast Two-Factor Authentication Method in Systems With a Centralized User's Database," *2022 IEEE 3rd KhPI Week on Advanced Technology (KhPIWeek)*, Kharkiv, Ukraine, pp. 1-5, doi: .DOI: 10.1109/KhPIWeek57572.2022.9916491

Riurean, P., Bolog, G., & Simona Mirela, , R. (2024). The Rise of Sophisticated Phishing. How AI Fuels Cybercrime. *Journal of Digital Science.*, *6*, 15–25. DOI: 10.33847/2686-8296.6.2_2

Rosado, D. G., Santos-Olmo, A., Sánchez, L. E., Serrano, M. A., Blanco, C., Mouratidis, H., & Fernández-Medina, E. (2022). Managing cybersecurity risks of cyber-physical systems: The MARISMA-CPS pattern. *Computers in Industry*, *142*, 103715. DOI: 10.1016/j.compind.2022.103715

Rosen, G. (2018, September 28). Security update. Facebook Newsroom. https://about.fb.com/news/2018/09/security-update/

Sabir, Z., Arbi, A., Hashem, A. F., & Abdelkawy, M. A. (2023). Morlet wavelet neural network investigations to present the numerical investigations of the prediction differential model. *Mathematics*, *11*(21), 4480. DOI: 10.3390/math11214480

Sabir, Z., Dirani, S., Bou Saleh, S., Mabsout, M. K., & Arbi, A. (2024). A novel radial basis and sigmoid neural network combination to solve the human immunodeficiency virus system in cancer patients. *Mathematics*, *12*(16), 2490. DOI: 10.3390/math12162490

Sabir, Z., Hashem, A. F., Arbi, A., & Abdelkawy, M. A. (2023). Designing a bayesian regularization approach to solve the fractional Layla and Majnun system. *Mathematics*, *11*(17), 3792. DOI: 10.3390/math11173792

Sadovykh, A., & Ivanov, V. V. (2024). Enhancing DevSecOps with continuous security requirements analysis and testing. *Компьютерные исследования и моделирование*, *16*(7), 1687-1702. DOI: 10.20537/2076-7633-2024-16-7-1687-1702

Saha, T., Aaraj, N., Ajjarapu, N., & Jha, N. K. (2022). SHARKS: Smart Hacking Approaches for RisK Scanning in Internet-of-Things and Cyber-Physical Systems Based on Machine Learning. *IEEE Transactions on Emerging Topics in Computing*, *10*(2). Advance online publication. DOI: 10.1109/TETC.2021.3050733

Saini, G. K., & Somani, G. (2024). *Resource Targeted Cybersecurity Attacks in Cloud Computing Environments*. Springer International Publishing. DOI: 10.1007/978-981-97-2644-8_9

Santana, C., & Albareda, L. (2022). Blockchain and the emergence of Decentralized Autonomous Organizations (DAOs): An integrative model and research agenda. *Technological Forecasting and Social Change*, *182*, 121806. DOI: 10.1016/j.techfore.2022.121806

Santoso, F., & Finn, A. (2022). A data-driven cyber–physical system using deep-learning convolutional neural networks: Study on false-data injection attacks in an unmanned ground vehicle under fault-tolerant conditions. *IEEE Transactions on Systems, Man, and Cybernetics. Systems*, *53*(1), 346–356.

Security, I. B. M. (2023). *Cost of a data breach report 2023*. IBM Corporation. https://www.ibm.com/reports/data-breach

Seelaboyina, R., Vadla, S. P. C., Teerthala, S. A., & Pedduri, V. V. (2022, November). Secure software development life cycle: an approach to reduce the risks of cyber attacks in cyber physical systems and digital twins. In *International Conference on Computational Intelligence in Machine Learning* (pp. 153-161). Springer Nature Singapore. DOI: 10.1007/978-981-99-7954-7_15

Segall, L. (2021, July 30). Amazon hit with record $887 million fine for alleged privacy violations. CNN Business. https://edition.cnn.com/2021/07/30/tech/amazon-eu-privacy-fine/index.html

Shafik, W. (2024d). Data-Driven Future Trends and Innovation in Telemedicine. In *Improving Security, Privacy, and Connectivity Among Telemedicine Platforms* (pp. 93–118). IGI Global. https://doi.org/DOI: 10.4018/979-8-3693-2141-6.ch005

Shafik, W. (2024e). Dissecting the Role of Women in Cybersecurity and Information Technology: A Medical Perspective. In *Next-Generation Cybersecurity: AI, ML, and Blockchain* (pp. 325–350). Springer. https://doi.org/DOI: 10.1007/978-981-97-1249-6_15

Shafik, W. (2025b). Generative Adversarial Networks: Security, Privacy, and Ethical Considerations. In *Generative Artificial Intelligence (AI) Approaches for Industrial Applications* (pp. 93–117). Springer.

Shafik, W. (2025c). Security, 15 Privacy, and Trust in Fintech. *FinTech and Financial Inclusion: Leveraging Digital Finance for Economic Empowerment and Sustainable Growth*, 216.

Shafik, W., & Kalinaki, K. (2023). Smart city ecosystem: An exploration of requirements, architecture, applications, security, and emerging motivations. In *Handbook of Research on Network-Enabled IoT Applications for Smart City Services*. https://doi.org/DOI: 10.4018/979-8-3693-0744-1.ch005

Shafik, W. (2023). Predicting Future Cybercrime Trends in the Metaverse Era. In *Forecasting cyber crimes in the age of the metaverse* (pp. 78–113). IGI Global., DOI: 10.4018/979-8-3693-0220-0.ch005

Shafik, W. (2024a). Agile Security Strategies. In *Smart and Agile Cybersecurity for IoT and IIoT Environments* (pp. 82–101). IGI Global., DOI: 10.4018/979-8-3693-3451-5.ch004

Shafik, W. (2024b). Artificial Intelligence and Machine Learning with Cyber Ethics for the Future World. In *Future Communication Systems Using Artificial Intelligence, Internet of Things and Data Science* (pp. 110–130). CRC Press., DOI: 10.1201/9781032648309-9

Shafik, W. (2024c). Blockchain's impetus for secure IoT-enabled applications in smart city. In *Big Data and Blockchain Technology for Secure IoT Applications* (pp. 48–71). CRC Press., DOI: 10.1201/9781032663005-4

Shafik, W. (2024f). IoT-Enabled Secure and Intelligent Smart Healthcare. In *Secure and Intelligent IoT-Enabled Smart Cities* (pp. 308–333). IGI Global., DOI: 10.4018/979-8-3693-2373-1.ch015

Shafik, W. (2024g). The Future of Healthcare: Data-Driven Trends and Innovation. In *Advancing Healthcare through Data-driven Innovations* (pp. 166–185). CRC Press.

Shafik, W. (2025a). Artificial Intelligence-Enabled Cybersecurity and Internet of Things Applications in Smart Cities. In *Building Tomorrow's Smart Cities With 6G Infrastructure Technology* (pp. 301–334). IGI Global Scientific Publishing.

Shafik, W., Matinkhah, S. M., & Ghasemzadeh, M. (2019). A fast machine learning for 5g beam selection for unmanned aerial vehicle applications. *Journal of Information Systems and Telecommunication, 7*(4). https://doi.org/https://doi.org/10.7508/jist.2019.04.003

Shafik, W., Mojtaba Matinkhah, S., & Shokoor, F. (2023). Cybersecurity in Unmanned Aerial Vehicles: A Review. *International Journal on Smart Sensing and Intelligent Systems, 16*(1). Advance online publication. DOI: 10.2478/ijssis-2023-0012

Shafik, W., Tufail, A., Apong, R. A. A. H. M., & Balasubramaniam, S. (2024). Future Directions in Cybersecurity, Digital Forensics and Biometric Systems. In *AI Based Advancements in Biometrics and its Applications* (pp. 238–263). CRC Press., DOI: 10.1201/9781032702377-13

Shan, C. P., Loon, W. H., Win, L. K., Din, D., & Seak, S. C. (2019, April). Automated login method selection in a multi-modal authentication system: Login method selection based on user behavior. In 2019 IEEE 9th Symposium on Computer Applications & Industrial Electronics (ISCAIE) (pp. 120-124). IEEE.

Sharghi, H., Ma, W., & Sartipi, K. (2015). "Federated Service-Based Authentication Provisioning for Distributed Diagnostic Imaging Systems," *2015 IEEE 28th International Symposium on Computer-Based Medical Systems*, Sao Carlos, Brazil, pp. 344-347, doi: DOI: 10.1109/CBMS.2015.85

Sharma, S., & Bhadula, S. (2023). Secure Federated Learning for Intelligent Industry 4.0 IoT Enabled Self Skin Care Application System. In 2023 2nd International Conference on Applied Artificial Intelligence and Computing (ICAAIC), 1164–1170. https://doi.org/DOI: 10.1109/icaaic56838.2023.10141028

Sharma, S., Gupta, A., & Tyagi, R. (2023). Sustainable Geo Political Strategic System for Global Peace Using Vedic Scripture, Artificial Intelligence, Blockchain, and Cloud Computing. In 2023 3rd International Conference on Smart Generation Computing, Communication and Networking (SMART GENCON), 1–7. https://doi.org/DOI: 10.1109/smartgencon60755.2023.10442904

Sharma, S., Tomar, M., & Tyagi, R. (2024). Federated learning enabled secure air transport and tourism system. 2022 13th International Conference on Computing Communication and Networking Technologies (ICCCNT), 1–6. https://doi.org/DOI: 10.1109/icccnt61001.2024.10724849

Sharma, S., Tyagi, R., & Bhardwaj, R. (2023). Sustainable Smart Society Development Based on Geo Sensitive Equality Using Vedic Structure, Artificial Intelligence, Blockchain and IoT. In 2023 1st International Conference on Circuits, Power and Intelligent Systems (CCPIS), 1–6. https://doi.org/DOI: 10.1109/ccpis59145.2023.10291593

Sharma, S., Tyagi, R., & Mohan, S. (2024). Edge Intelligence Decentralized Blockchain-Based Internet of Things (B-IoT) for sustainable healthcare. In Chapman and Hall/CRC eBooks (pp. 109–124). https://doi.org/DOI: 10.1201/9781003407096-7

Sheikh, Z. A., & Singh, Y. (2023). Minimizing Cost, Effort, and Implementation Complexity for Adopting Security Requirements in an Agile Development Process for Cyber-Physical Systems. In *Agile Software Development*. Trends, Challenges and Applications., DOI: 10.1002/9781119896838.ch6

Sheikh, Z. A., Singh, Y., Singh, P. K., & Ghafoor, K. Z. (2022). Intelligent and secure framework for critical infrastructure (CPS): Current trends, challenges, and future scope. *Computer Communications*, *193*, 302–331. DOI: 10.1016/j.comcom.2022.07.007

Shenfield, A., Day, D., & Ayesh, A. (2018). Intelligent intrusion detection systems using artificial neural networks. *ICT Express*, *4*(2), 95–99.

Shi, J., Wan, J., Yan, H., & Suo, H. (2011). A survey of cyber-physical systems. *In 2011 International Conference on Wireless Communications and Signal Processing (WCSP)*, Nanjing, China, (pp. 1-6): IEEE

Siahaan, C. N., Rufisanto, M., Nolasco, R., Achmad, S., & Siahaan, C. R. P. (2023). Study of cross-site request forgery on web-based application: Exploitations and preventions. *Procedia Computer Science*, *227*, 92–100.

Singh, S. P., Ansari, M. A., & Kumar, L. (2023, April). Analysis of website in web data mining using web log expert tool. In 2023 IEEE 12th International Conference on Communication Systems and Network Technologies (CSNT) (pp. 514-518). IEEE.

Singh, R., Shafik, W., Crowther, D., & Kumar, V. (Eds.). (2024). *Transforming Healthcare Sector Through Artificial Intelligence and Environmental Sustainability* (1st ed., Vol. 1). Springer Nature Singapore., DOI: 10.1007/978-981-97-9555-0

Sohn, I. (2021). Deep belief network-based intrusion detection techniques: A survey. *Expert Systems with Applications*, *167*, 114170.

Sokolowski, D. (2022, November). Infrastructure as code for dynamic deployments. In *Proceedings of the 30th ACM Joint European Software Engineering Conference and Symposium on the Foundations of Software Engineering* (pp. 1775-1779). DOI: 10.1145/3540250.3558912

Soon, J. P., Chan, R. Q., Lee, Q. H., Loke, D. E., Chun, S. L. H., & Yuen, P. K. (2024). User perceptions of artificial intelligence powered phishing attacks on Facebook's resilient infrastructure. *Int J Adv Appl Sci ISSN*, *2252*(8814), 8814.

Srivastav, S., Shukla, A. K., Kumar, S., & Muhuri, P. K. (2025). Hyride: A hybrid and robust intrusion detection approach to enhance cybersecurity in Industry 4.0. *Internet of Things : Engineering Cyber Physical Human Systems*, *30*, 101492.

Sule, A., Eyo-Udo, N. L., Onukwulu, E. C., Agho, M. O., & Azubuike, C. (2025). Implementing Blockchain for Secure and Efficient Cross-Border Payment Systems. *International Journal of Research and Innovation in Applied Science*, *IX*(XII), 508–535. DOI: 10.51584/ijrias.2024.912047

Suresh Babu, C. V., & Srisakthi, S. (2023). Cyber Physical Systems and Network Security: The Present Scenarios and Its Applications. In Thanigaivelan, R., Kaliappan, S., & Jegadheesan, C. (Eds.), *Cyber-Physical Systems and Supporting Technologies for Industrial Automation* (pp. 104–130). IGI Global. DOI: 10.4018/978-1-6684-9267-3.ch006

Sworna, Z. T., Mousavi, Z., & Babar, M. A. (2023). NLP methods in host-based intrusion detection systems: A systematic review and future directions. *Journal of Network and Computer Applications*, *220*, 103761.

Syarif, I., Prugel-Bennett, A., & Wills, G. (2012). Unsupervised clustering approach for network anomaly detection. In Networked Digital Technologies: 4th International Conference, NDT 2012, Dubai, UAE, April 24-26, 2012. Proceedings, Part I (pp. 135–145). Springer.

Sykes, P. (2023). *Combining ID's.* Attributes, and Policies in Hyperledger Fabric. DOI: 10.1007/978-3-031-31420-9_3

Takabi, H., Joshi, J. B. D., & Ahn, G. J. (2010). Security and privacy challenges in cloud computing environments. *IEEE Security and Privacy*, *8*(6), 24–31.

Tariq, M. U. (2024). Integration of IoMT for Enhanced Healthcare: Sleep Monitoring, Body Movement Detection, and Rehabilitation Evaluation. In Liu, H., Tripathy, R., & Bhattacharya, P. (Eds.), *Clinical Practice and Unmet Challenges in AI-Enhanced Healthcare Systems* (pp. 70–95). IGI Global., DOI: 10.4018/979-8-3693-2703-6.ch004

Tariq, M. U. (2025). Bridging Generations: Digital Transformation and Its Multifaceted Impact Across Societal Sectors. In Anshari, M., Almunawar, M., & Ordóñez de Pablos, P. (Eds.), *Impacts of Digital Technologies Across Generations* (pp. 1–22). IGI Global Scientific Publishing., DOI: 10.4018/979-8-3693-6366-9.ch001

Tariq, M. U. (2025). Innovative Business Models: Integrating Social, Economic, and Environmental Goals in Rural Manufacturing. In Prabhakar, A., Yu, P., & Erokhin, V. (Eds.), *Rural Social Entrepreneurship Development: Network-Based Manufacturing System Model* (pp. 147–174). IGI Global Scientific Publishing., DOI: 10.4018/979-8-3693-7515-0.ch005

Tariq, M. U. (2025). Integrating Digital Technologies to Optimize Sustainable Supply Chains. In Koç, E. (Ed.), *Developing Dynamic and Sustainable Supply Chains to Achieve Sustainable Development Goals* (pp. 33–64). IGI Global Scientific Publishing., DOI: 10.4018/979-8-3693-6284-6.ch002

Tariq, M. U. (2025). Integrating ICT for Enhanced Organizational Resilience: Strategies and Case Studies. In Carvalho, L., Reis, L., Neves de Almeida Baptista Figueiredo, A., & Russo, N. (Eds.), *Leveraging Technology for Organizational Adaptability* (pp. 59–80). IGI Global Scientific Publishing., DOI: 10.4018/979-8-3693-6045-3.ch004

Tavallaee, M., Bagheri, E., Lu, W., & Ghorbani, A. A. (2009). A detailed analysis of the KDD CUP99 dataset. In *2009 IEEE Symposium on Computational Intelligence for Security and Defense Applications* (pp. 1–6). IEEE.

Theodoropoulos, C., Koutras, D., Douligeris, C., & Kotzanikolaou, P. (2024). "An Edge Multi Factor Authentication System for Cyber Physical Systems Based on OTP," *2024 IEEE Symposium on Computers and Communications (ISCC)*, Paris, France, pp. 1-3, doi: DOI: 10.1109/ISCC61673.2024.10733619

Uriarte, R. B., & De Nicola, R. (2018). Blockchain-Based Decentralized Cloud/Fog Solutions: Challenges, Opportunities, and Standards. *IEEE Communications Standards Magazine*, *2*(3), 22–28. DOI: 10.1109/MCOMSTD.2018.1800020

Van Brussel, H. (1995). "Navigation" issues in intelligent autonomous systems. In Proceedings of the 4th *International Conference on Intelligent Autonomous Systems*, Karlsruhe, Germany, pp. 42–52

Van Loenhout, R., Ranasinghe, C., Degbelo, A., & Bouali, N. (2022). Physicalizing Sustainable Development Goals Data: An Example with SDG 7 (Affordable and Clean Energy). *Conference on Human Factors in Computing Systems - Proceedings*. https://doi.org/DOI: 10.1145/3491101.3519638

Vashishtha, L. K., Singh, A. P., & Chatterjee, K. (2023). HIDM: A hybrid intrusion detection model for cloud-based systems. *Wireless Personal Communications*, *128*(4), 2637–2666.

Vignesh, B., Chandrakumar, M., Divya, K., Prahadeeswaran, M., & Vanitha, G. (2025). Blockchain technology in agriculture: Ensuring transparency and traceability in the food supply chain. *Plant Science Today*, *12*(sp1). Advance online publication. DOI: 10.14719/pst.5970

Vliet, B. (2024). A Model of Decentralized Oversight for the Digital Asset Industry With an Example Anti-money Laundering/know-your-customer Standard. *Social Science Research Network*. DOI: 10.2139/ssrn.4771849

Wang, F., & Zhang, Y. (2009). "Study and Design of Intelligent Authentication System Based on Fingerprint Identification," *2009 Second International Symposium on Knowledge Acquisition and Modeling*, Wuhan, China, pp. 170-173, doi: DOI: 10.1109/KAM.2009.247

Wang, H., Wang, L., Yu, Q., Zheng, Z., & Yang, Z. (2018). "A proactive approach based on online reliability prediction for adaptation of service-oriented systems," *Journal of Parallel and Distributed Computing. Article*, *114*, 70–84.

Wang, N., Yang, W., Wang, X., Wu, L., Guan, Z., Du, X., & Guizani, M. (2022). A blockchain based privacy-preserving federated learning scheme for Internet of Vehicles. *Digital Communications and Networks*, *10*(1), 126–134. DOI: 10.1016/j.dcan.2022.05.020

Wang, Z., Wei, H., Wang, J., Zeng, X., & Chang, Y. (2022). Security issues and solutions for connected and autonomous vehicles in a sustainable city: A survey. *Sustainability*, *14*(19), 12409. DOI: 10.3390/su141912409

Wang, Z., Xie, W., Wang, B., Tao, J., & Wang, E. (2021). A survey on recent advanced research of CPS security. *Applied Sciences (Basel, Switzerland)*, *11*(9), 3751. DOI: 10.3390/app11093751

Weng, Y., & Wu, T. (2001). Car-following model of vehicular traffic. *In 2001 International Conferences on Info-Tech and Info-Net,* volume 4, 101–106 vol.4

Wu, S., Jiang, Y., Luo, H., Zhang, J., Yin, S., & Kaynak, O. (2022). An integrated data-driven scheme for the defense of typical cyber–physical attacks. *Reliability Engineering & System Safety*, *220*, 108257.

Xia, Z., Sun, J., & Tan, J. (2024). Privacy-Preserving Data Sharing in IOV: a federated learning and Blockchain-Based approach. 2022 IEEE International Conference on Communications Workshops (ICC Workshops), 511–516. https://doi.org/DOI: 10.1109/iccworkshops59551.2024.10615878

Xing, W., & Shen, J. (2024). Security control of cyber–physical systems under cyber attacks: A survey. *Sensors (Basel)*, *24*(12), 3815. PMID: 38931599

Xu, S., Xia, Y., & Shen, H. L. (2022). Cyber protection for malware attack resistance in cyber-physical power systems. *IEEE Systems Journal*, *16*(4), 5337–5345. DOI: 10.1109/JSYST.2022.3150576

Yang, J., & Tian, P. (2017). "Research on scheme of attribute identity authentication system in broadcasting monitoring system," *2017 IEEE 2nd International Conference on Big Data Analysis (ICBDA)*, Beijing, China, pp. 843-846, doi: DOI: 10.1109/ICBDA.2017.8078756

Yang, G., & Zhao, Y. (2010). Motion Stability Analysis of Vehicle with Four Wheel Steering System Considering Tire Nonlinearity. *In Proceedings of the 2010 3rd International Congress on Image and Signal Processing (CISP2010)*, Yantai, China, pp. 3433–3437.

Yan, Y., & Kunhui, Y. (2024). Novel cyber-physical architecture for optimal operation of renewable-based smart city considering false data injection attacks: Digital twin technologies for smart city infrastructure management. *Sustainable Energy Technologies and Assessments*, *65*. Advance online publication. DOI: 10.1016/j.seta.2024.103733

Yao, X., Zhou, J., Lin, Y., Li, Y., Yu, H., & Liu, Y. (2017). Smart manufacturing based on cyber-physical systems and beyond. *Journal of Intelligent Manufacturing*. Advance online publication. DOI: 10.1007/s10845-017-1384-5

Yasar, H., & Teplov, S. E. (2022, August). Devsecops in embedded systems: An empirical study of past literature. In *Proceedings of the 17th International Conference on Availability, Reliability and Security* (pp. 1-6). DOI: 10.1145/3538969.3544451

Zampetti, F., Nardone, V., & Di Penta, M. (2022, May). Problems and solutions in applying continuous integration and delivery to 20 open-source cyber-physical systems. In *Proceedings of the 19th International Conference on Mining Software Repositories* (pp. 646-657). DOI: 10.1145/3524842.3527948

Zampetti, F., Tamburri, D., Panichella, S., Panichella, A., Canfora, G., & Di Penta, M. (2023). Continuous integration and delivery practices for cyber-physical systems: An interview-based study. *ACM Transactions on Software Engineering and Methodology*, *32*(3), 1–44. DOI: 10.1145/3571854

Zeydan, E., Blanco, L., Mangues-Bafalluy, J., Arslan, S. S., Turk, Y., Yadav, A. K., & Liyanage, M. (2024). Blockchain-Based Self-Sovereign Identity: Taking control of identity in federated learning. *IEEE Open Journal of the Communications Society*, *5*, 5764–5781. DOI: 10.1109/ojcoms.2024.3449692

Zhang, B., Pan, H., Li, K., Xing, Y., Wang, L., Fan, D., & Zhang, W. (2024). A Blockchain and Zero Knowledge Proof Based Data Security Transaction Method in Distributed Computing. *Electronics (Basel)*, *13*(21), 4260. DOI: 10.3390/electronics13214260

Zhang, D., Li, C., Goh, H. H., Ahmad, T., Zhu, H., Liu, H., & Wu, T. (2022). A comprehensive overview of modeling approaches and optimal control strategies for cyber-physical resilience in power systems. *Renewable Energy*, *189*, 1383–1406.

Zhang, D., Shi, P., Lim, C. P., & Rudas, I. (2025). Resilient tracking control of cyber-physical systems against false data injection attacks and obstacle avoidance. *IEEE Transactions on Automation Science and Engineering*.

Zhang, J., Zhang, Z., Zhang, J., Fan, G., & Wu, D. (2021). A quantitative investigation on the benefit of various waste classifications. *Advances in Civil Engineering, 2021*(1), 6660927.

Zhang, Y., Fu, C., & Hu, L. (2014). Yellow light dilemma zone researches: A review. [English edition]. *Journal of Traffic and Transportation Engineering, 1*(5), 338–352.

Zhao, G., Li, Y., Du, L., & Zhao, X. (2015). "Asynchronous Challenge-Response Authentication Solution Based on Smart Card in Cloud Environment," 2015 2nd International Conference on Information Science and Control Engineering, Shanghai, China, pp. 156-159, doi: DOI: 10.1109/ICISCE.2015.42

Zhao, Z., Xu, Y., Li, Y., Zhen, Z., Yang, Y., & Shi, Y. (2022). Data-driven attack detection and identification for cyber-physical systems under sparse sensor attacks. *IEEE Transactions on Automatic Control, 68*(10), 6330–6337.

Zheng, Y., & Anubi, O. M. (2022). Resilient observer design for cyber-physical systems with data-driven measurement pruning. In *Security and Resilience in Cyber-Physical Systems: Detection, Estimation and Control* (pp. 85–117). Springer International Publishing.

Zhou, J., Sun, J., Zhang, M., & Ma, Y. (2020). Dependable scheduling for real-time workflows on cyber–physical cloud systems. *IEEE Transactions on Industrial Informatics, 17*(11), 7820–7829. DOI: 10.1109/TII.2020.3011506

Zhou, X., Ahmed, B., Aylor, J. H., Asare, P., & Alemzadeh, H. (2023). Hybrid knowledge and data driven synthesis of runtime monitors for cyber-physical systems. *IEEE Transactions on Dependable and Secure Computing, 21*(1), 12–30.

About the Contributors

Adnène Arbi is a distinguished academic affiliated with the University of Carthage in Tunisia, where he has contributed significantly to the fields of mathematics and engineering. His tenure at the university spans over a decade, during which he has held various positions, including roles at the Ecole Polytechnique de Tunisie and the National Institute of Applied Sciences and Technology. His research interests primarily focus on neural networks, dynamical systems, and mathematical modeling, with a particular emphasis on the stability and controllability of complex systems. Arbi's recent publications reflect his commitment to advancing knowledge in applied mathematics, particularly through innovative approaches such as wavelet neural networks and the dynamics of nonlinear systems. His work has been published in reputable journals, contributing to the understanding of mathematical phenomena in both theoretical and practical contexts. In addition to his academic pursuits, Arbi has collaborated with various prestigious institutions globally, including the University of the Witwatersrand and Imperial College London, showcasing his dedication to fostering international research partnerships. His contributions to the academic community continue to inspire emerging scholars and practitioners in the field. Actually, Dr. Arbi served as editor of various journal: -Frontiers in Applied Mathematics and Statistics, -Journal of Algorithms & Computational Technology, -Journal of Innovative Applied Mathematics and Computational Sciences, -International Journal of Sustainable Business and Management, -Karshi Multidisciplinary International Scientific Journal. Besides, he is author of more than 34 scientific peer-reviewed papers in international journals and conference proceedings, and he served as reviewer for many international conferences, workshops.

***

Sachin Vasant Chaudhari is a Ph.D. holder in Electronics Engineering. He is an Associate Professor in the Electronics and Telecommunication Engineering Department at Sanjivani College of Engineering, Kopargaon, which is affiliated with Savitribai Phule Pune University, Pune, India. He has worked on a broad range of topics including automated deep learning, UAV route planning, hybrid energy systems, and medical applications. His innovative research also addresses dynamic routing algorithms, channel estimation in OFDM, and advanced materials for medical implants. He has published over 35 papers in reputed International Journals. He is having professional membership of The Institution of Engineers (IEI) & International Association of Engineers (IANG) . He can be contacted at email: chaudharisachinetc@sanjivani.org.in,

Pramod Kumar is an accomplished academic leader with over 24 years of experience in the field. He currently serves as the Principal Swami Rama Himalayan University, Jolly grant, Dehradun, where he has been since April 2024. Prior to this, he held the position of Dean of Computer Science and Engineering at Krishna Engineering College in Ghaziabad and served as the director of Tula's Institute in Dehradun, Uttarakhand. Prof. Pramod Kumar holds a Ph.D. in Computer Science and Engineering, which he earned in 2011, as well as an M.Tech in CSE from 2006. He is a Senior Member of IEEE and an ex-joint secretary of the IEEE U.P. section. Through his research, he has made significant contributions to the fields of Computer Networks, IoT, and Machine Learning. He is the author or co-author of more than 70 research papers and has edited four books. He has also supervised and co-supervised several M.Tech and Ph.D. students. He has organized more than 12 IEEE international conferences and two Springer conferences both in India and abroad, which have made substantial contributions to the body of knowledge within the field. He has published more then 100 patents.

Bharathi M. Assistant Professor, Electronic and Communication Engineering, Mohan Babu University, Tirupati, Andhra Pradesh, India, bharathi.m@vidyanikethan.edu

Ved Prakash Mishra was born in India. He is working at Amity University Dubai as a Head of Academics- Engineering. He has published several research papers in reputed Journals, Magazines, International and National conferences of his field. His major area of interest is in Network Security, Data Mining and Process Mining. Currently working on Intrusion detection system with process mining approach. He also takes interest and successfully working in education management, curriculum development, students learning quality improvement etc..

Golla Sandhya Kumari, M.Tech, Ph.D, Currently Working as an Assistant Professor in the Department of Electronics and Communication Engineering at Siddartha Institute of Science and Technology, Puttur, Andhra Pradesh, India. She has completed her Ph.D in Koneru Lakshmaiah Education Foundation, Vijayawada, Andhra Pradesh, India. She has completed a Master of Technology in Digital Electronics and Communication Systems at Sri Padmavathi Mahila Visvavidyalayam, Tirupati, Andhra Pradesh and a Bachelor of Technology in Electronics and Communication Engineering at Sri Venkateswara Engineering College for Women, Tirupati under Jawaharlal Nehru Technological University, Anantapur. She has been worked as a research associate for the DST-CSRI project . Her research interests include Bio-Medical Signal Processing, Image Processing, Machine Learning and Deep Learning. She has published research papers in International journals and conferences. She is addressing as a reviewer for peer-reviewed journals as well as Web of Science,Scopus.

Wasswa Shafik (Member, IEEE) received a Bachelor of Science degree in information technology from Ndejje University, Uganda, a Master of Engineering degree in Information Technology (Computer and Communication Networks) from Yazd University, Iran, and a PhD in Computer Science with the School of Digital Science, Universiti Brunei Darussalam, Brunei Darussalam. He is also the Founder and Research Director of the Dig Connectivity Research Laboratory (DCRLab) after serving as a Research Associate at the Network Interconnectivity Research Laboratory at Yazd University. Prior to this, he worked as a Community Data Analyst at Population Services International (PSI-Uganda), a Community Data Officer at the Programme for Accessible Health Communication (PACE-Uganda), a Research Assistant at the Socio-Economic Data Centre (SEDC-Uganda), Uganda, an Assistant Data Officer at TechnoServe, Kampala, Uganda, and Asmaah Charity Organization as Cheif Executive Officer. He has hundreds of publications with renowned publishers. His research interests include Artificial Intelligence, Neural Networks, Computer Vision, Smart Agriculture, Digital Health, and Green Computing.

Sachin Sharma is currently working as a Professor at Amity School of Engineering and Technology, Amity University Punjab, Mohali, India. He also worked as Associate Dean of International Affairs and Professor, Department of Computer Science and Engineering at Graphic Era Deemed to be University, Dehradun, Uttarakhand, India. He has experience of 16+ years in industry and academia. He is also Co-founder and Chief Technology officer (CTO) of IntelliNexus LLC, Arkansas, USA based company. He also worked as a Senior Systems Engineer at Belkin International, Inc., Irvine, California, USA. He received his Philosophy of Doctorate (Ph.D.) degree in Engineering Science and Systems specialization in

Systems Engineering from University of Arkansas at Little Rock, USA with 4.0 out 4.0 GPA and M.S. degree in Systems engineering from University of Arkansas at Little Rock with 4.0 out 4.0 GPA. Dr. Sharma has authored/coauthored over 300+ publications in the form of books, book chapters, patents, and papers in refereed journals and conference proceedings. He holds 100+ US, Indian and international patents in the area of IoT, wireless communication.

C.V. Suresh Babu is a pioneer in content development. A true entrepreneur, he founded Anniyappa Publications, a company that is highly active in publishing books related to Computer Science and Management. Dr. C.V. Suresh Babu has also ventured into SB Institute, a center for knowledge transfer. He holds a Ph.D. in Engineering Education from the National Institute of Technical Teachers Training & Research in Chennai, along with seven master's degrees in various disciplines such as Engineering, Computer Applications, Management, Commerce, Economics, Psychology, Law, and Education. Additionally, he has UGC-NET/SET qualifications in the fields of Computer Science, Management, Commerce, and Education. Currently, Dr. C.V. Suresh Babu is a Professor in the Department of Information Technology at the School of Computing Science, Hindustan Institute of Technology and Science (Hindustan University) in Padur, Chennai, Tamil Nadu, India.

Muhammad Usman Tariq has more than 16+ year's experience in industry and academia. He has authored more than 200+ research articles, 110+ case studies, 130+ book chapters and several books other than 4 patents. He is founder and CEO of The Case HQ, a unique repository for courses, narrative and video case studies. He has been working as a consultant and trainer for industries representing six sigma, quality, health and safety, environmental systems, project management, and information security standards. His work has encompassed sectors in aviation, manufacturing, food, hospitality, education, finance, research, software and transportation. He has diverse and significant experience working with accreditation agencies of ABET, ACBSP, AACSB, WASC, CAA, EFQM and NCEAC. Additionally, Dr. Tariq has operational experience in incubators, research labs, government research projects, private sector startups, program creation and management at various industrial and academic levels. He is Certified Higher Education Teacher from Harvard University, USA, Certified Online Educator from HMBSU, Certified Six Sigma Master Black Belt and has been awarded PFHEA, SFSEDA, SMIEEE, and CMBE.

P. William is working as Dean, Research & Development at Sanjivani College of Engineering affiliated to SPPU, Pune. He is the Post Doctoral Fellow from Amity University, Dubai and adjunct faculty of Victorian Institute of Technology,

Australia. He is a member of IEEE, QCFI, ISTE and various other professional bodies. His research includes innovation and development of cutting-edge solutions in the fields of natural language processing, artificial intelligence, deep learning, machine learning, soft computing, cybersecurity, and cloud computing. He has published 135+ papers in Scopus indexed journals and Conferences. He has 30+ patents published with grants in his credit. He has authored and edited 10+ books with renowned publishers of global recognition. He has been associated with numerous Multi-National Companies and various Educational Groups for his expertise in research, corporate training and consulting where he has contributed to the advancement of knowledge and practice in his domain. A focused professional with experience of consulting in Research, Innovation and Development. He served as a Chairperson and Auditor in multiple committees of national recognition.

Index

www.ingramcontent.com/pod-product-compliance
Lightning Source LLC
LaVergne TN
LVHW081340300926
849161LV00008B/2028